D1001407

HOUGHTON MIFFLIN HARCOURT

Tennessee Science

Printed in the U.S.A.

ISBN: 978-0-547-08452-7

2 3 4 5 6 7 8 9 - 0918 - 17 16 15 14 13 12 11 10 09

Tennessee

Program Authors

William Badders
Director of the Cleveland Mathematics and Science Partnership
Cleveland Municipal School District,
Cleveland, Ohio

Douglas Carnine, Ph.D.
Professor of Education
University of Oregon,
Eugene, Oregon

Bobby Jeanpierre, Ph.D.
Assistant Professor, Science Education
University of Central Florida,
Orlando, Florida

James Feliciani
Supervisor of Instructional Media and Technology
Land O' Lakes, Florida

Carolyn Sumners, Ph.D.
Director of Astronomy and Physical Sciences
Houston Museum of Natural Science,
Houston, Texas

Catherine Valentino
Author-in-Residence
Houghton Mifflin,
West Kingston, Rhode Island

Contributing Author

Michael A. DiSpezio
Writer and Global Educator
JASON Project
Cape Cod, Massachusetts

Tennessee Teacher Reviewers

Melinda Carr
West View School
Limestone, Tennessee

Peggy Greene
Gray Elementary School
Gray, Tennessee

Loretta Harper
Goodlettsville Elementary
Goodlettsville, Tennessee

Donna Lachman
Boones Creek Middle School
Johnson City, Tennessee

Gloria R. Ramsey
Science Specialist
Memphis City Schools
Memphis, Tennessee

Richard Sherman
Warner Enhanced Option School
Nashville, Tennessee

Contents

UNIT A
Life Science

Contents

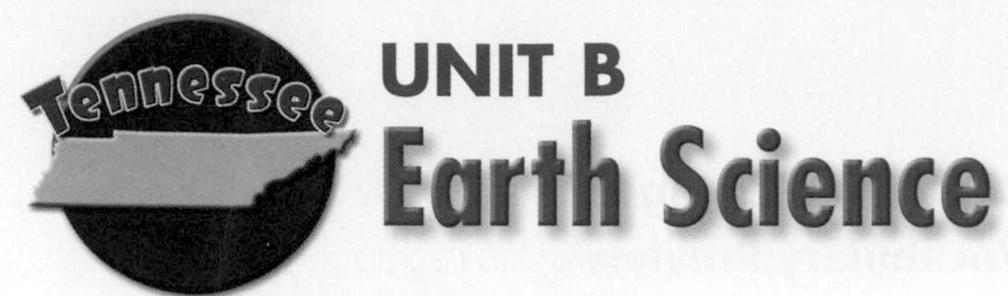

UNIT B
Earth Science

Tennessee River from Lookout Mountain, Chattanooga, Tennessee

UNIT C Physical Science

Inquiry Activities

LIFE SCIENCE

Technology and Engineering: Build a Bird Feeder

Directed Inquiry

Express Lab

Check for Understanding

EARTH SCIENCE

Technology and Engineering: Build a Spillway

Directed Inquiry

UNIT B EARTH SCIENCE

Express Lab

Check for Understanding

UNIT C PHYSICAL SCIENCE

Technology and Engineering: Build a Musical Instrument

Directed Inquiry

Express Lab

Check for Understanding

Grade 3 Embedded Inquiry

Grade Level Expectations

GLE 0307.Inq.1 Explore different scientific phenomena by asking questions, making logical predictions, planning investigations, and recording data.

GLE 0307.Inq.2 Select and use appropriate tools and simple equipment to conduct an investigation.

GLE 0307.Inq.3 Organize data into appropriate tables, graphs, drawings, or diagrams.

GLE 0307.Inq.4 Identify and interpret simple patterns of evidence to communicate the findings of multiple investigations.

GLE 0307.Inq.5 Recognize that people may interpret the same results in different ways.

GLE 0307.Inq.6 Compare the results of an investigation with what scientists already accept about this question.

Coverage of these standards occurs in Directed Inquiry, Guided Inquiry, and other features.

Grade 3 Embedded Technology & Engineering

Grade Level Expectations

GLE 0307.T/E.1 Describe how tools, technology, and inventions help to answer questions and solve problems.

GLE 0307.T/E.2 Recognize that new tools, technology, and inventions are always being developed.

GLE 0307.T/E.3 Identify appropriate materials, tools, and machines that can extend or enhance the ability to solve a specified problem.

GLE 0307.T/E.4 Recognize the connection between scientific advances, new knowledge, and the availability of new tools and technologies.

GLE 0307.T/E.5 Apply a creative design strategy to solve a particular problem generated by societal needs and wants.

Coverage of these standards occurs in Directed Inquiry, Guided Inquiry, Focus On, Technology and Engineering, and other features.

Valley Caves Cove, Smoky Mountains

Grade 3 Life Science

Standard 1 – Cells

GLE 0307.1.1 Use magnifiers to make observations of specific plant and body parts and describe their functions.

Chapter 1 How Living Things Function
Chapter 2 Survival of Living Things
Chapter 3 Organisms of Long Ago

Standard 2 – Interdependence

GLE 0307.2.1 Categorize things as living or non-living.

GLE 0307.2.2 Explain how organisms with similar needs compete with one another for resources.

Chapter 1 How Living Things Function
Chapter 2 Survival of Living Things

Standard 3 – Flow of Matter and Energy

GLE 0307.3.1 Describe how animals use food to obtain energy and materials for growth and repair

Chapter 3 Organisms of Long Ago

Standard 4 – Heredity

GLE 0307.4.1 Identify the different life stages through which plants and animals pass.

GLE 0307.4.2 Recognize common human characteristics that are transmitted from parents to offspring.

Chapter 1 How Living Things Function

Standard 5 – Biodiversity and Change

GLE 0307.5.1 Explore the relationship between an organism's characteristics and its ability to survive in a particular environment.

GLE 0307.5.2 Classify organisms as thriving, threatened, endangered, or extinct.

Chapter 2 Survival of Living Things
Chapter 3 Organisms of Long Ago

Grade 3 Earth and Space Science

Standard 6 – The Universe

GLE 0307.6.1 Identify and compare the major components of the solar system.

Chapter 4 Our Solar System

Standard 7 – The Earth

GLE 0307.7.1 Use information and illustrations to identify the earth's major landforms and water bodies.

GLE 0307.7.2 Recognize that rocks can be composed of one or more minerals.

GLE 0307.7.3 Distinguish between natural and manmade objects.

GLE 0307.7.4 Design a simple investigation to demonstrate how earth materials can be conserved or recycled.

Chapter 5 Earth's Surface and Resources

Standard 8 – The Atmosphere

GLE 0307.8.1 Recognize that there are a variety of atmospheric conditions that can be measured.

GLE 0307.8.2 Use tools such as the barometer, thermometer, anemometer, and rain gauge to measure atmospheric conditions.

GLE 0307.8.3 Identify cloud types associated with particular atmospheric conditions.

GLE 0307.8.4 Predict the weather based on cloud observations.

Chapter 6 Patterns in Earth's Atmosphere

Grade 3 Physical Science

Standard 9 – Matter

GLE 0307.9.1 Design a simple experiment to determine how the physical properties of matter can change over time and under different conditions.

GLE 0307.9.2 Investigate different types of mixtures.

GLE 0307.9.3 Describe different methods to separate mixtures.

Chapter 7 Matter

Standard 10 – Energy

GLE 0307.10.1 Investigate phenomena that produce heat.

GLE 0307.10.2 Design and conduct an experiment to investigate the ability of different materials to conduct heat.

Chapter 8 Heat and Sound Energy

Standard 11 – Motion

GLE 0307.11.1 Explore how the direction of a moving object is affected by unbalanced forces.

GLE 0307.11.2 Recognize the relationship between the mass of an object and the force needed to move it.

GLE 0307.11.3 Investigate how the pitch and volume of a sound can be changed.

Chapter 8 Heat and Sound Energy
Chapter 9 Force and Motion

Standard 12 – Forces in Nature

GLE 0307.12.1 Explore how magnets attract objects made of certain metals.

Chapter 9 Force and Motion

The Nature of Science

You Can...

Do What Scientists Do

Meet Dr. Paula Mikkelsen. She works at the American Museum of Natural History in New York City. She is in charge of the museum's collection of mollusks. The collection includes clamshells, snail shells, and the remains of slugs and squids. Dr. Mikkelsen helps other scientists find the mollusks they want to study.

Scientists ask questions. Then they answer them by investigating and experimenting.

In the Florida Keys, Dr. Mikkelsen has found 1,700 kinds of ocean mollusks. That number surprised her. It is three times the number other scientists predicted.

STANDARDS GLE 0307.Inq.1 Explore different scientific phenomena by asking questions, making logical predictions, planning investigations, and recording data.
GLE 0307.T/E.1 Describe how tools, technology, and inventions help to answer questions and solve problems.

Dr. Mikkelsen has many questions about mollusks. For example, she wants to know how many kinds of mollusks live in the ocean around islands called the Florida Keys. To find out, she scuba dives to collect mollusks.

Back at the museum, Dr. Mikkelsen records the name of each new mollusk. Like all scientists, she keeps careful records of science information, or **data.**

Science investigations take many forms.

Dr. Mikkelsen collects animals to analyze. Other scientists make observations. Still others carry out experiments. Dr. Mikkelsen shares what she discovers with other scientists. They ask her questions about her data. Dr. Mikkelsen also shares her results with people in charge of protecting Florida wildlife. This helps them make decisions about how much scuba diving, boating, and fishing they can allow around the Keys.

Dr. Paula Mikkelsen uses tools such as these magnifying goggles to observe tiny mollusk shells.

You Can...

Think Like a Scientist

The ways scientists ask and answer questions about the world around them is called **scientific inquiry.** Scientific inquiry requires certain attitudes, or ways of thinking. To think like a scientist you have to be:

- curious and ask a lot of questions.
- creative and think up new ways to do things.
- willing to listen to the ideas of others but reach your own conclusions.
- open to change what you think when your investigation results surprise you.
- willing to question what other people tell you.

What attracts the bee to the flower? Is it color, odor, or something else?

STANDARDS GLE 0307.Inq.6 Compare the results of an investigation with what scientists already accept about this question.
GLE 0307.Inq.5 Recognize that people may interpret the same results in different ways.

Use Critical Thinking

When you think critically you make decisions about what others tell you or what you read. Is what you heard or read fact or opinion? A *fact* can be checked to make sure it is true. An *opinion* is what you think about the facts.

Did anyone ever tell you a story that was hard to believe? When you think, "That just can't be true," you are thinking critically. Critical thinkers question what they hear or read in a book.

It looks like bees are attracted to certain flowers. I wonder if they use color, smell, or something else, to tell one flower from another?

I read that bees are attracted to flowers by their smell, but they identify different flowers by their color and shape.

Science Inquiry

Applying scientific inquiry helps you understand the world around you. Say you have decided to keep Triops, or tadpole shrimp.

Observe You watch the baby Triops swim around in their tank. You notice how they swim.

Ask a Question When you think about what you saw, heard, or read you may have questions.

Hypothesis Think about facts you already know. Do you have an idea about the answer? Write it down. That is your hypothesis.

Experiment Plan a test that will tell if the hypothesis is true or not. List the materials you will need. Write the steps you will follow. Make sure that you keep all conditions the same except the one you are testing. That condition is called the *variable.*

Conclusion Think about your results. What do they tell you? Did your results support your hypothesis or show it to be false?

Describe your experiment to others. Communicate your results and conclusion. You can use words, charts, or graphs.

STANDARDS GLE 0307.Inq.1 Explore different scientific phenomena by asking questions, making logical predictions, planning investigations, and recording data.
GLE 0307.Inq.2 Select and use appropriate tools and simple equipment to conduct an investigation.

My Triops Experiment

Observe Light appears to cause Triops to change how they move.

Ask a Question I wonder, do Triops like to swim more in the daytime or the nighttime?

Hypothesis Triops move differently in dim light than they do in bright light.

Experiment I'm going to observe how the Triops move in dim light. Then I'm going to turn on a light and observe any changes.

Conclusion When I turn on a bright light, the Triops speed up in the water. The results support my hypothesis. Triops are more active in bright light than in dim light.

Inquiry Process

Here is a process that some scientists follow to answer questions and make new discoveries.

Make Observations → Ask Questions → Hypothesize → Do an Experiment → Draw a Conclusion → Hypothesis Is Supported / Hypothesis Is Not Supported (→ back to Make Observations)

Science Inquiry Skills

You'll use many of these inquiry skills when you investigate and experiment.

- Ask Questions
- Observe
- Compare
- Classify
- Predict
- Measure
- Hypothesize
- Use Variables
- Experiment
- Use Models
- Communicate
- Use Numbers
- Record Data
- Analyze Data
- Infer
- Collaborate
- Research

Try It Yourself!

Experiment With a Matter Masher

To use the Matter Masher, put foam cubes or mini marshmallows in the bottle and screw on the cap. Then, push the top part of the cap up and down to pump air into the bottle.

1. Make a list of questions you have about the Matter Masher.
2. Think about how you could find out the answers.
3. Describe your experiment. If you did your experiment, what do you think the results would be?

You Can...

Be an Inventor

Jonathan Santos has been an inventor all his life. His first invention was a system of strings he used to switch off the lights without getting out of bed.

As a teenager, Jonathan invented a throwing toy called the J-Boom. He read about boomerangs. Then he planned his own toy with four arms instead of two. He built a sample, tried it out, and made improvements. Then he sold it in science museum gift shops.

Today, Jonathan works as a computer software engineer. He invents new ways to use computers. Jonathan is still inventing toys. His latest idea is a new kind of roller coaster!

His invention earned him his own trading card!

"As a kid I quickly discovered that by using inventiveness you can design things and build things by using almost anything."

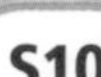

What Is Technology?

The tools people make and use and the things they build with tools are all **technology.** A wooden flying toy is technology. So is a space shuttle.

Scientists use technology, too. For example, a microscope makes it possible for them to see things that cannot be seen with just the eyes. They also use measurement tools to make their observations more exact.

Many technologies make the world a better place to live. But sometimes a technology that solves one problem can cause other problems. For example, riding in cars or buses makes it easier for people to travel long distances. But the fuel that powers cars and buses pollutes the air. Air pollution causes health problems for people and other living things.

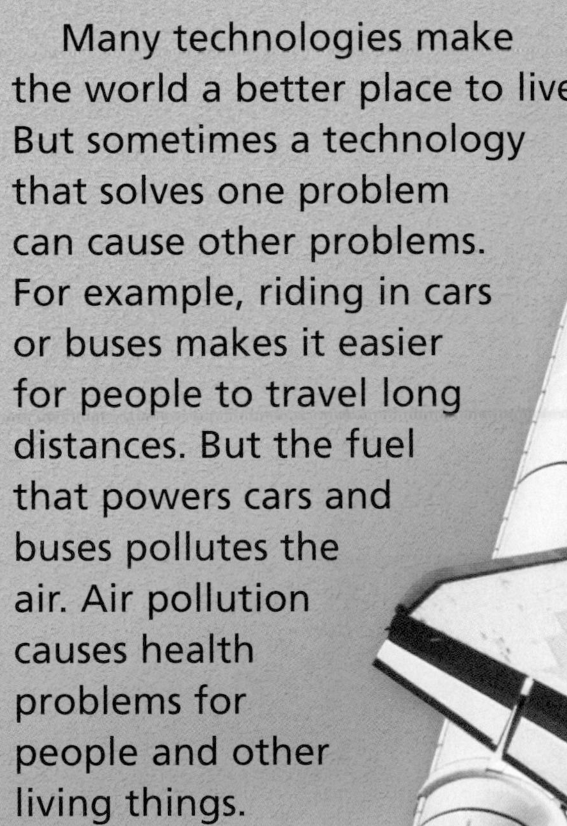

A Better Idea

"I wish I had a better way to _____". How would you fill in the blank? Everyone wishes they could find a way to do their jobs more easily or have more fun. Inventors try to make those wishes come true. Inventing or improving an invention requires time and patience.

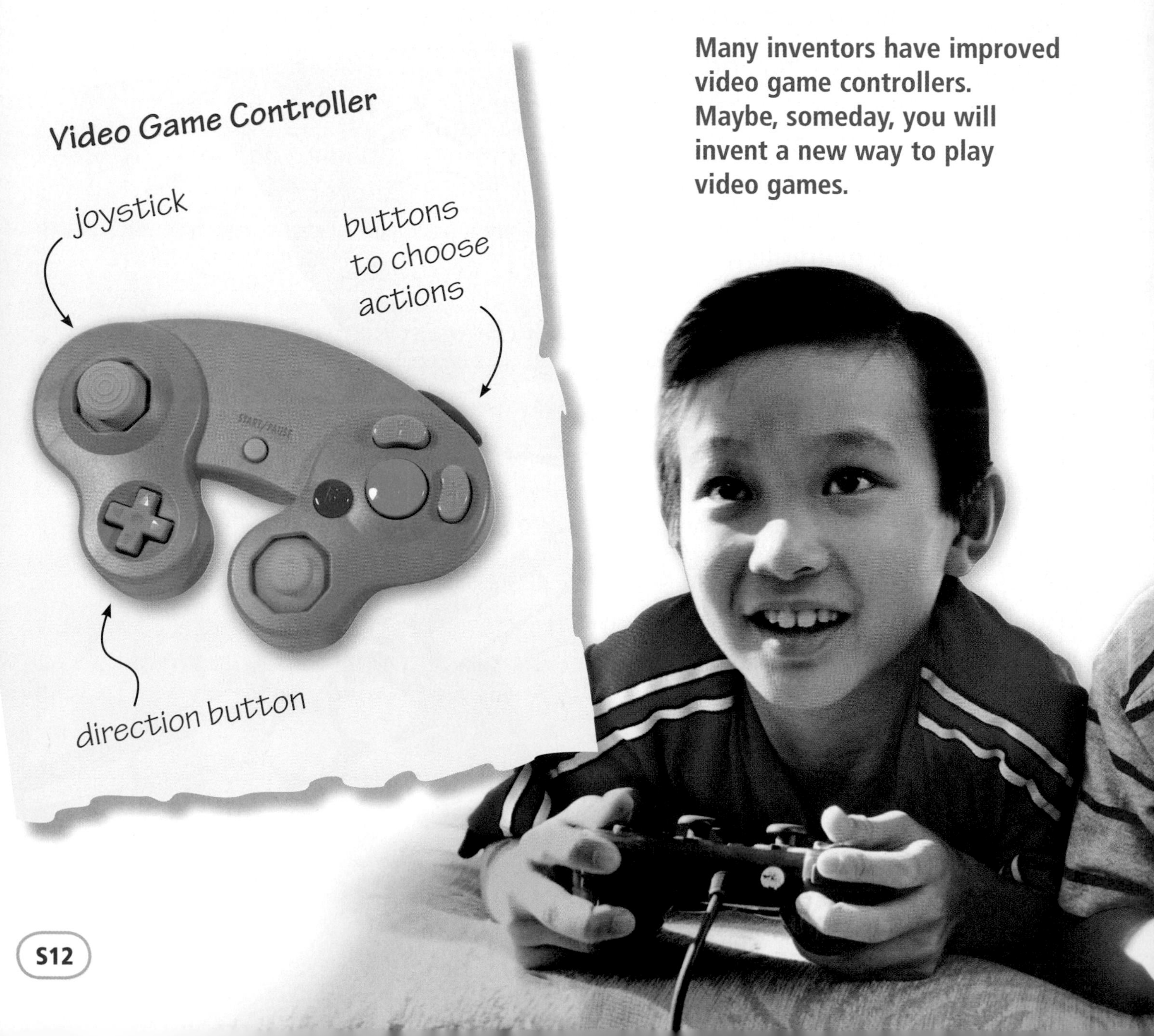

Many inventors have improved video game controllers. Maybe, someday, you will invent a new way to play video games.

How to Be a Good Inventor

1. **Identify a problem.** It may be a problem at school, at home, or in your community.
2. **Think of a solution.** Sometimes the solution is a new tool. Other times it may be a new way of doing an old job or activity. Decide which idea will work best. Think about which one you can carry out.
3. **Plan and build.** A sample, called a *prototype,* is the first try. Your idea may need many materials or none at all. Choose measuring tools that will help your design work better.
4. **Test and improve.** Use your prototype or ask someone else to try it. Keep a record of how it works and what problems you find. Use what you learned to make your design work better. Draw or write about the changes you made and why you made them.
5. **Communicate.** Show your invention to others. Explain how it works. Tell how it makes an activity easier or more fun. If it did not work as well as you wanted, tell why.

You Can...

Make Decisions

Troubles for Baby Turtles

Each spring adult female sea turtles come out of the ocean in the dark of night. They crawl onto sandy beaches and dig nest holes. They lay their eggs, cover them with sand, and slip back into the ocean.

A few weeks later, and all at once, the babies hatch and climb out of the nest. Attracted to nature's bright lights, the turtles should crawl toward the lights of the night sky shining on the ocean. But on many beaches, the lights from streetlights or houses are much brighter. The baby turtles crawl away from the ocean and toward the electric lights. Instead of finding their home in the sea, many of them die.

STANDARDS GLE 0307.T/E.5 Apply a creative design strategy to solve a particular problem generated by societal needs and wants.

Deciding What to Do

How could you help save the most baby turtles?

Here's how to make your decision about the baby turtles. You can use the same steps to help solve problems in your home, in your school, and in your community.

Learn → Learn about the problem. Take the time needed to get the facts. You could talk to an expert, read a science book, or explore a website.

List → Make a list of actions you could take. Add actions other people could take.

Decide → Think about each action on your list. Decide which choice is the best one for you or your community.

Share → Communicate your decision to others.

Science Safety

- ☑ Know the safety rules of your school and classroom and follow them.
- ☑ Read and follow the safety tips in each Directed Inquiry activity.
- ☑ When you plan your own investigations, write down how to keep safe.
- ☑ Know how to clean up and put away science materials. Keep your work area clean and tell your teacher about spills right away.
- ☑ Know how to safely plug in electrical devices.
- ☑ Wear safety goggles when your teacher tells you.
- ☑ Unless your teacher tells you to, never put any science materials in or near your ears, eyes, or mouth.
- ☑ Wear gloves when handling live animals.
- ☑ Wash your hands when your investigation is done.

Caring for Living Things

- ☑ Learn how to care for the plants and animals in your classroom so that they stay healthy and safe. Learn how to hold animals carefully.

TENNESSEE

Tennessee Excursions and Engineering Project

UNIT A

The Cumberland River

The Cumberland River winds like a snake through parts of northern Tennessee. On summer afternoons, the river is a popular place for boating and fishing. The river also supplies drinking water to the city of Nashville. Like other rivers, the Cumberland River is home to many kinds of living things.

You probably know the names of some of the common plants and animals found in Tennessee. In the Cumberland River, channel catfish and striped bass are common. A plant or an animal that is common and easy to find is one that is thriving.

A living thing that is thriving is doing well in its environment. It is growing and reproducing without problems. In the Cumberland River, the goldeye fish is thriving. In the river, it easily finds everything it needs to survive.

Cumberland River

goldeye fish

A Place to Call Home

In some places, such as Wisconsin, goldeye fish are endangered. *Endangered* means that there are few goldeye fish remaining. If they are not protected, they may all die. In other places, such as Pennsylvania, goldeye fish are threatened. *Threatened* means that the number of individuals has decreased. Threatened plants and animals can become endangered if not protected.

Have you ever wondered why there are not more fish in a river? Plants and animals need certain things to survive. These things are called resources. For example, fish need food, air, water, and shelter. Because the fish in a river all use these same resources, there may not be enough for all the fish. So some fish will die.

Think and Write

1. **Scientific Inquiry** A science teacher gave her students 20 seeds, 3 cups, soil, and water. How could they design an experiment to test how the amount of water available affects growing plants?
2. **Scientific Thinking** Draw a bar graph with three bars to show the difference between thriving, threatened, and endangered.

Tennessee National Wildlife Refuge

On a warm spring day at the Tennessee National Wildlife Refuge, you can see flowers blooming and hear birds singing. The birds are building nests and raising their young. More than 100 kinds of birds build nests at this refuge near Kentucky Lake. A refuge is land that people set aside for plants and animals to live on.

Some of the loudest and largest birds at the refuge are Canada geese. You may hear them honking as they fly overhead. They migrate north each spring, and south each fall. When they fly, they form V-shaped flocks.

Least terns

Looking Like Your Parents

Canada geese build nests from dried grasses and reeds. A female usually lays between 2 and 8 eggs in the nest. When the young hatch, they do not look much like their parents.

The way a living thing looks is based on features that are passed from parents to their young. Young Canada geese will grow up to look much like their parents.

Humans pass features to their children in much the same way. You got some of your features from your mother, and some from your father.

Young Canada geese don't look like their parents until they are grown.

Protecting Endangered Species

At the refuge, there are lots of Canada geese—they're thriving. Other kinds of living things there are endangered. For example, birds called least terns build nests on the sandy shores of rivers. There are very few least terns in Tennessee. Workers at the refuge help protect the nests of these birds.

Think and Write

1. **Scientific Thinking** On a sheet of paper, draw a picture of a person. Circle and label two features that the person inherited.
2. **Science and Technology** Scientists can use binoculars and video cameras to study least terns and watch them on their nests. Why is a video camera a better tool than binoculars?

The Memphis Zoo and Endangered Animals

At the Memphis Zoo, you can see all kinds of animals. Orangutans swing through their home in Primate Canyon. Bats fly through the Animals of the Night exhibit. Zebras, giraffes, and rhinos stomp across the grasslands of the African Veldt exhibit.

The Memphis Zoo

Caring for Animals

The giant pandas are among the zoo's most famous residents. In the wild, pandas are endangered. There are fewer than 4,000 living. That may seem like a lot, but there were once many more.

One goal of a zoo is to help protect endangered species. A zoo provides good food, medical care, and a safe place for animals to live. Many giant pandas have been born in zoos. Some zoo pandas might have to be returned to the wild to help increase the number of wild pandas.

Zoo visitors can watch giant pandas eat bamboo.

A Helping Hand

Many kinds of living things are endangered because people have made changes to the environment. Zoos are not the only way people work to protect endangered animals. The United States and the State of Tennessee also have laws that help protect endangered plants and animals.

Think And Write

1. **Science and Technology** Suppose you are designing a new exhibit for a zoo. What information about the kinds of animals that would live there is important to find out?
2. **Scientific Thinking** Why is it important to have laws to protect endangered plants and animals?

Build a Bird Feeder

Identify the Problem Your class will be studying cardinals to observe how they eat.

Think of a Solution To observe cardinals, you could build a feeder for them. List the features a bird feeder must have. For example, it must have places for birds to perch on as they eat.

Plan and Build Use your list to design the feeder. Sketch and label it. Think of materials you could use. Then build it.

Test and Improve Test your bird feeder. Provide sketches, explanations, and the results of your test. Try to improve your feeder.

Communicate

1. What part of your bird feeder design was successful?
2. Was there any part of your feeder design that didn't work? If so, explain what the problem was.
3. Describe one improvement you made to your design.

Possible Materials

- masking tape
- plastic plates and bowls
- paper-towel rolls
- scissors
- craft sticks
- twigs
- glue
- scrap cardboard
- bird food
- string
- pole

GLE 0307.T/E.5 Apply a creative design strategy to solve a particular problem generated by societal needs and wants.

TENNESSEE  SCIENCE

Life Science

Tennessee

Guiding Question

How do the parts of living things help them survive and produce young?

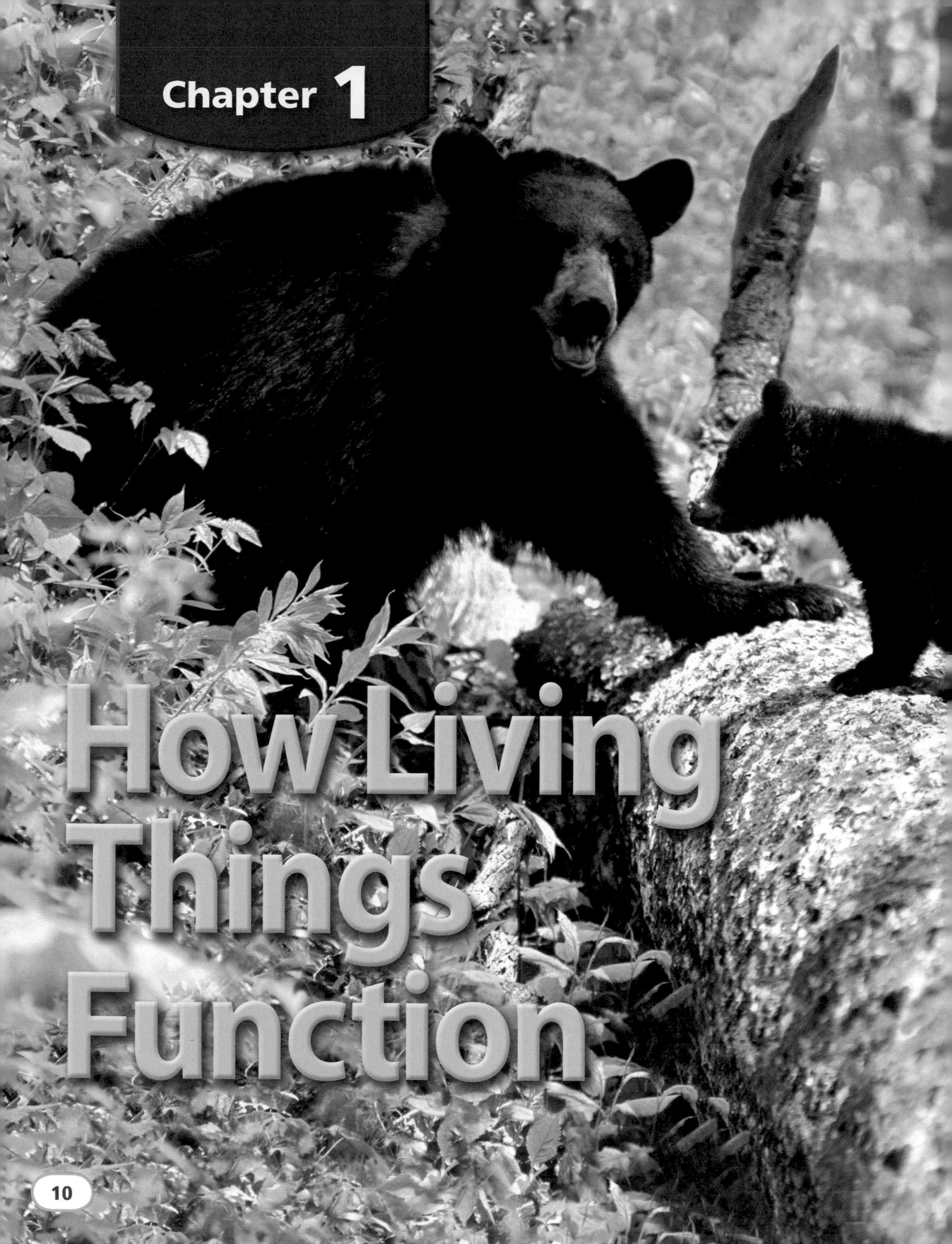

Chapter 1

How Living Things Function

Lesson Preview

LESSON 1

Carrots, radishes, turnips, and beets are all vegetables. What plant parts are they?

LESSON 2

How do a flower, a fruit, and an insect each help a plant produce new plants?

LESSON 3

A turtle hatches from an egg and a caterpillar becomes a butterfly. How do the life cycles of animals compare?

LESSON 4

A dog might be large or small. Why do living things of the same kind sometimes look different?

Fun Facts

The seeds of an Indian Lotus plant can sprout even after 300 years.

See you in 300 years.

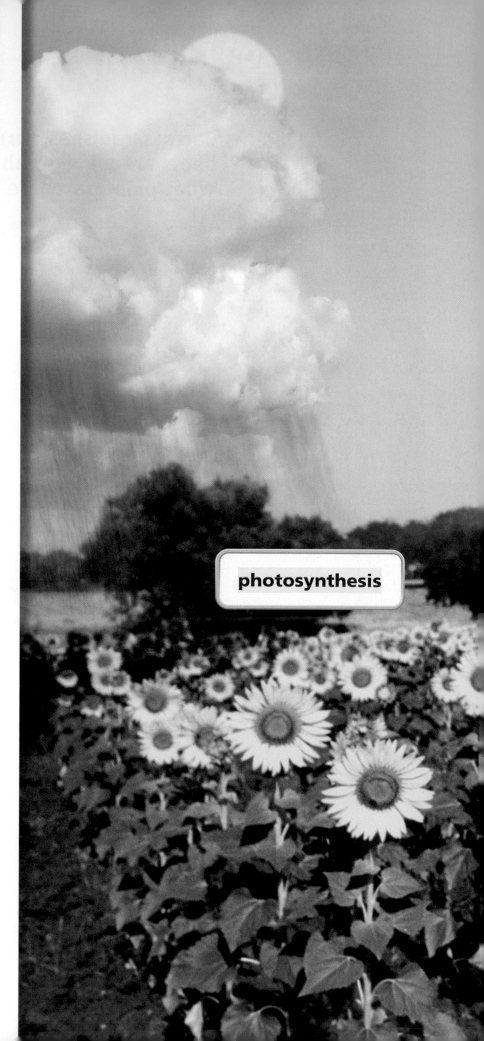

Vocabulary Preview

cell
conifer
fruit
individual
larva
leaf
★ life cycle
nutrient
★ offspring
★ photosynthesis
pupa
root
seed
stem

★ = Tennessee Academic Vocabulary

Vocabulary Strategies

Have you ever seen any of these terms before? Do you know what they mean?

Describe, explain, or give an example of the vocabulary terms in your own words.

Draw a picture, symbol, example, or other image that describes the term.

Glossary p. H16

photosynthesis

life cycle

offspring

pupa

Start with Your Standards

Inquiry

GLE 0307.Inq.1 Explore different scientific phenomena by asking questions, making logical predictions, planning investigations, and recording data.

GLE 0307.Inq.3 Organize data into appropriate tables, graphs, drawings, or diagrams.

GLE 0307.Inq.4 Identify and interpret simple patterns of evidence to communicate the findings of multiple investigations.

Technology and Engineering

GLE 0307.T/E.1 Describe how tools, technology, and inventions help to answer questions and solve problems.

Life Science

Standard 1 Cells

GLE 0307.1.1 Use magnifiers to make observations of specific plant and body parts and describe their functions.

Standard 4 Heredity

GLE 0307.4.1 Identify the different life stages through which plants and animals pass.

GLE 0307.4.2 Recognize common human characteristics that are transmitted from parents to offspring.

Interact with this chapter.

www.eduplace.com/tnscp

Lesson 1

TENNESSEE STANDARDS

GLE 0307.Inq.1 Explore different scientific phenomena by asking questions, making logical predictions, planning investigations, and recording data.

GLE 0307.1.1 Use magnifiers to make observations of specific plant and body parts and describe their functions.

Guiding Question

How Do Plants Use Their Parts?

Why It Matters...

Plants are living things that people use for many purposes. If you have ever enjoyed the shade of a tree on a warm day, then you have used plants. Plants provide people with food to eat, material for clothing and buildings, and many other items.

PREPARE TO INVESTIGATE

Inquiry Skill

Observe When you observe, you gather information about the environment by using your senses of sight, hearing, smell, and touch.

Materials

- bean seed
- plastic bag with seal
- stapler
- paper towels
- water
- hand lens
- masking tape
- metric ruler

Science and Math Toolbox

For steps 2 and 3, review **Using a Hand Lens** on page H2.

Directed Inquiry

Bean Bags

Procedure

STEP 1

1. **Collaborate** Work with a partner. Wet a paper towel until it is damp, but not dripping. Fold the paper towel and slide it into a plastic bag, as shown. Staple the bag about 2 cm from the bottom.

STEP 2

2. **Observe** Look closely at a bean seed with your hand lens. In your Science Notebook, draw a picture of the bean seed. Label the picture *Day 1*. Place the bean seed in the bag. Seal the bag.

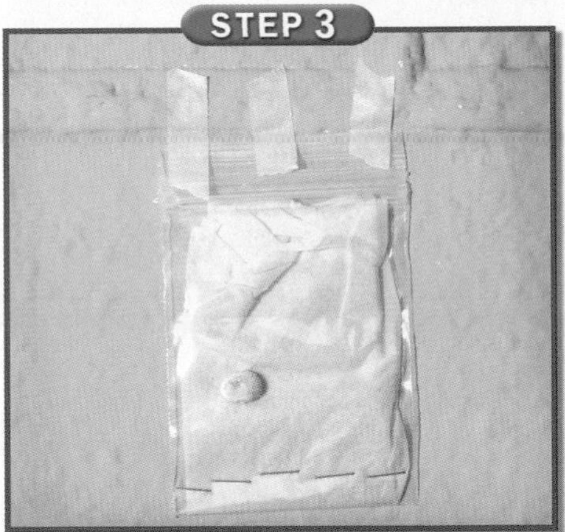
STEP 3

3. **Observe** Tape the bag so it hangs in a sunny spot. Use your hand lens to observe the bean seed each day. Look for roots and tiny hairs on the roots. Draw and label a picture of the bean seed each day. Add water as needed to keep the paper towel damp.

4. **Research** After you have observed a change in the bean seed, use library books or the Internet to learn how to plant the bean seed in soil and how to care for it.

Think and Write

1. **Classify** Would you say that a bean seed is a living thing? Why or why not?
2. **Infer** Based on your observations, what does a bean seed need to grow?

✓ 0307.1.1

Guided Inquiry

Design an Experiment

Use scissors to cut off a small part of the bean plant. Use a hand lens to observe changes to the plant every day. Draw what you see.

Reading Science

Plants Meet Their Needs

VOCABULARY

cell
leaf
nutrient
★ photosynthesis
root
stem

GRAPHIC ORGANIZER

Compare and Contrast
As you read, use the chart to compare how each plant part helps a plant meet its needs.

GLE 0307.1.1 Use magnifiers to make observations of specific plant and body parts and describe their functions.

Plants

Living things, or things that are alive, are found all over Earth. All of the living things on Earth can be separated into groups. Two groups of living things are plants and animals. A plant is a living thing that grows on land or in the water. It cannot move from place to place, and usually has green leaves.

These sunflowers need sunlight and air to grow. They also need water and nutrients from soil.

The Needs of Plants

Humans and other animals need air to breathe, water to drink, and food to eat. Plants need certain things to live too. They need air, water, and sunlight. Most plants also need soil, which provides nutrients (NOO tree uhnts). A **nutrient** is a substance that living things need to survive and grow.

FOCUS CHECK What are two things that both plants and animals need to live?

Parts of Plants

Like animals and all other living things, plants are made of cells (sehlz). A **cell** is the smallest and most basic unit of a living thing. Plant cells have stiff walls that support the plant and give it shape.

Plants cannot move from place to place to find food and water as animals can. So how do plants meet their needs? They have parts that help them get the things they need to survive.

Almost all plants have three parts. Each part does a job that helps the plant live. A **root** takes in water and nutrients and provides support for the plant. A **stem** holds up the leaves and carries water and nutrients through the plant. A **leaf** collects sunlight and gases from the air. It uses them to make food for the plant.

The zebra plant is unusual because it has leaves patterned like zebra fur. What features does it have in common with other plants? ▶

Roots

You usually don't see the roots of a plant. The roots of most plants grow underground. The most important job of roots is to take in water and nutrients from the soil. Roots have tiny hairlike parts that help them do this. These parts are called root hairs.

The roots of most plants also have another job. Roots hold the plant in place in the soil and help it stand up. Tall trees have huge roots that help keep them from tipping over. Roots of grasses help hold them in place.

Sometimes roots store food for the plant. The carrots you eat are actually roots. They contain many nutrients that they store for use by the carrot plant. Radishes, turnips, beets, and some other vegetables that people eat are also roots.

FOCUS CHECK Describe two jobs that plant roots do.

Root hairs viewed through a microscope ▶

Carrots are roots. They have tiny hairlike parts, called root hairs, that help take in water and nutrients from soil. ▶

▲ Stems help a plant grow tall. These bamboo plants have long, strong stems that grow very quickly.

Stems

The stems of many plants are long and thin. They contain small tubes. These tubes carry water and nutrients throughout the plant. The stems hold up the leaves. This allows the leaves to collect sunlight.

Some stems, such as the stems of sugar cane, can store food. In a cactus plant, the stems store water. Tree trunks are also stems. Celery stalks and asparagus are examples of stems eaten by people.

This Japanese maple bonsai (bahn SY) is a tiny form of a full-size tree. It has roots, stems, and leaves, just like a large tree. ▼

Express Lab

Activity Card
Observe Skin and Nails

Leaves

Leaves grow out of the stem of a plant. Most plants have many leaves. The leaf is the part of the plant that makes food. The process by which a plant makes food is called **photosynthesis** (foh toh SIHN-thih sihs). In photosynthesis, leaf cells use water, sunlight, and air to make sugar. The sugar is food that the plant needs to stay alive.

Leaves usually grow near the top of the plant, where they can take in a lot of sunlight. Different types of plants usually have differently shaped leaves. The pads on water lilies are leaves. So are the needles of a pine tree. You might eat the leaves of some plants, such as lettuce, spinach, or cabbage.

FOCUS CHECK How do leaves help a plant stay alive?

▲ **This Japanese maple leaf is divided into sections called lobes.**

This plant is called a ponytail palm. Its leaves are long and narrow. ▶

How Plants Meet Needs

The roots, stems, and leaves of a plant are all connected. They work together to help the plant meet its needs. To live and grow, a plant must meet its needs. Roots take in water and nutrients from soil. Stems carry the water and nutrients to the leaves and other parts of the plant. Leaves use sunlight, water, and air to make sugar.

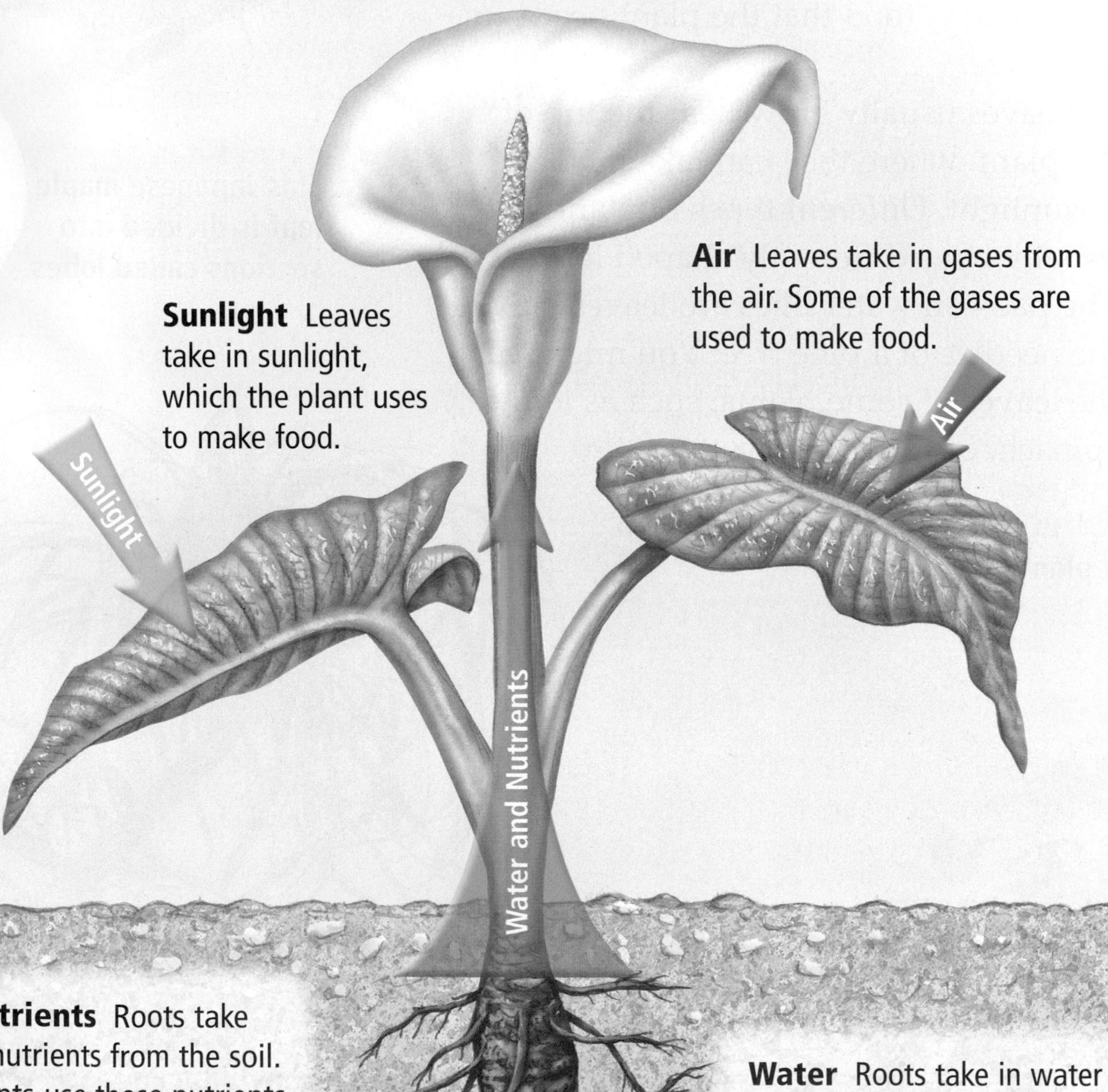

Sunlight Leaves take in sunlight, which the plant uses to make food.

Air Leaves take in gases from the air. Some of the gases are used to make food.

Nutrients Roots take in nutrients from the soil. Plants use these nutrients to live and grow.

Water Roots take in water from the soil. Plants use water to make food. Water helps hold the plant upright.

Lesson Wrap-Up

Visual Summary

Plants need air, water, sunlight, and nutrients to live.

Plants have roots, stems, and leaves and are made of cells.

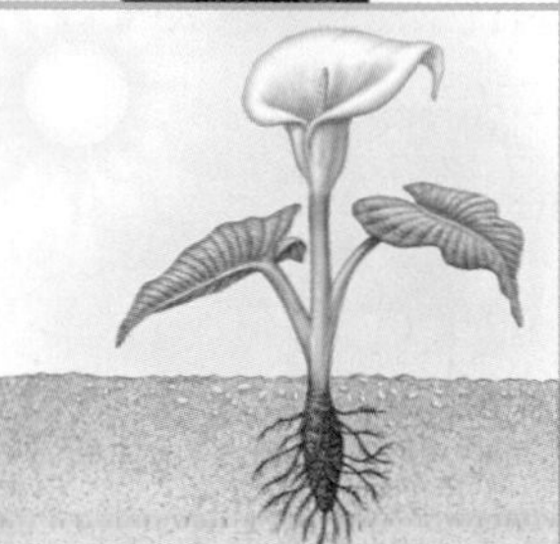

The roots, stems, and leaves of a plant work together to help the plant meet its needs.

Check for Understanding

TELL ABOUT PLANT PARTS

With your teacher's permission, use a hand lens to examine the leaves, cut stem, and roots of a plant. Make a drawing of what you see. Label the leaf veins, stem, roots, and root hairs. For each labeled part, write how that part helps a plant meet its needs.

✓ 0307.1.1

Review

1. **MAIN IDEA** How does a plant meet its needs?
2. **VOCABULARY** What is the job of roots?
3. **READING SKILL: Compare and Contrast** Choose two plant parts. Compare the job that each part does in keeping a plant alive.
4. **CRITICAL THINKING: Synthesize** Describe how stems and leaves of a plant work to help the plant live.
5. **INQUIRY SKILL: Observe** Suppose a plant has plenty of light, soil, and air. Its leaves are turning brown and becoming dry. Which of its needs is not being met?

TCAP Prep

Which part needs sunlight to make food for most plants?

Ⓐ root hair
Ⓑ stem
Ⓒ leaf
Ⓓ root

SPI 0307.1.1

Go Digital Technology

Visit **www.eduplace.com/tnscp** to learn more about the needs of plants.

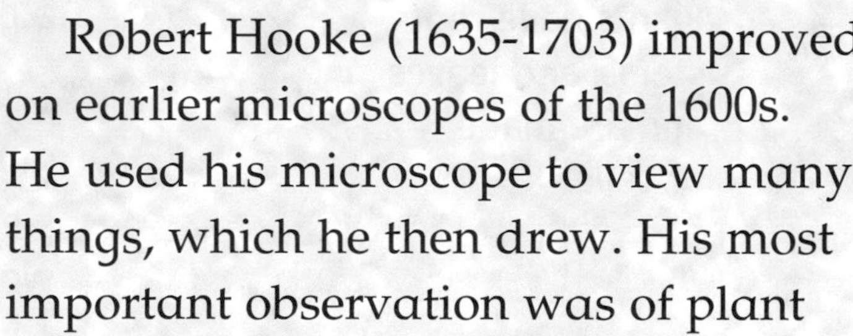

Micrographia:

A Big Book About Tiny Things

▲ Robert Hooke made discoveries in physics, astronomy, and meteorology.

Robert Hooke (1635-1703) improved on earlier microscopes of the 1600s. He used his microscope to view many things, which he then drew. His most important observation was of plant cells. He looked at a slice of cork under the microscope and saw "hollow" spaces with walls around them. He named the spaces "cells." Hooke's work helped lead to the discovery that all living things are made of cells.

Hooke shared his observations with the world when he published *Micrographia* in 1665. His book included detailed drawings of plant cells, insects, and snowflakes.

Hooke's microscope magnified objects to about 30 times their actual size. ▶

Human skin

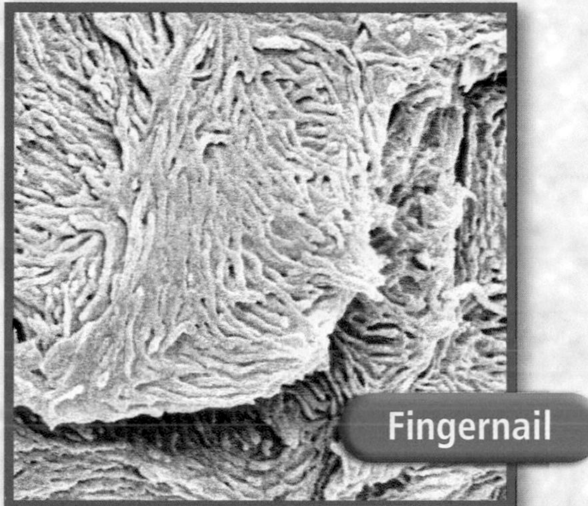

Fingernail

Microscopes have been improved greatly since Hooke's time. The pictures above show human skin and a fingernail as seen through modern microscopes. Compare the pictures with what you can see when you use a hand lens to look at your own skin and fingernail.

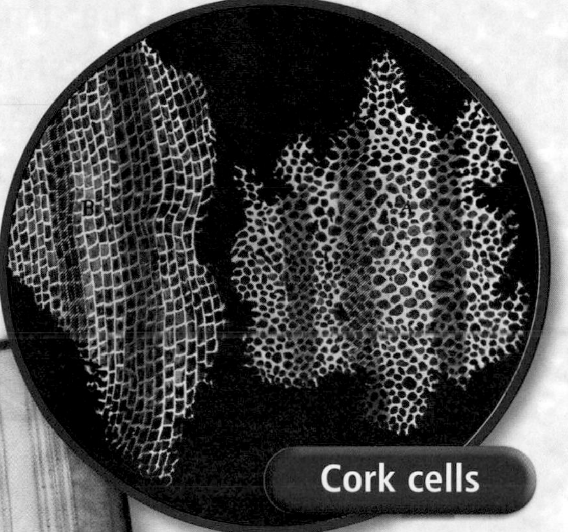

Cork cells

Sharing Ideas

1. **READING CHECK** What drawings did Hooke's book include?
2. **WRITE ABOUT IT** What scientific discovery did Hooke's observations of cork cells lead to?
3. **TALK ABOUT IT** Discuss the effect of Hooke's work on other scientists.

Lesson 2

TENNESSEE STANDARDS

GLE 0307.Inq.3 Organize data into appropriate tables, graphs, drawings, or diagrams.
GLE 0307.4.1 Identify the different life stages through which plants and animals pass.

What Are Plant Life Cycles?

Why It Matters...

When you look outside, you probably see many types of plants. You may see huge trees or small flowers. Perhaps you see vegetables in a garden or fruits on a vine. By understanding how plants grow, people can produce the food supplies that they need.

PREPARE TO INVESTIGATE

Inquiry Skill

Observe When you observe, you gather information by using your senses and tools such as hand lenses.

Materials

- clear plastic cup
- gravel
- potting soil
- pea seed
- plastic spoon
- water
- pencil
- metric ruler
- hand lens
- goggles

Science and Math Toolbox

For step 2, review **Using a Tape Measure or Ruler** on page H6.

Directed Inquiry

Growing Greens

Procedure

1. **Observe** In your Science Notebook, make a chart like the one shown. Use a hand lens to look closely at a pea seed. Draw the seed and record your observations. **Safety:** Wear goggles.
2. **Measure** Place a 2-cm layer of gravel in the bottom of a cup. Use a ruler to help you measure. Then fill the cup with soil.
3. **Experiment** Use a pencil to make a small hole in the soil. Place the pea seed in the hole and cover it with soil. Add a few spoonfuls of water. Place the cup near a sunny window.
4. **Observe** After a few days, measure the plant and observe it with a hand lens. Add water if the soil is dry. Make a drawing. Record your observations and measurements in your chart.
5. **Observe** Repeat step 4 each day for the next four days. Then put all five drawings in the correct order.

STEP 1

Seed Growth	Drawing	Observation
Day 1		
Day 2		
Day 3		
Day 4		
Day 5		

STEP 2

STEP 3

Think and Write

1. **Compare** Exchange charts with a partner. How are your observations alike?
2. **Predict** You have seen two stages in a plant's life cycle. What stage will you see next if your plant keeps growing?

✓ 0307.4.1

Guided Inquiry

Design an Experiment

Observe the inside of a tomato. Based on your observation, infer how a tomato plant grows. Design an experiment to test your idea.

Reading Science

Plant Life Cycles

VOCABULARY

conifer
fruit
★ life cycle
seed

GRAPHIC ORGANIZER

Main Idea and Details
Use a chart to show three details about the life cycle of a flowering plant.

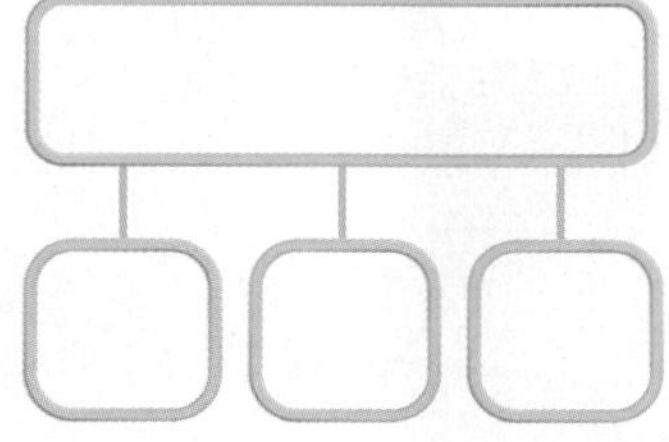

GLE 0307.4.1 Identify the different life stages through which plants and animals pass.

Flowering Plants

Both plants and animals have life cycles (SY kuhlz). A **life cycle** is the series of changes that a living thing goes through during its lifetime. Different living things have different life cycles. Flowering plants, such as this apple tree, have similar life cycles.

A flower, or blossom, is the part of the plant that makes fruit and seeds. A **seed** is the first stage in the life of most plants. For a plant to produce seeds, pollen (PAHL uhn) must first move from one part of a flower to another. Pollen is a powdery material found inside flowers. The wind, insects, and other animals can move pollen.

A **fruit** is the part of the plant that contains the seeds. The apple blossoms on this tree will produce many apples. The seeds inside the apples can grow into new apple trees.

When a seed is planted in the soil, it will sprout and develop into a seedling. As the seedling grows it becomes a young tree, or sapling. When the sapling becomes an adult, the life cycle begins again. Most plants continue this cycle for many years until they die.

FOCUS CHECK What part of a flowering plant contains seeds?

Activity Card
Observe Seeds in Fruit

Life Cycle of an Apple Tree
blossom
fruit
seed in fruit
seedling
sapling

Conifers

Not all plants have flowers. Some plants have cones instead of flowers. A **conifer** (KAHN uh fur) is a plant that makes seeds inside cones. Pine trees are conifers. Conifer seeds produce new conifer plants . The diagram below shows the stages in the life cycle of a conifer.

FOCUS CHECK **What is a conifer?**

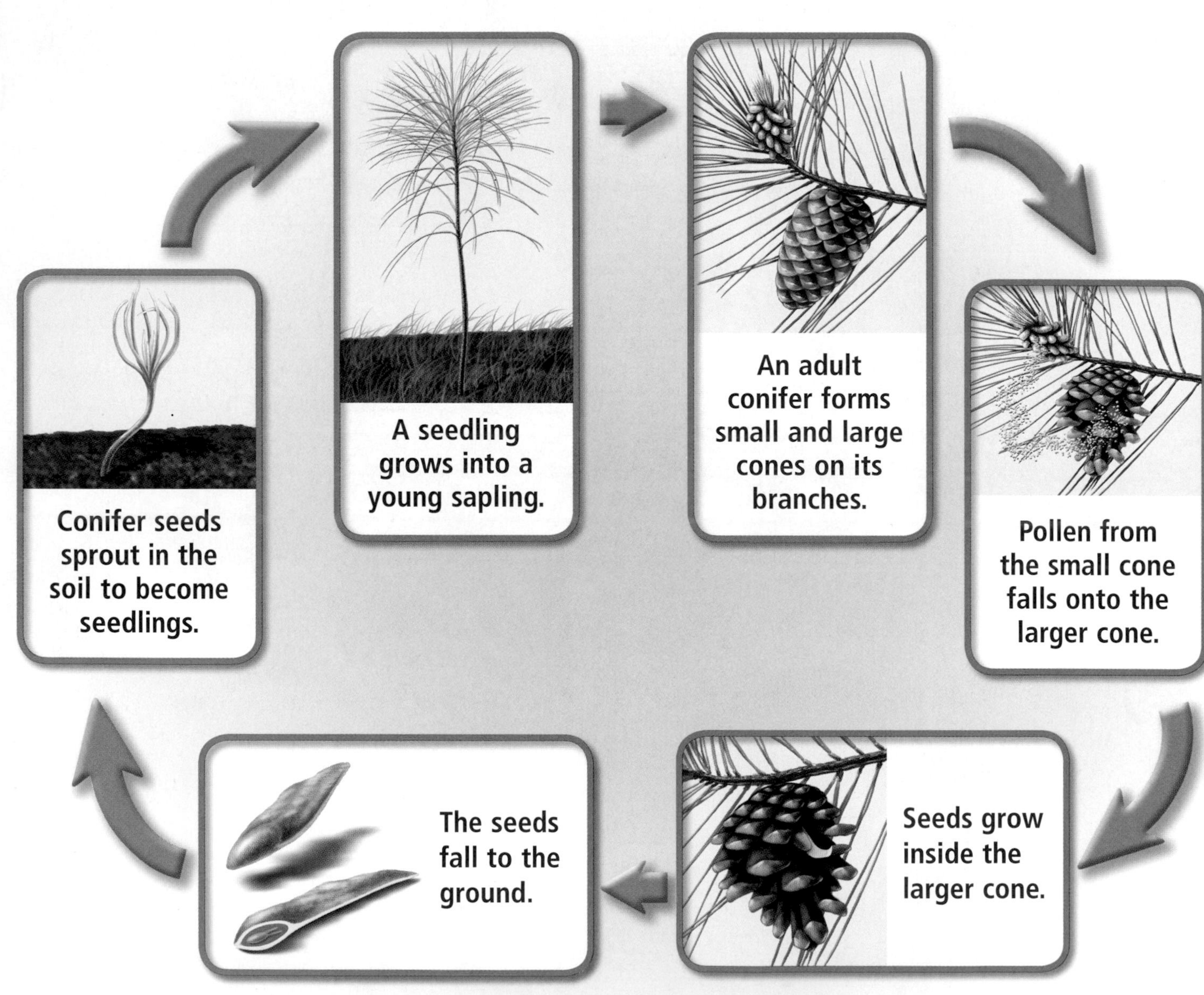

A seedling grows into a young sapling.
An adult conifer forms small and large cones on its branches.
Pollen from the small cone falls onto the larger cone.
Seeds grow inside the larger cone.
The seeds fall to the ground.
Conifer seeds sprout in the soil to become seedlings.

Lesson Wrap-Up

Visual Summary

Flowering plants grow and reproduce by making fruits and seeds from flowers.

Conifers grow and reproduce by making seeds from cones.

SEQUENCE A LIFE CYCLE

Look at the pictures below. Write the letter of each picture in the correct order to show the stages in the life cycle of a pine tree. Start with picture *D*.

0307.4.1

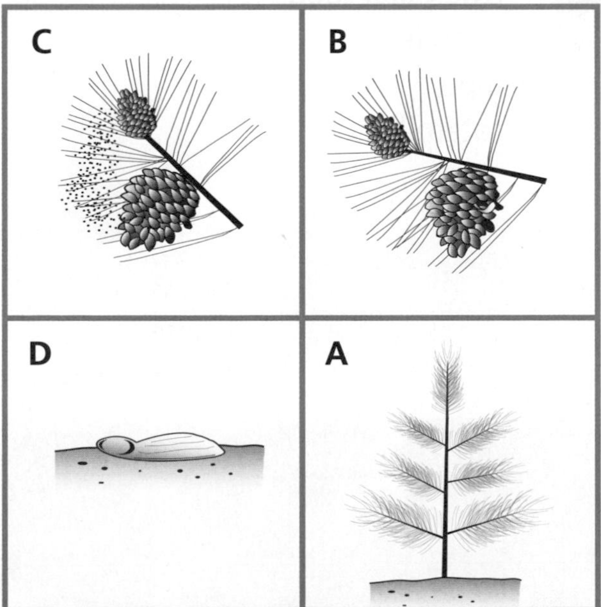

Review

1. **MAIN IDEA** What are two things that happen during a plant's life cycle?

2. **VOCABULARY** Write a sentence using the term *life cycle*.

3. **READING SKILL: Main Idea and Details** List three details about the life cycle of a conifer.

4. **CRITICAL THINKING: Analyze** How is the seed of a flowering plant different from the seed of a conifer?

5. **INQUIRY SKILL: Observe** You see a plant that has white blossoms and small berries with seeds inside. Is the plant a flowering plant or a conifer? Explain.

TCAP Prep

Look back at the photos on page 29. Which one shows the growing plant part that contains the developing seeds?

Ⓐ seedling
Ⓑ fruit
Ⓒ blossom
Ⓓ sapling

SPI 0307.4.1

Go Digital Technology

Visit **www.eduplace.com/tnscp** to find out more about the life cycles of plants.

Lesson 3

TENNESSEE STANDARDS

GLE 0307.Inq.3 Organize data into appropriate tables, graphs, drawings, or diagrams.

GLE 0307.4.1 Identify the different life stages through which plants and animals pass.

GLE 0307.4.2 Recognize common human characteristics that are transmitted from parents to offspring.

Guiding Question

What Are Some Animal Life Cycles?

Why It Matters...

Like some kinds of animals, an elephant grows inside its mother's body until it is born. Other kinds of animals hatch from eggs. Some animals grow in size until they become adults. Some animals may change form. You can learn a lot about animals by studying their life cycles.

PREPARE TO INVESTIGATE

Inquiry Skill

Communicate **When you communicate, you present information by using words, sketches, charts, and diagrams.**

Materials

- disposable gloves
- plastic container and lid
- butterfly habitat
- paper towel
- leaves
- twigs
- caterpillar food
- hand lens
- tape
- caterpillars

Directed Inquiry

Caterpillar Change

Procedure

1. In your Science Notebook, make a chart like the one shown.
2. **Experiment** Place a folded paper towel, leaves, and twigs in a plastic container. Carefully put caterpillars and their food in the container and close the lid. **Safety:** Wear gloves and handle the caterpillars gently.
3. **Observe** Look closely at the caterpillars with a hand lens. Make a dated drawing. Record your observations in your chart.
4. Repeat step 3 every other day for 7 to 10 days. When the caterpillars are hanging from the paper disk at the top of the container and are enclosed in a casing, remove the paper disk with the casings attached. Tape it to the wall of the habitat, as shown.
5. Repeat step 3 every other day for another 7 to 10 days.

STEP 1

Drawing	Observation

STEP 3

STEP 4

Think and Write

1. **Compare** Compare two stages of the butterfly life cycle.
2. **Communicate** Sequence your drawings to explain how a caterpillar becomes a butterfly.

✓ 0307.4.2

Guided Inquiry

Research Choose an animal that lives in your area. Use library books or search the Internet to find out how the animal is born and how it changes as it grows.

Reading Science

Animal Life Cycles

VOCABULARY

larva
★ offspring
pupa

GRAPHIC ORGANIZER

Sequence Use a chart to show the life cycle of an animal.

1	
2	
3	
4	

GLE 0307.4.1 Identify the different life stages through which plants and animals pass.

GLE 0307.4.2 Recognize common human characteristics that are transmitted from parents to offspring.

Life Cycle of Insects

Animals follow similar stages in their life cycles. They are born, grow, reproduce, and die. But butterflies and most other insects change more than many other animals do.

The first stage in the life cycle of most insects is the egg. The second stage is a wormlike stage called the **larva** (LAHR vuh). The third stage is the **pupa** (PYOO puh). During the pupa stage, the butterfly changes into an adult. Butterflies form a case called a chrysalis (KRIHS uh lihs). The fourth stage is the adult. The life cycle starts again when the adult female butterfly lays eggs.

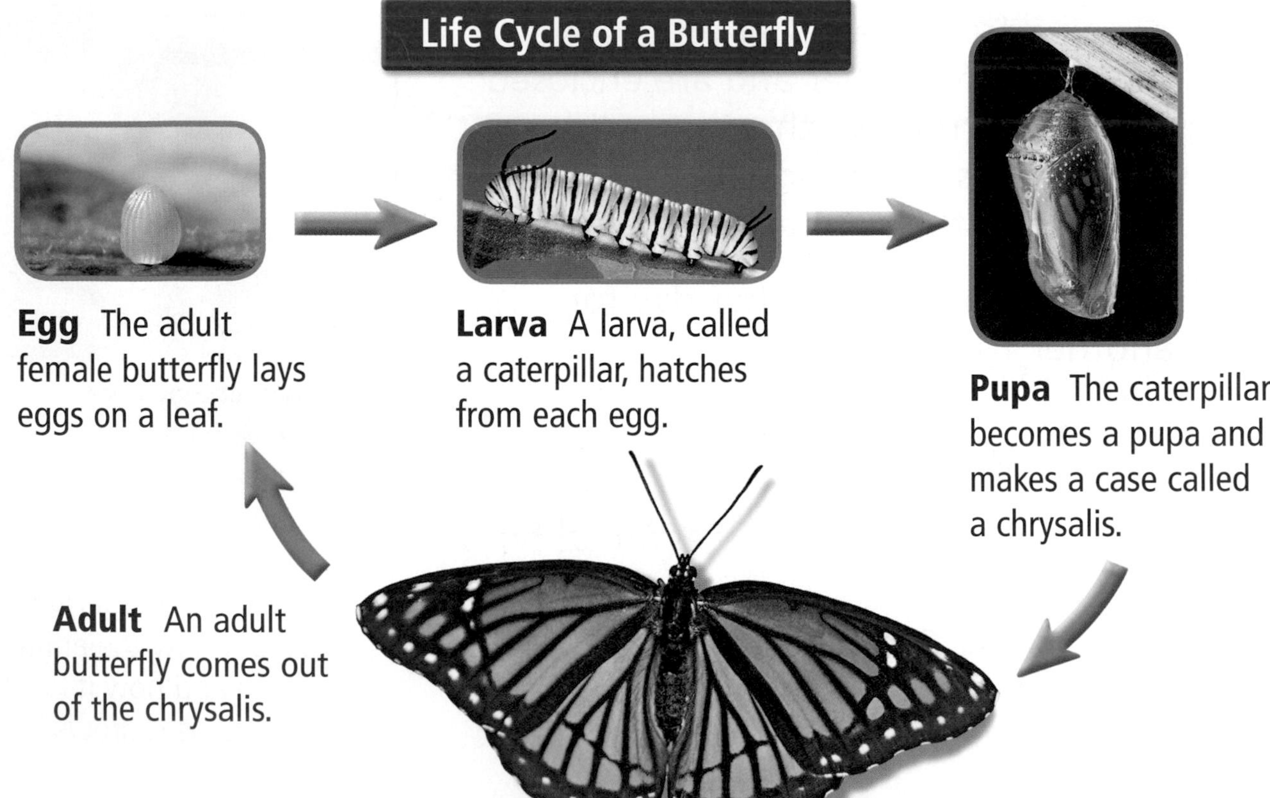

Life Cycle of a Butterfly

Egg The adult female butterfly lays eggs on a leaf.

Larva A larva, called a caterpillar, hatches from each egg.

Pupa The caterpillar becomes a pupa and makes a case called a chrysalis.

Adult An adult butterfly comes out of the chrysalis.

Life Cycle of a Frog

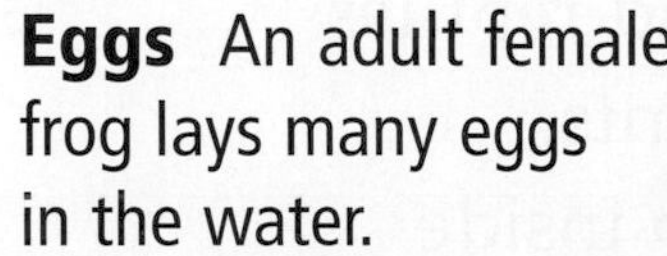

Eggs An adult female frog lays many eggs in the water.

Tadpole A tadpole hatches from an egg.

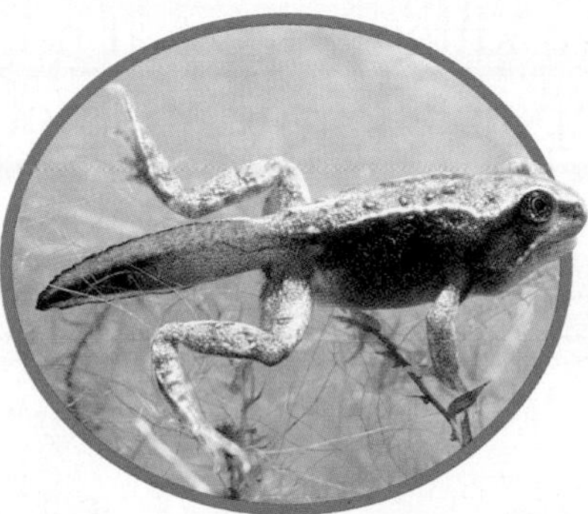

Young frog The tadpole becomes a small frog with legs and a tail.

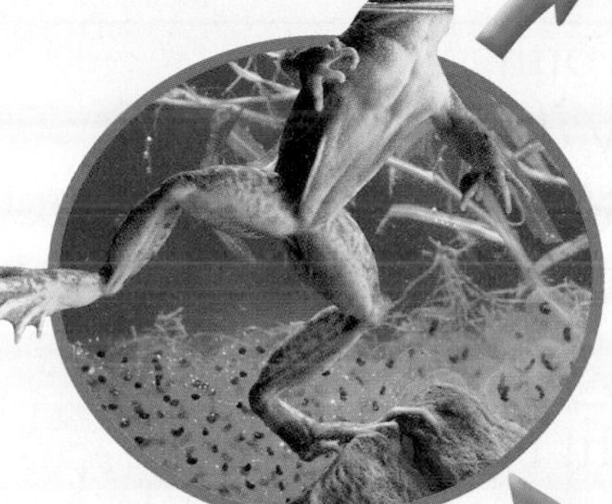

Frog The adult frog has no tail and breathes with lungs.

Life Cycles of Amphibians and Reptiles

Like insects, amphibians, such as frogs, change form during their life cycles. After a frog hatches from its egg, it is called a tadpole. A tadpole lives in water and has a long tail, gills, and no legs. It looks very different from an adult frog.

Reptiles have a different life cycle from amphibians. The adult female reptile lays eggs, usually on land. After the eggs hatch, young reptiles increase in size and grow into adults. Unlike amphibians, reptiles do not change form as they grow. A young reptile looks similar to its parents.

FOCUS CHECK Amphibians lay eggs during which stage of their life cycle?

Express Lab

Activity Card
Model an Insect Life Cycle

Life Cycles of Birds and Mammals

Birds lay eggs, just as insects, amphibians, and reptiles do. Young birds have traits similar to their parents.

The offspring of mammals grow and develop inside the bodies of adult females. **Offspring** are the living things that result when an animal produces its young.

The offspring of mammals are born live. They do not hatch from eggs. Dogs, cats, and humans grow and develop in this way. In mammals, the newborn offspring look much like their adult parents. For example, you can tell a puppy is a dog and a kitten is a cat. It might be harder to know that a tadpole is a frog and not a fish.

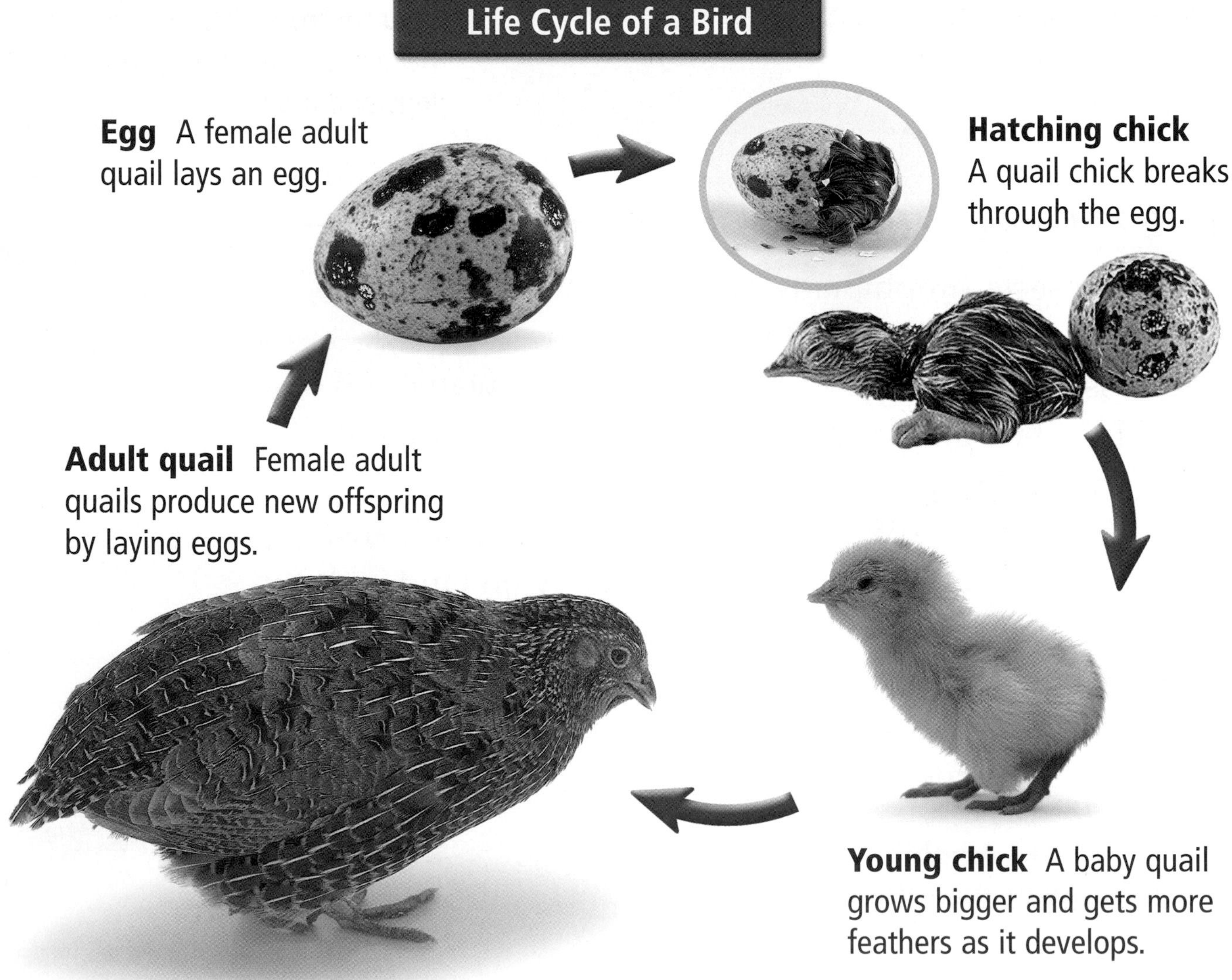

Life Cycle of a Bird
Egg A female adult quail lays an egg.
Hatching chick A quail chick breaks through the egg.
Young chick A baby quail grows bigger and gets more feathers as it develops.
Adult quail Female adult quails produce new offspring by laying eggs.

Lesson Wrap-Up

Visual Summary

Some animals are born live and other animals hatch from eggs.

Animals grow in size or change into different forms as they develop.

Adult animals reproduce and make new offspring.

COMPARE LIFE CYCLES

Make a two-column chart to compare the stages in the life cycle of a butterfly with the stages in the life cycle of a frog.

0307.4.3

Review

1. **MAIN IDEA** What do the life cycles of all animals have in common?
2. **VOCABULARY** Write a sentence using the terms *offspring* and *tadpole.*
3. **READING SKILL: Sequence** Describe the stages in the life cycle of a bird.
4. **CRITICAL THINKING: Analyze** Suppose that Animal A is an adult animal that hatched from an egg, once had gills, and once had a tail. What type of animal is Animal A?
5. **INQUIRY SKILL: Communicate** Draw a diagram of the life cycle of a reptile.

TCAP Prep

Look back at the life cycle of a butterfly shown on page 34. What is the form of the butterfly right after it hatches from an egg?

Ⓐ adult butterfly
Ⓑ pupa
Ⓒ chrysalis
Ⓓ larva

SPI 0307.4.1

Technology

Visit **www.eduplace.com/tnscp** to find out more about animal life cycles.

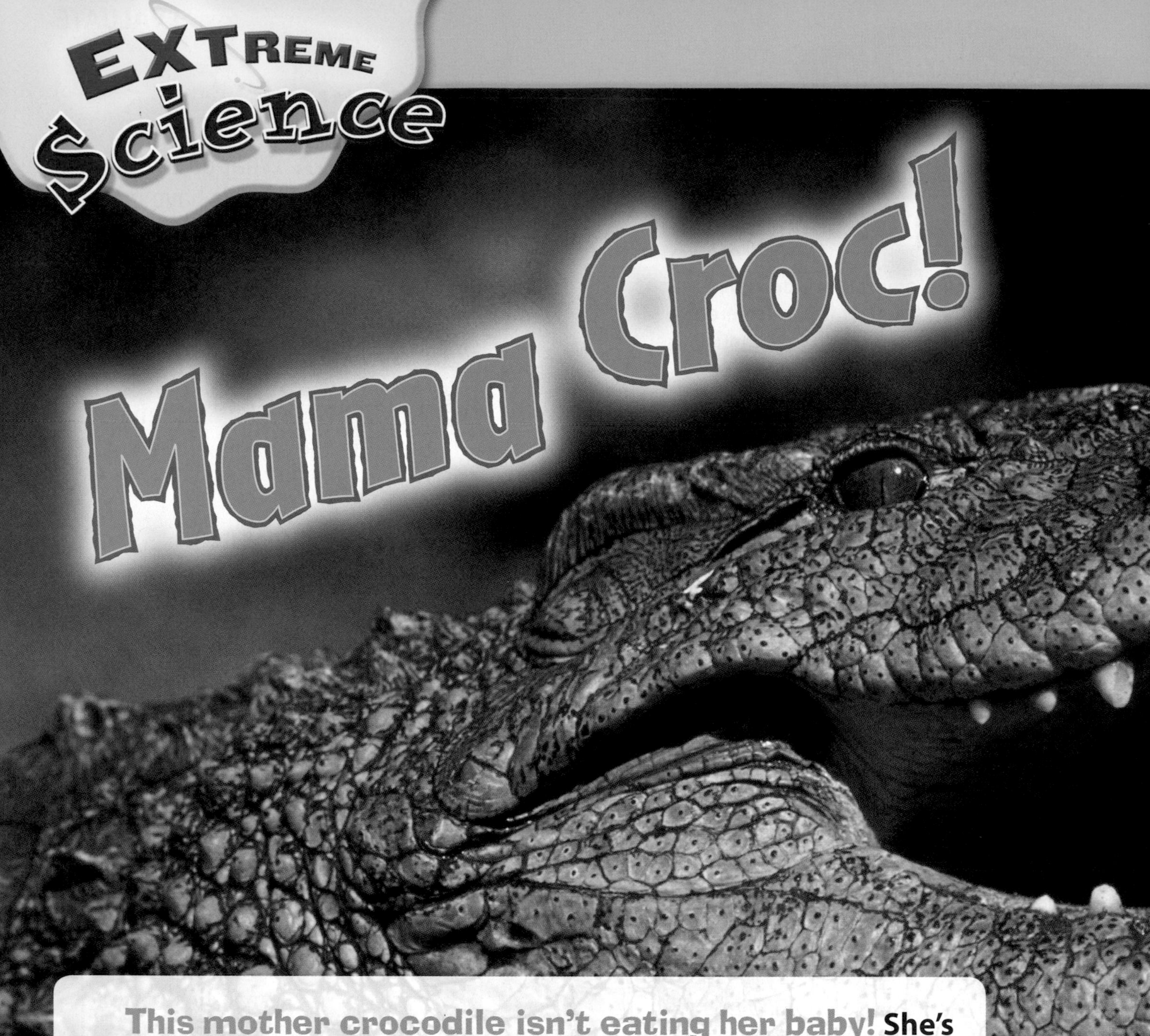

This mother crocodile isn't eating her baby! She's carrying it in her mouth to keep it safe from harm. Most reptiles just bury their eggs and leave them. The crocodile fiercely guards her buried eggs from other predators.

When she hears peeping from the buried eggs, she digs them out. Sometimes she even uses her huge teeth to help her babies out of their shells. After carrying them to the water, she watches over them until they are big enough to protect themselves.

This baby will grow fast—and big. Some full-grown crocodiles are longer than a family car and weigh more than a ton!

Lesson 4

TENNESSEE STANDARDS

GLE 0307.Inq.4 Identify and interpret simple patterns of evidence to communicate the findings of multiple investigations.
GLE 0307.4.2 Recognize common human characteristics that are transmitted from parents to offspring.

How Can Living Things Vary?

Why It Matters...

These two animals look very different from each other, but they are both dogs. Living things of the same kind do not always look the same. Some may be tall and some may be short. Some may have spots and some are a solid color. Scientists study living things of the same kind to learn how they are alike and different.

PREPARE TO INVESTIGATE

Inquiry Skill

Use Numbers You use numbers when you measure, estimate, and record data.

Materials

- 4 pea pods
- 4 index cards
- marking pen
- metric ruler

Science and Math Toolbox

For step 6, review **Making a Bar Graph** on page H3.

Directed Inquiry

Peas in a Pod

Procedure

1. In your Science Notebook, make a chart like the one shown.
2. **Experiment** Label four index cards *A, B, C,* and *D*. Place a pea pod on each of the labeled cards.
3. **Measure** Use a ruler to measure the length of each pea pod. Record the data in your chart.
4. **Record Data** Open each pea pod. Count the number of peas in each pod. Record the data in your chart.
5. **Observe** Look at the color of the peas in in each pod. Record your observations.
6. **Record Data** In your Science Notebook, copy the graph grid shown. Use the data in your chart to complete a bar graph.

STEP 1

Pea Pod	Length of Pod	Number of Peas	Color of Peas
A			
B			
C			
D			

STEP 4

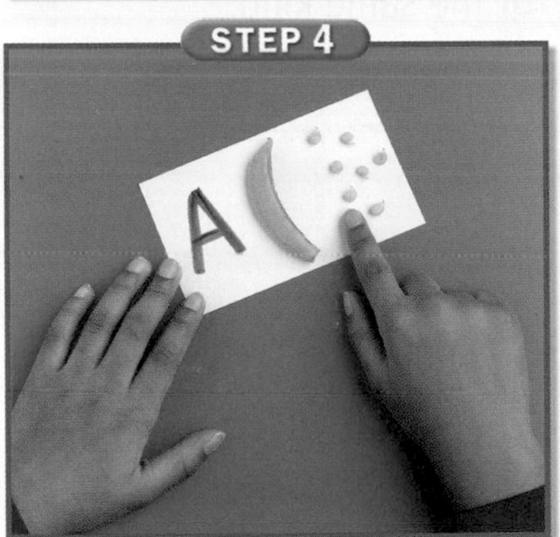

STEP 6

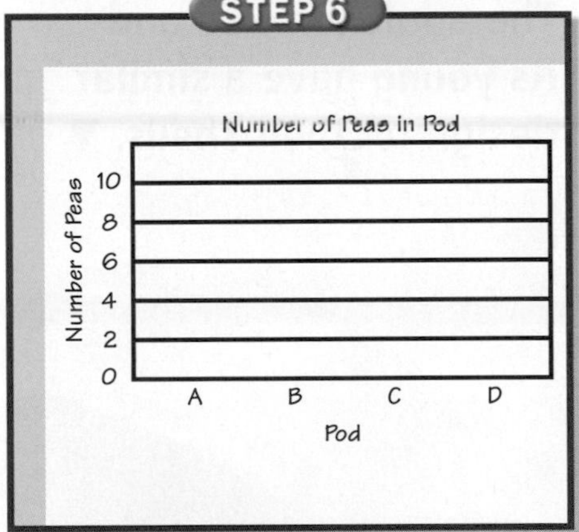

Think and Write

1. **Analyze Data** Find the greatest and the least number of peas in your data. Combine this data with that of your classmates. Make a line plot to show the class data.
2. **Predict** Suppose you measured and observed four additional pea pods. Would you expect the data to be similar to the class data? Explain your answer.

Guided Inquiry

Research Use books or the Internet to learn about one type of apple. Write a report about that apple type. Find out if all apples of that type have the same number of seeds.

✓ 0307.Inq.4

Reading Science

VOCABULARY

individual

GRAPHIC ORGANIZER

Compare and Contrast
Use a chart to compare and contrast living things of the same kind.

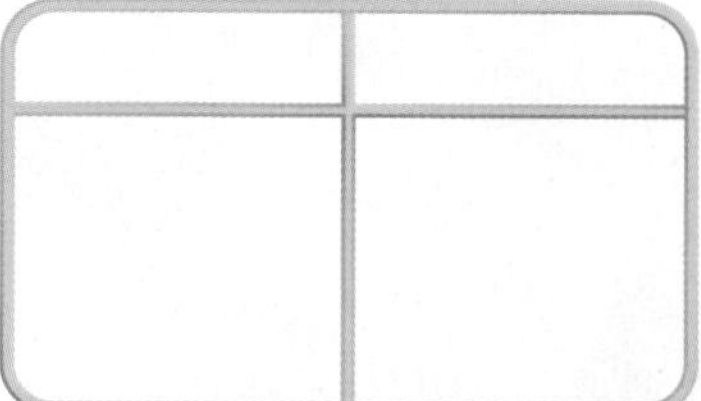

GLE 0307.4.2 Recognize common human characteristics that are transmitted from parents to offspring.

Similarities and Differences

Family Resemblance

"He has his father's eyes!" "Oh, she has her mother's smile!" You may have heard people talk about children in this way. In some families, children look similar to their parents. Young plants and animals also often look like their parents. They grow to be about the same height as their parents. The color of a plant's flowers is usually similar to that of its parent plant. The color of an animal's fur is often similar to the fur of one or both of its parents.

The adult tortoise and its young have a similar design on their shells. ▼

▲ The adult and baby rabbit look very similar.

Although offspring and their parents may look similar, they do not look exactly alike. A young horse may grow to be taller or a different color than its parents. A child may have a different eye color than either parent. An adult tree may have fewer flowers or fruit than the tree from which it came.

Differences in appearance between parents and offspring are not extreme. Have you ever seen a turtle the size of a house? A turtle may grow to be larger than either of its parents. But a turtle cannot grow to be as large as a house. Similarly, a large animal, such as a giraffe, does not produce offspring that stay very small.

FOCUS CHECK Compare ways in which plants and animals may resemble their parents.

▲ The adult penguin and its offspring do not look exactly alike.

This adult orca whale and its baby have a similar pattern on their skin.

Express Lab

Activity Card

Graph a Human Trait

Individuals Vary

In a crowd, you can see lots of different people—some are tall, some are short, some have blue eyes, some have brown eyes—but they are all humans. Although all people are humans, each person has different features, or traits.

There are also many differences within groups of plants. For example, some petunia flowers have red petals and others have pink petals.

Animals also show many differences in traits. One dog may have short fur. Another dog may be so furry you cannot see its face! Cats also show great variety in their traits. You can see examples of this in the pictures below.

▲ These petunias come in many different colors.

These are all domestic cats. Notice how different they look from one another. ▼

Petal color and fur length are just two examples of differences among individuals (ihn duh VIHJ oo uhlz). An **individual** is a single member of a species. Can you think of some other differences among individuals?

When living things reproduce, they pass on traits to their offspring. This explains why offspring usually look similar to their parents. Look at the three sheep shown here. The parents of the first sheep probably also had black heads. The parents of the second sheep likely had curled horns. The wooly third sheep probably had wooly parents, as well.

FOCUS CHECK Name two traits that can be different among individuals.

▲ These animals look different, but they are all sheep.

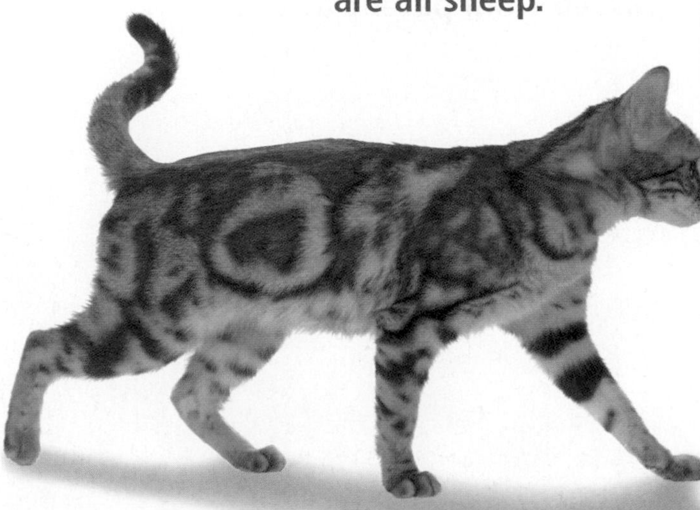

Human Traits

In humans, many traits are passed from parents to offspring. Examples include having curly or straight hair, or having dimples or not having dimples. The shape of the hairline and the shape of the ears are other traits passed to offspring.

Some traits of individuals come from the environment. The environment is everything that surrounds and affects a living thing. For example, a plant that does not get enough sunlight may not grow as tall as its parent plant. A child that does not eat healthful foods may not grow as tall as its parents.

Individuals may also get traits when they interact with their environment. But these traits are not passed on to their offspring. For example, suppose a woman cuts her hand and the cut leaves a scar. The woman did not get this trait from her parents. She also will not pass it on to any children she might have.

FOCUS CHECK Identify one trait that can be passed from parent to child.

▲ facial dimples when smiling

▲ no facial dimples when smiling

▲ widow's peak hairline

▲ straight hairline

Lesson Wrap-Up

Visual Summary

Living things usually look similar to, but not exactly like, their parents.

Individuals of the same kind usually vary in appearance.

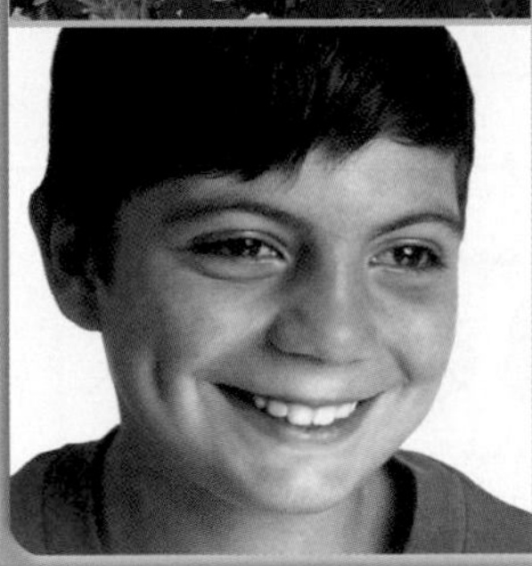

In humans, some traits are passed from parents to offspring. Other traits result from the environment.

Check for Understanding

TELL ABOUT TRAITS

Identify three traits in humans that are passed from parents to offspring. Make a titled poster that shows these traits. Use photos from magazines or make drawings to illustrate each trait. Label the pictures.

✓ **0307.4.5, 0307.4.4**

Review

1. **MAIN IDEA** Why do most offspring look similar to their parents?
2. **VOCABULARY** Define the term *individual.*
3. **READING SKILL: Compare and Contrast** How are the sheep on page 45 similar? How are they different?
4. **CRITICAL THINKING: Evaluate** Two flowers are the same color. Your friend says they must be the same species. Is this correct? Explain.
5. **INQUIRY SKILL: Use Numbers** The number of eggs laid by six birds of the same kind are: 2, 3, 2, 3, 3, 4. What can you infer about the number of eggs usually laid by this kind of bird?

TCAP Prep

Which trait cannot be passed from human parents to their child?

Ⓐ a straight hairline
Ⓑ curly hair
Ⓒ a sprained ankle
Ⓓ dimples

SPI 0307.4.2

Go Digital Technology

Visit **www.eduplace.com/tnscp** to learn more about how individuals vary.

GLE 0307.4.2 Recognize common human characteristics that are transmitted from parents to offspring. **Math GLE 0306.5.1** Organize, display, and analyze data using various representations to solve problems. **ELA GLE 0301.3.3** Write in a variety of modes and genres, including narration, literary response, personal experience, and subject matter content.

Math Counting Petunias

A group of students planted a package of petunia seeds in the school garden. The package contained 125 seeds of mixed colors.

After several months, most of the seeds had grown into adult petunia plants. Look at the pictograph. It shows the number of plants of each flower color that grew.

Use the pictograph to answer the questions.

Petunia Plants

Pink

Purple

White

Red

= 10 plants

1. How many plants of each color grew?
2. How many petunia plants in all grew?
3. How many seeds failed to grow into adult plants?

Tell a Story

Imagine that you are a frog. Write your life story. Tell how your body changes as you grow from an egg to an adult frog.

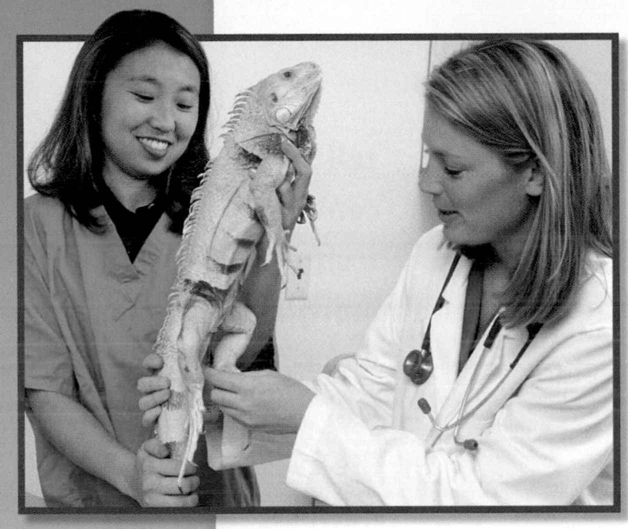

Veterinary Assistant

Do you enjoy caring for animals? As a veterinary assistant, you might help a veterinarian bandage the broken leg of a dog or calm a cat during an exam. You would also feed, water, and exercise animals. You would clean cages and exam rooms. Veterinary assistants work at animal shelters, humane societies, and animal hospitals.

What It Takes!

- High-school diploma
- Courses in biology; some knowledge of medicine

Botanist

The next time you bite into a sweet juicy apple, think about the plant that produced it. If you are interested in plants, you might want to become a botanist—a plant scientist. As a botanist, you might study plant disease. Or you might find ways to improve crops. Some botanists are looking for ways to save Earth's rain forests.

What It Takes!

- Degree in botany or biology
- Love of plants

Chapter 1 Review and TCAP Prep

Vocabulary

Complete each sentence with a term from the list.

1. The process by which plants make food is called ______.
2. The part of the plant that contains seeds is the ______.
3. The third stage of an insect's life cycle is the ______.
4. The series of changes that a living thing goes through during its lifetime is called a/an ______.
5. A single member of a species is called a/an ______.
6. Living things that result when animals produce young are called ______.
7. The first stage in the life cycle of most plants is the ______.
8. The part of most plants that grows underground is the ______.
9. A plant that grows cones is a/an ______.
10. The wormlike stage of an insect's life cycle is called the ______.

cell
conifer
fruit
individual
larva
leaf
★ **life cycle**
nutrient
★ **offspring**
★ **photosynthesis**
pupa
root
seed
stem

TCAP Inquiry Skills

11. **Communicate** Make a diagram to show the life cycle of a bird. Write labels to explain each part of your drawing. **GLE 0307.Inq.3, GLE 0307.4.1**

12. **Predict** A male and a female dog both have long fur. If their fur is cut short, will their puppies be likely to have long fur or short fur? Explain. **GLE 0307.Inq.1**

13. **Observe** Describe what must happen for an orange tree with blossoms to produce fruits and seeds. **GLE 0307.4.1**

Map the Concept

Place the following terms in the concept map to describe the life cycle of an insect.

pupa **egg**
adult **larva**

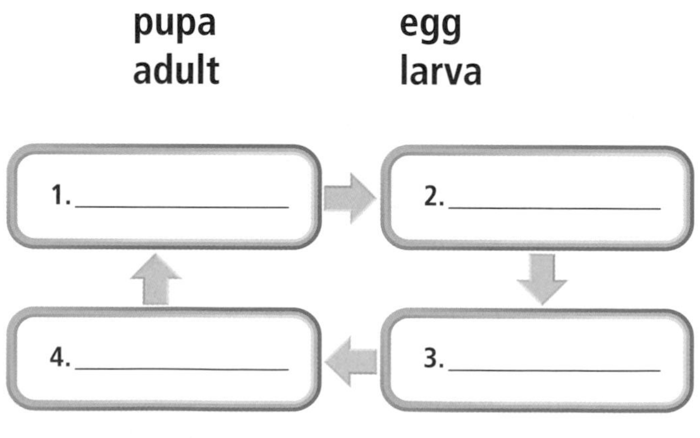

GLE 0307.4.1

Critical Thinking

14. Synthesize A man with dimples has a scar on his arm. Could one, both, or neither of these of traits be passed on to the man's children? Explain your answer. **GLE 0307.4.2**

15. Evaluate Your classmate says that an apple seed is similar to a frog's egg. Do you agree or disagree with this statement? Explain your answer. **GLE 0307.4.1**

16. Analyze The outer surface of many kinds of leaves has a waxy covering that is waterproof. What human body part is such a covering most like? How are they alike? **GLE 0307.1.1**

Compare Life Cycles

Do research in books or on the Internet to find out about the stages in the life cycle of a mealworm. The adult insect is called a darkling beetle. Make labeled drawings of the life cycle. Compare the mealworm's life cycle to that of a butterfly. Tell how are they alike.

0307.4.3

TCAP Prep

Answer the following questions.

17 Which picture below shows the pupa stage in the life cycle of a butterfly?

Ⓐ 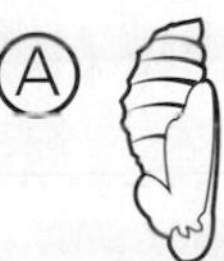

Ⓒ 

Ⓑ

Ⓓ 

SPI 0307.4.1

18 Which trait would not be passed from parent to offspring?

Ⓕ ear shape
Ⓖ broken fingernail
Ⓗ cheek dimples
Ⓙ curly hair

SPI 0307.4.2

19 Which is true of adult frogs?

Ⓐ They give birth to live young.
Ⓑ They live only in water.
Ⓒ They have tails.
Ⓓ They breathe with lungs, not with gills.

SPI 0307.4.1

20 Photosynthesis is carried out in which part of a plant?

Ⓕ leaf
Ⓖ root
Ⓗ stem
Ⓙ flower

SPI 0307.1.1

Chapter 2

Survival of Living Things

Lesson Preview

LESSON 1

You cannot live without water, air, and a place to live. Why do you need these things to survive?

LESSON 2

Bald eagles and bears both eat fish. What happens to these animals if there are not enough fish?

LESSON 3

Plants have leaves and ducks have webbed feet. How do their parts help living things survive?

LESSON 4

A fire spreads through a forest. Can a fire ever be helpful to living things?

Fun Facts

A shrimp's heart is in its head.

Vocabulary Preview

adaptation
behavior
community
ecosystem
★ energy
environment
habitat
★ organism
★ pollution
population
★ predator
★ prey

★ = Tennessee Academic Vocabulary

Vocabulary Strategies

Have you ever seen any of these terms before? Do you know what they mean?

Describe, explain, or give an example of the vocabulary terms in your own words.

Draw a picture, symbol, example, or other image that describes the term.

Glossary p. H16

predator

prey

pollution

population

Start with Your Standards

Inquiry

GLE 0307.Inq.2 Select and use appropriate tools and simple equipment to conduct an investigation.

GLE 0307.Inq.3 Organize data into appropriate tables, graphs, drawings, or diagrams.

GLE 0307.Inq.4 Identify and interpret simple patterns of evidence to communicate the findings of multiple investigations.

GLE 0307.Inq.5 Recognize that people may interpret the same results in different ways.

Life Science

Standard 2 Interdependence

GLE 0307.2.1 Categorize things as living or non-living.

GLE 0307.2.2 Explain how organisms with similar needs compete with one another for resources.

Standard 3 Flow of Matter and Energy

GLE 0307.3.1 Describe how animals use food to obtain energy and materials for growth and repair.

Standard 5 Biodiversity and Change

GLE 0307.5.1 Explore the relationship between an organism's characteristics and its ability to survive in a particular environment.

Interact with this chapter.

www.eduplace.com/tnscp

TENNESSEE STANDARDS

GLE 0307.Inq.5 Recognize that people may interpret the same results in different ways.
GLE 0307.2.1 Categorize things as living or non-living.
GLE 0307.3.1 Describe how animals use food to obtain energy and materials for growth and repair.

Guiding Question

What Are the Needs of Living Things?

Why It Matters...

You probably know that a turtle is alive and that a rock is not alive. But how do you know this? What does it mean to be alive? You and all other living things share some of the same traits. All living things also share the same basic needs.

PREPARE TO INVESTIGATE

Inquiry Skill

Collaborate When you collaborate, you work with others to share ideas, data, and observations.

Materials

- aquarium
- water
- gravel
- goldfish
- fish food
- piece of elodea plant

Science and Math Toolbox

For step 2, review **Making a Chart to Organize Data** on page H10.

Directed Inquiry

Staying Alive

Procedure

1. **Collaborate** Work with a partner. One partner should observe a goldfish. The other partner should observe an elodea (ih LOH dee ah), which is a type of water plant. In your Science Notebook, make a chart like the one shown.
2. **Observe** Watch your living thing for a few minutes. In your chart, record the name of the living thing and everything that you observe. Include its surroundings and any movements it makes.
3. **Infer** Based on your observations, write two or three things that you think your living thing needs to stay alive.
4. **Collaborate** Compare charts with your partner. Circle the needs that are alike for the fish and the plant.

STEP 1

Observing Living Things	
Observations	Needs

STEP 2

STEP 4

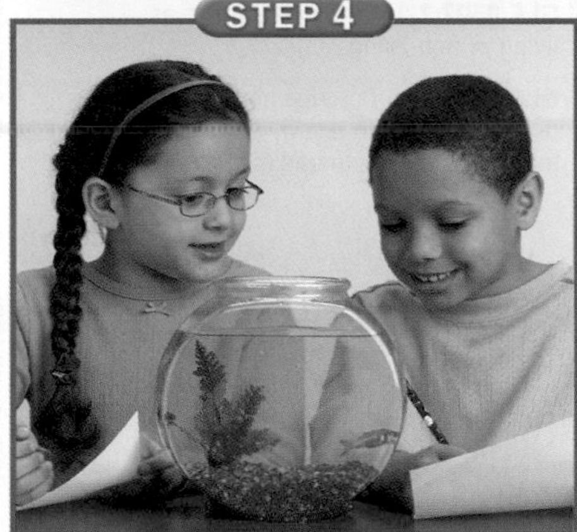

Think and Write

1. **Compare** What does the goldfish need that the elodea plant does not need?
2. **Hypothesize** If you put the elodea plant in sunlight, it releases tiny bubbles of gas. Where do you think this gas comes from? What does the goldfish do that might be similar?

Guided Inquiry

Research What animal would you like to have as a pet? Use the library or Internet to find books about what that animal needs to stay alive and healthy.

✓ 0307.3.2 ✓ 0307.3.4

Reading Science

▶ VOCABULARY

ecosystem
★ energy
environment
★ organism

▶ GRAPHIC ORGANIZER

Draw Conclusions Fill in the diagram with details about an object. Conclude whether the object is alive or not.

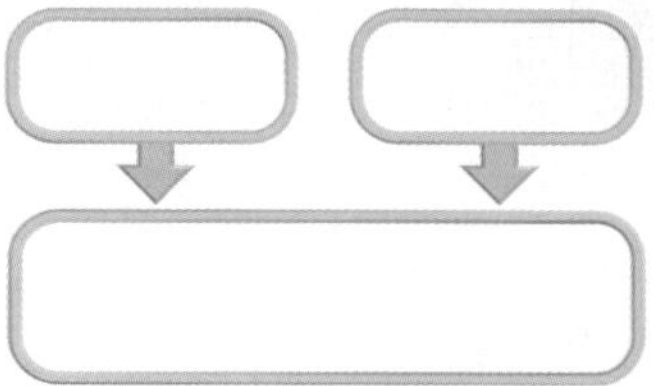

GLE 0307.2.1 Categorize things as living or non-living.

GLE 0307.3.1 Describe how animals use food to obtain energy and materials for growth and repair.

Needs of Living Things

Living and Nonliving Things

As you look at the picture on this page, you see many things. There are flowers, bushes, sunlight, soil, chairs, and humans. Some of these things are living, and others are nonliving. A living thing is alive. Only a living thing is able to carry out the life processes (PRAHS ehs ihz).

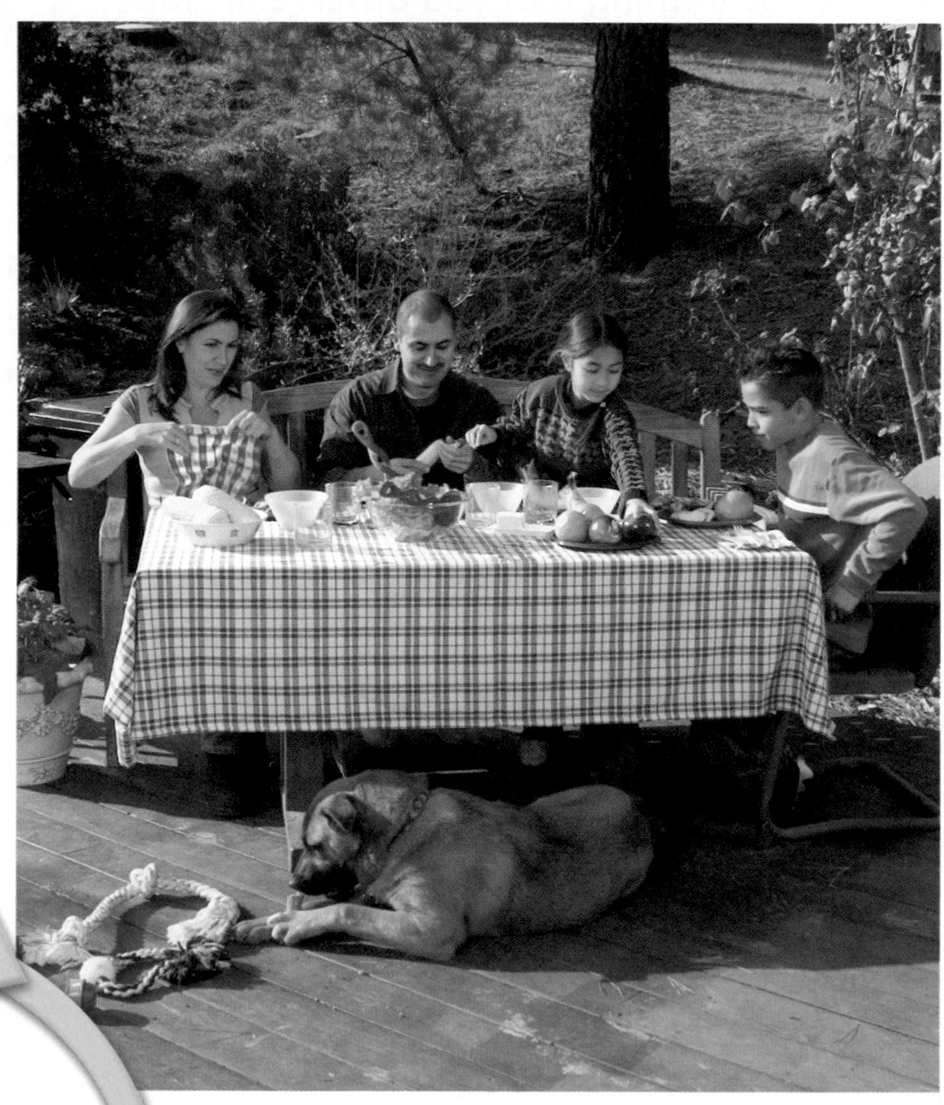

There are living and nonliving things in this picture. Identify as many of each kind as you can. ▶

Express Lab

Activity Card
Draw a Habitat

What are life processes? Think of the things your body does. For example, you grow and develop. You also react to the things around you. Another life process is the ability to reproduce (ree pruh DOOS), or to produce young. All of these life processes use energy (EHN ur jee). **Energy** is the ability to cause change.

Not all things are alive. Nonliving things cannot carry out life processes. What traits could you look for to decide whether something is living? The five traits of living things are described in the table below.

FOCUS CHECK What are three traits you would look for to decide whether something is a toy dog or a living dog?

Traits of Living Things

Trait	Description
Made of Cells	All living things are made of tiny parts called cells. Some living things are made up of only one cell. Humans are made of many millions of cells!
Obtain and Use Energy	Plants, such as apple trees, get energy from the Sun. Apples contain food energy. Animals obtain energy from food and use that energy for growth, repair of parts, and other life activities.
Respond to Surroundings	When a plant bends toward the light, it is responding to its surroundings. All living things react to changes in their surroundings.
Grow and Develop	All living things grow and develop. When you get taller, you are growing. When your body changes during your lifetime, you are developing.
Reproduce	All living things have the ability to reproduce. This means that they can produce offspring, or young that are like themselves.

Needs of Living Things

You watch a bee flying just above a flower. A bee and a plant don't seem to have much in common, but both are organisms (AWR guh nihz uhmz). An **organism** is a living thing. All organisms carry out the same life processes. They also have similar basic needs. What do plants, animals, and all other organisms need to survive?

Energy Moving, growing, and breathing all require energy. All living things need a source of energy. They use food as a source of energy, but they get this food in different ways. Plants use energy from sunlight to make food. Animals cannot make food. They get energy by eating plants or other animals.

Nutrients Nutrients are materials in food and in soil that living things need for energy and for growth.

Air Air is a mixture of gases that living things need. One of the gases in air is oxygen. Most living things need oxygen to survive. When plants make food, they give off oxygen into the air. Animals depend on this oxygen to survive.

Energy Leaves capture the energy in sunlight. The plant uses this energy to make food.

Nutrients Roots and stems carry nutrients and water from the soil to all parts of the plant.

Shelter All animals need a place to live. An animal's home gives it shelter and provides it with protection from enemies. Some animals use plants for shelter.

Water Living things are made mostly of water. In fact, more than three fourths of your blood is water. Most living things can live for only a short time without water.

FOCUS CHECK Could most plants live in soil that contains no nutrients? Why or why not?

Air **When you exercise, you need a lot of oxygen. Oxygen is used to break down nutrients.**

Shelter **Caves give bats shelter. The insects that bats eat and the water that bats drink are found in or near caves.**

Water **The body needs water to break down food, to move things from place to place, and to make cells.**

Interactions

Living things are found in every kind of environment (ehn VY ruhn muhnt). An **environment** is all the living and nonliving things that surround an organism.

A Florida mangrove swamp is one kind of ecosystem (EE koh sihs tuhm). An **ecosystem** is all the living and nonliving things that exist and interact in one place. To survive, the organisms in an ecosystem depend on each other and on the nonliving things that share their ecosystem.

FOCUS CHECK What might happen if all of one type of organism in an ecosystem died?

Herons build nests in the leafy branches.
Mangrove trees use sunlight to make food.
Mangrove roots prevent soil from washing away.
Pelicans depend on fish for food.
Red snapper and other fish live in the water.
Oysters and crabs use mangrove roots for shelter.

Lesson Wrap-Up

Visual Summary

Living things are made up of cells, obtain and use energy, react, grow and develop, and produce offspring.

Living things need energy, nutrients, air, water, and shelter.

In an ecosystem, organisms interact with other organisms and with nonliving parts of their environment.

Check for Understanding

COMPARE LIVING AND NONLIVING THINGS

Make a two-column chart. Write the heading *Living Thing* at the top of one column and the heading *Nonliving Thing* at the top of the other. Then select one living and one nonliving thing. Draw a picture of each thing in the correct column. Below each picture, write the traits that make that thing either living or nonliving.

✓ 0307.2.1

Review

1. **MAIN IDEA** What are the five traits of living things?
2. **VOCABULARY** Write a sentence using the term *environment*.
3. **READING SKILL: Draw Conclusions** You receive a gift that grows in sunlight and does not need to be fed. Would you conclude that this gift is a plant or an animal? Explain.
4. **CRITICAL THINKING: Apply** Give an example of how a nonliving thing might affect the living things in a desert ecosystem.
5. **INQUIRY SKILL: Collaborate** Name a basic need of living things. Explain to a classmate how that basic need can be met for a mouse.

TCAP Prep

Which of the following is true only of a living thing?

Ⓐ It breaks down.
Ⓑ It uses energy.
Ⓒ It is made of cells.
Ⓓ It is warm to the touch.

SPI 0307.2.1

Go Digital Technology

Visit **www.eduplace.com/tnscp** to find out more about the needs of living things.

Lesson 2

TENNESSEE STANDARDS

GLE 0307.Inq.3 Organize data into appropriate tables, graphs, drawings, or diagrams.

GLE 0307.2.2 Explain how organisms with similar needs compete with one another for resources.

How Do Living Things Compete?

Why It Matters...

"It's mine!" "No, it's mine!" If birds and squirrels could speak to each other, this is what they might say. When food is limited in an environment, animals must compete. An animal that loses a competition might lose a meal or a place to live.

PREPARE TO INVESTIGATE

Inquiry Skill

Use Variables A variable is the condition that is being tested in an experiment. All conditions in an experiment must be kept the same, except for the variable.

Materials

- 4 paper plates
- 4 sheets of paper
- pretzels (1 per student)

Science and Math Toolbox

For step 5, review **Making a Bar Graph** on page H3.

Directed Inquiry

Competition

Procedure

1. **Use Variables** Your teacher will set up four model ecosystems. Each ecosystem is represented by a plate covered with a sheet of paper. Some plates contain many pretzels, some contain few pretzels, and some contain no pretzels.

2. **Use Models** Stand in the center of the room. When your teacher says "Go," choose an ecosystem and walk to it. **Safety:** Do not run or push others.

3. Peek under the paper. If there is a pretzel, take the pretzel and stand by the ecosystem. If there are no pretzels, move on to another ecosystem.

4. Repeat step 3 until you find a pretzel.

5. **Communicate** When every student has found a pretzel, make a bar graph like the one shown. The graph should show how many ecosystems each student visited before finding food.

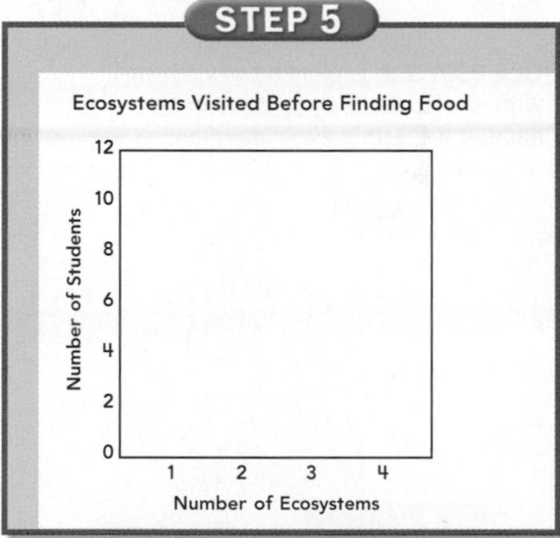

Think and Write

1. **Analyze Data** How many ecosystems did most people visit before they found food? Why?

2. **Predict** How might an organism be affected if the food in its ecosystem were eaten by other organisms?

Guided Inquiry

Solve a Problem Take away several pretzels, then repeat the activity. Think of ways that each student could still get some food. Share your ideas with your classmates.

✔ **0307.Inq.3**

Reading Science

▶ **VOCABULARY**

community
population
★ predator
★ prey

▶ **GRAPHIC ORGANIZER**

Main Idea and Details
As you read, write down details that describe the ways in which organisms compete.

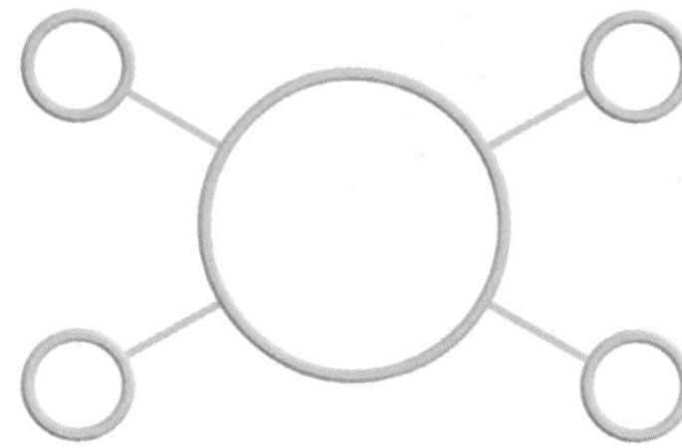

GLE 0307.2.2 Explain how organisms with similar needs compete with one another for resources.

Living Things Compete

Competing for Food and Water

Look around. You, your classmates, your teachers, your family, and all the people who live in your neighborhood make up a population (pahp yuh LAY shuhn) of humans. A **population** is all the organisms of the same kind that live together in an ecosystem. All the ants living in a forest make up the ant population of that forest ecosystem. Every oak tree in a forest is a member of the oak tree population of that ecosystem.

In a prairie ecosystem, coyotes, snakes, and skunks compete with each other for prairie chicken eggs.

All the populations in an ecosystem make up a community (kuh MYOO nih tee). A **community** is a group of plants and animals that live in the same area and interact with each other. The ants, oak trees, robins, and other living things in a forest ecosystem are part of the same community.

A pond ecosystem is home to animal populations such as fish, frogs, and insects. Plants such as cattails and populations of algae also live there. Living things in nature must be able to get enough resources (REE-sawrs ehz) to survive. A resource is a thing found in nature that is useful to organisms. Food, water, shelter, and air are resources. If there is not enough of a resource for all the organisms that need it, they must compete for that resource.

In a pond community, plants such as cattails and algae compete for nutrients in the water. Members of the same population may also compete for a resource. If there are not enough resources to meet the needs of all the organisms, some will die. For example, if there are too many frogs, some will not catch enough insects and will not survive.

FOCUS CHECK What are four resources for which living things compete?

above surface

below surface

▲ **Pond Community**
Competition in a community keeps populations from getting too large.

Activity Card
Compete for Resources

Competing for Space

In addition to food and water, organisms need living space. Many birds need tree branches and holes in tree trunks to build nests. Trees need space underground for their roots to spread out. They need space above ground for their leafy branches to capture energy from sunlight.

Wolves live in family groups called packs. Sometimes there isn't enough space for all the wolf packs in an area to live and raise offspring. Some of the packs may leave the area to find more space.

Sea lions live on rocks at the edge of the ocean. If a sea lion population in a rocky area becomes too crowded, the animals will fight for space. Some sea lions are injured or killed as a result of those fights.

▲ **Wolf packs may move to new areas to find more space.**

Sea lions compete with each other for space. ▼

Moose are big animals. They need large areas where they can roam in search of food, water, and shelter. Sometimes humans build houses in areas where moose live. Then the moose no longer have enough space to meet their needs. As moose populations become crowded, moose wander into areas where humans live. This can be dangerous for both the moose and the humans.

People need space, too. When people are crowded together, as in some large cities, they may compete for space. Competition for space might take place on a busy street or on a crowded bus.

▲ In a crowded city, people compete for space.

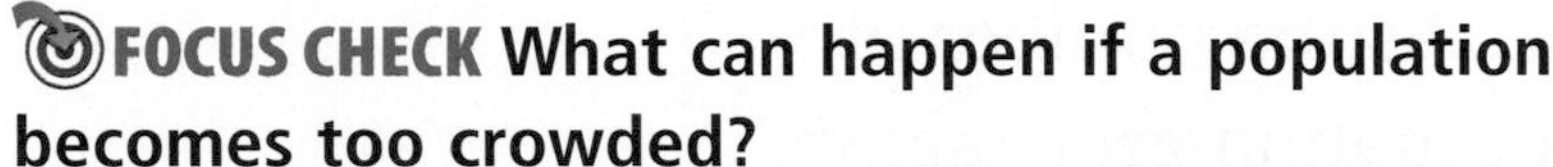

FOCUS CHECK What can happen if a population becomes too crowded?

Moose often roam into areas where humans live. ▼

Resources and Population Size

The resources in an area affect the size of the populations that depend on those resources. About one hundred years ago, wild horses roamed southern Nevada. They ate grasses and small shrubs. Some horses were killed by other animals, such as mountain lions. Mountain lions are predators. A **predator** is an animal that hunts other animals for food. The horses are prey. A **prey** is any animal that is hunted for food by a predator. The predators kept the horse population from becoming too large.

As humans moved into the area, they hunted many mountain lions. With fewer predators, the wild horse population grew. More horses ate more grass and shrubs. As plant resources disappeared, horses began to starve and die. As the number of horses decreased, the plant population grew again.

Today, when the number of horses becomes too great for the amount of plant resources, the United States government captures some horses. The government finds new homes for them.

FOCUS CHECK What caused the wild horse population to decrease?

Population size is limited by the amount of food resources available. ▼

Lesson Wrap-Up

Visual Summary

All the populations that live in an area and interact make up a community.

Organisms in a region compete for resources such as food, water, air, and space.

The size of a population depends on the available resources in an area.

Check for Understanding

SHOW PLANT AND ANIMAL RELATIONSHIPS

Deer, mice, crickets, and rabbits live in a forest. All of these animals eat grass plants. Make a drawing to show how these animals compete. Write a caption for your drawing.

✓ **0307.2.2**

Review

1. **MAIN IDEA** When do living things compete for resources?
2. **VOCABULARY** How is a population different from a community?
3. **READING SKILL: Main Idea and Details** Explain how frogs compete for resources in a pond.
4. **CRITICAL THINKING: Apply** How might a community of rabbits, grass, and coyotes change if a lot of grass died?
5. **INQUIRY SKILL: Use Variables** An experiment is designed to find out how the amount of food in a fish tank affects the size of the fish. What is the variable?

TCAP Prep

A robin and a blue jay try to build their nests on the same branch. For what resource are the birds competing?

Ⓐ food
Ⓑ space
Ⓒ water
Ⓓ air

SPI 0307.2.2

Go Digital Technology

Visit **www.eduplace.com/tnscp** to learn more about competition.

Lesson 3

TENNESSEE STANDARDS

GLE 0307.Inq.4 Identify and interpret simple patterns of evidence to communicate the findings of multiple investigations.
GLE 0307.5.1 Explore the relationship between an organism's characteristics and its ability to survive in a particular environment.

Guiding Question

How Do Adaptations Help Living Things?

Why It Matters...

Suppose you were an insect that lived on green leaves. What would be a good way to hide from birds that wanted to make you their dinner? Green katydids look just like the leaves they live on. All living things have special body parts or ways in which they act that help them stay alive.

PREPARE TO INVESTIGATE

Inquiry Skill

Infer When you infer, you use facts you know and observations you have made to draw a conclusion.

Materials

- foods: wheat nugget cereal, shredded wheat cereal softened in water, sunflower seeds, grapes
- water bottle with water
- tools: tweezers, chopsticks, dropper, salad tongs, pliers, hand-held strainer or slotted spoon
- goggles

Science and Math Toolbox

For step 1, review **Making a Chart to Organize Data** page H10.

Directed Inquiry

Best Bird Beak

Procedure

1. **Record Data** In your Science Notebook, make a chart like the one shown. **Safety:** Wear goggles during this activity. Do not eat any of the foods.
2. **Experiment** Use each tool to pick up softened shredded wheat. Each tool represents a type of bird beak. Which tool works best? Write the name of that tool next to "softened shredded wheat" on your chart.
3. Repeat step 2 for each of the other materials. Record results in your chart.
4. The bottle of water represents a trumpet-shaped flower containing a sweet liquid called nectar. Repeat step 2 to find out which tool works best to remove water from the bottle.
5. **Communicate** Compare your results with those of your classmates. Then decide which tool you think is best for handling each material.

Think and Write

1. **Use Models** Which tool would be best for getting nectar from a flower?
2. **Infer** From your results, make an inference about how the shape of a bird's beak is related to what it eats.

✓ 0307.5.1, ✓ 0307.5.2

STEP 1

Material	Best Tool
softened shredded wheat	
wheat nuggets	
sunflower seeds	
grapes	
water	

STEP 2

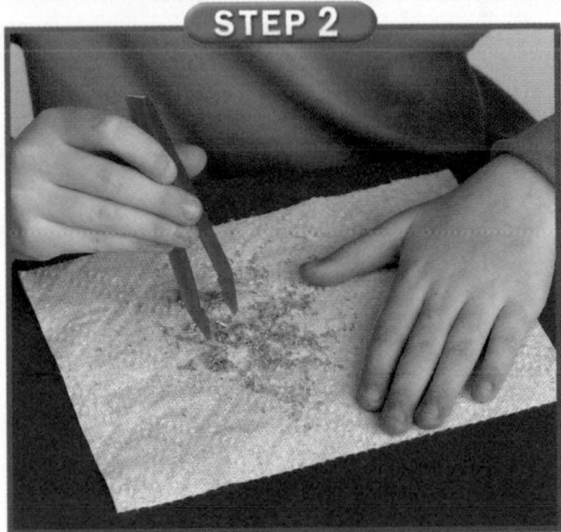

STEP 4

Guided Inquiry

Research Look in books, in magazines, and on the Internet for pictures of bird beaks that work like the tools in the activity. Try to find one beak for each tool. How does each bird's beak help it eat?

Reading Science

▶ **VOCABULARY**

adaptation

behavior

▶ **GRAPHIC ORGANIZER**

Problem-Solution Use the chart to identify an extreme environment. Give an example of an organism that has body structures that allow it to survive in that environment.

GLE 0307.5.1 Explore the relationship between an organism's characteristics and its ability to survive in a particular environment.

Adaptations Help Living Things

Getting Food

Did you ever wish that you were invisible so you could take a snack without being seen? Many animals have adaptations (ad dap TAY shuhnz) that let them become almost invisible. Then they can sneak up on food or hide from enemies. An **adaptation** is a behavior (bi HAYV yur) or a body part that helps a living thing survive in its environment. A **behavior** is the way an animal typically acts in a certain situation.

A cat's ability to sneak up on a mouse is a behavior that is an adaptation. ▼

▲ Some spiders have body parts that enable them to spin webs. Webs trap insects that spiders use for food.

Many types of animal behaviors are adaptations. A bee dancing to tell other bees where food can be found is an adaptation that helps that population of bees survive.

Adaptations for getting food help an organism survive. Certain adaptations let an organism get food that others cannot get. A hummingbird has a long, thin beak that can reach nectar deep inside a flower. The arms of sea stars have strong suction cups that are used to pull open the shells of clams.

Plants have adapted parts, too. Some plants are climbing vines. Their long stems grow up trunks to the tops of trees. Although their roots are in the ground, their leaves are up high where sunlight can shine on them.

FOCUS CHECK What two kinds of adaptations help a living thing survive?

▲ Venus' flytraps live where soil has few nutrients. They get nutrients by trapping insects.

▼ The long-necked giraffe can eat tree leaves that are out of reach of other animals.

Surviving Harsh Conditions

Living conditions in an alpine, or high-mountain, ecosystem are harsh. Temperatures are low and it often snows. The land is steep and rocky. Organisms there have adaptations that help them survive.

The growing season is short. The fact that plants sprout, grow, and produce seeds quickly is an adaptation. Many plants are small. Small plants lose little water when it's windy.

Animals also have adaptations that help them survive the cold. Thick fur and layers of fat keep some animals, such as marmots and sheep, warm. Some animals sleep during very cold periods.

Some plants and animals have adaptations that are slightly better than those of others. These organisms are more likely to survive than others of their kind.

FOCUS CHECK Describe an adaptation that helps an animal survive in cold temperatures.

Needle-shaped leaves of some trees help prevent water loss.

Ptarmigans have white feathers in winter, which helps them blend in with the snow. In summer their feathers are brown, which helps them hide on rocky ground.

ptarmigans

Alpine Ecosystem
bighorn sheep
The feet of mountain goats and bighorn sheep are adapted to walking on rocks and steep slopes.
mountain goat
The marmot's thick fur protects it from cold temperatures.
marmot
Express Lab
Activity Card
Match Structures to Food

▲ A barrel cactus is covered with long, sharp spines. The spines help keep animals away.

Self-Defense

Most organisms have adaptations for self-defense. These are behaviors or structures that help keep an organism from being eaten by enemies. For example, when an enemy approaches, many animals will run away or hide. Some plants have spines or thorns that prevent them from being eaten. Some plants and insects contain bad-tasting chemicals. The bad taste makes them a poor choice for a meal.

Some organisms have coloring or markings, such as spots or stripes, that make it hard to see them in their environment. For example, a green insect is hard to see on a green plant. Still other plants and animals look like other organisms that are poisonous. These harmless organisms fool their enemies into thinking they are poisonous, so they are left alone.

FOCUS CHECK How does a self-defense adaptation help an organism survive?

An octopus can change its color or release a cloud of ink to help it hide. ▼

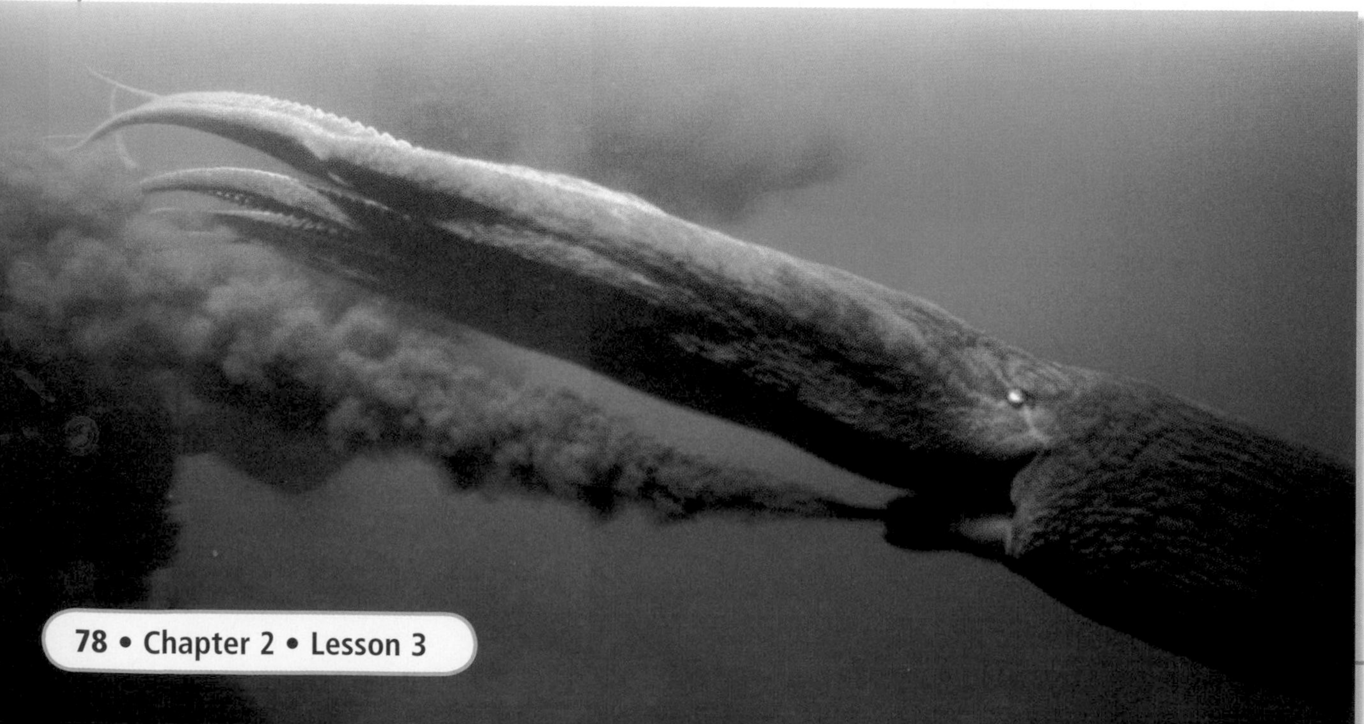

Lesson Wrap-Up

Visual Summary

Adaptations help organisms:
- get food
- survive harsh conditions
- defend themselves from enemies

Body structures help organisms:
- survive
- grow
- reproduce

Behaviors help organisms:
- survive
- grow
- reproduce

DESCRIBE ADAPTATIONS

Make a two-column chart. Head one column *Organism* and the other column *Adaptation for Getting Food*. In the first column, write the name of each of the following organisms: sea star, Venus' flytrap, giraffe, climbing vine, hummingbird. In the second column write a brief description of an adaptation that the organism has for getting food.

0307.3.3

Review

1. **MAIN IDEA** Why are adaptations important?
2. **VOCABULARY** Use the term *behavior* in a sentence about animal adaptations.
3. **READING SKILL: Problem-Solution** How might a plant be adapted to life in a desert?
4. **CRITICAL THINKING: Apply** Describe an adaptation an organism might have if it lived on ice and ate animals that lived under the ice.
5. **INQUIRY SKILL: Infer** An animal can store a lot of water in its body. What can you infer about its environment?

TCAP Prep

Which is not an example of self-defense?

Ⓐ An octopus squirts a cloud of ink.
Ⓑ A bee injects poison with a stinger.
Ⓒ A harmless butterfly looks like a poisonous butterfly.
Ⓓ A sea star uses its suction cups to open clam shells.

SPI 0307.5.1

Go Digital Technology

Visit **www.eduplace.com/tnscp** to learn more about adaptations.

Big Mouth!

Its jaws are as long as a rowboat. The underside of its throat can expand like an accordion. Its nostrils are at the top of its head. Everything about the humpback whale is an adaptation for gulping gallons of seawater.

Why would a whale take in so much water? Huge humpback whales eat tiny animals called krill. But they don't eat them one at a time—they eat them by the ton! The whale takes in a huge amount of water and krill in one gulp. Then it pushes the water out between comb-like plates in its jaw called baleen. The krill are left behind for the whale's meal.

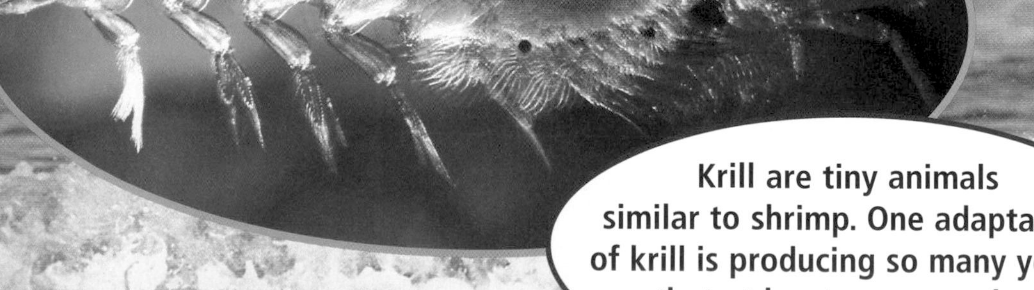

Krill are tiny animals similar to shrimp. One adaptation of krill is producing so many young that at least some survive.

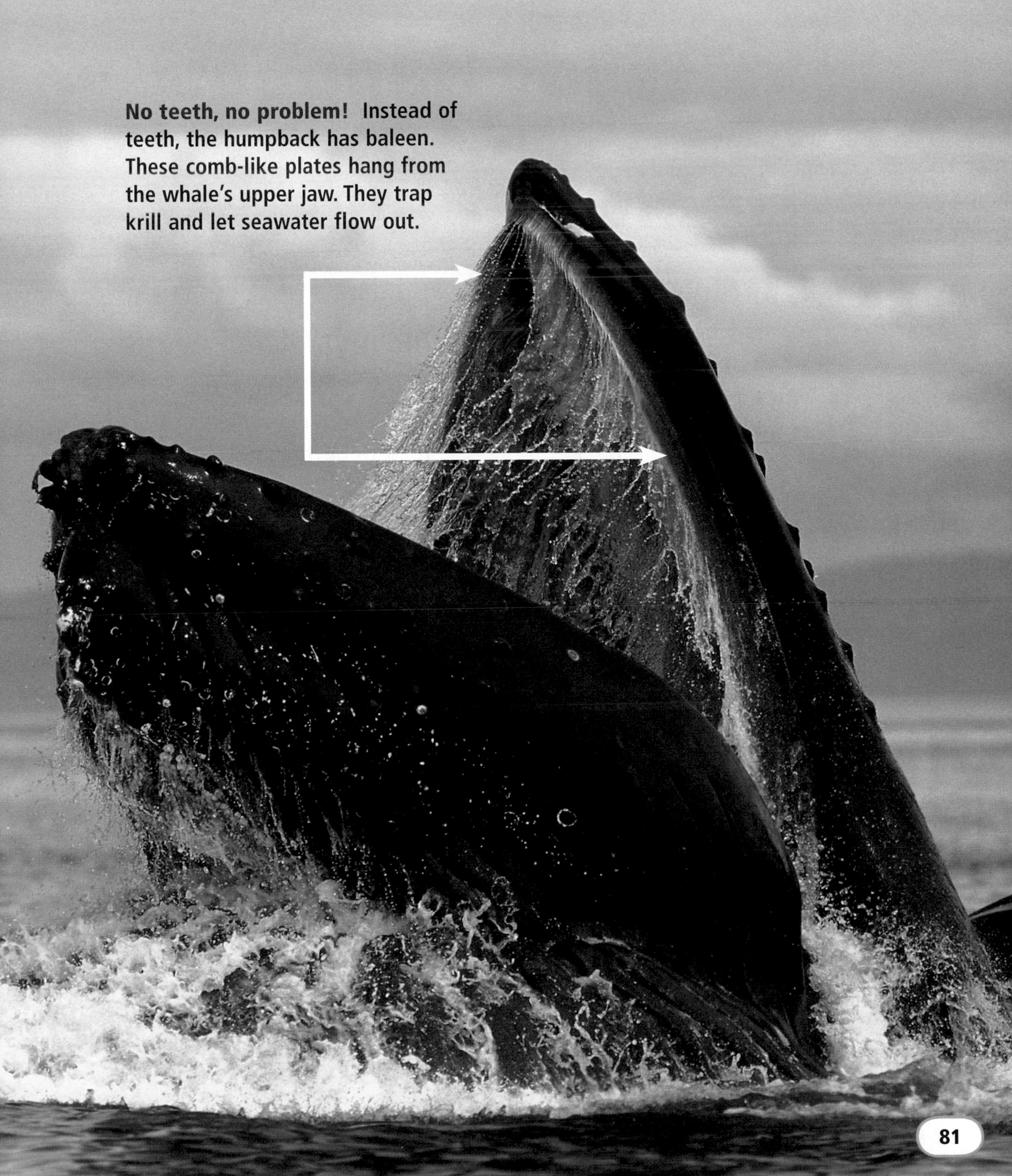

No teeth, no problem! Instead of teeth, the humpback has baleen. These comb-like plates hang from the whale's upper jaw. They trap krill and let seawater flow out.

Lesson 4

TENNESSEE STANDARDS

GLE 0307.Inq.2 Select and use appropriate tools and simple equipment to conduct an investigation.

GLE 0307.5.1 Explore the relationship between an organism's characteristics and its ability to survive in a particular environment.

Guiding Question

What Happens When Habitats Change?

Why It Matters...

You may have seen headlines about an oil tanker accidentally spilling oil into water. The oil coats the fur and feathers of water animals. An animal can't keep warm with oil on its body. Oil-coated birds can't float or fly, and may drown. Organisms are affected in different ways when their environments change.

PREPARE TO INVESTIGATE

Inquiry Skill

Use Models You can use a model of an object, process, or idea to better understand or describe how it works.

Materials

- large feather
- baby oil
- balance
- water
- dropper
- disposable gloves
- aluminum pan

Science and Math Toolbox

For step 3, review **Using a Balance** on page H9.

Directed Inquiry

Feather Failure

Procedure

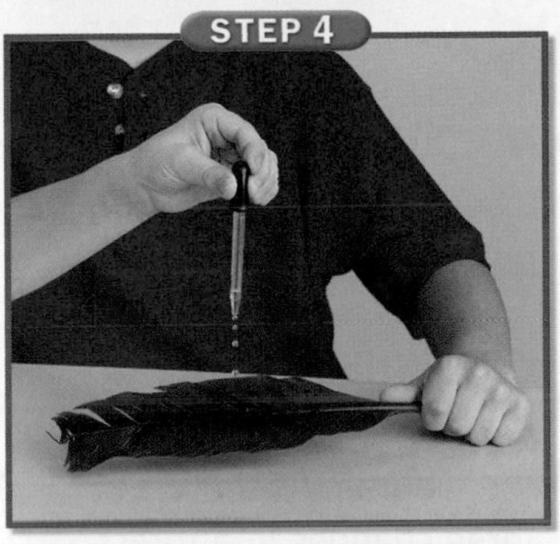

STEP 4

STEP 5

STEP 6

1. **Communicate** Work with a partner. In your Science Notebook, make a two-column chart with the headings *Dry* and *Oily*.
2. **Observe** Examine a dry feather. Smooth it with your fingers. Wave it in the air. Record your observations.
3. **Measure** Use a balance to find the mass of the feather. Record the mass.
4. **Experiment** Smooth the feather. With a dropper, sprinkle several drops of water on the feather. Record your observations.
5. Put on disposable gloves. Pour baby oil into an aluminum pan. Dip the feather into the oil. Spread the oil over the entire feather.
6. Using the oily feather, repeat steps 2, 3, and 4.

Think and Write

1. **Use Models** What features of the dry feather might help a bird survive?
2. **Hypothesize** How did the oil affect the feather? How might an oil spill affect the bird population of an ecosystem?

Guided Inquiry

Design an Experiment

Make a plan to find out how to remove the oil from bird feathers. Choose your materials and get permission from your teacher to carry out your plan. Share your results.

✓ 0307.5.4, ✓ 0307.T/E.1

Reading Science

Habitats Change

VOCABULARY

habitat

★ pollution

GRAPHIC ORGANIZER

Cause and Effect Use the diagram to show three changes in a forest habitat that are caused by a forest fire.

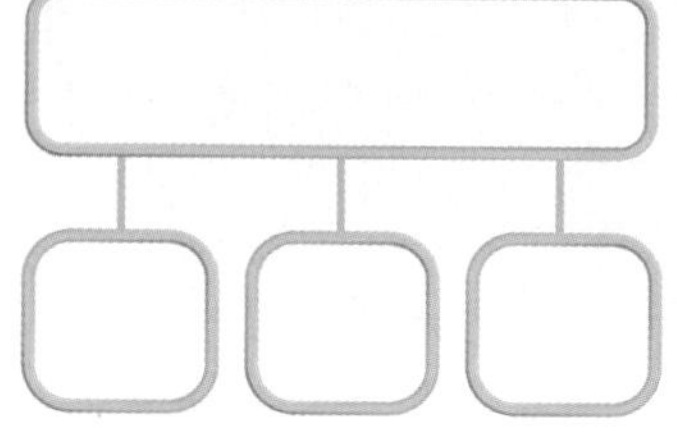

GLE 0307.5.1 Explore the relationship between an organism's characteristics and its ability to survive in a particular environment.

Fire and Water

How does a fire change a forest? Small plants that some animals eat are destroyed. Thick bushes that provide shelter may vanish.

But a change that is harmful to some organisms can be good for others. A fire can create new habitats (HAB ih tats). A **habitat** is a place where an organism lives.

After a flood, people and animals may lose their homes. Plants die as muddy water covers them and blocks sunlight. But when the water dries up, nutrient-rich soil is left behind. New plants can grow where they might not have grown before the flood.

Forest fires destroy habitats, but they also create conditions that allow new plants and animals to live. ▶

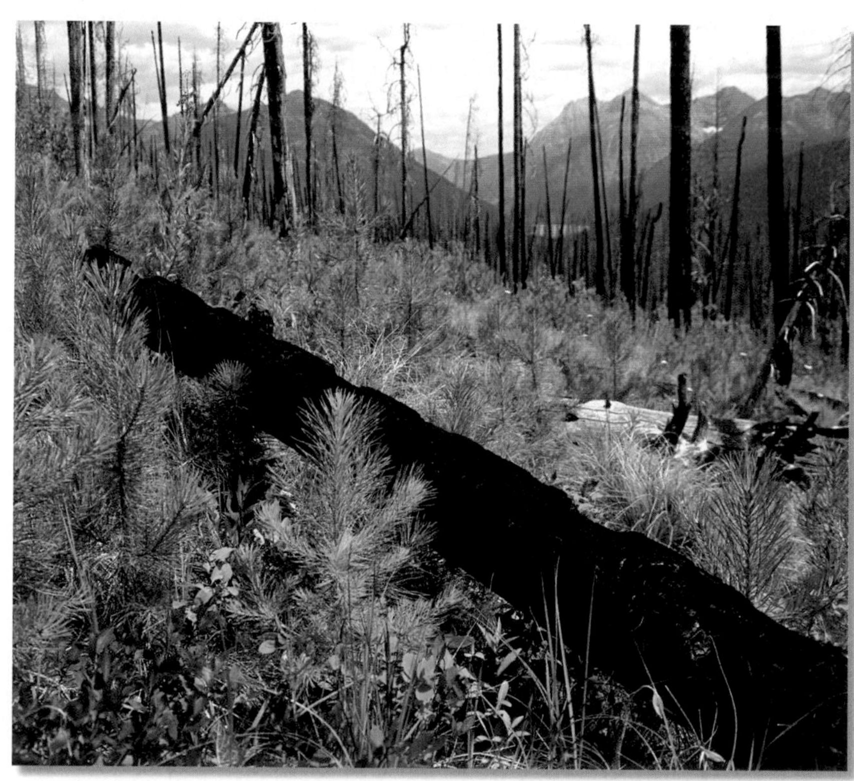

Plants and Animals

Living things change an environment in many ways. When beavers build a dam across a stream, the water builds up behind the dam. A pond may form. Plants or animals that lived in the once-dry area may die, or they may have to find new homes. However, new plants and animals may make the pond their habitat.

Kudzu (KUD zoo) is a fast-growing vine. It was brought to the United States from Japan. It rapidly changes the environment in which it grows. Kudzu vines grow so fast that they can cover houses and trees in a short time. The trees die because they cannot get enough sunlight.

FOCUS CHECK How is a forest fire harmful to the organisms that live in a forest?

Beavers cut down trees to build dams. The areas where the trees once grew get more sunlight. ▼

Pollution

Some human activities harm the environment, and some help it. People build houses, roads, farms, and cities. In the process, they may destroy the habitats of plants and animals.

Human activities can produce pollution (puh-LOO shuhn). **Pollution** is any harmful material in the environment. For example, chemicals dumped into rivers can cause fish to die. Smoke can pollute air, harming organisms that breathe it. Garbage dumps pollute land when harmful materials in them leak into water or soil.

It's not all bad news, though. Humans can also help the environment. People have passed laws to protect natural resources. Laws that limit hunting and fishing can help protect wildlife populations. Wildlife habitats are also protected by laws. In some places, land has been set aside for parks and wildlife reserves. And farmers plant crops in ways that keep soil healthy.

FOCUS CHECK What human activities can improve the environment?

Pollution can destroy wildlife habitats. ►

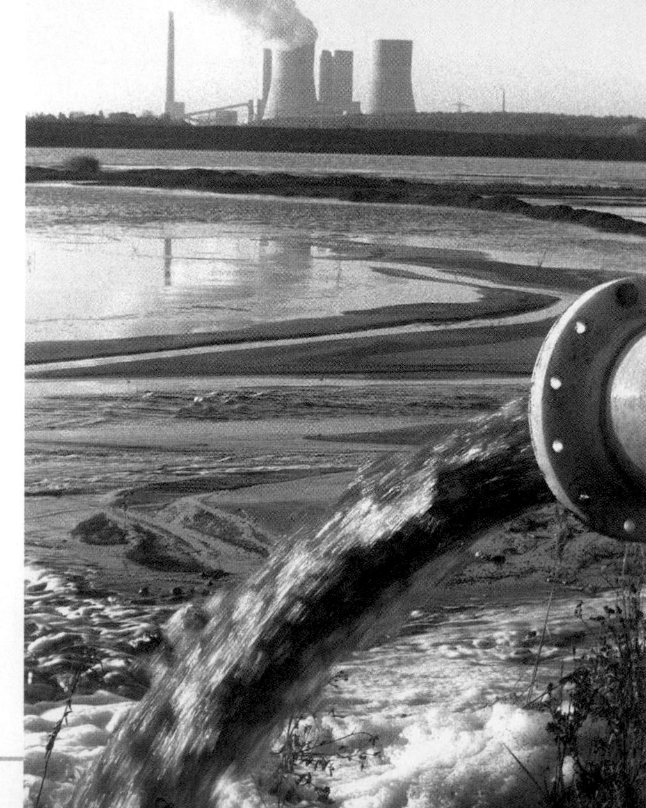

Express Lab

Activity Card

Experience Feather Failure

Lesson Wrap-Up

Visual Summary

Fires and floods destroy natural habitats, but they also create new ones.

Plants and animals can cause both good and bad changes in their environment.

Humans create pollution, but they also work to protect the environment.

Check for Understanding

TELL ABOUT CHANGES IN THE ENVIRONMENT

A river overflows its banks and floods a large field. What is likely to happen to the plants in the field? Once the water dries up, explain how the flood might actually have helped improve the environment for the future.

0307.5.3

Review

1. **MAIN IDEA** How might a change in the environment affect an organism that lives in that environment?
2. **VOCABULARY** Define the word *habitat*.
3. **READING SKILL: Cause and Effect** How can a beaver dam cause a pond to form?
4. **CRITICAL THINKING: Evaluate** A forest fire can benefit living things. Give evidence to support this statement.
5. **INQUIRY SKILL: Use Models** Describe a model that shows how thick vines covering a tree can cause harm to the tree.

TCAP Prep

Which trait of the kudzu vine is the reason it causes harmful changes to the environment in which it grows?

Ⓐ It came from Japan.
Ⓑ It needs soil.
Ⓒ It is fast growing.
Ⓓ It uses water.

SPI 0307.5.1

Go Digital Technology

Visit **www.eduplace.com/tnscp** to find out more about changing environments.

The Wump World is a story about fictional creatures that must adapt to a changing environment. The Wumps are forced to live underground when their planet becomes polluted. Read an excerpt from *The Wump World* below. In *Deer, Moose, Elk, & Caribou,* read about how real-life animals adapt to changes in their environment.

The Wump World

by Bill Peet

...the poor Wumps remained underground wandering aimlessly through the caverns feeding on the fuzzy green moss growing on the ledges and the mushrooms clustered in the crannies, and sipping the sweet water from pools fed by underground springs. But they were very unhappy. For all they knew, they might have had to spend the rest of their days down there.

Deer, Moose, Elk, & Caribou

by Deborah Hodge

To survive, the deer family needs wild, wooded areas. When people clear land for houses and roads, wild areas get smaller. The number of cougars and wolves also shrinks. With fewer enemies, too many deer end up in one area. Food becomes scarce, and some deer die. Others eat farmers' crops to stay alive.

Sharing Ideas

1. **READING CHECK** How did the Wumps adapt when their environment became polluted?
2. **WRITE ABOUT IT** Do you think that deer are able to adapt? Give reasons for your answer. If you think deer are able to adapt, compare the way that the Wumps adapted to the way that deer adapt.
3. **TALK ABOUT IT** Tell a story about a group of fictional characters that must adapt to a changing environment.

GLE 0307.5.1 Explore the relationship between an organism's characteristics and its ability to survive in a particular environment. **Math GLE 0306.5.1** Organize, display, and analyze data using various representations to solve problems. **ELA GLE 0301.3.1** Write for a variety of purposes and to a variety of audiences.

MATH Reading a Bar Graph

The peppered moth is a common insect in England. It has two forms, one with light-colored wings and the other with dark-colored wings. Moths that can blend with their environment are less likely to be eaten by birds.

Light-colored moths were most common before air pollution darkened the tree bark on which they lived. Then the dark-colored moths became more plentiful. As air pollution was cleaned up, light-colored moths returned. Use the graph to answer these questions.

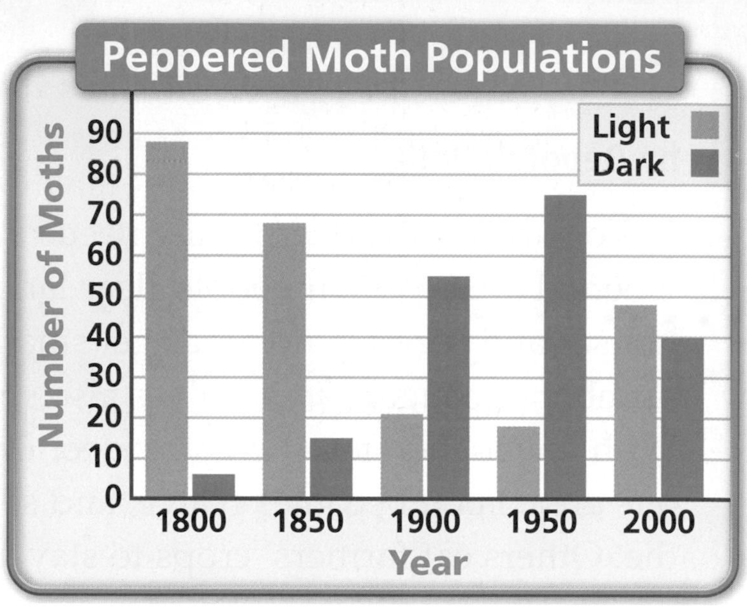

1. In which year was the population of light moths the greatest and dark moths the least?
2. In which year was the population of dark and light moths almost the same?

Letter

Think of a place where you have seen some form of pollution. Write a letter to a person in your local government. Describe the pollution problem. Ask for help correcting the situation.

Soil Conservationist

Soil conservationists are experts on soil. They develop ways to help farmers keep their land fertile, moist, and rich in nutrients. They also advise government agencies and businesses on how to use land without harming it.

What It Takes!

- A degree in environmental studies, forestry, or agriculture
- Investigative and research skills

Ecotourist Guide

As an ecotourist guide, you could find yourself leading safaris in Africa, exploring South American rainforests, or hiking glaciers in Alaska. Ecotourist guides take adventure-seekers on vacations to natural areas. They teach people about protecting wildlife and the environment.

What It Takes!

- A high-school diploma
- An interest in nature, ecology, and adventure

Chapter 2 Review and TCAP Prep

Vocabulary

Complete each sentence with a term from the list.

1. All the living and nonliving things that exist and interact in one place are a/an ______.
2. A living thing is also called a/an ______.
3. The ability to cause change is ______.
4. A behavior that helps a living thing survive is a/an ______.
5. All living things of the same kind in an ecosystem are a/an______.
6. An animal that hunts other animals for food is a/an ______.
7. The way an animal acts in a situation is called ______.
8. Harmful chemicals in a water supply are a kind of ______.
9. The place where a plant or animal lives is its ______.
10. Plants and animals that live in the same area and interact with each other are members of a/an ______.

adaptation
behavior
community
ecosystem
★ **energy**
environment
habitat
★ **organism**
★ **pollution**
population
★ **predator**
★ **prey**

TCAP Inquiry Skills

11. **Infer** Half the mice in a field have white fur and half have brown. Owls eat mice. In fall, only brown mice are left. What can you infer about the color of the grass in the meadow? Explain. **GLE 0307.5.1**

12. **Use Variables** You plant one group of bean seeds 5 cm apart. Another group you plant 2 cm apart. How do you think the variable of space will affect each group? Explain. **GLE 0307.2.2**

Map the Concept

Use the diagram to classify the terms listed. Show whether they are adaptations of plants, animals, or both.

sharp thorns
grows toward light
spins webs
bad-tasting chemicals
thick layer of fat
looks like poisonous organism

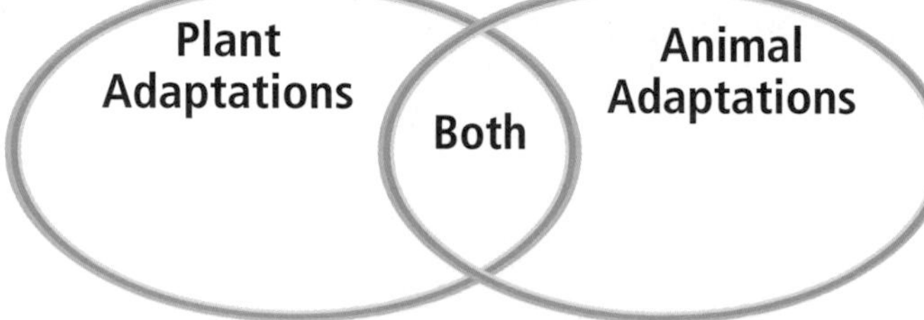

GLE 0307.5.1

Critical Thinking

13. **Synthesize** Without touching, how can you tell a real plant from a fake one? **GLE 0307.2.1**

14. **Apply** Two kinds of birds live in a habitat. Both eat insects. How is it possible that the two populations do not compete for food? **GLE 0307.2.2**

15. **Synthesize** The cones of some types of pine trees release seeds only after they have been heated. How can this adaptation increase the chance of the pine trees producing new trees after a fire? **GLE 0307.5.1**

16. **Evaluate** You know that all living things need energy to survive. A friend says animals and plants get energy in the same way. Explain why you agree or disagree. **GLE 0307.3.1**

Show Interactions in an Ecosystem

Select an ecosystem such as a forest, rainforest, desert, lake, or pond. Make a poster that shows how the plants and animals in that ecosystem interact with each other and with their environment.

✓ 0307.2.3, ✓ 0307.3.1

TCAP Prep

Answer the following questions.

17 Which of the following is not a need of all living things?

Ⓐ water
Ⓑ energy
Ⓒ nutrients
Ⓓ carbon dioxide **SPI 0307.3.1**

18 Sea lions on the same crowded rock are competing for which resource?

Ⓕ space
Ⓖ energy
Ⓗ water
Ⓙ algae **SPI 0307.2.2**

19 Which is an example of a behavior that is an adaptation for getting food?

Ⓐ the markings on a giraffe
Ⓑ a spider spinning a web
Ⓒ the thick fur of a polar bear
Ⓓ the spines of a cactus **SPI 0307.5.1**

20 Which of the following is an organism that uses sunlight to make its food?

Ⓕ oyster
Ⓖ mangrove tree
Ⓗ red snapper
Ⓙ heron **SPI 0307.3.2**

Chapter 3

Organisms of Long Ago

Lesson Preview

LESSON 1

Some kinds of living things, such as this riparian brush rabbit, are in danger of dying out. Why does an animal population decrease in size?

LESSON 2

Pieces of bone, feathers, and leaves become trapped inside rocks. What can these fossils tell scientists about life in the past?

LESSON 3

Scientists compare fossils to living things that seem to be similar. What organisms from the past are like living things of today?

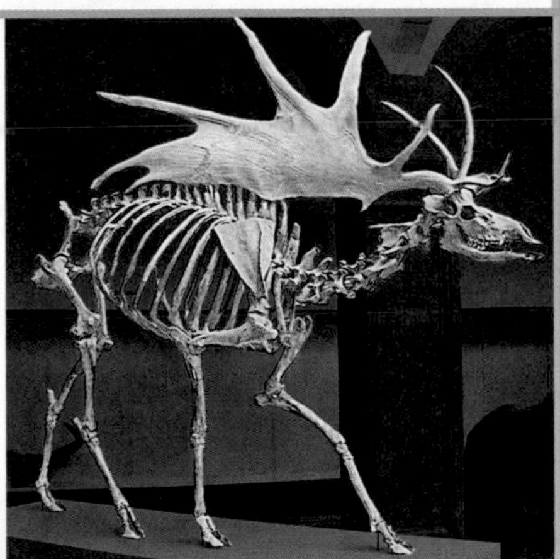

Fun Facts

The largest dinosaur ever discovered, *Seismosaurus*, was over 100 feet long.

Vocabulary Preview

ancestor
endangered species
era
★ extinct species
fossil
paleontologist
relative
species
trait

★ = Tennessee Academic Vocabulary

Vocabulary Strategies

Have you ever seen any of these terms before? Do you know what they mean?

Describe, explain, or give an example of the vocabulary terms in your own words.

Draw a picture, symbol, example, or other image that describes the term.

Glossary p. H16

endangered species

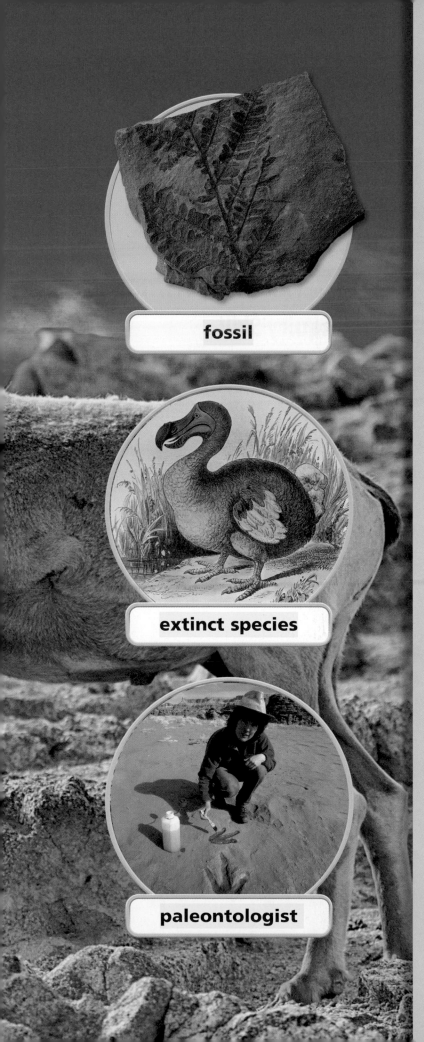

fossil

extinct species

paleontologist

Start with Your Standards

Inquiry

GLE 0307.Inq.2 Select and use appropriate tools and simple equipment to conduct an investigation.

GLE 0307.Inq.3 Organize data into appropriate tables, graphs, drawings, or diagrams.

GLE 0307.Inq.4 Identify and interpret simple patterns of evidence to communicate the findings of multiple investigations.

Life Science

Standard 5 Biodiversity and Change

GLE 0307.5.1 Explore the relationship between an organism's characteristics and its ability to survive in a particular environment.

GLE 0307.5.2 Classify organisms as thriving, threatened, endangered, or extinct.

Interact with this chapter.

www.eduplace.com/tnscp

Lesson 1

TENNESSEE STANDARDS

GLE 0307.Inq.4 Identify and interpret simple patterns of evidence to communicate the findings of multiple investigations.

GLE 0307.5.1 Explore the relationship between an organism's characteristics and its ability to survive in a particular environment.

GLE 0307.5.2 Classify organisms as thriving, threatened, endangered, or extinct.

What Threatens the Survival of Species?

Why It Matters...

The giant panda eats only bamboo. To survive, it needs to eat large amounts of this plant. People have cut down bamboo plants to use the land it grows on for other purposes. Because there is less bamboo for pandas to eat, their survival is in danger.

PREPARE TO INVESTIGATE

Inquiry Skill

Use Numbers You use numbers to describe and compare objects, events, and measurements.

Materials

- number cube
- Mammoth Key A Support Master
- Mammoth Key B Support Master

Directed Inquiry

Causes of Extinction

Procedure

1 Record Data Use a chart like the one shown. You will model what can happen to a herd of 10 woolly mammoths over 40 years. Each roll of a number cube represents what happens to one mammoth in a 20-year period.

2 Use Models You and a partner will use different Mammoth Keys. Roll the cube once. Follow the directions on your Mammoth Key for that number. Record what happens to the first mammoth.

3 Use Numbers Roll the cube once for each remaining mammoth. Record on the chart what happens to each animal. Record the total mammoths left in the herd at the end of 20 years (Trial 1).

4 Use Numbers For Trial 2, draw circles to represent the number of remaining mammoths in the herd. Repeat step 3 for the remaining mammoths. Record the total mammoths left in the herd at the end of 40 years (Trial 2).

STEP 1

Trial	Mammoths at Start of Trial	Mammoths at End of Trial
1	OOOOO OOOOO	
2		

STEP 2

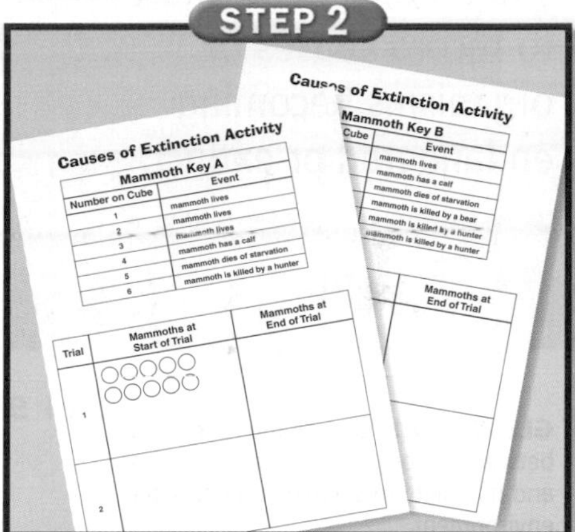
Causes of Extinction Activity

Mammoth Key A	
Number on Cube	Event
1	mammoth lives
2	mammoth lives
3	mammoth lives
4	mammoth has a calf
5	mammoth dies of starvation
6	mammoth is killed by a hunter

Trial	Mammoths at Start of Trial	Mammoths at End of Trial
1		
2		

Causes of Extinction Activity

Mammoth Key B	
Cube	Event
	mammoth lives
	mammoth has a calf
	mammoth dies of starvation
	mammoth is killed by a bear
	mammoth is killed by a hunter
	mammoth is killed by a hunter

STEP 3

Think and Write

1. **Use Numbers** Share your results with your partner. How does the number of mammoths left in each herd compare?
2. **Hypothesize** What do the results suggest about how a type of living thing can become extinct, or die off? ✓ 0307.5.7

Guided Inquiry

Ask Questions Ask a question about what happened to real woolly mammoths. Based on the activity, infer what happened to them. Then do research to check your inference.

Lesson 2

TENNESSEE STANDARDS

GLE 0307.Inq.2 Select and use appropriate tools and simple equipment to conduct an investigation.
GLE 0307.5.1 Explore the relationship between an organism's characteristics and its ability to survive in a particular environment.
GLE 0307.5.2 Classify organisms as thriving, threatened, endangered, or extinct.

Guiding Question

What Can Be Learned from Fossils?

Why It Matters...

Parts of a long-dead animal are discovered in rock. Scientists try to answer questions about the discovery. What type of animal was it? When did it die? They study the remains of organisms that lived long ago. They hope to learn more about them. Often they look for ways in which extinct organisms are like living things of today.

PREPARE TO INVESTIGATE

Inquiry Skill

Hypothesize If you think you know why something that you observe happens, you can make a hypothesis, or an educated guess, about it.

Materials

- modeling clay
- small object (shell, leaf, twig)
- hand lens

Science and Math Toolbox

For step 3, review **Using a Hand Lens** on page H2.

Directed Inquiry

Make a Fossil

Procedure

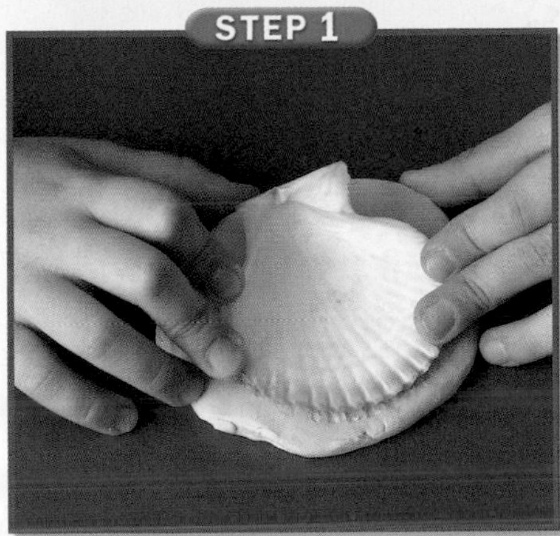
STEP 1

1. **Use Models** Make a model of a fossil (FAHS uhl). A **fossil** is the remains, or traces, of a living thing preserved in some way. Mold a piece of clay into a thick, flat layer. Press an object into the clay until the object makes an imprint. Carefully remove the object.

STEP 2

2. Exchange imprints with a partner. Do not let your partner see the object that you used to make the imprint.

STEP 3

3. **Record Data** Use a hand lens to look closely at your partner's imprint. Record your observations of the imprint.
4. **Hypothesize** Based on your observations, try to identify the object that was used to make your partner's imprint.
5. **Use Models** Now exchange objects with your partner. Record the similarities and differences between your partner's object and the imprint made from it.

Think and Write

1. **Infer** What clues about organisms can scientists learn from studying fossils?
2. **Infer** What cannot be learned from fossils? What other evidence can scientists use to study organisms of long ago?

✓ 0307.5.6

Guided Inquiry

Experiment Collect other natural objects to make into fossils. Hypothesize which objects will make good fossils. Carry out an experiment to test your hypotheses.

Reading Science

Fossils

VOCABULARY

era
fossil
paleontologist

GRAPHIC ORGANIZER

Sequence Use the chart below to show a simple version of the geologic time scale.

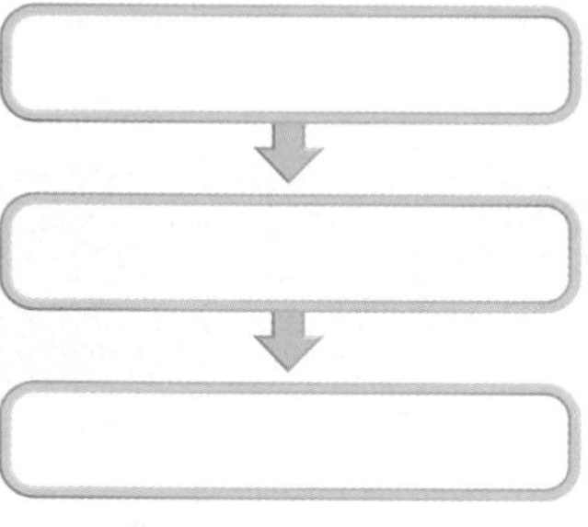

GLE 0307.5.2 Classify organisms as thriving, threatened, endangered, or extinct.

Why Scientists Study Fossils

How do scientists know what Earth was like millions of years ago? Studying fossils (FAHS uhlz) gives them some clues. A **fossil** is the preserved remains of an organism that lived long ago. Fossils can include bones, teeth, shells, and imprints of organisms that were pressed into mud and sand.

Scientists study fossils to find out how organisms of long ago lived, what they looked like, and what they ate. For example, the shape of a dinosaur's teeth can tell scientists something about what food that dinosaur ate. What kind of food do you think a dinosaur with sharp teeth might have eaten?

This fossil is from a giant tree fern that lived about 300 million years ago. It looks much like ferns that exist today. ▶

Express Lab

Activity Card
Find Fossil Clues

A scientist who studies fossils and forms of life that no longer exist is called a **paleontologist** (pay lee ahn TAHL uh-jihst). Paleontologists can learn many things by looking at fossils. Often, they can use what they learn to make hypotheses about how the organism lived and what its environment was like.

For example, suppose a paleontologist finds a fossil of a fish skeleton. The fossil provides information about the size and shape of the fish. The shape of the teeth gives clues about what the fish ate. Scientists know that all fish must live in water. If they find many fish fossils in rock on dry land, they can hypothesize that the area was once underwater.

Fossils are often only part of the remains of an ancient organism. That is why studying a fossil does not always provide complete information about the organism that formed it.

FOCUS CHECK Describe how an organism becomes a fossil.

Most fossils form from hard parts of living things, such as bone, shell, and wood.

How Fossils Form

1

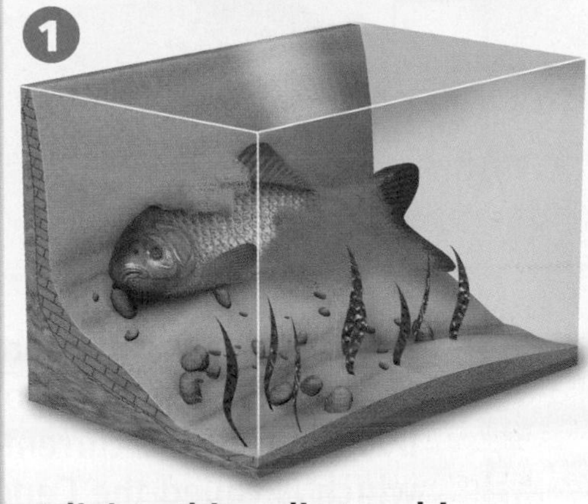

A living thing dies and is buried under layers of sand and soil.

2

Over a long period of time, the sand and soil harden and turn into rock.

3

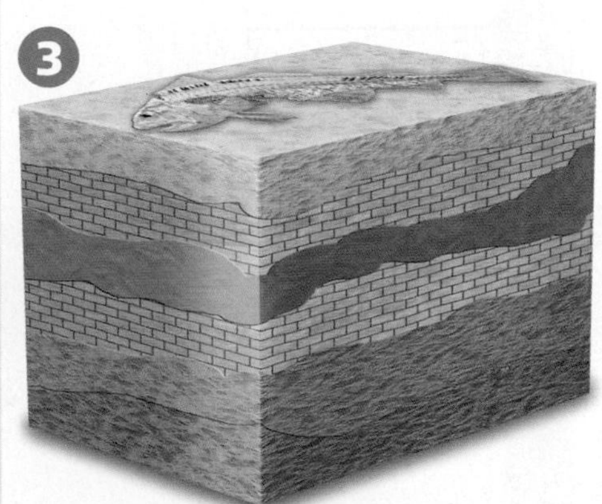

Over time, the rock covering the fossil wears away. The fossil appears on the surface.

Geologic Time Scale

65 million years ago to present

Cenozoic Era

Saber-toothed cats were alive about 16,000 years ago. They lived during the current era, which is called the Cenozoic Era.

248–65 million years ago

Mesozoic Era

The velociraptor (vuh lahs ih-RAP tur) was a small dinosaur. It lived about 70 million years ago during the Mesozoic Era.

544–248 million years ago

Paleozoic Era

Trilobites (TRY luh byts) lived over 300 million years ago. They lived during the Paleozoic (pay lee oh ZOH ihk) Era.

Dating Fossils

Paleontologists find the age of fossils in different ways. In one method, scientists compare the ages of fossils by looking at how deeply the fossils are buried. Fossils in deeper layers of rock are likely older.

Scientists can also use materials in some fossils to find out how old the fossils are. They find the age of most fossils by measuring the ages of the rocks in which the fossils are found.

Scientists have made a timeline, called the geologic (jee uh LAH jihk) time scale. It shows important events in Earth's history. It also tells about the kinds of organisms that lived at different times. A simple version of this scale is shown.

The time scale is broken down into sections called eras. An **era** is a major division of time. Each era lasted many millions of years. An era is defined by the events that took place during that time.

FOCUS CHECK Look at the geologic time scale. Which era came just before the Cenozoic Era?

Lesson Wrap-Up

Visual Summary

	A fossil is the preserved remains of an organism that lived long ago. Fossils can include bones, teeth, and shells.
	Scientists study fossils to learn about organisms that were once alive.
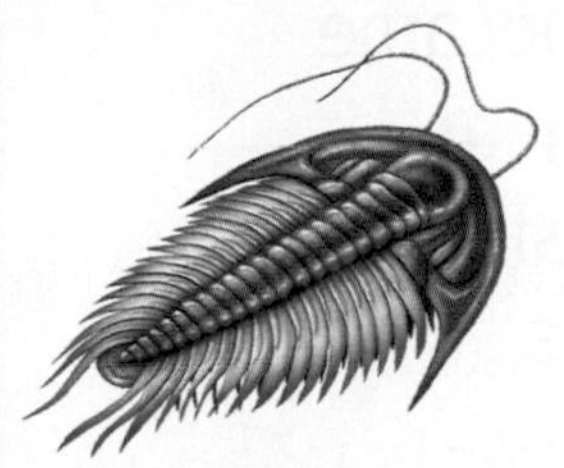	Different methods of studying fossils help scientists determine when a long-dead organism lived.

Check for Understanding

REPORT ON THE EVIDENCE

Use the library or Internet to research three extinct species. Choose one from each of the geologic eras—Paleozoic, Mesozoic, and Cenozoic—shown on page 110. Find out what evidence scientists have that the species ever existed. Report your findings to your class.

✓ **0307.5.6**

Review

1. **MAIN IDEA** What can scientists learn from fossils?
2. **VOCABULARY** What is an era?
3. **READING SKILL: Sequence** In order, what are three eras of the geologic time scale?
4. **CRITICAL THINKING: Analyze** Can scientists tell what color an animal was by looking at a fossil? Why or why not?
5. **INQUIRY SKILL: Hypothesize** Suppose you find a fossil that looks like a leaf. Hypothesize about the type of environment that this fossil came from.

TCAP Prep

Which is most likely the kind of evidence that helped scientists learn that saber-toothed cats once lived?

Ⓐ leaf imprints
Ⓑ fossil bones and teeth
Ⓒ shell imprints
Ⓓ fish scale fossils

SPI 0307.5.3

Go Digital Technology

Visit **www.eduplace.com/tnscp** to learn more about fossils.

Readers' Theater

Fossil Find

In ancient times when people found the skeletons of unusual animals, they thought they had found the bones of mythical creatures. In more recent times, scientists have learned about the true nature of the long-dead organisms that left fossil clues.

In the early 1800s, a girl named Mary Anning became a successful fossil hunter. She explored the cliffs near her house at the seashore in England. The fossils she found helped scientists learn about extinct species.

Characters

Mary Anning: a young girl

Joseph Anning: Mary's brother

Mrs. Anning: Mary's mother

Thomas Birch: a trained fossil collector

Mrs. Anning: Thank you so much for coming all the way from London, Mr. Birch.

Thomas Birch: I heard that you had many unusual fossils to sell. They may be of great interest to scientists.

Joseph Anning: Scientists! But I thought these bones were just the remains of strange animals that people collected for fun.

Thomas Birch: Oh, no. These bones are actually fossils. That means that they were left by animals that lived long ago. One day, we may be able to tell what Earth was like millions of years ago. You deserve a lot of thanks for finding these fossils, Mrs. Anning.

Mrs. Anning: Actually, you should thank my daughter Mary. She found most of them.

Thomas Birch: Wonderful job, Mary. Why don't you show us your latest find?

Mary Anning: *(showing a fossil)* It's a strange sea creature that my brother and I found.

Joseph Anning: I found its head.

Mary Anning: And I dug it out of the cliff.

Thomas Birch: Wait a moment, how do you know that it's a sea creature?

Mary Anning: Well, its skull looks a bit like a crocodile. Plus, it has fins like a dolphin. Crocodiles and dolphins both live in water, so this creature probably did too.

Joseph Anning: They don't live around here, do they? They're scary looking.

Thomas Birch: Scientists think that they died out long ago.

Mrs. Anning: How did the bones come to be here?

Thomas Birch: Well, we're still not sure. We think the animals may have been buried in sand when they died. Over many years, the sand turned into rock. Then, as the ocean wore away the rock, it uncovered the creatures' bones.

Mary Anning: I've found another strange animal. It's much larger than the sea creature, and it has a neck like that of a snake.

Thomas Birch: I'd be very interested to see it.

Mary Anning: I've just begun to get it out of the cliff. You'll have to come down to see! *[Mary runs off.]*

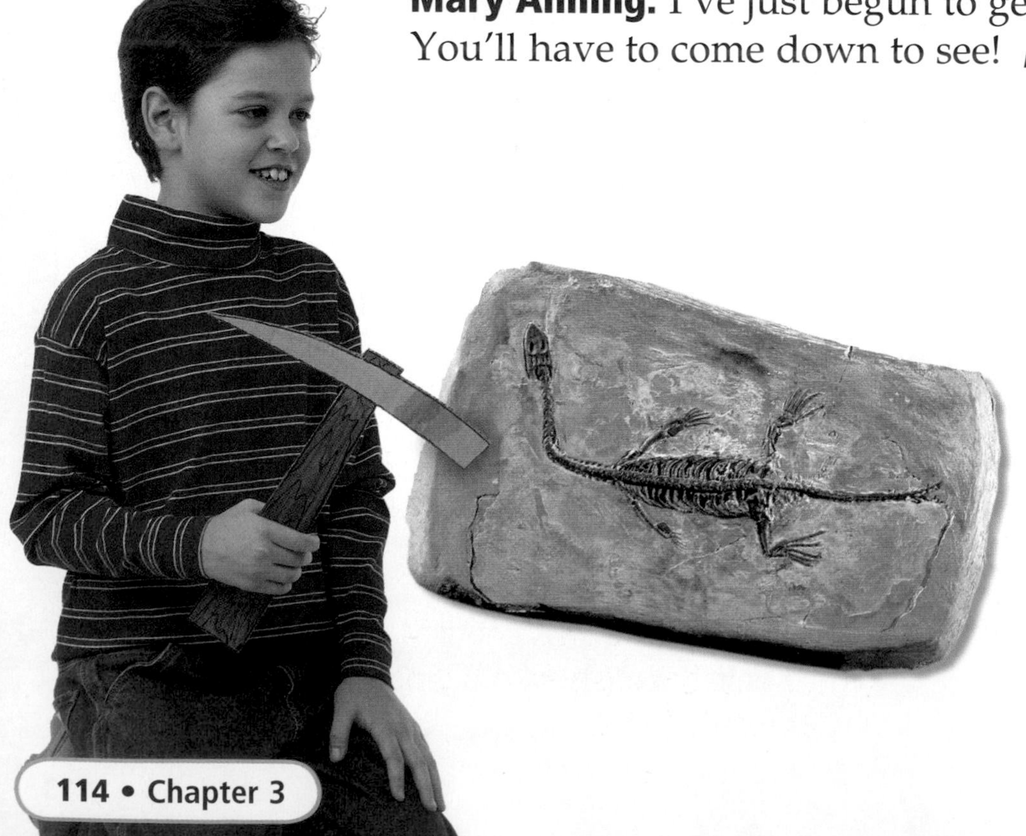

◀ **Mary found many fossils of plesiosaurs. These extinct reptiles lived in water, had four flippers, long necks, tiny heads, and wide bodies.**

Thomas Birch: Your daughter is very brave and smart.

Joseph Anning: She always seems to know things about the bones she finds.

Mary Anning: *[reappearing]* Here's a fish I found the other day. It looks like a shark.

Thomas Birch: Mary, I have a feeling that you and your family are going to be a great help to scientists studying fossils.

Mary Anning uncovered the skeleton of an ichthyosaur. This extinct sea animal was a fishlike reptile. ▼

In 1828, Mary discovered the fossil of a pterodactyl. These ancient reptiles had large, featherless wings. ▼

Sharing Ideas

1. **READING CHECK** How did fossil remains of sea animals come to be in the cliffs near Mary's house?
2. **WRITE ABOUT IT** What facts did Mary Anning use to hypothesize that the animal she found was a sea creature?
3. **TALK ABOUT IT** Discuss how Mary's discoveries could help scientists who did not yet understand what fossils were.

Lesson 3

TENNESSEE STANDARDS

GLE 0307.Inq.3 Organize data into appropriate tables, graphs, drawings, or diagrams.
GLE 0307.5.2 Classify organisms as thriving, threatened, endangered, or extinct.

How Are Extinct and Living Things Alike?

Why It Matters...

Most people would say a woolly mammoth looked like an elephant with thick fur. Scientists use similarities between modern and extinct species to learn about extinct species. Scientists believe that woolly mammoths, like modern-day elephants, ate plants and roamed in herds.

PREPARE TO INVESTIGATE

Inquiry Skill

Classify When you classify, you sort objects according to their properties.

Materials

- Extinct and Living Animal Species cards Support Master

Directed Inquiry

Extinct and Living

Procedure

1. Make a chart like the one shown. Cut out the picture cards of extinct and living animal species. Arrange the cards in two sets—extinct species and living species.
2. **Observe** Look at the set of cards showing extinct species. Note the features of each species.
3. **Compare** Repeat step 2 for the cards showing living species. Compare the appearance of each extinct species with the appearance of each living species.
4. **Classify** Match each extinct species with the living species it most resembles. Then place each matched pair of cards on your chart in the correct columns.
5. **Hypothesize** Write a hypothesis about whether or not the species in each paired set might be related.

STEP 1

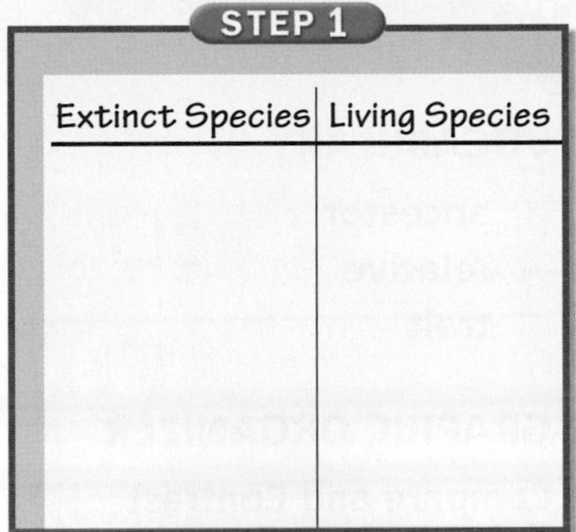

STEP 2

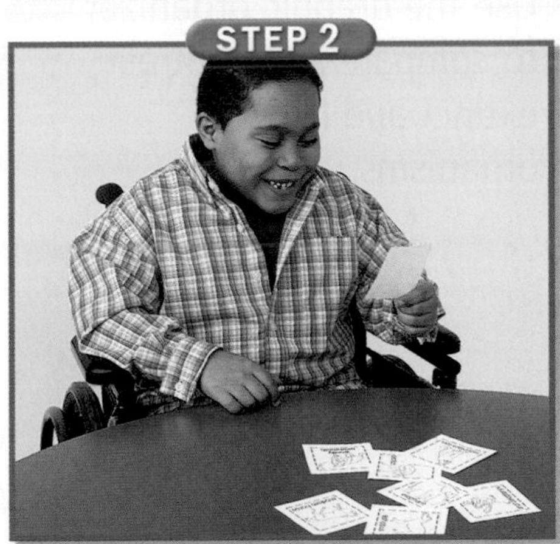

STEP 4

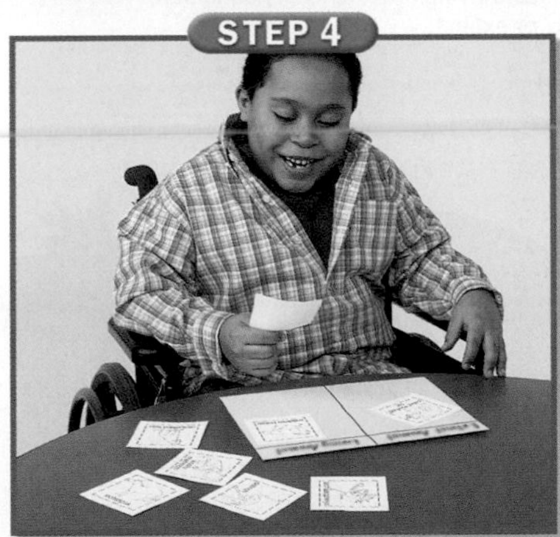

Think and Write

1. **Infer** What kind of information can you gather by comparing the appearance of extinct and living species?
2. What other evidence might scientists look for to determine whether an extinct species and a living species are actually related?

✔ 0307.5.7

Guided Inquiry

Ask Questions How was a _____ like a ______? Fill in the name of an extinct species in the first blank. Fill in the name of a living species in the second blank. Research the answer to your question.

Reading Science

Extinct and Modern Animals

VOCABULARY

ancestor
relative
trait

GRAPHIC ORGANIZER

Compare and Contrast
Use the graphic organizer to compare and contrast extinct and living organisms.

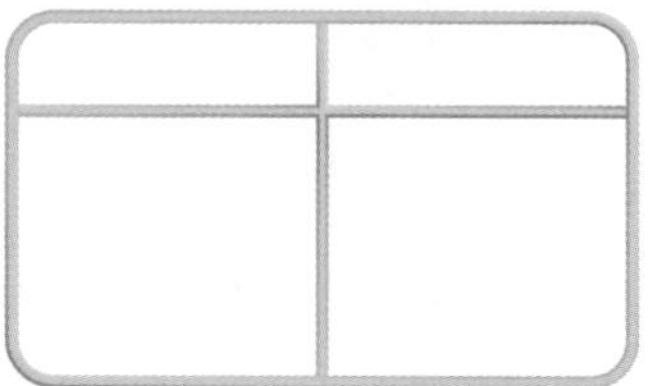

GLE 0307.5.2 Classify organisms as thriving, threatened, endangered, or extinct.

Elephant Ancestors

There are only two species of elephant alive today—African elephants and Asian elephants. And there are no other animals that look like elephants. Both these modern elephants share animal ancestors. An **ancestor** is a species or form of a species that lived long ago and to which modern species may be traced back.

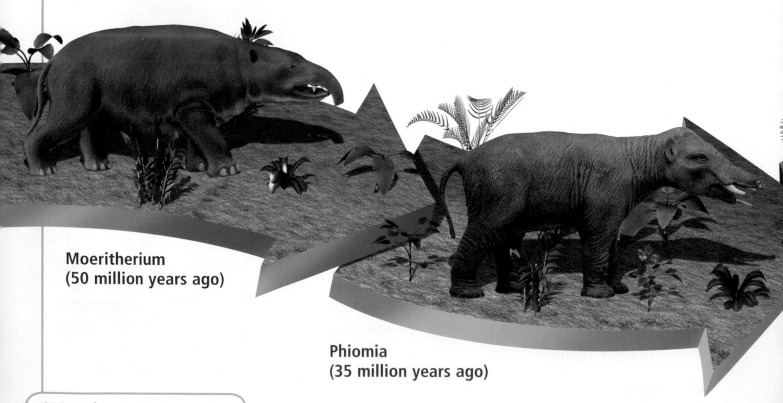

Moeritherium
(50 million years ago)

Phiomia
(35 million years ago)

Elephants do not have any close living relatives. A **relative** is a species that shares a common ancestor with another species. A relative also shares many traits with that other species. A **trait** is a feature such as a body part or a behavior. For example, large ears are a trait of both African and Asian elephants.

Though they lack close living relatives, elephants have many extinct ancestors and relatives. Some elephant ancestors looked a lot like modern elephants.

Other elephant ancestors looked very different from modern elephants. For example, Phiomia (fee OH mee uh) had tusks but a very small trunk. The woolly mammoth was covered with fur.

Usually, ancestors that had very different traits from modern animals lived longer ago. Ancestors that had many of the same traits lived more recently.

FOCUS CHECK In what ways are modern elephants and their ancestors alike and different?

Deinotherium (10 million years ago)

Elephants (alive today)

Animal Look-Alikes

Like the elephant, other modern species look similar to extinct species. However, not all of these look-alikes are related. For example, the emu is a large bird that cannot fly. It shares several traits with the extinct diatryma (dih AH trih mah). But fossils show that the birds are not related. The diatryma was a meat-eater. Emus eat seeds and insects.

Fossils show that the rhinoceros and the extinct indricothere (IHN druh koh-THIHR) are related. Like the indricothere, rhinos are mammals that eat leaves and have feet with three toes.

Diatryma

A diatryma was a large bird that is now extinct. It could not fly. It hunted small animals.

▲ **The emu is a large bird from Australia. It cannot fly.**

Indricothere

The indricothere was the largest land mammal ever known. It was 5.5 m (18 ft) tall.

◀ **Although the modern rhinoceros looks fierce, it eats only leaves and grass.**

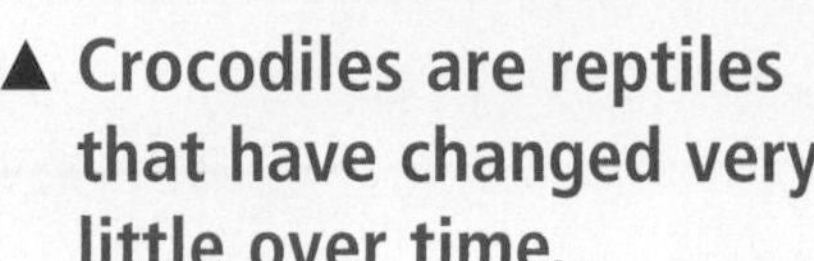

▲ Crocodiles are reptiles that have changed very little over time.

The saber-toothed cat was a fierce-looking mammal. It had two teeth, each 18 cm (7 in.) long. It used its jaws to rip apart the animals it hunted. It was not a fast runner because its legs were short.

This animal is not closely related to modern wild cats. Bengal tigers are larger, have shorter teeth, and have longer legs than saber-toothed cats.

FOCUS CHECK How is a diatryma like an emu?

Extinct Crocodile

This extinct crocodile species was similar to modern crocodiles. Its behavior was probably also similar.

Saber-toothed Cat

Saber-toothed cats likely became extinct when the animals they ate died out.

◀ The Bengal tiger and saber-toothed cat share some traits, but they are not closely related.

◀ This animal, thought by some scientists to be one of the first birds, is called archaeopteryx (ark ee OP tuh riks). It was related to dinosaurs, had wings, and was covered with feathers.

▲ Modern birds look different from dinosaurs, but share some of their traits.

Dinosaur-Bird Connections

Dinosaurs became extinct about 65 million years ago. There are no modern species that have all the traits of dinosaurs. But some modern species, such as birds, may have had dinosaurs as ancestors.

Recently, scientists have found fossils of dinosaurs that had wings and feathers. These small, winged, meat-eating dinosaurs share other traits with birds. The shape of their hips and the ways in which their hearts and lungs work are similar to those traits in birds. Many scientists believe that these dinosaurs are the ancestors of modern birds.

FOCUS CHECK What are two ways that modern birds are similar to their ancestors?

Activity Card
Classify Animals

Lesson Wrap-Up

Visual Summary

An ancestor is a species or form of a species that lived long ago and to which, through fossil evidence, modern species can be traced back.

Fossil evidence shows that some modern species resemble extinct species.

Check for Understanding

MAKE DIORAMAS OF ANIMALS PAST AND PRESENT

Work with a partner to select a pair of animals. One animal should be extinct. The other should be a modern animal that resembles it but that is alive. Each partner should make a diorama that shows one of the animals in its environment.

Research to learn the kind of climate and plant life found in each animal's environment. For each diorama, prepare an index card giving the name of the animal, a brief description of it, and information about when and where it lived or lives. Display the paired dioramas.

✓ 0307.5.5

Review

1. **MAIN IDEA** How do scientists learn about extinct species?
2. **VOCABULARY** Define the term *ancestor*.
3. **READING SKILL: Compare and Contrast** How are saber-toothed cats and Bengal tigers alike and different?
4. **CRITICAL THINKING: Evaluate** A fossil looks like the skeleton of a modern wolf. Can you conclude that the extinct animal is related to modern wolves? Explain.
5. **INQUIRY SKILL: Classify** Why can the rhinoceros and the indricothere be classified as relatives?

TCAP Prep

Fossils of a large land mammal show the animal ate leaves and had feet with three toes. It is most likely related to which of these modern animals?

(A) emu
(B) crocodile
(C) rhinoceros
(D) vulture

SPI 0307.5.3

Go Digital Technology

Visit **www.eduplace.com/tnscp** to learn more about animal ancestors.

SuperCroc!

How big can crocodiles get? Modern crocodiles can reach about 5 m (16 ft) long and weigh almost a metric ton (about 2,000 pounds). Now imagine coming face-to-face with a creature that would make those crocs look puny. Meet SuperCroc—the largest crocodile that ever lived.

This huge animal's scientific name means "emperor of the flesh-eating crocodiles." But when paleontologists discovered its huge fossil in Africa, they called it "SuperCroc." You can see why. This beast could easily have eaten a 20-foot dinosaur. And it probably did!

GLE 0307.5.1 Explore the relationship between an organism's characteristics and its ability to survive in a particular environment.

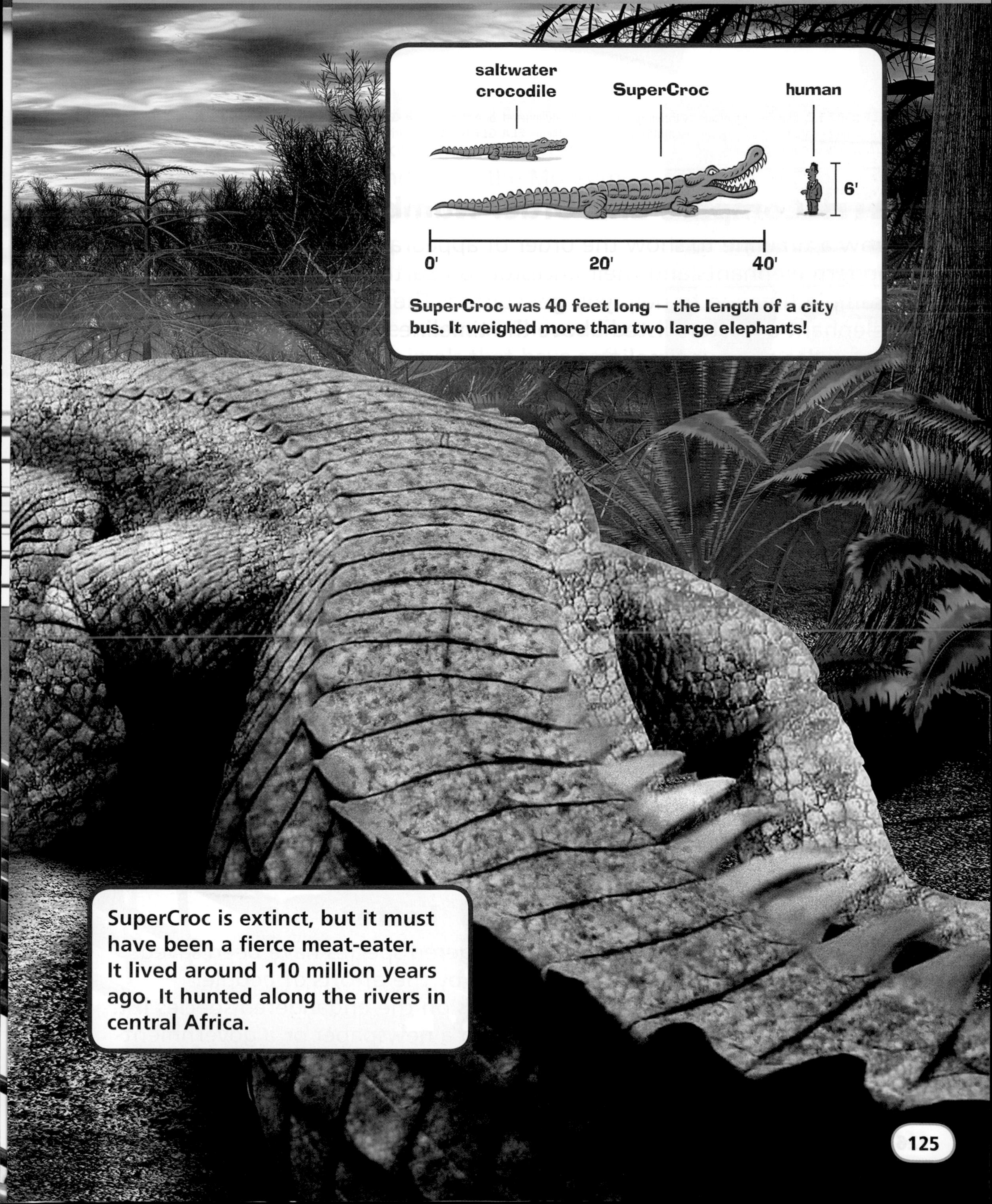
saltwater crocodile
SuperCroc
human
6'
0'
20'
40'

SuperCroc was 40 feet long — the length of a city bus. It weighed more than two large elephants!

SuperCroc is extinct, but it must have been a fierce meat-eater. It lived around 110 million years ago. It hunted along the rivers in central Africa.

Chapter 3 Review and TCAP Prep

Vocabulary

Complete each sentence with a term from the list.

1. A species or form of a species that lived long ago and to which modern species may be traced back is a/an ______.
2. The preserved remains of an organism is a/an ______.
3. A scientist who studies fossils is a/an ______.
4. A species that shares a common ancestor and has many traits in common with another species is a/an ______ of that species.
5. A group of the same type of living thing that can mate and produce living things of the same kind is a/an ______.
6. A major division of time is a/an ______.
7. A species that is at risk of dying out is a/an ______.
8. A feature, such as a body part or behavior, is a/an ______.
9. A species that has died off is called a/an ______.

ancestor
endangered species
era
★ **extinct species**
fossil
paleontologist
relative
species
trait

TCAP Inquiry Skills

10. **Classify** An extinct organism lived 300 million years ago. Use the geologic scale on page 110 to tell in which era it lived. **GLE 0307.5.2**
11. **Use Numbers** There are 10,000 ducks of a species. Hunters kill 50 a week. In how many weeks will that species of duck become extinct? **GLE 0307.5.2**
12. **Hypothesize** Name two human activities that might cause a species to become extinct. **GLE 0307.5.2**

Map the Concept

Use the terms from the list to fill in the concept map.

behavior
bones
food sources
relatives
shells
teeth

GLE 0307.5.1

Fossils of existing animals

can be formed from ______ ______

provide clues about ______ ______ ______

Critical Thinking

13. **Apply** Because of overhunting, the number of a species of bird drops from 75 to 10. Is this species endangered or extinct? Explain. **GLE 0307.5.2**

14. **Analyze** A magazine article tells about an extinct ancestor of modern lions. What are some traits the extinct ancestor might have? **GLE 0307.5.2**

15. **Evaluate** Suppose a fossil is found on a mountain. The animal that formed the fossil had fins, a tail, and a flat body. What evidence is there to support the idea that the mountain was once under the ocean? Explain. **GLE 0307.5.2**

16. **Apply** What might people do to save a species that is endangered because of destruction of its habitat? **GLE 0307.5.2**

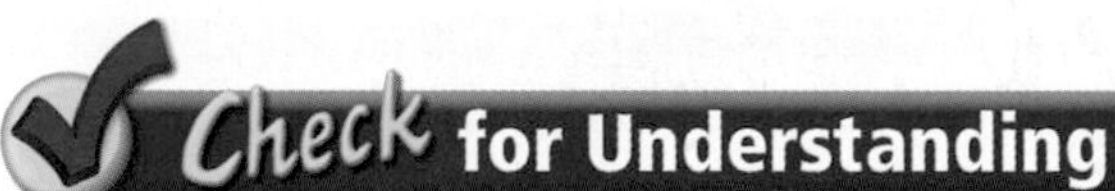

Research an Extinct Animal

Steller's sea cow is an extinct animal that lived in the cold waters of the Bering Sea. The sea cow looked like a large manatee. Do research to learn about when these animals became extinct and the cause of their extinction. Find out what evidence there is that these animals existed. **0307.5.6**

TCAP Prep

Answer the following questions.

17 A dodo is an example of a/an

Ⓐ ancestor of the elephant
Ⓑ endangered species
Ⓒ relative of the saber-toothed cat
Ⓓ extinct species **SPI 0307.5.2**

18 Which of the following would a paleontologist most likely study?

Ⓕ why tigers have become endangered
Ⓖ whether dinosaurs are related to birds
Ⓗ how fish breathe with gills
Ⓙ what modern wolves eat **SPI 0307.5.2**

19 Which best describes why dinosaurs became extinct?

Ⓐ natural causes and human activities
Ⓑ human activities
Ⓒ natural causes
Ⓓ water pollution **SPI 0307.5.2**

20 The modern elephant and its ancestors

Ⓕ share no traits
Ⓖ share some traits
Ⓗ share all traits
Ⓙ are not related **SPI 0307.5.3**

UNIT A TCAP Prep

1 Cells

Performance Indicator **SPI 0307.1.1 Identify specific parts of a plant and describe their function.**

1 Which is the main job of leaves?

Ⓐ hold up the plant
Ⓑ make food for the plant
Ⓒ take in water and nutrients
Ⓓ store food for the plant

2 Interdependence

Performance Indicator **SPI 0307.2.1 Distinguish between living and non-living things.**

2 Which trait would help you decide if an object you found was a living thing?

Ⓕ It could move.
Ⓖ It is made up of cells.
Ⓗ It is soft.
Ⓙ It breaks easily.

Performance Indicator **SPI 0307.2.2 Determine how plants and animals compete for resources such as food, space, water, air, and shelter.**

3 Which of these is most likely to compete with a coyote for food?

Ⓐ panther 

Ⓒ grass 

Ⓑ rabbit 

Ⓓ mouse 

5 Biodiversity and Change

Performance Indicator **SPI 0307.5.2 Investigate populations of different organisms and classify them as thriving, threatened, endangered, or extinct.**

4 Which species shares traits with the extinct woolly mammoth?

Ⓕ rhinoceros
Ⓖ emu
Ⓗ elephant
Ⓙ crocodile

3 Flow of Matter and Energy

Performance Indicator **SPI 0307.3.2 Recognize that animals obtain their food by eating plants and other animals.**

5 Which adaptation helps an organism get food?

Ⓐ thorns of a rose bush
Ⓑ thick fur of a bighorn sheep
Ⓒ seeds of a maple tree
Ⓓ web of a spider

4 Heredity

Performance Indicator **SPI 0307.4.1 Select an illustration that shows how an organism changes as it develops.**

6 Which shows the life cycle of a frog in the correct order.

Ⓕ 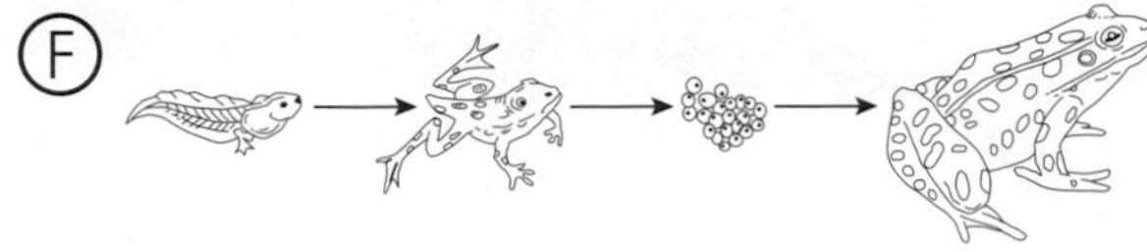

Ⓗ 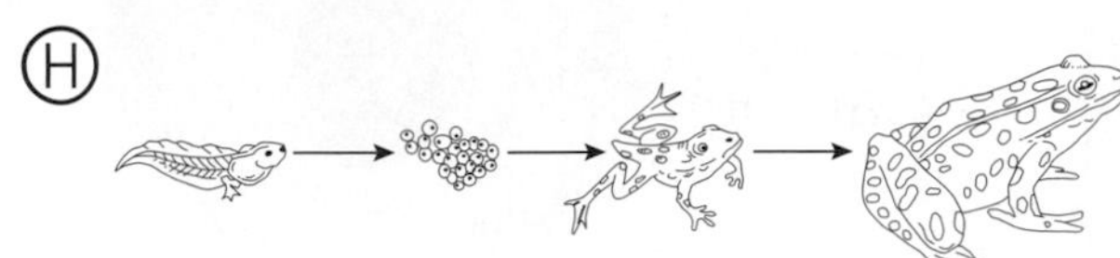

Ⓖ 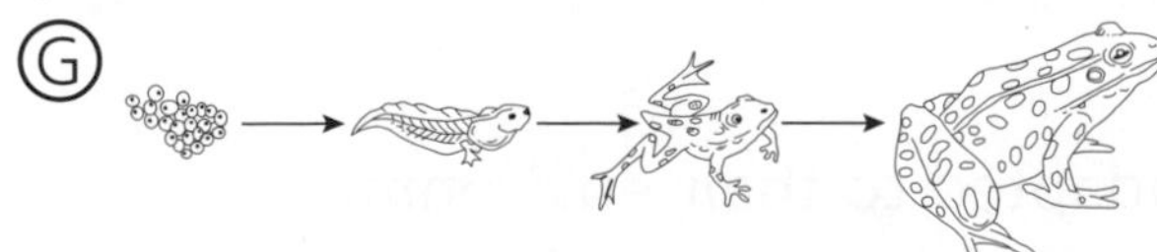

Ⓙ 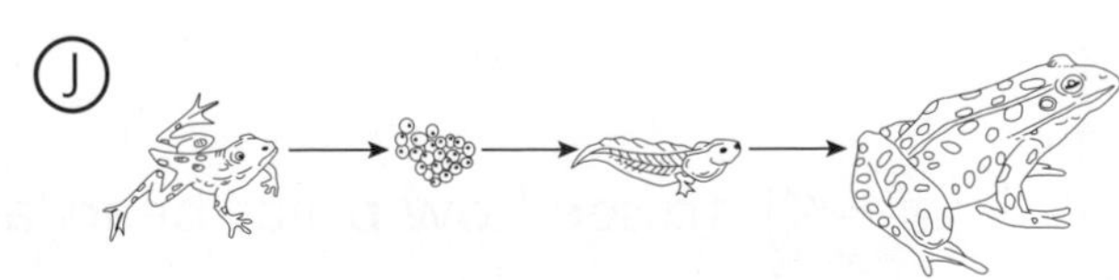

www.eduplace.com/tnscp

Discover More

Simulate adaptations to environments. Polar bears are adapted to the cold, icy environment of the Arctic. Thick fur and a layer of fat keep them warm in freezing temperatures. Even their paws are adapted for their environment.

Polar bears have four paws that can be over 25 cm (about 10 in.) wide. Each paw has five toes, and each toe has a long, sharp claw. These claws help polar bears grip the ice. Each polar bear paw has seven foot pads that are covered with small bumps. The bumps are like the treads on a sport shoe. They grip the ice and keep the bear from slipping when it runs.

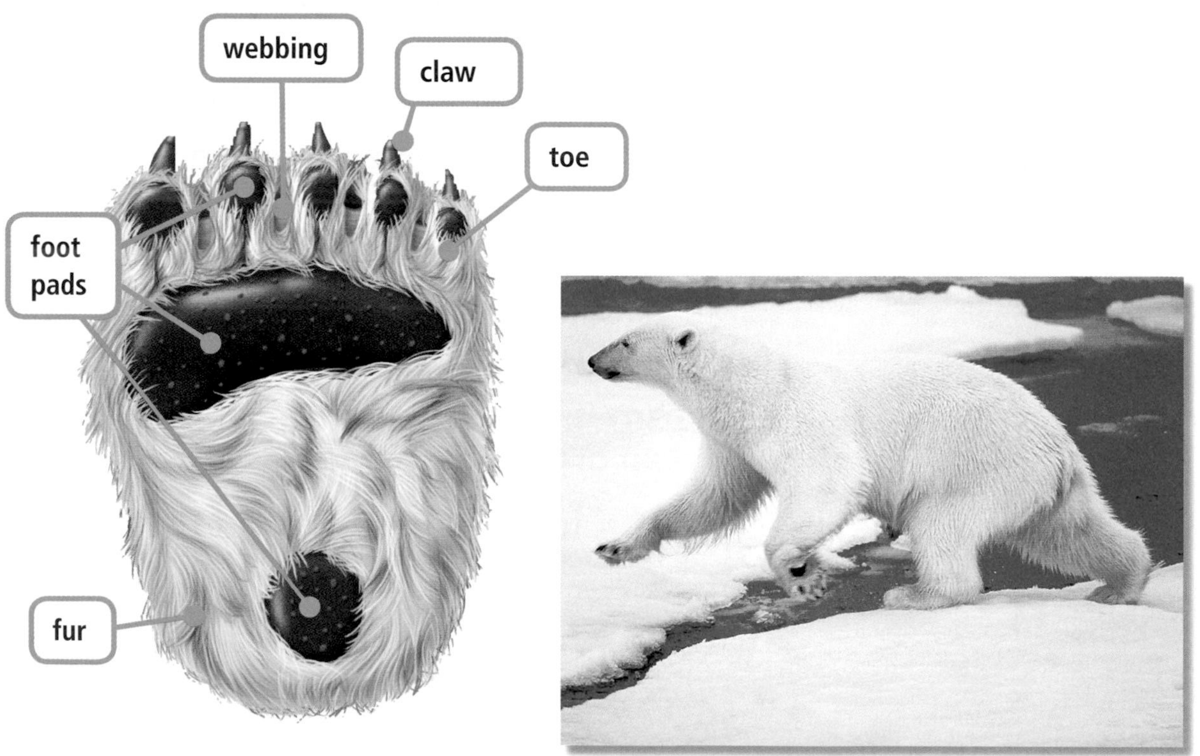

to see how polar bears are adapted to their environment.

EARTH  SCIENCE

TENNESSEE

Tennessee Excursions and Engineering Project

Our Solar System

Have you ever heard of solar energy? Why is it called solar? Well, *solar* refers to things that come from the Sun or are related to the Sun. Earth revolves around the Sun. Many other objects also revolve around the Sun. The Sun and all of these objects make up the solar system. The Sun is a star, and it keeps all the other objects in place. Because of the Sun, Earth has light and many other forms of energy.

Jupiter has the most moons of any planet in our solar system.

Parts of the Solar System

The Sun is the largest object in our solar system. Jupiter is the largest planet, but it is far away from the Sun. The smallest planet, Mercury, is the closest to the Sun. Earth is bigger than some planets and smaller than others. It is also the only planet known to have liquid water and living things.

All the planets in the solar system, except for Mercury, have at least one moon. A moon orbits a planet. Jupiter has 63 moons, but Earth has only one.

The M. D. Anderson Planetarium in Jackson, Tennessee, features many shows about our solar system. There, you can learn about the planets, moons, comets, and asteroids. You can learn about dwarf planets and other objects that exist very far from the Sun. You can also learn how the objects are alike and how they are different. At the planetarium, you can compare all the different parts of our solar system.

Think and Write

1. **Science and Technology** Astronomers have known for thousands of years that other objects are in our solar system. Do some research about technologies that are related to astronomy. How have scientific advances helped us view our solar system?
2. **Scientific Thinking** Why do you think only Earth is known to have liquid water and living things?

M. D. Anderson Planetarium

Clouds and Weather

People many, many years ago didn't have accurate ways to predict weather. They didn't have satellites or radar to tell them what the weather was going to be like later in the week. People in Knoxville, Tennessee, didn't have weather forecasters from WATE Channel 6 to tell them what kind of weather was headed their way. People relied on other ways to tell the weather. One of the main ways was to observe clouds. Different kinds of clouds bring different types of weather. Some clouds show that fair weather is on the way. Other clouds show that light rain or snow is coming. Still other clouds warn people to look out for severe weather, such as thunderstorms or tornados. Even with satellites and radar, observing clouds helps people know what's on the way.

Weather forecasters use education and technology to predict the weather.

What do the clouds over WATE Channel 6 tell you about the weather?

Activity

Using Clouds to Predict Weather

1. Research different kinds of clouds and the types of weather they indicate.
2. Observe the clouds in your area every day for two weeks. Record your observations.
3. Use your research to predict what kind of weather may be in your area over the next day or two.
4. Use online resources to see what weather forecasters have predicted for the next day or two.
5. Compare and contrast your predictions and the weather forecasters' predictions.

Draw Conclusions

1. How were your predictions the same as or different from the weather forecasters' predictions?
2. Whose predictions were more accurate?

Think and Write

1. **Scientific Inquiry** Research other ways people in the past predicted weather. How are the old ways similar to and different from the ways weather is predicted today?
2. **Science and Technology** What are some ways technology has affected how weather is predicted? Research modern weather prediction methods. Report on important technologies you learn about.

Earthquake Lake!

In northwest Tennessee sits a lake unlike most other lakes. Reelfoot Lake, near Tiptonville, formed as a result of an earthquake. Four earthquakes, which together are called the New Madrid earthquakes, hit the area in 1811 and 1812. They are named after the seismic zone in the area. A seismic zone is a place where earthquakes can happen. These earthquakes were some of the most powerful ever to strike the United States.

A Lake Forms

These earthquakes changed the shape of the land. They also affected the path of the Mississippi River. The river even flowed backward for a little while. Some of the land in the area sank because of the earthquakes. The Mississippi River flowed into one of the areas that sank. The river water filled in the sunken area and formed a lake. That lake is Reelfoot Lake.

Walkways crisscross Reelfoot Lake's shallow water.

Reelfoot Lake is a major body of water in Tennessee because it is the largest natural lake in the state. However, the lake is unusual in a couple of ways. The lake is very shallow, and cypress trees are able to live in the water. There are also many dead trees in the lake because the area was a forest before the Mississippi River flowed over the land. As a result, boaters on the lake must be very careful not to damage their boats on sunken trees. Still, the lake is a popular fishing spot. Bald eagles often nest around the lake. Reelfoot Lake's unusual formation makes it a unique place in Tennessee.

Think and Write

1. **Scientific Inquiry** Do research on the formation of other lakes in Tennessee. Describe how their formation was the same as or different from that of Reelfoot Lake.
2. **Scientific Thinking** The New Madrid earthquakes forever changed the landscape of northwestern Tennessee. What is another change, besides forming Reelfoot Lake, that the earthquakes brought to the land?

Build a Spillway

Identify the Problem You and some friends like to play soccer in a field next to a lake. When there is a lot of rain, however, the lake may flood and the field is too wet to use.

Think of a Solution A spillway can keep a lake from flooding areas around it. List the characteristics that a spillway must have. For example, it must provide a pathway for the extra water to follow.

Plan and Build Using the ideas from your list, sketch and label a model of a spillway. Think of materials you could use to make it. Then build the model.

Test and Improve Test your model spillway. Make improvements as needed to make sure your model works.

Communicate

1. Describe how a spillway like your model would solve the problem.
2. Explain how you used your listed ideas to build your spillway.
3. Tell what you did to improve your design and how the improvement affected the outcome.

Possible Materials

- clay
- cardboard tubes
- scissors
- craft sticks
- aquarium rocks
- straws
- aluminum foil
- plastic wrap

GLE 0307.T/E.5 Apply a creative design strategy to solve a particular problem generated by societal needs and wants.

Earth Science

Tennessee

Guiding Question

What is Earth like, and what is its place in the solar system?

Chapter 4

Our Solar System

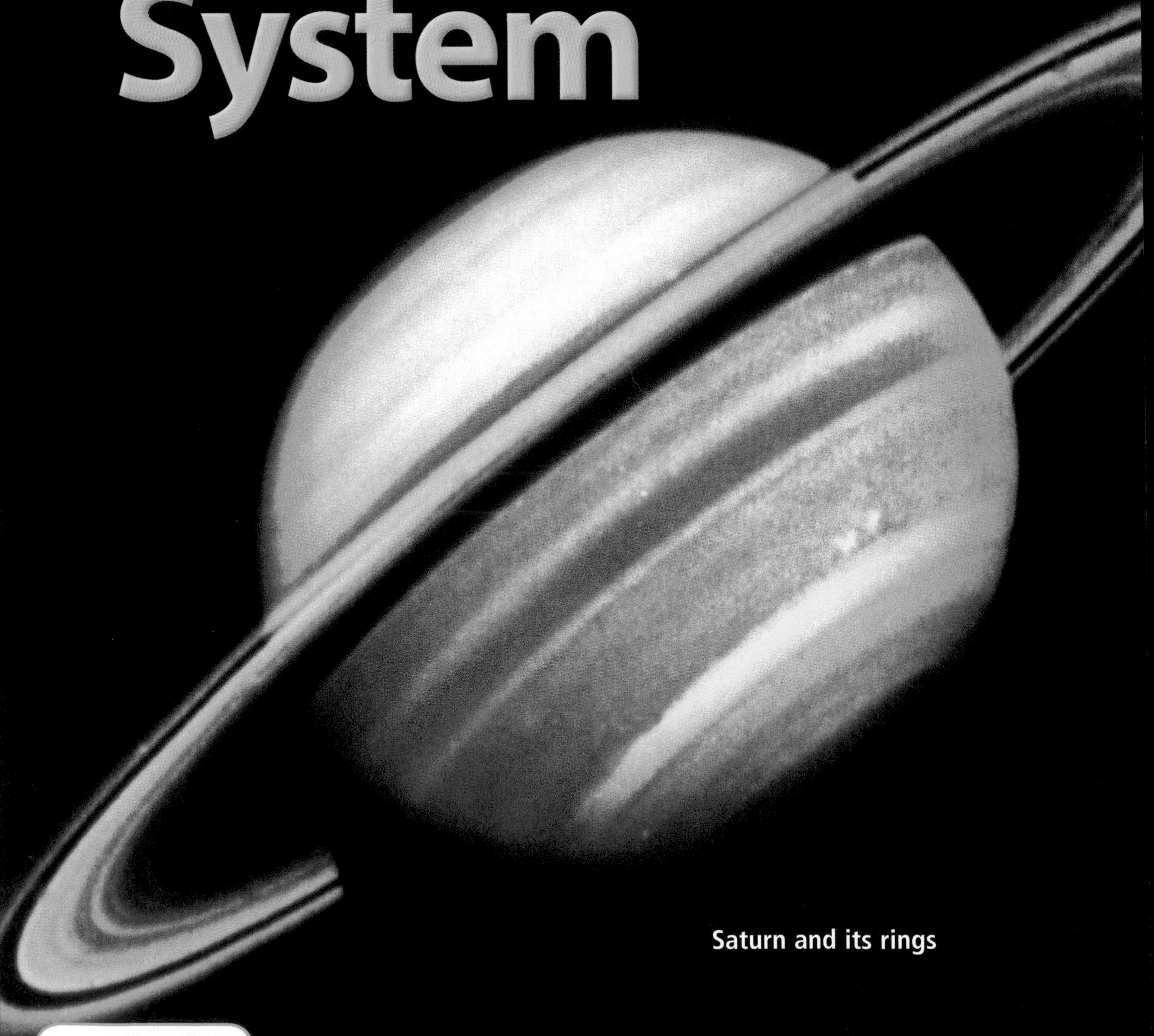

Saturn and its rings

Lesson Preview

LESSON 1

They're on mountaintops, in backyards, and in outer space. How do telescopes help people study objects in space?

LESSON 2

Eight planets, dwarf planets, many moons, and other objects travel in paths around the Sun. What are Earth's neighbors in space?

LESSON 3

Mercury, Venus, and Mars have some things in common with Earth. What do scientists know about the planets closest to the Sun?

LESSON 4

Jupiter, Saturn, Uranus, and Neptune are the planets farthest from the Sun. What are these planets like?

Vocabulary Preview

gas giant
inner planet
magnify
moon
★ orbit
outer planet
planet
★ rotation
★ solar system
space probe
Sun
telescope

★ = Tennessee Academic Vocabulary

Vocabulary Strategies

Have you ever seen any of these terms before? Do you know what they mean?

Describe, explain, or give an example of the vocabulary terms in your own words.

Draw a picture, symbol, example, or other image that describes the term.

Glossary p. H16

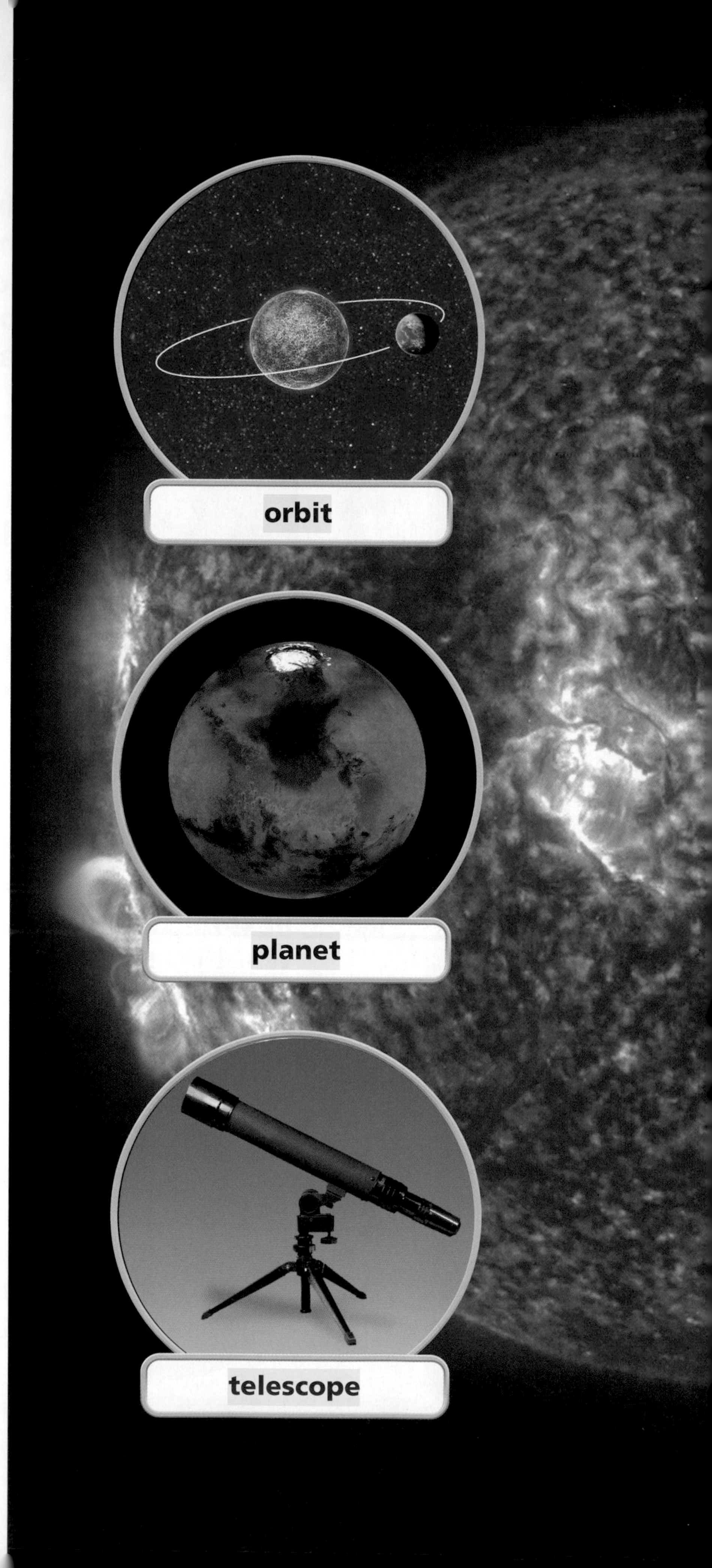

orbit

planet

telescope

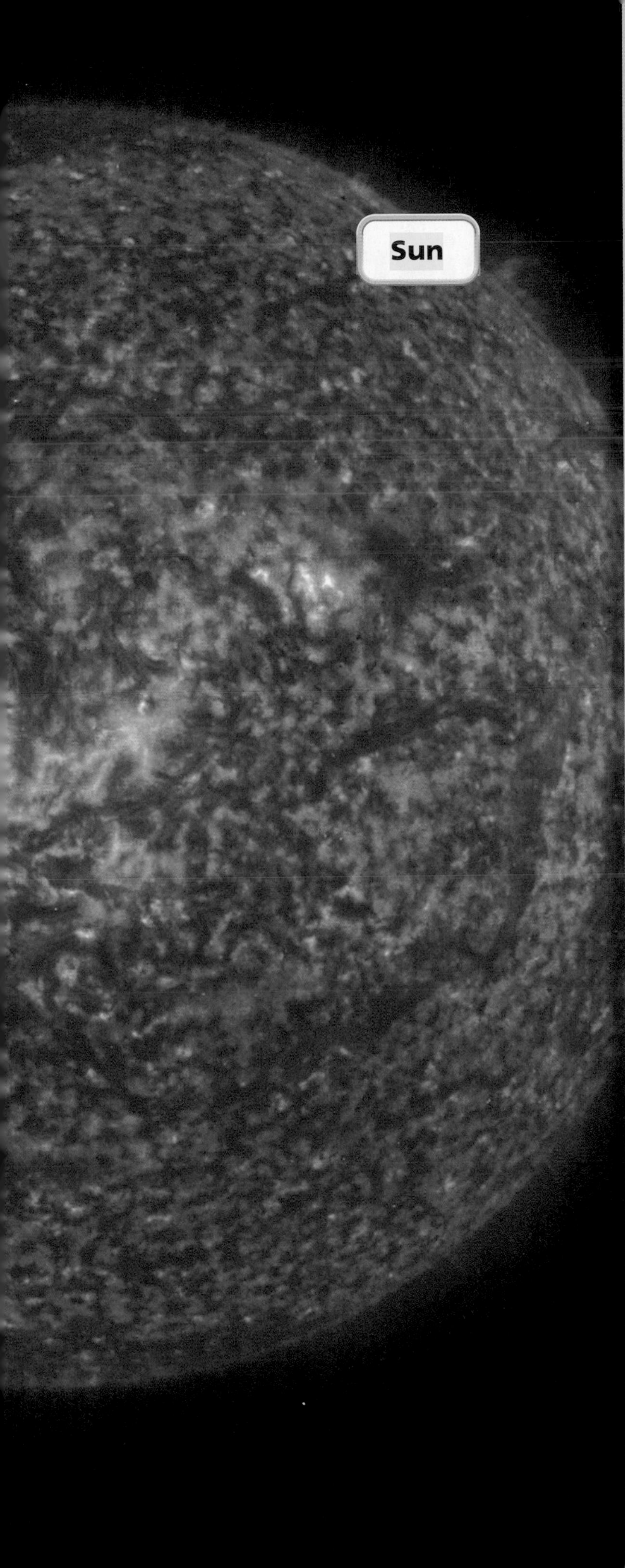

Sun

Start with Your Standards

Inquiry

GLE 0307.Inq.1 Explore different scientific phenomena by asking questions, making logical predictions, planning investigations, and recording data.

GLE 0307.Inq.2 Select and use appropriate tools and simple equipment to conduct an investigation.

GLE 0307.Inq.4 Identify and interpret simple patterns of evidence to communicate the findings of multiple investigations.

Technology and Engineering

GLE 0307.T/E.1 Describe how tools, technology, and inventions help to answer questions and solve problems.

GLE 0307.T/E.3 Identify appropriate materials, tools, and machines that can extend or enhance the ability to solve a specified problem.

GLE 0307.T/E.4 Recognize the connection between scientific advances, new knowledge, and the availability of new tools and technologies.

Earth and Space Science

Standard 6 The Universe

GLE 0307.6.1 Identify and compare the major components of the solar system.

Interact with this chapter.

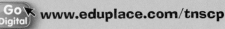

Go Digital www.eduplace.com/tnscp

Lesson 1

TENNESSEE STANDARDS

GLE 0307.Inq.1 Explore different scientific phenomena by asking questions, making logical predictions, planning investigations, and recording data.
GLE 0307.T/E.1 Describe how tools, technology, and inventions help to answer questions and solve problems.
GLE 0307.T/E.3 Identify appropriate materials, tools, and machines that can extend or enhance the ability to solve a specified problem.

How Do Scientists Use Telescopes?

Why It Matters...

Stars and planets look like tiny points of light in the night sky. The Moon looks white and flat. How have scientists learned what distant objects in space really look like? They use telescopes to view these objects more clearly.

PREPARE TO INVESTIGATE

Inquiry Skill

Compare When you compare, you describe how objects or events are alike and how they are different, often by using numbers.

Materials

- 2 cardboard tubes
- transparent tape
- convex lens A (15-cm focal length)
- convex lens B (5-cm focal length)

Directed Inquiry

Making a Telescope

Procedure

1. Make a telescope. Slip a smaller tube inside a larger tube to make a telescope tube. Tape lens A, the larger, thinner lens, to the larger end of the telescope tube. Tape lens B, the smaller, thicker lens, to the smaller end of the tube.

2. **Observe** Without using the telescope, observe three objects that are across the room. In your Science Notebook, record how the objects look.

3. **Record Data** Use the telescope to observe the same three objects. Hold the smaller end of the telescope to your eye and look through the lens. Slowly slide the larger tube forward and back until you can see each object clearly. Record how the objects look.

4. **Compare** Exchange telescopes with a partner and repeat step 3.

STEP 1

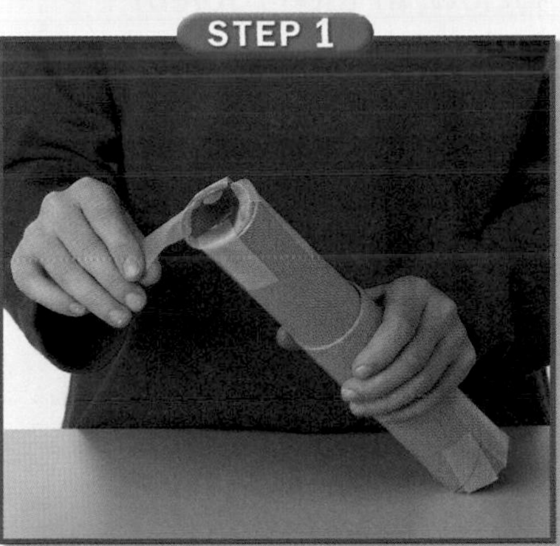

STEP 1

STEP 3

Think and Write

1. **Compare** What differences did you notice when you viewed the objects with just your eyes, and then with the telescope? What differences did you notice with your partner's telescope?
2. **Infer** Why do you think telescopes are useful to scientists who study space?

✓ 0307.6.1

Guided Inquiry

Experiment With an adult, take your telescope outside at night. Observe the Moon with just your eyes. Then use your telescope to observe the Moon.

Reading Science

Seeing Into Space

VOCABULARY

magnify
telescope

GRAPHIC ORGANIZER

Problem-Solution Use a chart like the one below. In the *Problem* column, write "Earth's atmosphere keeps people from having a clear view of the planets." In the *Solution* column, write a possible solution to the problem.

GLE 0307.T/E.1 Describe how tools, technology, and inventions help to answer questions and solve problems.

GLE 0307.T/E.3 Identify appropriate materials, tools, and machines that can extend or enhance the ability to solve a specified problem.

GLE 0307.T/E.4 Recognize the connection between scientific advances, new knowledge, and the availability of new tools and technologies.

Telescopes

If you look up at the night sky, you can see the Moon. You can also see small points of light. Most of these points of light are stars. A few of them are planets. How can you see these objects more clearly?

A telescope can help you see details of objects in the sky. A **telescope** is a tool that makes distant objects appear larger, brighter, and sharper. When you make an object appear larger, you **magnify** it. Because some telescopes make objects appear brighter, more stars can be seen through a telescope than can be seen with just your eyes.

▼ **This optical telescope is on Mount Palomar in California.**

▲ **This radio telescope in Arecibo, Puerto Rico, is the largest in the world.**

It is dangerous to look directly at the Sun. Looking directly at the Sun can damage your eyes. People observing the Sun should never look straight at it, even with a telescope. It is safe to look directly at other stars, which are more distant.

There are different kinds of telescopes. One kind of telescope magnifies distant objects by collecting light. This is called an optical (AHP tihk uhl) telescope. A radio telescope collects radio waves instead of light. Computers use the radio waves to make pictures of space. As more powerful telescopes are invented, scientists learn more about objects in space.

The Hubble Space Telescope is an optical telescope. It travels around Earth 575 km (360 mi) above the surface. ▼

FOCUS CHECK What tool can you use to see objects in space more clearly?

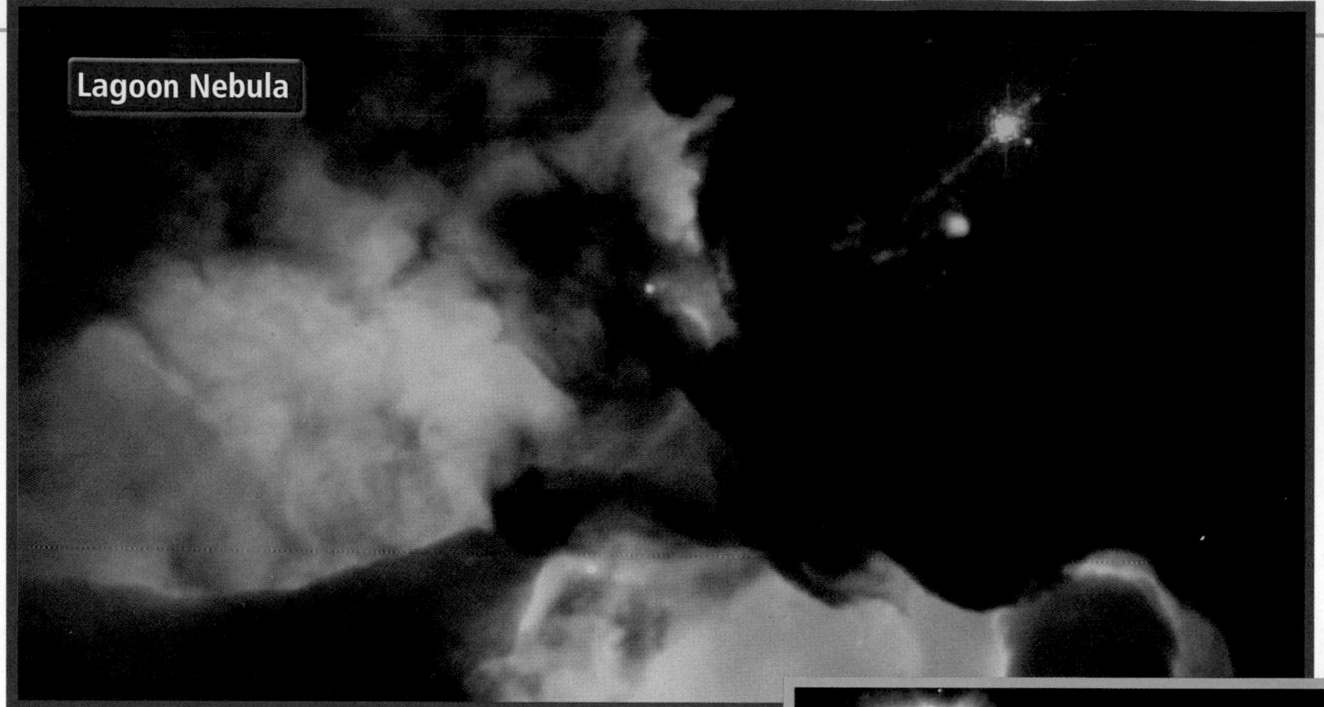

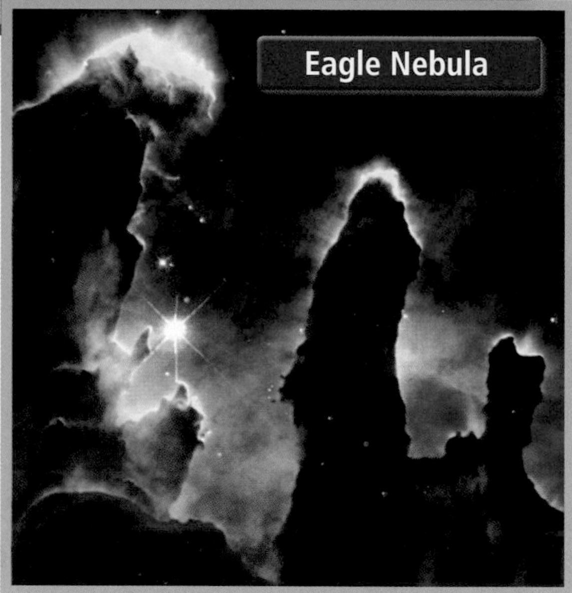

These nebula photos were taken by the Hubble. A nebula is a place where stars form.

A Hubble Scrapbook

The Hubble Space Telescope is different from other telescopes because it is in space. It moves around Earth every 97 minutes. The Hubble was launched in 1990 from a space shuttle.

Earth's atmosphere, the blanket of air around the planet, contains clouds, dust, and water. The atmosphere blurs our view of objects in space. But the Hubble is beyond Earth's atmosphere. It gives scientists a clearer view of distant regions of space.

FOCUS CHECK How is the Hubble able to help scientists see objects in space more clearly?

Express Lab

Activity Card

Show What Magnification Does

Lesson Wrap-Up

Visual Summary

Telescopes are tools that make distant objects appear larger, brighter, and sharper so they can be seen more clearly.

Optical telescopes magnify distant objects, such as planets. Radio telescopes collect radio waves.

The Hubble Space Telescope is in space. It helps scientists to clearly see objects beyond Earth's atmosphere.

Check for Understanding

CHOOSE A TELESCOPE

Think about the Hubble Space Telescope and the one you made for this lesson. Which would be better for identifying an object at the far end of the playground? Explain. **0307.T/E.4**

Review

1. **MAIN IDEA** Why do scientists use telescopes?
2. **VOCABULARY** Use the terms *telescope* and *magnify* in a sentence.
3. **READING SKILL: Problem-Solution** Suggest a problem that could be solved by using a telescope.
4. **CRITICAL THINKING: Evaluate** Why do you think it is dangerous to look directly at the Sun?
5. **INQUIRY SKILL: Compare** How is a radio telescope different from an optical telescope?

TCAP Prep

The Hubble Space Telescope is

Ⓐ a radio telescope
Ⓑ above Earth's atmosphere
Ⓒ on a mountaintop
Ⓓ always in the same place

SPI 0307.T/E.1

Go Digital Technology

Visit **www.eduplace.com/tnscp/** to learn more about telescopes.

Technology

Deep Impact!

A comet is a small ball of dust, ice, and rock traveling around the Sun. Most comets are billions of kilometers from Earth. But some follow paths that bring them closer to Earth once every few thousand years. These objects can tell scientists many things about how the Sun and planets formed.

How can scientists learn a comet's secrets? In July of 2005, the spacecraft Deep Impact approached the comet Tempel 1. It fired a 370-kg object at the comet. The impact sent an explosion of dust and gases into space. It left behind a crater, or hole, in the comet's surface.

Telescopes all over Earth recorded the impact. Scientists took photographs of the dust cloud and the crater. These photographs gave them many clues about the inside of the comet. Scientists can use these clues to learn about the comet's history.

A bright explosion of dust and gas flies off the Tempel 1 comet. This photograph was taken by the Deep Impact spacecraft.

Large radio telescopes like this one in the Deep Space Network recorded the comet's impact. This radio telescope dish is 70 m (about 230 feet) across. But smaller telescopes could see the impact as well. People were encouraged to watch the impact through backyard telescopes and send scientists their observations. ▼

▲ Drawing of the Deep Impact spacecraft firing at the comet

Sharing Ideas

1. **READING CHECK** What two tools did scientists use to study the comet Tempel 1?
2. **WRITE ABOUT IT** Suppose you used a small telescope to observe the impact of Tempel 1. Write a descriptive paragraph telling what you might see.
3. **TALK ABOUT IT** Would scientists have been able to learn as much from Tempel 1 if they did not have telescopes? Why or why not?

Lesson 2

TENNESSEE STANDARDS

GLE 0307.Inq.2 Select and use appropriate tools and simple equipment to conduct an investigation.

GLE 0307.6.1 Identify and compare the major components of the solar system.

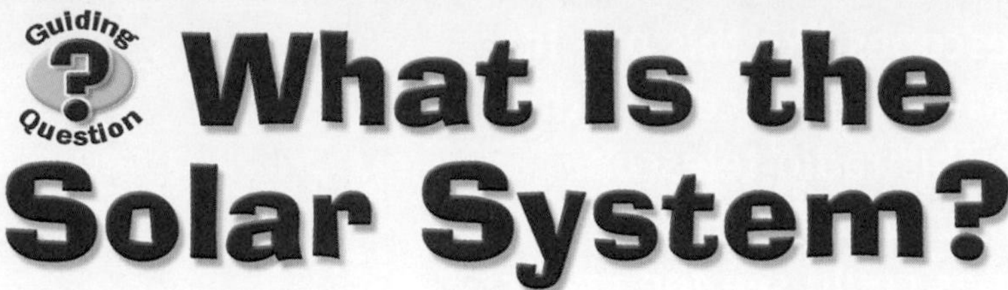

What Is the Solar System?

Why It Matters...

Earth is part of a group of objects including planets, moons, and one star—the Sun. The Sun is in the center of all these other objects. Each of eight planets, including Earth, moves in a path around the Sun.

PREPARE TO INVESTIGATE

Inquiry Skill

Use Models You can use a model of an object, a process, or an idea to better understand or describe how it works.

Materials

- drinking straw
- scissors
- metric ruler
- string (1 m long)
- small plastic-foam ball
- metal washer
- tape
- goggles

Science and Math Toolbox

For step 1, review **Using a Tape Measure or Ruler** on page H6.

Directed Inquiry

Planet Movements

Procedure

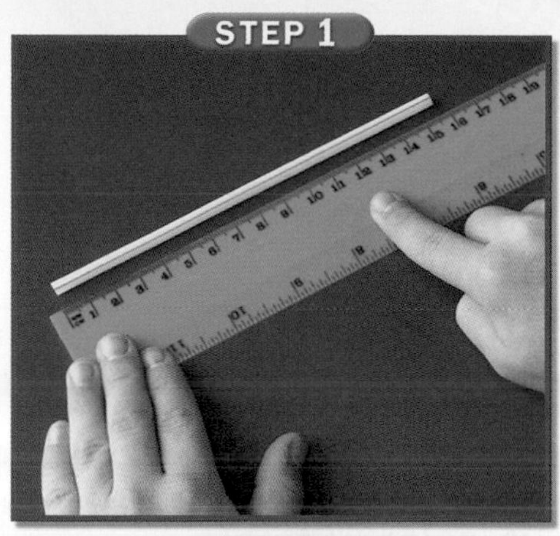
STEP 1

1. **Measure** Cut a drinking straw so that it is 12 cm long. Thread a piece of string that is 1 m long through the straw.

STEP 2

2. Tie one end of the string to a washer. Wrap the other end of the string around a plastic-foam ball and tie it tightly. Use tape to secure the string to the ball.

STEP 3

3. **Use Models** Hold the straw upright with one hand. Rest the washer in your other hand. Hold the washer so that there is 10 cm of string between the ball and the top of the straw. Stand away from your classmates. Move the straw in a circular motion above your head so the ball swings in a circle around the straw. In your Science Notebook, describe the motion of the ball. **Safety:** Wear goggles.

4. **Experiment** Repeat step 3, using 15 cm of string and then 60 cm of string.

Think and Write

1. **Use Models** What do you think the ball represents in the model?

2. **Infer** Venus is closer to the Sun than is Jupiter. Which planet travels farther around the Sun?

✓ 0307.6.1

Guided Inquiry

Ask Questions Write a question about how a planet's distance from the Sun affects the time it takes to go around the Sun. Use the Internet to compare the lengths of a "year" on each planet.

The Solar System

VOCABULARY

- inner planets
- moon
- ★ orbit
- outer planets
- planet
- ★ rotation
- ★ solar system
- Sun

GRAPHIC ORGANIZER

Compare and Contrast Compare a moon and a planet in the diagram.

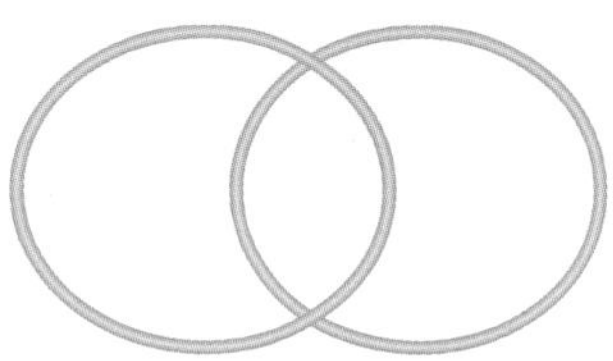

GLE 0307.6.1 Identify and compare the major components of the solar system.

The Sun and Planets

Each day, the Sun fills our sky with light. The **Sun** is the nearest star to Earth. Like all stars, the Sun is a huge sphere of hot gases that gives off heat and light. We can see more distant stars at night.

Throughout time, people have also noticed starlike objects that move among the fixed patterns of stars. These objects came to be called "wanderers," or planets. A **planet** is a large body in space that moves around a star.

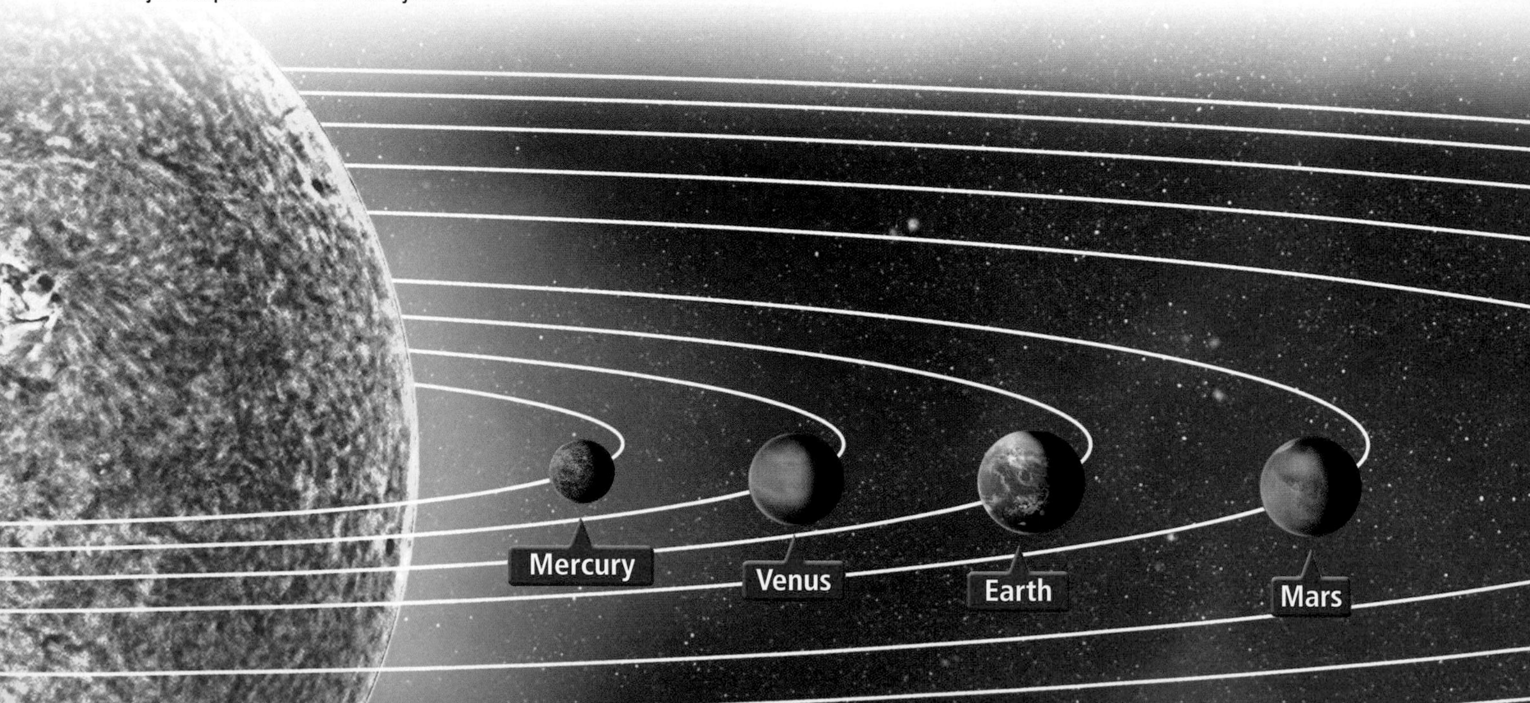

A planet does not produce light of its own. We are able to see planets shining in the night sky when light from the Sun reflects, or bounces, off them. Earth is one of eight planets that **orbit**, or move in a path, around the Sun.

You can also see Earth's moon in the night sky. A **moon** is a small, rounded body in orbit around a planet. A moon does not produce its own light. It reflects light from the Sun. Most planets have one or more moons. The Sun, planets, moons, and other objects that orbit the Sun make up the **solar system** (SOH lur SIHS tuhm). Planets and moons have oval-shaped orbits.

FOCUS CHECK What is one way that planets and moons are similar?

Eight planets orbit the Sun in the solar system. Pluto is classified as a dwarf planet.

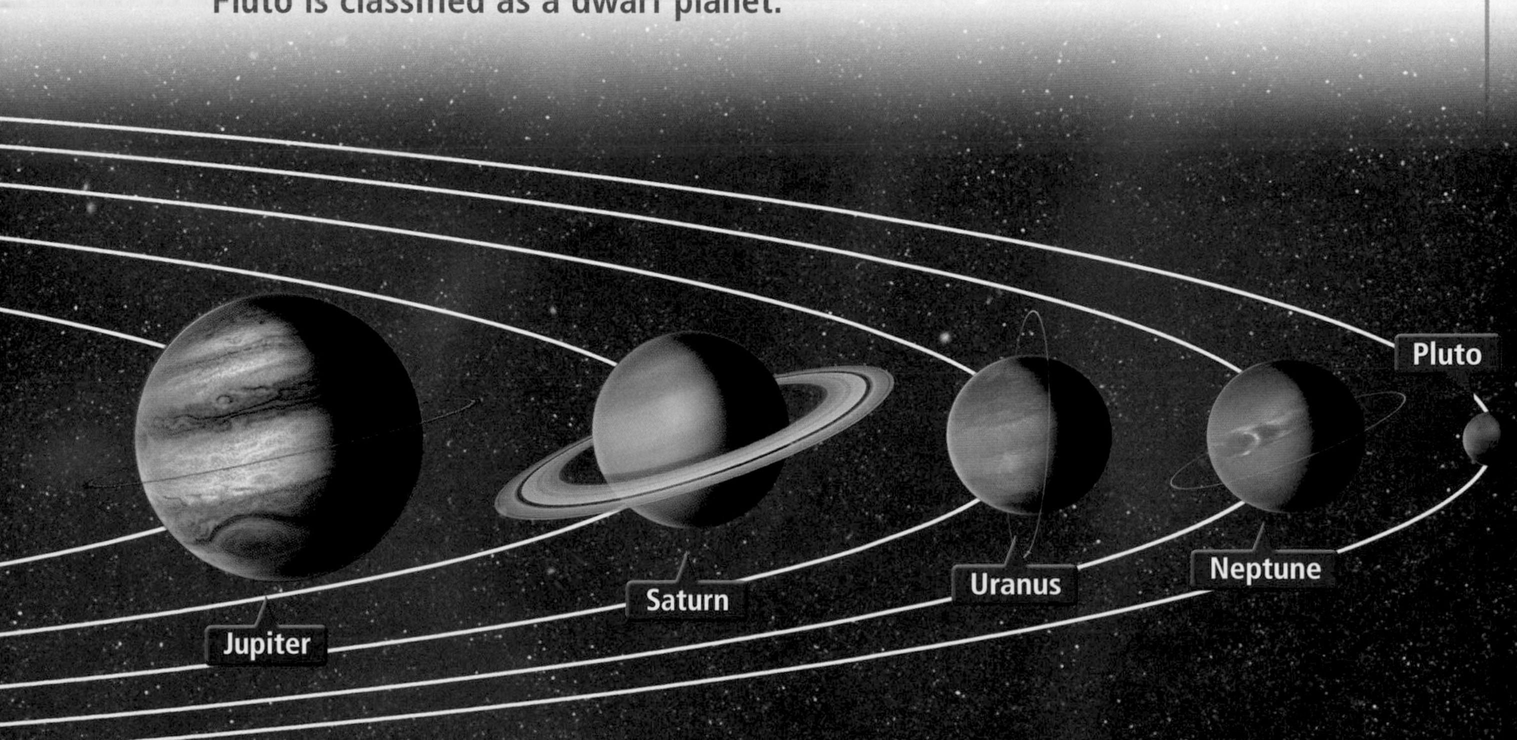

The Inner Planets

Mercury, Venus, Earth, and Mars are called the **inner planets**. These planets get a lot of heat and light because they are close to the Sun. The inner planets are small and are made of solid rock materials. Their surfaces have mountains and craters.

Venus (VEE nuhs) is the second planet from the Sun. It is covered by thick clouds of gas. The clouds trap heat and make the planet very hot.

Earth is the third planet from the Sun. It is the only planet known to support life. Earth has an atmosphere.

Mercury (MUR kyuh ree) is the closest planet to the Sun. Mercury is very hot during the day and very cold at night.

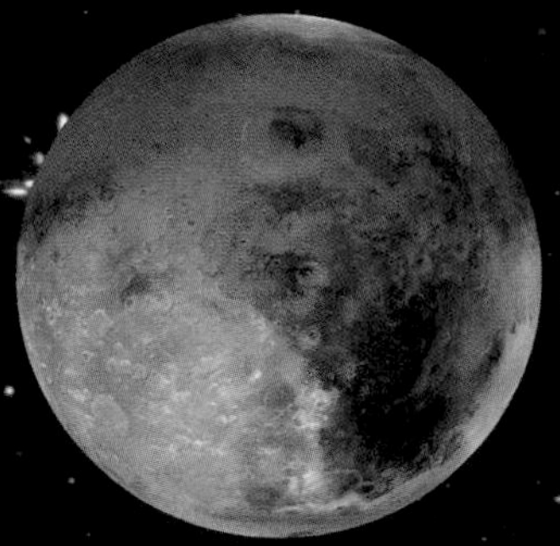

Mars (mahrz) is the fourth planet from the Sun. The surface of Mars has many craters, mountains, and volcanoes. Mars has the largest volcano ever discovered in the solar system.

Activity Card
Model Different Orbits

The Outer Planets

Jupiter, Saturn, Uranus, and Neptune are called the **outer planets**. They are cold and dark because they are far from the Sun. They are large, made of gases, and have many moons. Each also has a system of rings.

Pluto is classified as a dwarf planet. It is small and is made of rocks and frozen gases. Pluto has no rings and three known moons.

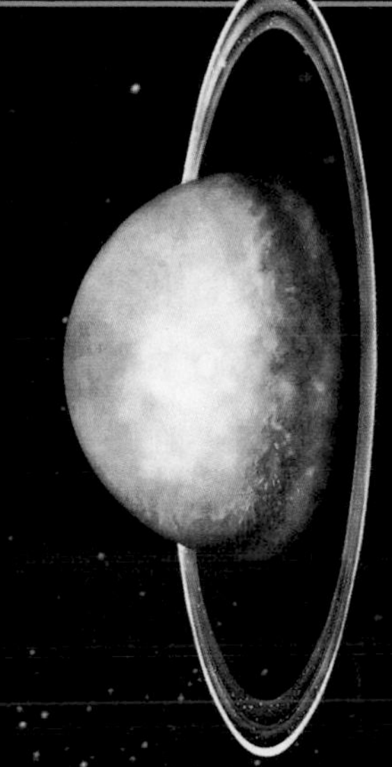

Uranus (YUR uh nuhs) is the seventh planet from the Sun. Unlike any other planet, Uranus spins on its side.

Jupiter (JOO pih tur) is the fifth planet from the Sun and is the largest planet. The Great Red Spot is a large storm.

Neptune (NEHP toon) is the eighth planet from the Sun. Methane in its atmosphere gives Neptune its blue color.

Saturn (SAT urn) is the sixth planet from the Sun. It has beautiful rings made of dust, ice, and rocks.

Pluto (PLOO toh) is a dwarf planet. It is smaller than the planets and very far from the Sun .

Planets in Motion

As it orbits the Sun, each planet spins, or rotates, like a top. Earth's day is 24 hours long. It takes one day for Earth to make one **rotation**, or complete turn. Some planets spin more quickly than Earth; some more slowly. Jupiter's rotation takes about 10 Earth hours. Venus takes 243 Earth days.

The farther a planet is from the Sun, the longer it takes to orbit. The time it takes to complete one trip around the Sun is called a year. Earth's year is about 365 days long. Mercury takes only 88 Earth days.

Because Earth spins and orbits, it is hard to measure the orbits of the other planets. Only in the past few hundred years have people figured out how Earth, the Moon, and the planets move.

FOCUS CHECK What two ways do planets move?

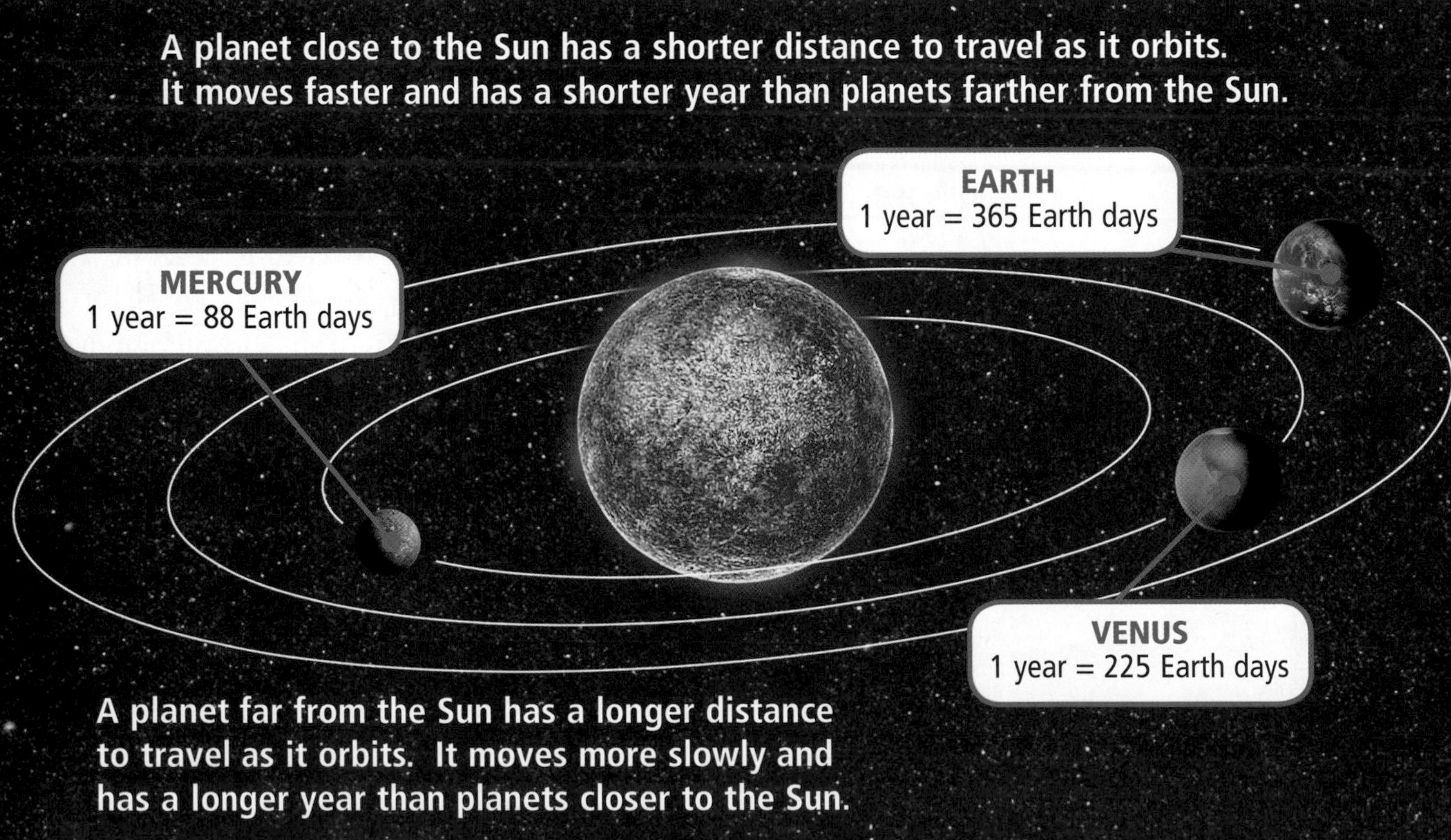
A planet close to the Sun has a shorter distance to travel as it orbits. It moves faster and has a shorter year than planets farther from the Sun.
EARTH
1 year = 365 Earth days
MERCURY
1 year = 88 Earth days
VENUS
1 year = 225 Earth days
A planet far from the Sun has a longer distance to travel as it orbits. It moves more slowly and has a longer year than planets closer to the Sun.

Lesson Wrap-Up

Visual Summary

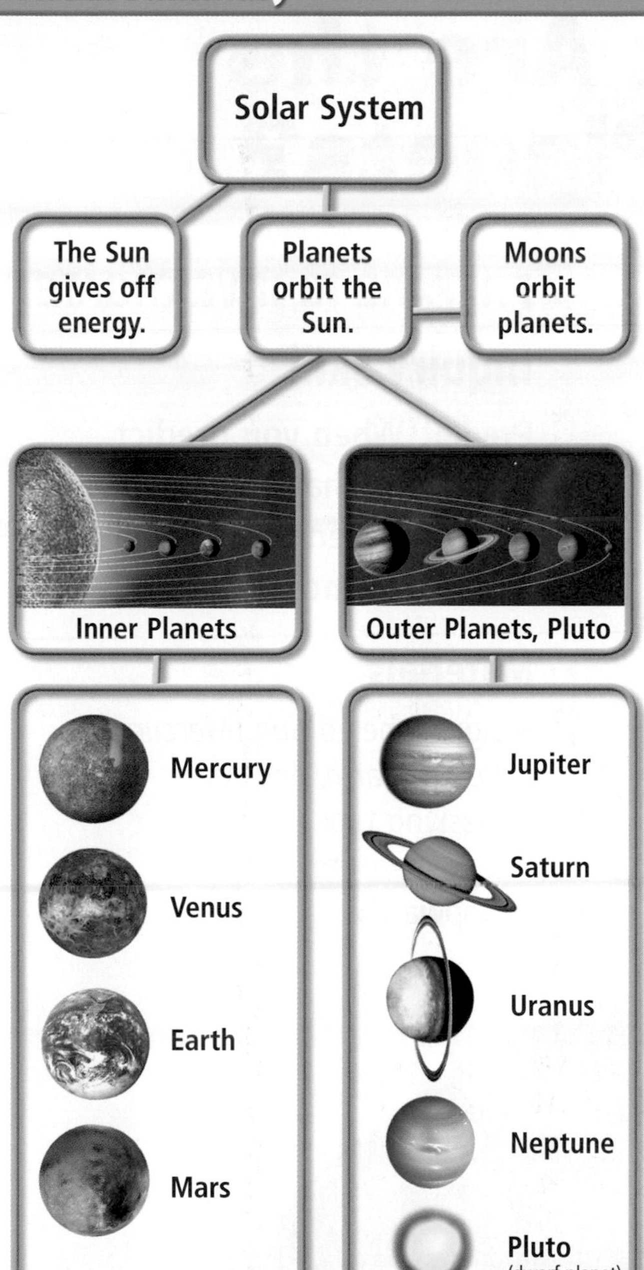

COMPARE YEAR LENGTH

Make a table showing the length of year for each planet. Use the art on page 160 to help you. Then skim Lessons 3 and 4 to find any more information you need. You may decorate the chart with pictures of the planets.

✓ 0307.6.2

Review

1. **MAIN IDEA** Name the planets of the solar system in order of their distance from the Sun.
2. **VOCABULARY** Write a sentence that uses the terms *planet* and *orbit*.
3. **READING SKILL: Compare and Contrast** How are the inner planets and outer planets alike? How are they different?
4. **CRITICAL THINKING: Analyze** A planet has a very long year compared to Earth's year. Do you think that this planet is closer to or farther from the Sun than Earth?
5. **INQUIRY SKILL: Use Models** Suppose you want to use balls to make a model of the Sun and planets of the solar system. How many balls would you need?

TCAP Prep

Which statement about the Sun is true?

Ⓐ It gives off light.
Ⓑ It orbits the planets.
Ⓒ It is made of rock.
Ⓓ It has one moon.

SPI 0307.6.1

Go Digital Technology

Visit **www.eduplace.com/tnscp** to learn more about the solar system.

Lesson 3

TENNESSEE STANDARDS

GLE 0307.Inq.4 Identify and interpret simple patterns of evidence to communicate the findings of multiple investigations.
GLE 0307.6.1 Identify and compare the major components of the solar system.

Guiding Question

What Are the Inner Planets?

Why It Matters...

The inner planets—Mercury, Venus, Earth, and Mars—are alike in some ways. They are small, they are made of rock, and they have few moons. Within your lifetime, people may be traveling to other inner planets.

PREPARE TO INVESTIGATE

Inquiry Skill

Predict When you predict, you state what you think will happen based on observations and experiences.

Materials

- Signs labeled *Sun, Mercury, Venus, Earth,* and *Mars*
- masking tape
- tape measure
- stopwatch

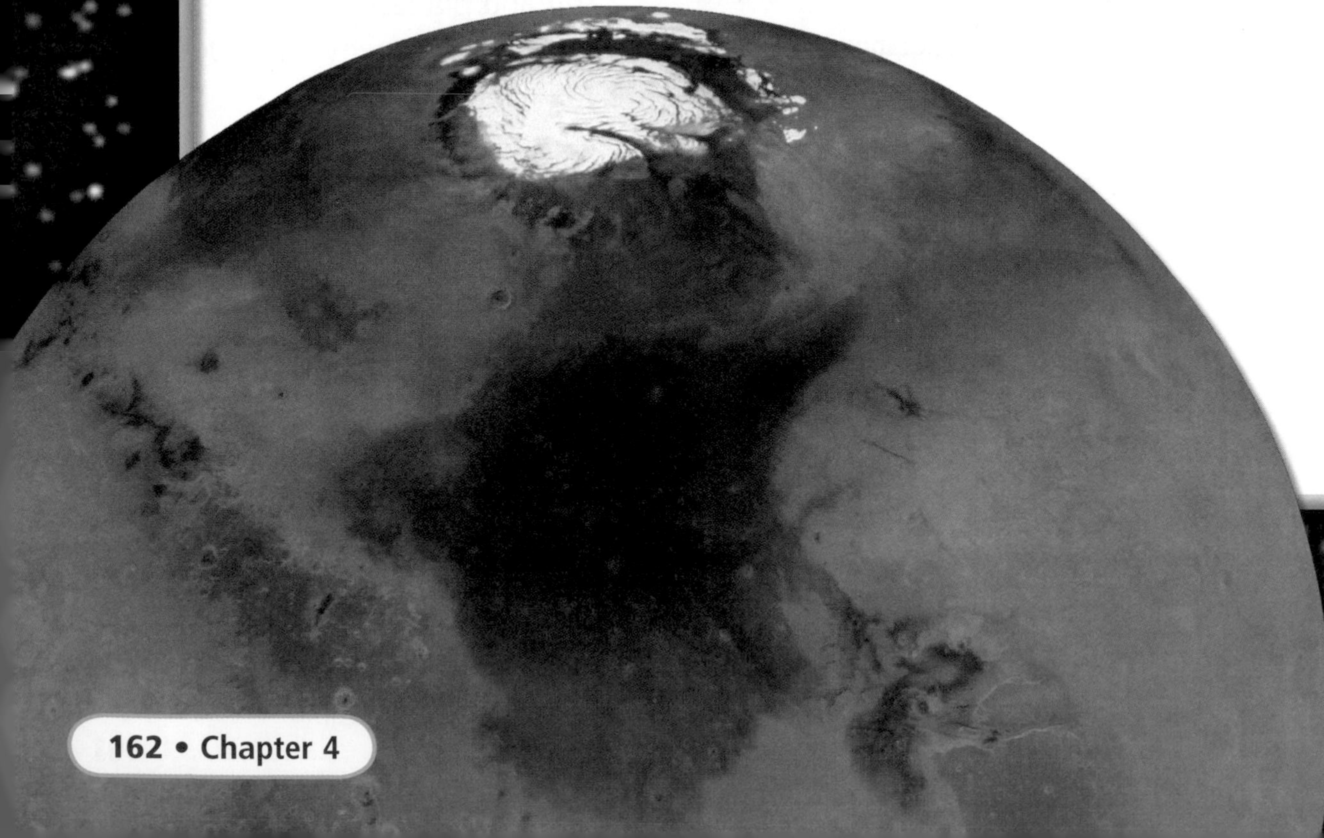

Directed Inquiry

Orbiting the Sun

Procedure

1. **Measure** Make a simple model of the solar system. Use masking tape to make an X on the floor to mark the Sun's position. Mark an orbit around the Sun by placing pieces of tape in a circle 1 m from the X. Make three more orbits with tape, each 1 m farther out from the X.
2. **Collaborate** Five students should hold signs to model the inner planets and the Sun. Use the data in the table to arrange the "planets" in their orbits.
3. **Predict** Predict where each "planet" will be after walking for 5 seconds. Mercury should move most quickly. Venus should move slightly slower. Earth should move more slowly than Venus. Mars should move the slowest.
4. **Use Models** When a timekeeper says to start, the "planets" should walk in their own orbits as described in step 3. After 5 seconds, the timekeeper will tell the "planets" to stop. Draw the position of each "planet."

STEP 1

STEP 2

Distance of Planets from Sun

Planet	Average distance from Sun (millions of km)
Mercury	58
Venus	108
Earth	150
Mars	228

STEP 2

Think and Write

1. **Compare** Which planet has the greatest distance to travel to complete its orbit?
2. **Infer** What can you infer about how a planet's distance from the Sun and its speed affect the length of its year?

✓ 0307.6.1

Guided Inquiry

Experiment Extend your model to include Jupiter. How should Jupiter move? Infer how the length of a year on Jupiter and a year on Mars differs.

Reading Science

The Inner Planets

VOCABULARY

space probe

GRAPHIC ORGANIZER

Main Idea and Details

As you read, write down details that describe each of the inner planets.

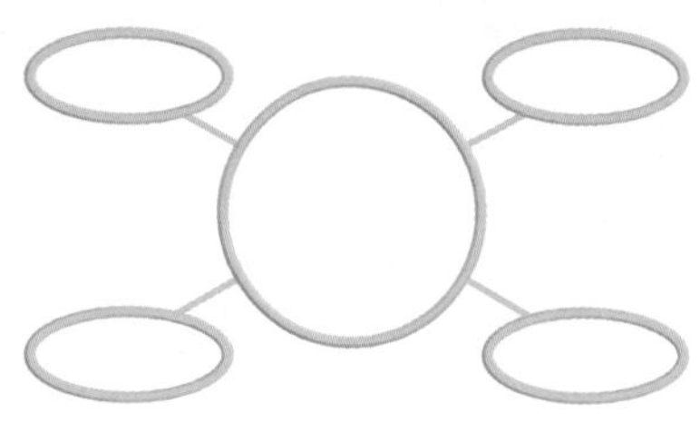

GLE 0307.6.1 Identify and compare the major components of the solar system.

Mercury

Mercury is the planet nearest to the Sun. It is a tiny planet not much larger than Earth's moon. Mercury is so close to the Sun that its surface gets broiling hot during its day. During its night, almost all the heat escapes, and its surface becomes very cold.

Mercury moves very quickly through space. Its year is only 88 Earth days long. This is because Mercury's orbit is so close to the Sun.

Mercury

Length of day	59 Earth days
Length of year	88 Earth days
Distance from Sun	58 million km (36 million mi)
Average temperature	Day: 427°C (800°F); Night: –173°C (–279°F)
Diameter	4,878 km (3,029 mi)
Number of moons	none

Mercury orbits quickly, but spins slowly.

Venus

Venus is the second planet from the Sun. Venus has been called Earth's twin. This is because Venus is about the same size as Earth and its orbit is next to Earth's orbit. Venus is a very bright planet in Earth's sky. Often Venus can be seen low in the sky, just after sunset.

Venus's motion is very different from Earth's. Venus spins in the opposite direction of most of the other planets. It also spins extremely slowly. In fact, a "day" on Venus is longer than its year. That means that Venus orbits all the way around the Sun before it completes a full spin.

FOCUS CHECK Describe two types of motions of both Mercury and Venus.

Venus	
Length of day	243 Earth days
Length of year	225 Earth days
Distance from Sun	108 million km (67 million mi)
Average temperature	482°C (900°F)
Diameter	12,104 km (7,519 mi)
Number of moons	none

Venus's surface is covered by very thick clouds.

Earth

Earth, the third planet, is your home. It is the only planet in the solar system that is known to support life. Earth has both liquid water and oxygen, which most living things need. In addition, Earth's atmosphere keeps the planet from getting too hot or too cold.

Earth's motion causes many of the events you are familiar with from your daily life. Earth spins every 24 hours, causing day and night. It orbits around the Sun about every 365 days, or one year.

Earth

Length of day	24 hours
Length of year	about 365 Earth days
Distance from Sun	150 million km (93 million mi)
Average temperature	15°C (59°F)
Diameter	12,712 km (7,926 mi)
Number of moons	1

Earth's atmosphere and its distance from the Sun keep it at the right temperature to support life.

Mars

Mars, the fourth planet, is called the Red Planet. It is covered with red rocks and soil that contain rust. Canyons, craters, and valleys can be found on its surface. Many scientists believe that liquid water and perhaps life may have once existed on Mars. But no signs of life have yet been found.

Mars and Earth spin at similar speeds. A day on Mars is only slightly longer than a day on Earth. However, a year on Mars is almost twice as long as a year on Earth.

FOCUS CHECK In what way is Mars's motion similar to that of Earth?

Mars	
Length of day	$24\frac{1}{2}$ hours
Length of year	687 Earth days
Distance from Sun	228 million km (141 million mi)
Average temperature	–63°C (–81°F)
Diameter	6,746 km (4,223 mi)
Number of moons	2

Mars's atmosphere is thinner than Earth's. Mars is also farther from the Sun than Earth is, so its temperature is colder.

Express Lab
Activity Card
Show the Spin of Venus

Exploring the Inner Planets

The planets of our solar system are difficult to study because they are so far away from Earth. Scientists were first able to study the planets in detail by using telescopes. More recently, scientists have had the chance to see the planets up close by using space probes. A **space probe** is a craft that helps scientists explore outer space. Space probes carry instruments, but not people.

Space probes carry cameras, lab equipment, and other tools to take pictures and collect data. They send the information back to Earth to be studied.

FOCUS CHECK How do space probes help scientists study other planets?

Mariner 10
Mariner 10 was the first space probe ever to collect data about two planets—Mercury and Venus.

Magellan
The Magellan probe was launched in 1989 to map the surface of Venus.

Mars Rovers
Two rovers, Spirit and Opportunity, landed on Mars in 2004. They studied rocks and soil. They also looked for signs that water was once on Mars.

Lesson Wrap-Up

Visual Summary

Mercury is the planet closest to the Sun. It has the shortest orbit.

Venus is between Earth and Mercury. It has the hottest surface of all the planets.

Earth is the only planet known to have liquid water and life.

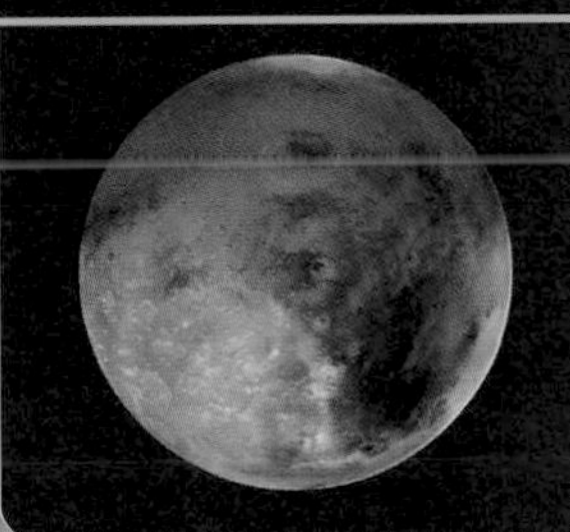

Mars has red soil and rocks. Its day is almost the same length as Earth's.

Check for Understanding

MODEL THE INNER PLANETS

Make a table model to show the relative sizes of the inner planets. Use these objects:

- Sun—a ball or balloon with an 8-inch diameter
- Mercury and Mars—a piece of sand about the size of a pinhead for each
- Venus and Earth—a peppercorn for each

Glue each object to a large sheet of paper. Label the Sun and each of the inner planets in your model.

✓ **0307.6.1**

Review

1. **MAIN IDEA** What do the inner planets have in common?
2. **VOCABULARY** What is a space probe?
3. **READING SKILL: Main Idea and Details** What are four details that could be used to describe Mars?
4. **CRITICAL THINKING: Apply** Suppose water and oxygen had been found on Mars. Why would it still be hard for living things to survive there?
5. **INQUIRY SKILL: Predict** Suppose the distance between Venus and the Sun increased. What might happen to the length of a year on Venus?

TCAP Prep

Which invention helped scientists learn more about the planets?

- (A) telephone
- (B) microphone
- (C) telescope
- (D) phonograph

SPI 0307.T/E.2

Go Digital Technology

Visit **www.eduplace.com/tnscp/** to learn more about the inner planets.

Lesson 4

TENNESSEE STANDARDS

GLE 0307.Inq.4 Identify and interpret simple patterns of evidence to communicate the findings of multiple investigations.
GLE 0307.6.1 Identify and compare the major components of the solar system.

Guiding Question

What Are the Outer Planets?

Why It Matters...

Using probes like this one, scientists have learned a lot about the planets farthest from the Sun. These planets are very different from Earth. They are huge and made mainly of gas. They have dozens of moons, and all have rings.

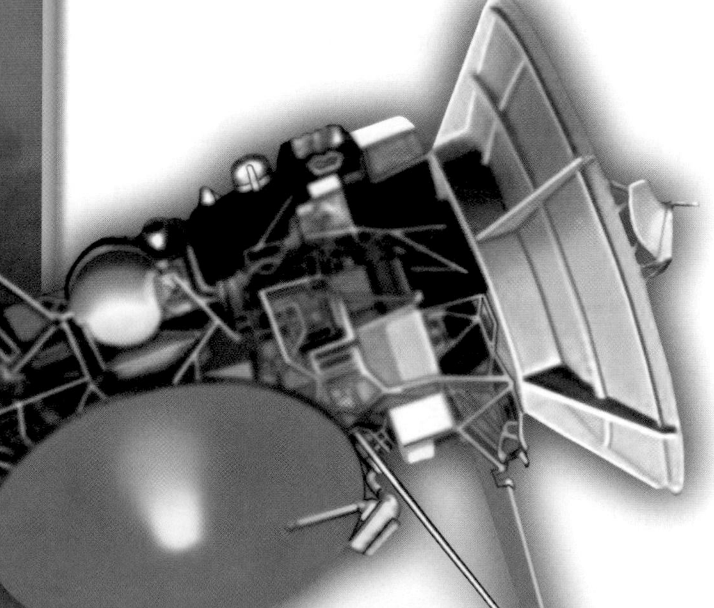

PREPARE TO INVESTIGATE

Inquiry Skill

Analyze Data When you analyze data, you look for patterns that can help you draw conclusions.

Materials

- 2 large sheets of construction paper
- metric ruler
- pencil
- scissors

Science and Math Toolbox

For step 1, review **Using a Tape Measure or Ruler** on page H6.

Directed Inquiry

Outer Planets

Procedure

STEP 1

STEP 2

1. **Measure** For each measurement below, use a metric ruler to draw a line of that length on construction paper. Draw another line perpendicular to the first line. Connect the lines to make a circle, as shown. Label each circle with the name of the planet it represents.

   Jupiter 23 cm   Uranus 8.2 cm
   Saturn 19 cm   Neptune 7.6 cm
   Pluto (dwarf planet) 0.4 cm (4 mm)

2. **Use Models** Cut out and label each planet. Put the model planets in the order they are in the solar system, as listed. Record this data in your Science Notebook.

3. **Compare** Now put your model planets in order from smallest to largest. Record the data. Now put your model planets in order from largest to smallest. Record the data.

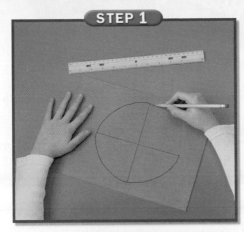

Data Table

Planet	Diameter (km)
Jupiter	142,980
Saturn	120,540
Uranus	51,120
Neptune	49,530
Pluto (dwarf planet)	2,390

Think and Write

1. **Analyze Data** Compare your data. Which two sets of data are similar?
2. **Infer** Refer to the data table on this page. What can you infer about the general relationship between planet size and distance from the Sun?

Guided Inquiry

Experiment Predict the mass of each planet based on its diameter. Then use the Internet or the library to find the actual masses of the planets. Compare them to your predictions.

0307.6.1

Reading Science

VOCABULARY

gas giant

GRAPHIC ORGANIZER

Sequence Use a diagram like the one below to order the outer planets.

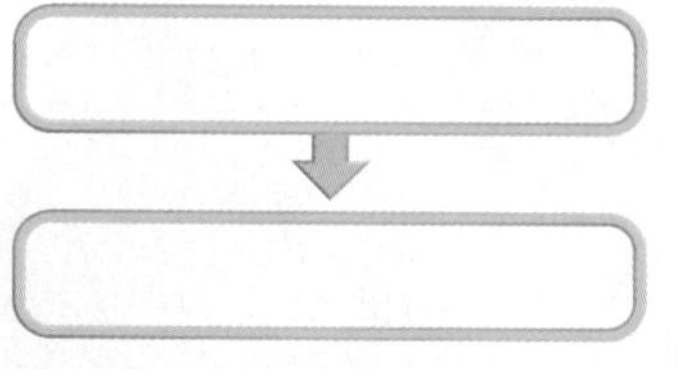

GLE 0307.6.1 Identify and compare the major components of the solar system.

The Outer Planets

Jupiter

The four planets farthest from the Sun are called the outer planets. Jupiter is the largest planet. In fact, all the other planets could fit inside it! A huge storm in Jupiter's atmosphere, called the Great Red Spot, is more than twice the size of Earth. Jupiter rotates so quickly that its day is only about 10 hours long.

Jupiter is one of four gas giants. Saturn, Uranus, and Neptune are the others. A **gas giant** is a very large planet made up mostly of gases. Jupiter has a very deep atmosphere with high and low clouds. Jupiter has at least 63 moons. Scientists think that more moons will be discovered.

Jupiter	
Length of day	9.8 hours
Length of year	12 Earth years
Distance from Sun	780 million km (480 million mi)
Average temperature	–150°C (–238°F)
Diameter	142,980 km (88,844 mi)
Number of moons	63 discovered so far

The Great Red Spot has been observed from Earth through telescopes for more than 300 years.

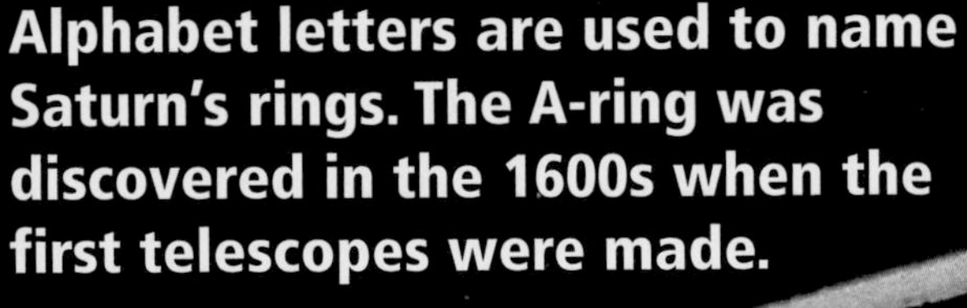

Alphabet letters are used to name Saturn's rings. The A-ring was discovered in the 1600s when the first telescopes were made.

Saturn	
Length of day	$10\frac{1}{2}$ hours
Length of year	$29\frac{1}{2}$ Earth years
Distance from Sun	1.4 billion km (860 million mi)
Average temperature	–170°C (–274°F)
Diameter	120,540 km (74,900 mi)
Number of moons	47 discovered so far

Saturn

Saturn is the second-largest planet. Like the other gas giants, it is covered by thick clouds. Saturn has many moons. Like Jupiter, Saturn spins very quickly. A day on Saturn is about 11 hours long. Saturn spins so quickly that it has a slightly flattened shape.

In 2004, the Cassini spacecraft began sending close-up images of Saturn's bright, beautiful rings back to Earth. The rings are made of pieces of ice, dust, and rocks that orbit the planet. Most pieces are only a few centimeters across. Some are as large as a house.

FOCUS CHECK **Which two planets are next to Jupiter?**

Pluto

Pluto once was known as the ninth planet. Today it is classified as a dwarf planet. The dwarf planets are round, orbiting bodies much like planets, but smaller.

Pluto is rocky and icy. Its orbit is tilted compared with the orbits of the planets. In addition, its orbit is so stretched out that once every 248 years, Pluto moves inside Neptune's orbit.

Scientists continue to discuss Pluto and the best way to classify it. Their decision may change.

FOCUS CHECK What is unusual about Pluto's position in the solar system?

Pluto	
Length of day	6 hours
Length of year	248 Earth years
Distance from Sun	6 billion km (3.7 billion mi)
Average temperature	–229°C (–380°F)
Diameter	2,390 km (1,485 mi)
Number of moons	3

From 1979 to 1999 Pluto was inside the orbit of Neptune. This switch happened because their orbits cross.

Lesson Wrap-Up

Visual Summary

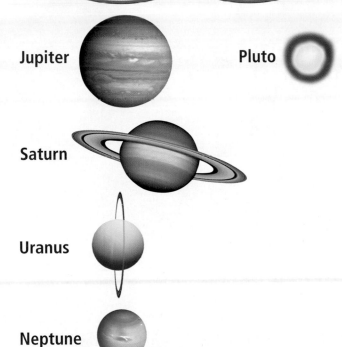

Outer Planets
- Larger than inner planets
- Made up mostly of gases

Both
- Far from Sun

Pluto
- A dwarf planet
- Rocky and icy
- Orbit more extreme oval and tilted

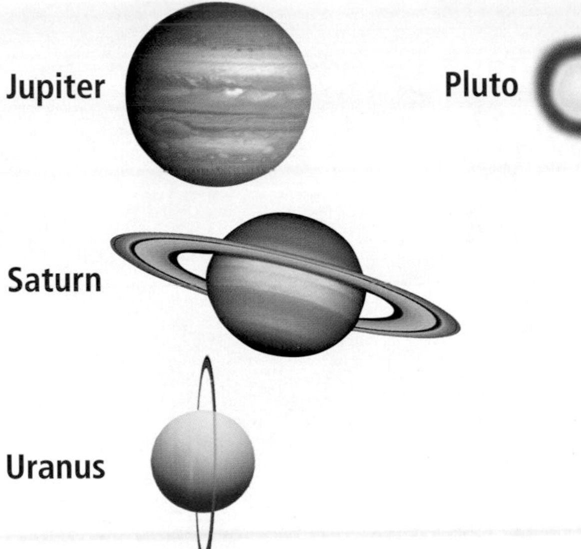

Check for Understanding

MODEL THE OUTER PLANETS

Add the outer planets to the table model you began in Lesson 3. Use these objects to represent the outer planets:

- Jupiter—a chestnut or a pecan
- Saturn—a hazelnut or an acorn
- Uranus and Neptune—a peanut or a coffee bean for each.

Glue each object as you did before. Then label each of the outer planets and display your completed model solar system. ✓ **0307.6.1**

Review

1. **MAIN IDEA** List the outer planets in order, starting with the planet nearest the Sun.
2. **VOCABULARY** What is a gas giant?
3. **READING SKILL: Sequence** List the outer planets in order from smallest to largest.
4. **CRITICAL THINKING: Synthesize** Based on its description, would you group Pluto with the outer planets or the inner planets? Why?
5. **INQUIRY SKILL: Analyze Data** A year on Jupiter is 12 Earth years. What does this data tell about Jupiter's distance from the Sun as compared to Earth's?

TCAP Prep

Which is an outer planet?

Ⓐ Mars
Ⓑ Earth
Ⓒ Saturn
Ⓓ Venus

SPI 0307.6.1

Go Digital Technology

Visit **www.eduplace.com/tnscp** to find out more about the outer planets.

Eyes on the Skies

Look at those rings! The planet Saturn is a beautiful sight even in a small backyard telescope. How much more exciting would it be to look at Saturn through the biggest telescope in the world?

Compare these two images of Saturn. An amateur astronomer recorded the smaller image with his home telescope. The larger image comes from one of the mighty Keck telescopes on top of Mauna Kea in Hawaii. At the Keck Observatory, astronomers have not one, but two giant eyes on the sky. Each telescope is the largest of its type anywhere.

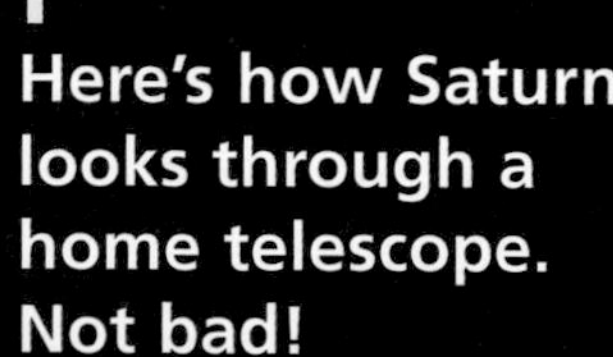

Here's how Saturn looks through a home telescope. Not bad!

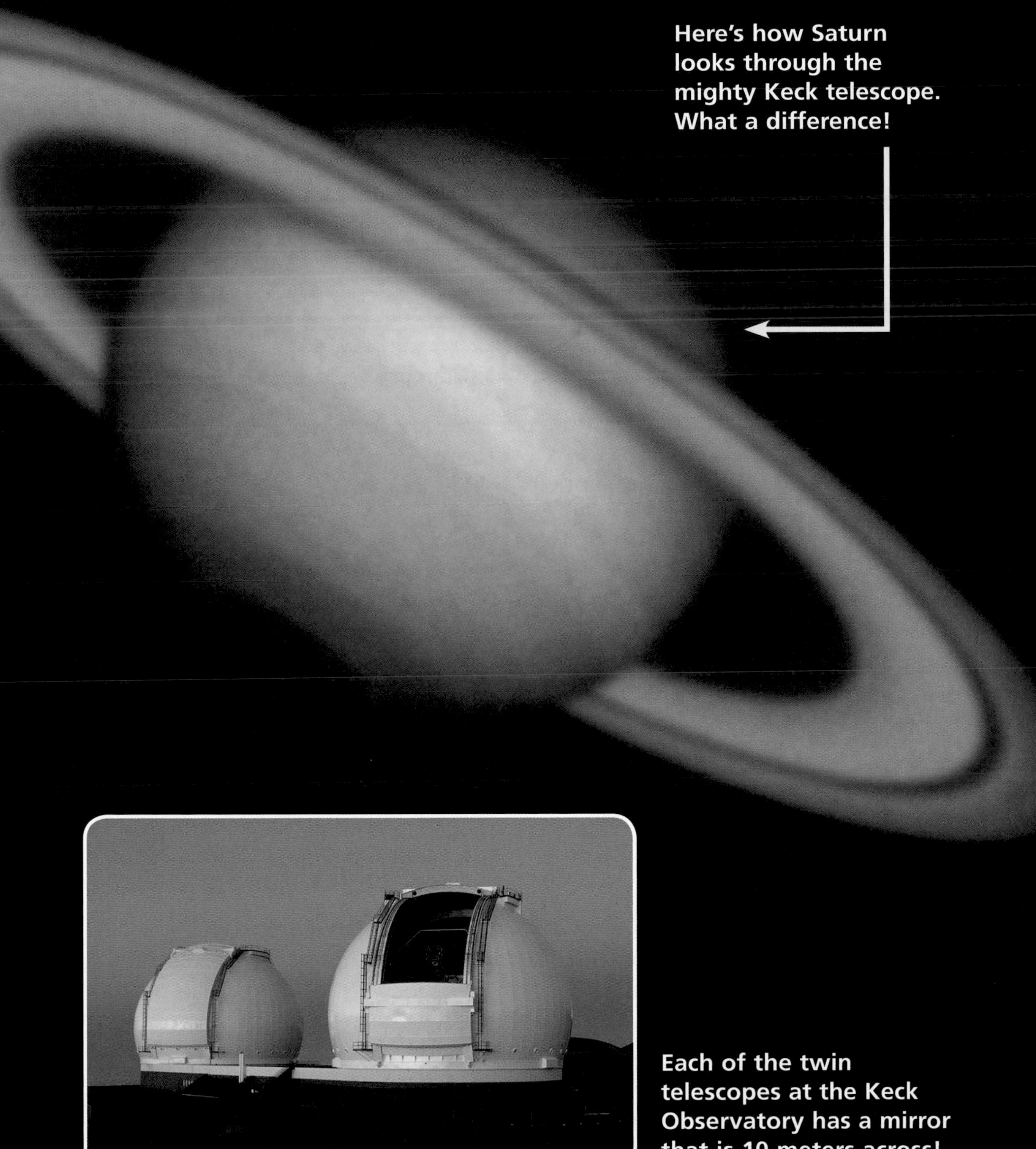

Here's how Saturn looks through the mighty Keck telescope. What a difference!

Each of the twin telescopes at the Keck Observatory has a mirror that is 10 meters across!

Math GLE 0306.1.2 Apply and adapt a variety of appropriate strategies to problem solving, including estimation, and reasonableness of the solution. **GLE 0306.5.1** Organize, display, and analyze data using various representations to solve problems. **ELA GLE 0301.3.1** Write for a variety of purposes and to a variety of audiences.

Math Estimate Results

Two of the inner planets have at least one moon. All outer planets have moons. The chart shows the number of known moons in our solar system.

1. Suppose you read in a book that the total number of known moons in our solar system is about 160. Is this estimate accurate? Show your work to explain why or why not.
2. Find the total number of outer planet moons, including Pluto's. Round the number to the nearest ten. Is this number different from the estimated total? Why or why not?
3. Round the total number of known moons in our solar system to the nearest hundred.

Number of Known Moons

Planet	Number of Moons
Mercury	0
Venus	0
Earth	1
Mars	2
Jupiter	63
Saturn	47
Uranus	27
Neptune	13
Pluto (dwarf planet)	3

Descriptive

Within your lifetime, people may be able to land on Mercury, Venus, or Mars. Imagine that you are able to travel to, and live on, one of those planets. Describe what living on the planet is like. Explain what type of home you live in. Do you need any special equipment to survive on this planet? How is living on this planet different from living on Earth?

Dr. Adriana Ocampo

Dr. Adriana Ocampo has been studying planets and the solar system since she was a teenager. Today, she speaks about these subjects to scientists around the world.

Through her research, Dr. Ocampo has discovered some important facts about Earth's history. For many years, she studied the land over a buried crater in Central America. She helped show how an asteroid formed the crater. The asteroid, or piece of rock from space, hit Earth 65 million years ago.

Dr. Ocampo also works with NASA, the government agency that explores space. One of her goals is to join the crew of a Space Shuttle mission.

Chapter 4 Review and TCAP Prep

Vocabulary

Complete each sentence with a term from the list.

1. When you make an object look larger, you _____ the object.
2. The Sun and the objects that orbit it make up the _____.
3. When planets move around the Sun, they _____ it.
4. A small, rounded body that orbits a planet is a/an _____.
5. A craft that carries instruments to explore space is a/an _____.
6. Mercury, Venus, Earth, and Mars are called the _____.
7. Jupiter, Saturn, Uranus, and Neptune are called _____ because of their size and makeup.
8. Earth takes 24 hours to make one _____.
9. Jupiter, Saturn, Uranus, and Neptune make up the _____.
10. A body that orbits the Sun and does not produce light is a/an _____.

gas giants
inner planets
magnify
moon
★ **orbit**
outer planets
planet
★ **rotation**
★ **solar system**
space probe
Sun
telescope

TCAP Inquiry Skills

11. **Use Models** Suppose you want to make a model of the solar system with planets and moons that move. How will the motion of the moons compare with the motion of the planets? **GLE 0307.Inq.2**

12. Suppose you look through a telescope at Jupiter and see its Great Red Spot facing Earth. Predict whether or not you would see the Great Red Spot in the same position each time you looked at Jupiter. **GLE 0307.Inq.1**

Map the Concept

Use these terms to fill in the map.

Mercury **Jupiter** **Neptune**
Mars **Venus** **Uranus**

Inner Planets
1. __________
2. __________
Earth
3. __________

Outer Planets
4. __________
Saturn
5. __________
6. __________

Critical Thinking

13. **Apply** In 2006, scientists decided to classify Pluto as a dwarf planet. How is Pluto different from the eight planets? **GLE 0307.6.1**

14. **Synthesize** You have learned about the advantages that the Hubble telescope offers to scientists. What disadvantages might it offer? **GLE 0307.T/E.1**

15. **Evaluate** Someone tells you that Earth's moon produces its own light. They say that the proof of this is that the Moon is very bright at night. Evaluate this statement. **GLE 0307.6.1**

16. **Analyze** Venus turns on its axis every 243 Earth days. What does this tell you about the speed at which Venus spins compared to the speed at which Earth spins? **GLE 0307.6.1**

Compare Planets

Make a table of the inner planets, using these three column headings: *Planet*, *Surface*, and *Atmosphere*. Review Lessons 2 and 3 to find information to use in the table. Don't forget to check picture captions for information.

0307.6.2

TCAP Prep

Answer the following questions.

17 The Hubble Space Telescope helps scientists view space from

Ⓐ the surface of Mars
Ⓑ a mountaintop
Ⓒ within Earth's atmosphere
Ⓓ beyond Earth's atmosphere

SPI 0307.T/E.1

18 The body in the solar system from which Earth gets light is

Ⓕ the Moon
Ⓖ Jupiter
Ⓗ Mars
Ⓙ the Sun

SPI 0307.6.1

19 Which is true of all the inner planets?

Ⓐ They are made of frozen gases.
Ⓑ They are made of rocky materials.
Ⓒ They have no moons.
Ⓓ They orbit a planet.

SPI 0307.6.1

20 The time it takes a planet to orbit the Sun exactly once is called a

Ⓕ day
Ⓖ season
Ⓗ year
Ⓙ decade

SPI 0307.6.1

Chapter 5

Earth's Surface and Resources

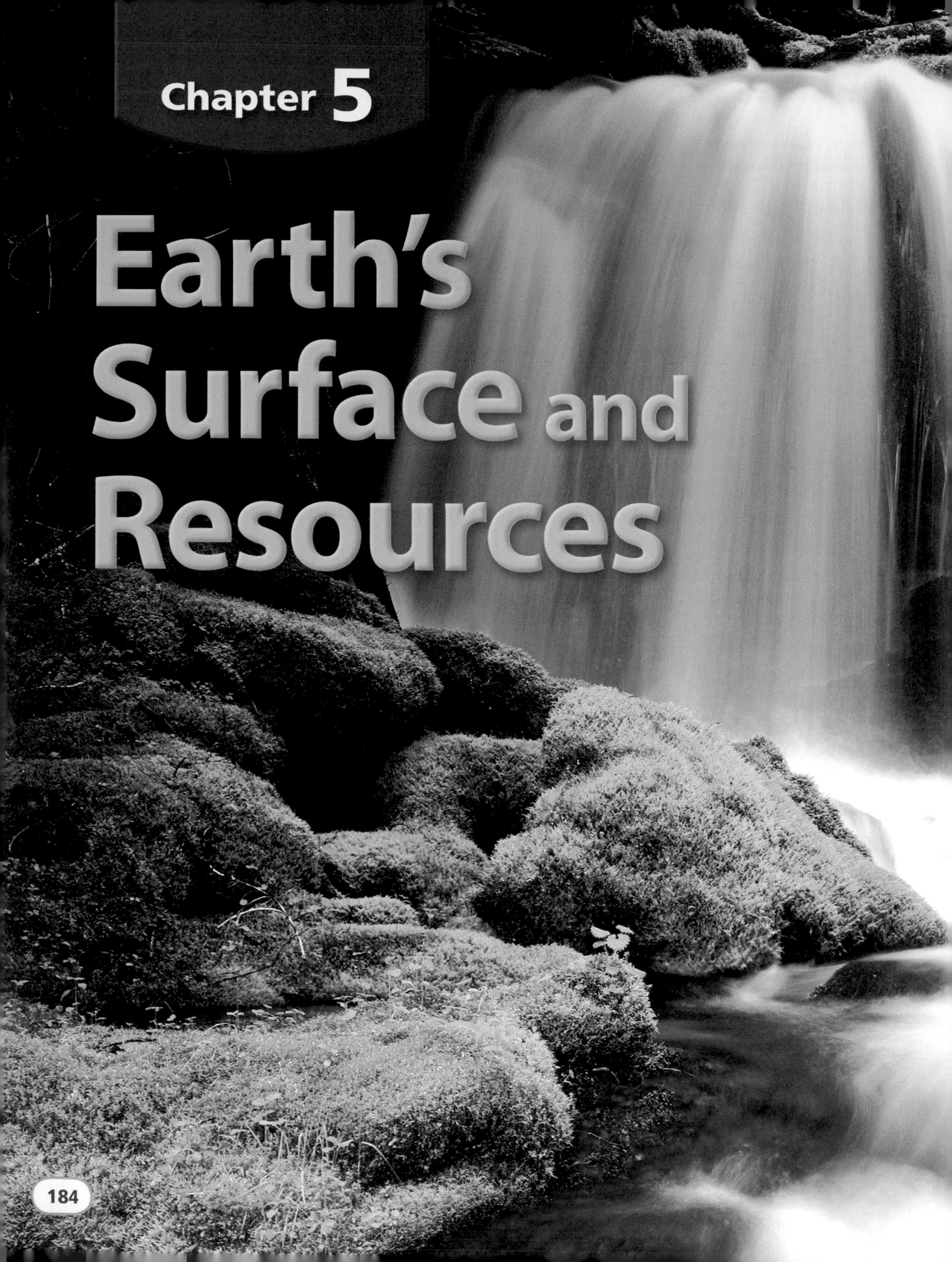

Lesson Preview

LESSON **1**

Tall mountains and huge oceans are features of Earth's surface. What other features can you find on a map?

LESSON **2**

There are three main types of rock. What are some properties of each type?

LESSON **3**

Would gasoline in a car, water in a lake, or a rock on the ground be replaced naturally?

LESSON **4**

How do reducing, reusing, and recycling help save Earth's resources?

Fun Facts

Recycling one glass bottle saves enough energy to run a TV for 90 minutes.

Vocabulary Preview

★ conservation
★ geological feature
igneous rock
metamorphic rock
mineral
★ natural resource
nonrenewable resource
ore
★ pollution
recycle
renewable resource
rock
sedimentary rock
★ weathering

★ = Tennessee Academic Vocabulary

Vocabulary Strategies

Have you ever seen any of these terms before? Do you know what they mean?

Describe, explain, or give an example of the vocabulary terms in your own words.

Draw a picture, symbol, example, or other image that describes the term.

Glossary p. H16

natural resource

pollution

recycle

sedimentary rock

Start with Your Standards

Inquiry

GLE 0307.Inq.1 Explore different scientific phenomena by asking questions, making logical predictions, planning investigations, and recording data.

GLE 0307.Inq.3 Organize data into appropriate tables, graphs, drawings, or diagrams.

Technology and Engineering

GLE 0307.T/E.1 Describe how tools, technology, and inventions help to answer questions and solve problems.

Earth and Space Science

Standard 7 The Earth

GLE 0307.7.1 Use information and illustrations to identify the earth's major landforms and water bodies.

GLE 0307.7.2 Recognize that rocks can be composed of one or more minerals.

GLE 0307.7.3 Distinguish between natural and manmade objects.

GLE 0307.7.4 Design a simple investigation to demonstrate how earth materials can be conserved or recycled.

Interact with this chapter.

www.eduplace.com/tnscp

Lesson 1

TENNESSEE STANDARDS

GLE 0307.Inq.1 Explore different scientific phenomena by asking questions, making logical predictions, planning investigations, and recording data.

GLE 0307.7.1 Use information and illustrations to identify the earth's major landforms and water bodies.

What Is Earth's Surface Like?

Why It Matters...

This island in the southern Pacific Ocean looks like a giant mushroom. Of course, it's made of rock. As surrounding ocean water wears away the edges of the rock, the island becomes mushroom-shaped. Like this island in the ocean, the surface of Earth is made of rock.

PREPARE TO INVESTIGATE

Inquiry Skill

Compare When you compare two things, you observe how they are alike and how they are different.

Materials

- 4 clear plastic cups
- metric measuring cup
- water
- sand
- marking pen

Science and Math Toolbox

For steps 2, 3, and 4, review **Measuring Volume** on page H7.

Directed Inquiry

Earth's Surface

Procedure

1. **Use Models** Work with a partner. Use a marking pen to label each of three clear plastic cups *Water*. Label another clear plastic cup *Land*.
2. **Measure** Measure 150 mL of sand. Pour the sand into the cup labeled *Land*. The sand in this cup represents the amount of land on Earth's surface.
3. **Measure** Measure 150 mL of water. Pour the water into one cup labeled *Water*.
4. Repeat step 3 twice, adding water to the remaining two cups labeled *Water*. The water in these three cups represents the amount of water on Earth's surface.
5. **Use Models** Look at the cups of sand and water. Compare the amount of sand with the amount of water. Record your comparison in your Science Notebook.

STEP 2

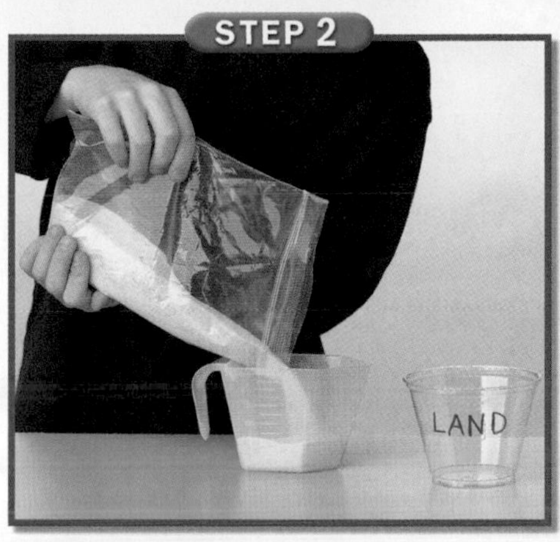

STEP 4

STEP 5

Think and Write

1. **Compare** How does the amount of land on Earth compare with the amount of water?
2. **Use Numbers** Use numbers to complete this sentence: The Earth's surface is ____ parts water and ____ part land.

Guided Inquiry

Research Use resource books or the Internet to find out how much of the water on Earth's surface is fresh water and how much is salt water. Write two fractions to show these amounts in hundredths.

0307.Inq.1

Reading Science

Surface of Earth

VOCABULARY

★ geological features

GRAPHIC ORGANIZER

Classify Use a chart to classify geological features as *Land* or *Water*.

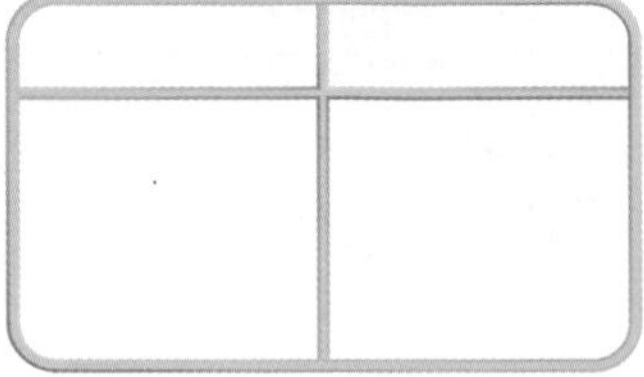

GLE 0307.7.1 Use information and illustrations to identify the earth's major landforms and water bodies.

Water on Earth's Surface

People looking at Earth from space say it looks like a big blue marble. Earth is sometimes called the blue planet because about three-fourths of its surface is covered by water. The remaining one-fourth of the surface is land.

Most of Earth's water is salt water. Salt water is found in the oceans and seas. Lakes, rivers, and streams have a different kind of water, called fresh water. Water you use for drinking, washing, and cooking is fresh water.

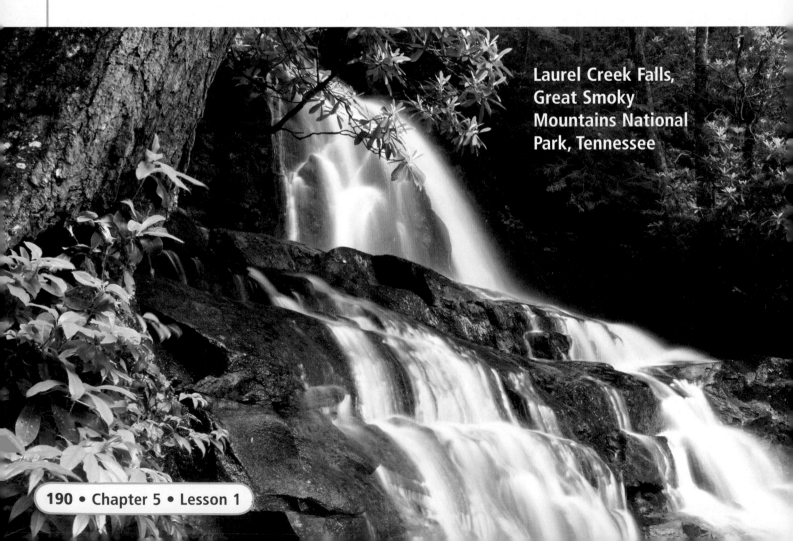

Laurel Creek Falls, Great Smoky Mountains National Park, Tennessee

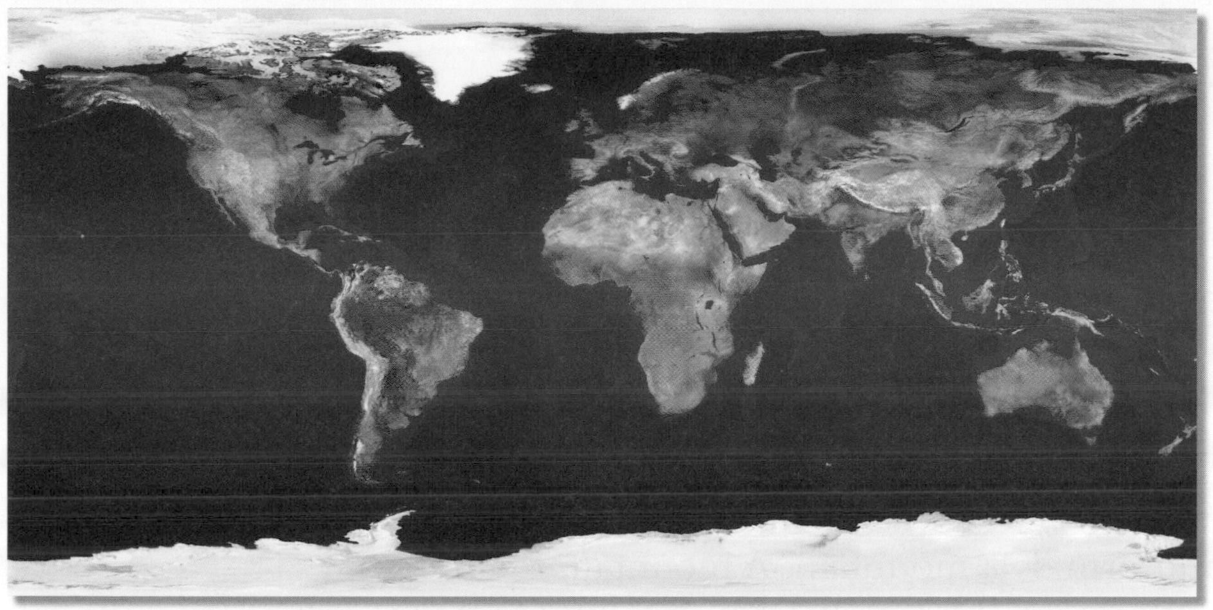

Satellite photos show that almost three-fourths of Earth's surface is water.

Only a very small amount of all the water on Earth is fresh water. And only a tiny amount of this fresh water is usable by living things. The rest of the fresh water cannot be used. It is frozen in huge masses of ice called glaciers (GLAY shurz).

You have already learned that fresh water is found in rivers, lakes, and streams. It's also found in soil, air, and large spaces in deep underground rock.

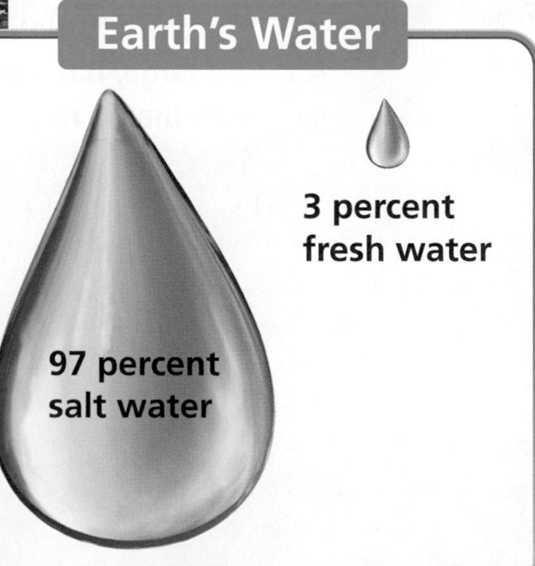

FOCUS CHECK Is there more salt water or fresh water on Earth's surface?

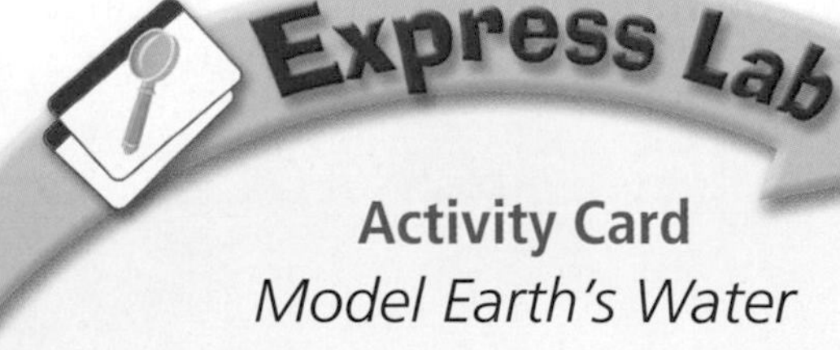

Activity Card
Model Earth's Water

Earth's Geological Features

You have probably seen several different features of the land. Perhaps you have gone hiking to the top of a mountain. A mountain is a geological feature. A **geological feature** is a part of Earth's surface that has a certain shape and is formed naturally. Earth has many kinds of geological features, both land and water.

The most visible geological land feature, or landform, is a mountain. A mountain is a raised part of the land, usually with steep sides, that rises above the area around it. Some mountains are high, rocky, and topped with snow. Others are lower and tree-covered.

Plateau A plateau is a large, flat land area that is raised.

Valley A valley is a low area surrounded by mountains.

The low area of land between mountains, hills, or other high areas is called a valley (VAL ee). Some valleys are wide and flat. Others are narrow with steep sides. A canyon (KAN yuhn) is a narrow and deep valley that often has a stream or river flowing through it.

A plain is a large land area that is mostly flat. The middle part of the United States is a large plain. Plains often have rich soil and make good farmland. Another type of landform is a plateau (pla TOH). Plateaus are flat areas of land that are higher than the land around them. The sides of a plateau may be steep.

FOCUS CHECK **How are plateaus and plains different?**

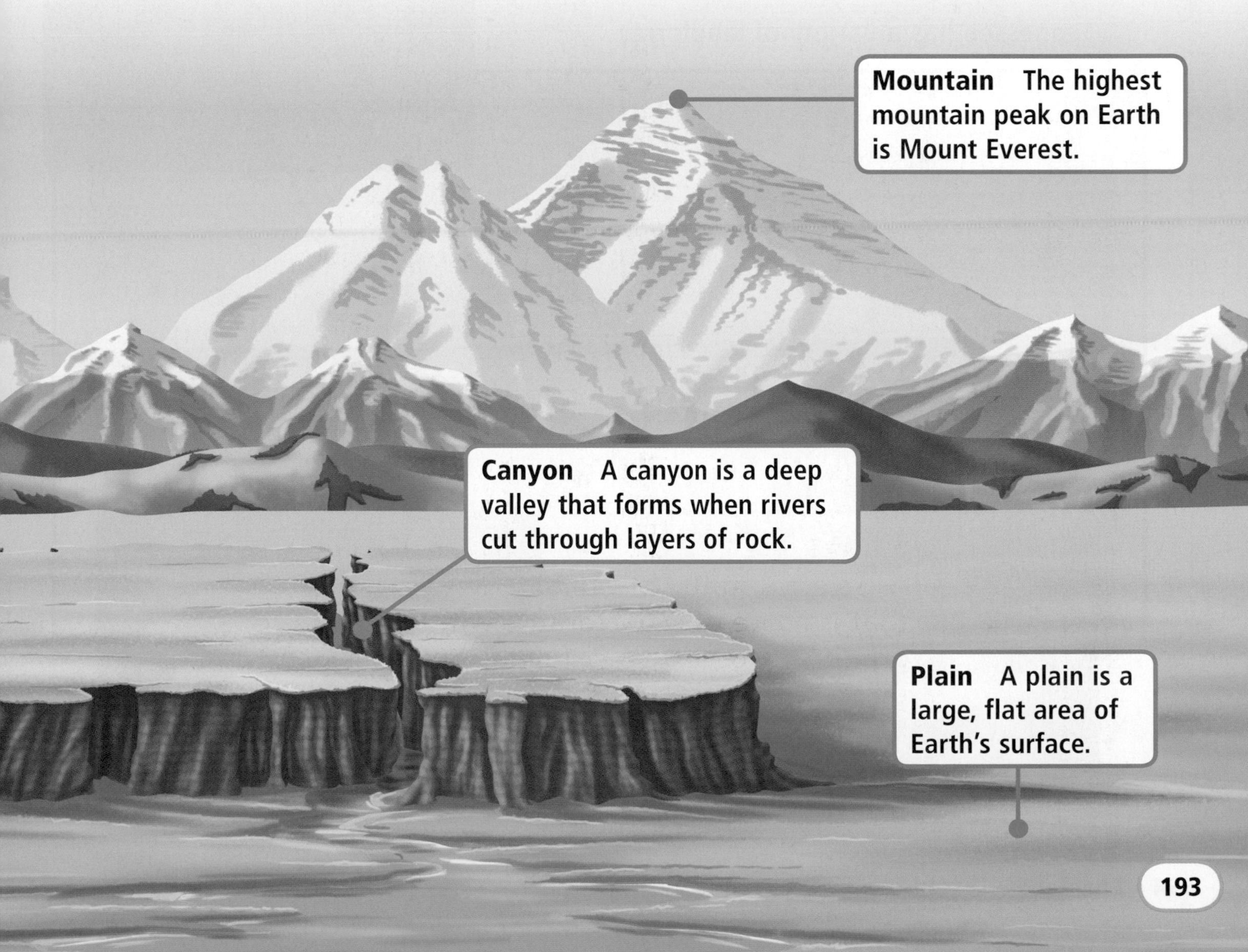

Mountain The highest mountain peak on Earth is Mount Everest.
Canyon A canyon is a deep valley that forms when rivers cut through layers of rock.
Plain A plain is a large, flat area of Earth's surface.

Mapping Geological Features

If you want to know what kinds of geological features are found in an area, you can look at a map. Many maps show rivers, mountains, and valleys. A physical map tells you about the shape of the land's surface. Mountains are drawn to look like mountains and valleys are drawn to look like valleys.

Some maps use symbols to represent different kinds of features. On these maps, a key tells what each symbol stands for.

FOCUS CHECK What are two different ways that maps show geographical features?

Tennessee has a variety of landforms.

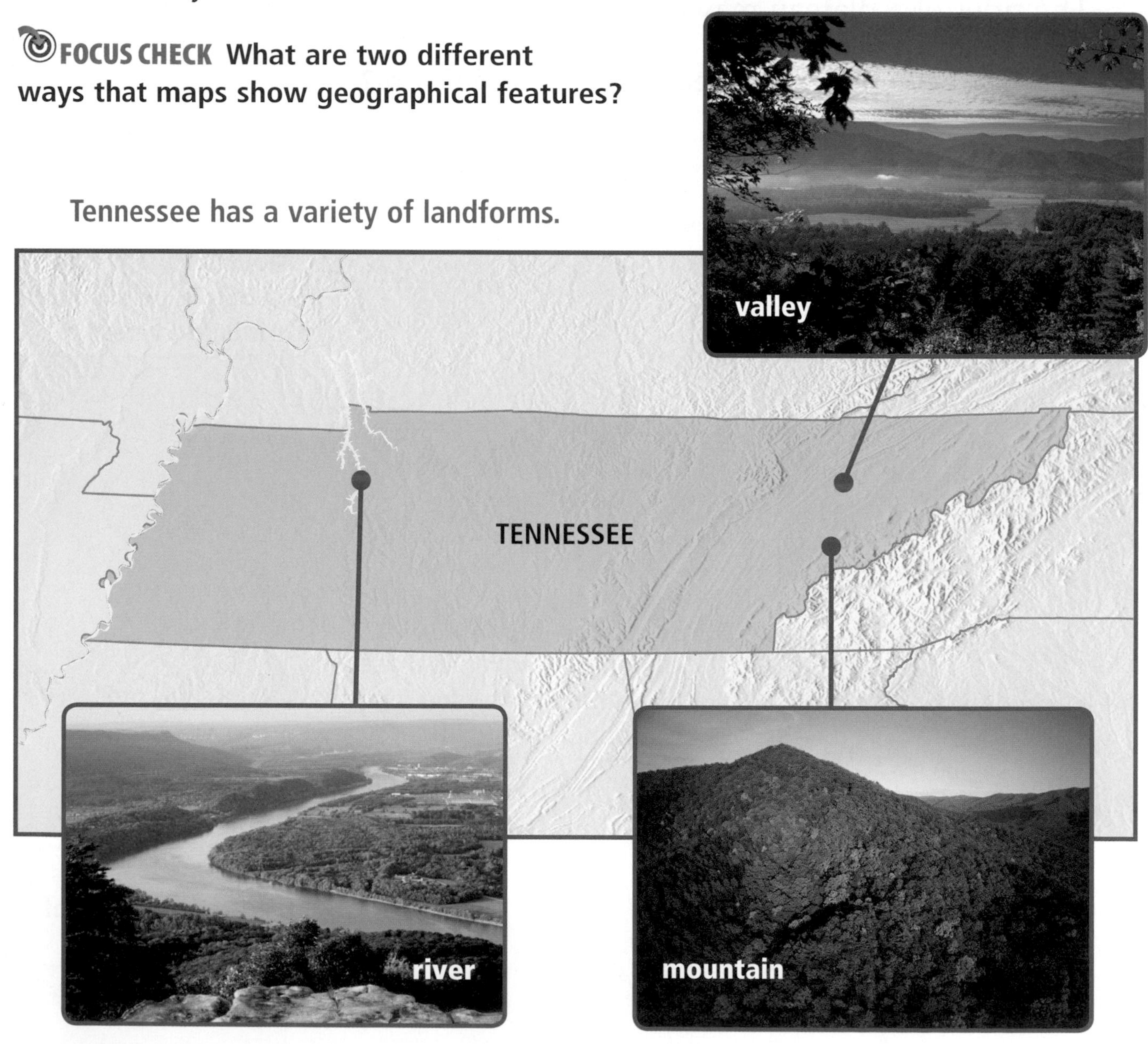

Lesson Wrap-Up

Visual Summary

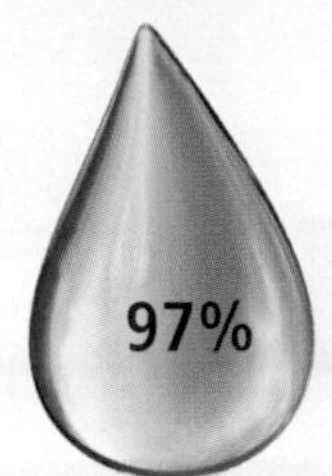	About three-fourths of Earth's surface is covered by water. And 97 percent of that water is salt water.
	Earth's surface has mountains, valleys, canyons, plains, and plateaus.
	Some maps show the shape of the land's surface.

Check for Understanding

COMPARE GEOLOGICAL FEATURES

Look at the drawing on pages 192–193. Then make a Venn diagram to compare a plateau and a mountain. You may use the Internet to find a picture of each feature and add the pictures to the diagram.

0307.7.1

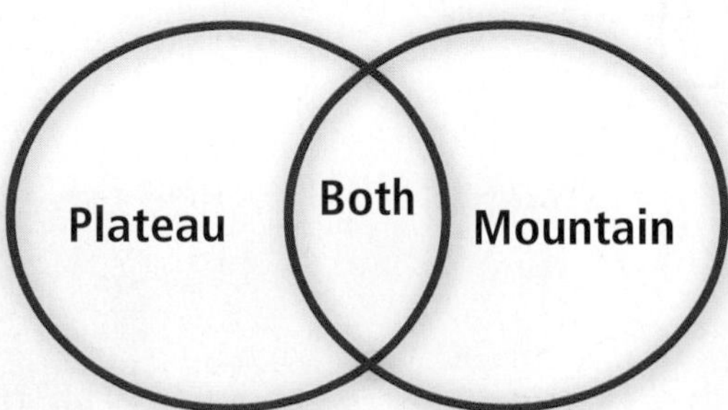

Review

1. **MAIN IDEA** How does the amount of land on Earth's surface compare with the amount of water?
2. **VOCABULARY** What does the term *geological feature* mean?
3. **READING SKILL: Compare and Contrast** What is the difference between a valley and a canyon?
4. **CRITICAL THINKING: Apply** When your friend looks out the windows, he sees mountains rising high above him on both sides. Identify the kind of geological feature where he is likely to be located.
5. **INQUIRY SKILL: Compare** Compare the features of a mountain with those of a valley.

TCAP Prep

A very narrow and deep valley is called a

Ⓐ plateau
Ⓑ plain
Ⓒ mountain
Ⓓ canyon

SPI 0307.7.1

Go Digital Technology

Visit **www.eduplace.com/tnscp** to learn more about Earth's surface.

Lesson 2

TENNESSEE STANDARDS

GLE 0307.Inq.3 Organize data into appropriate tables, graphs, drawings, or diagrams.

GLE 0307.7.2 Recognize that rocks can be composed of one or more minerals.

What Are Rocks and Minerals?

Why It Matters...

The way a rock looks depends on the minerals it contains. The properties of a rock also depend on how it formed. Like minerals, rocks can be identified by their properties. Some rocks have properties that make them useful as building materials. This famous statue of Abraham Lincoln is carved from strong marble.

PREPARE TO INVESTIGATE

Inquiry Skill

Infer When you infer, you interpret your observations.

Materials

- rock specimen set
- marker
- paper labels
- hand lens

Science and Math Toolbox

For step 4, review **Using a Hand Lens** on page H2.

Directed Inquiry

Looking at Rocks

Procedure

1. In your Science Notebook, make a chart like the one shown.
2. **Collaborate** Work with a partner. Choose six rocks from the rock specimen set. Using paper labels and a marker, label the rocks *A, B, C, D, E,* and *F.*
3. **Observe** Closely observe each rock for different colored pieces or layers. Record your observations in your chart. Run your fingers over each rock to feel its texture. Record the texture as *rough* or *smooth* in your chart.
4. **Experiment** Use a hand lens to observe each sample. Rub each rock with your fingers to see if any bits of rock break off. Record each rock's grain as *no grain, large grain,* or *small grain.*
5. **Classify** Combine your rock collection with another team's and group similar rocks. Record the properties you used to classify each group.

STEP 1

	Colors	Texture	Grain
A			
B			
C			
D			
E			
F			

STEP 2

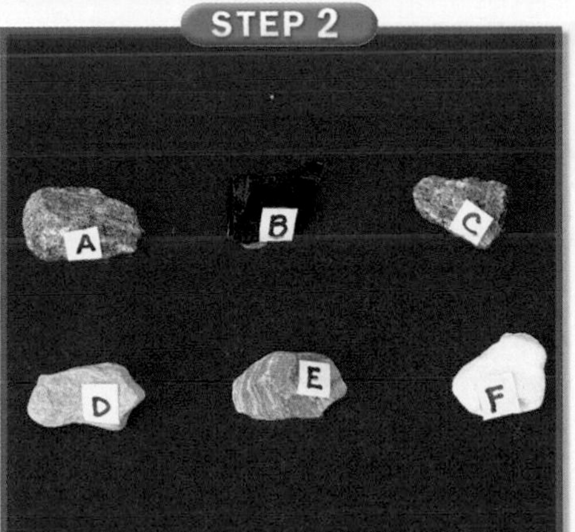

STEP 4

Think and Write

1. **Classify** Discuss with your classmates other ways you may classify the rocks.
2. **Infer** How do you think these rocks formed? For example, which might have formed by melting? by pressure?

✓ 0307.2

Guided Inquiry

Experiment Suppose you want to classify your rocks by other properties. Make a plan to test for two properties. Then, with your teacher's permission, carry out your plan. Record your results.

Reading Science

The Solid Earth

VOCABULARY

igneous rock
metamorphic rock
mineral
rock
sedimentary rock
★ weathering

GRAPHIC ORGANIZER

Compare and Contrast
Use a chart to compare and contrast the properties of the three types of rock.

GLE 0307.7.2 Recognize that rocks can be composed of one or more minerals.

Minerals

If you play a game to guess an unknown object, the first question is usually whether it is an animal, a vegetable, or a mineral (MIHN ur uhl). A **mineral** is a material that is found in nature and that has never been alive. Among the many kinds of minerals are metals, such as gold and iron. The graphite (GRAF yt) in your pencil is a mineral, too. Salt that you put on food is also a mineral.

Minerals have certain properties that can be used to identify them. Color, hardness, and texture are some properties of minerals. Gold is yellow and shiny. Graphite is black and soft, and feels greasy. The mineral talc is so soft you can scratch it with a fingernail.

◀ **Rock** Gabbro is a rock that contains the minerals shown below.

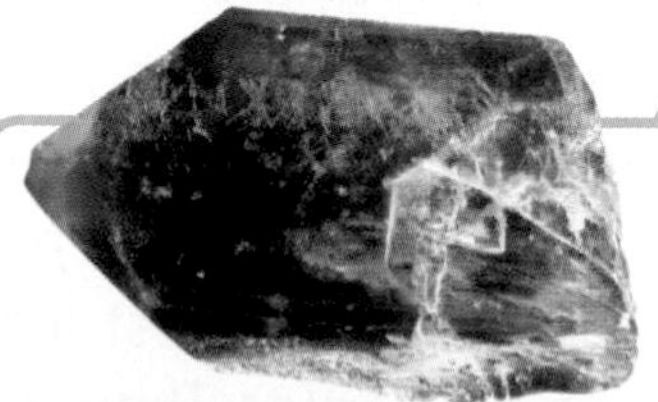

Mineral Olivine is a hard, dark-green mineral.

Mineral Pyroxenes are important rock-forming minerals.

Mineral Feldspars are common minerals in Earth's crust.

How Minerals Are Used

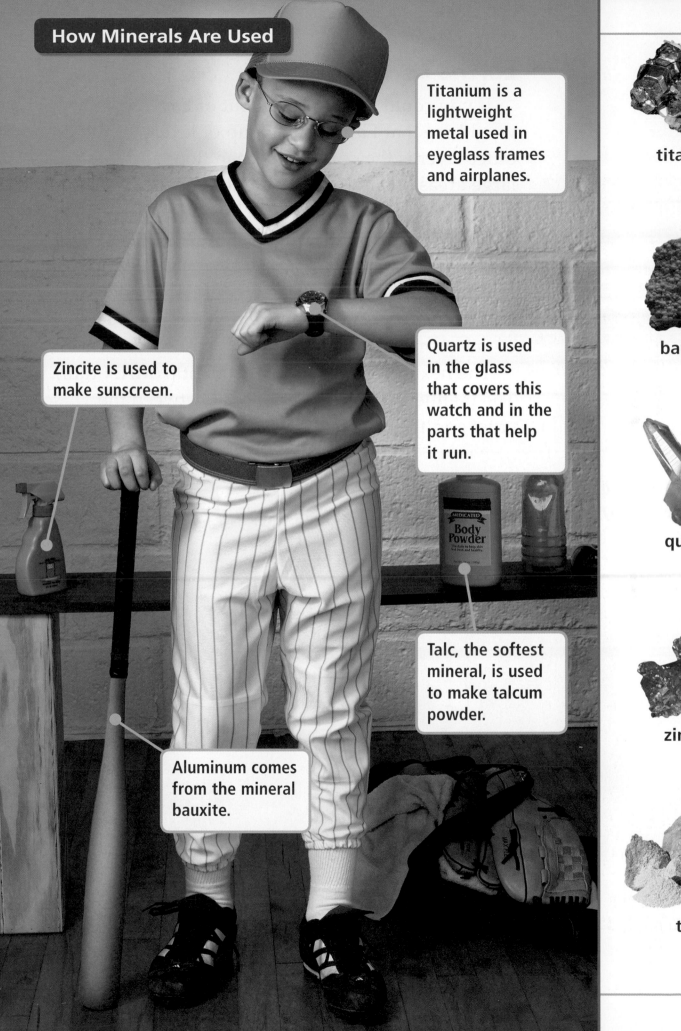

Titanium is a lightweight metal used in eyeglass frames and airplanes.

Zincite is used to make sunscreen.

Quartz is used in the glass that covers this watch and in the parts that help it run.

Talc, the softest mineral, is used to make talcum powder.

Aluminum comes from the mineral bauxite.

titanium

bauxite

quartz

zincite

talc

Earth's Layers

If you could take a section out of Earth, you would see that Earth is made up of layers. The outer layer is the crust. The ocean floor and the large areas of land called continents (KAHN tuh nuhnts) are part of the crust. The continents are North America, South America, Europe, Asia, Africa, Australia, and Antarctica.

The crust is the thinnest layer of Earth, and is made up of rock. **Rock** is a solid material made up of one or more minerals.

The next layer of Earth is the mantle (MAN tuhl). The mantle is a thick layer of rock between the crust and the core.

Earth is made up of different layers. ▶

The lower part of the mantle is solid. In the upper part of the mantle, the rock is soft enough to move like modeling clay.

The innermost layer of Earth is the core. The core is a dense ball. It has a liquid outer part and a solid inner part, which is the hottest part of Earth.

FOCUS CHECK What are rocks made of?

Earth's Layers

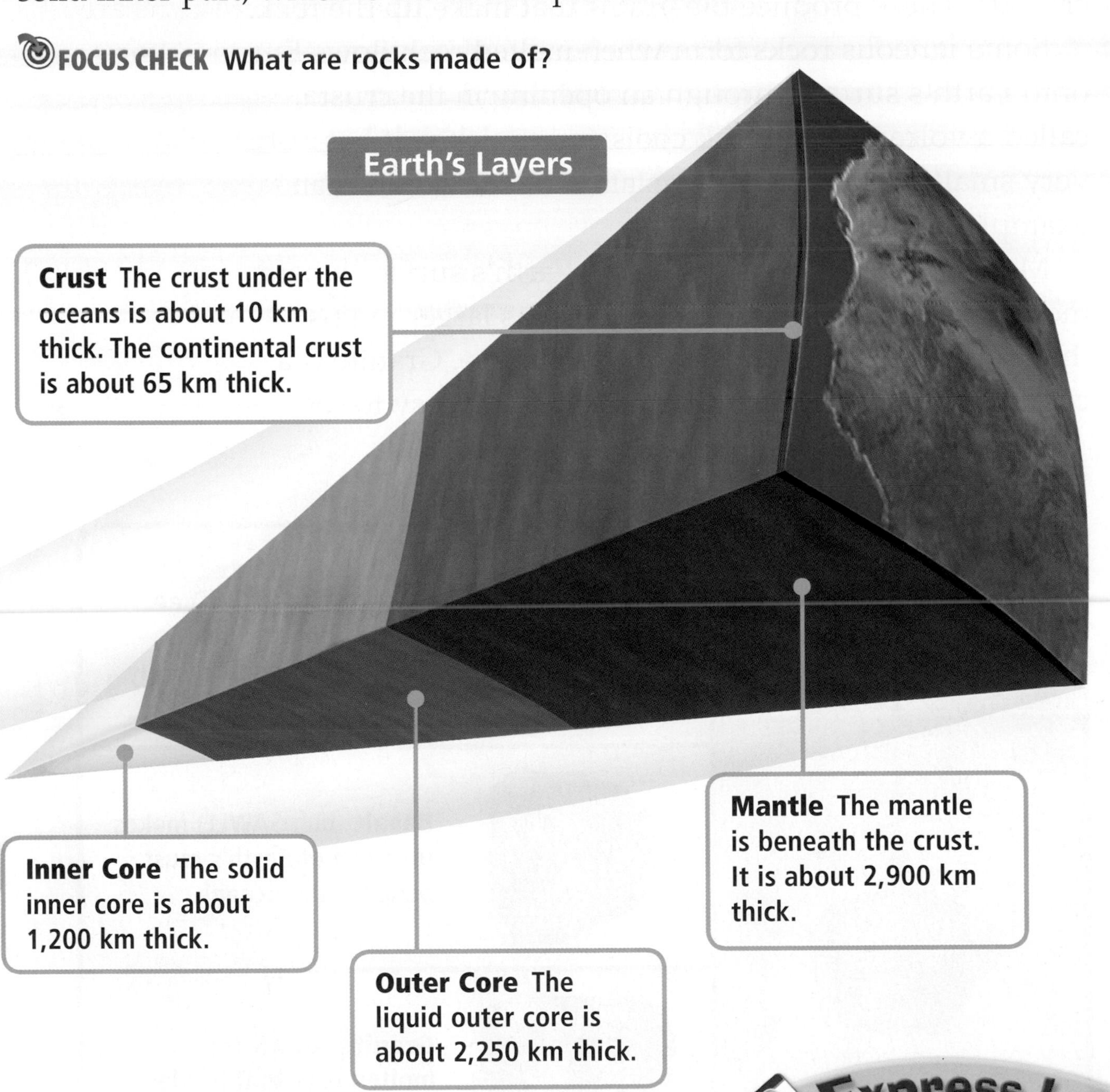

Crust The crust under the oceans is about 10 km thick. The continental crust is about 65 km thick.

Inner Core The solid inner core is about 1,200 km thick.

Outer Core The liquid outer core is about 2,250 km thick.

Mantle The mantle is beneath the crust. It is about 2,900 km thick.

Express Lab

Activity Card

Diagram Earth's Layers

Igneous Rock

Three types of rock make up Earth's crust. Each forms in a different way. **Igneous** (IHG nee uhs) **rock** forms when melted rock from deep below Earth's surface cools and hardens. As it cools, minerals in the rock form crystals. These produce the grains that make up the rock.

Some igneous rocks form when melted rock flows onto Earth's surface through an opening in the crust called a volcano. This rock cools very quickly. It has very small crystals, or no crystals at all. Obsidian is an example of such a rock.

Most igneous rock forms below Earth's surface where molten rock cools slowly. Such rock has larger grains than does rock that cools at Earth's surface. Granite is a common igneous rock with grains that are easy to see.

Igneous Rock

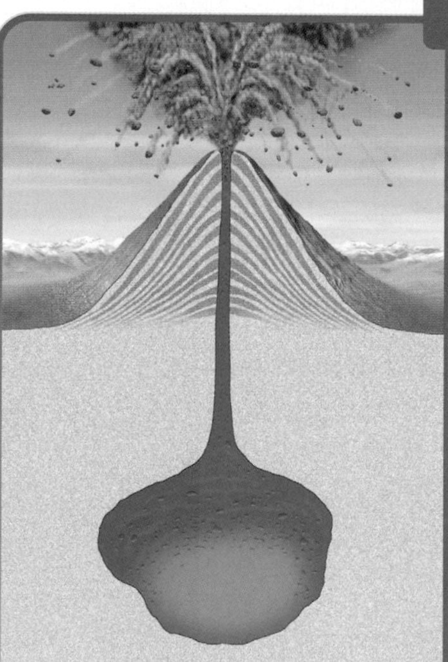

Molten rock hardens to form igneous rock.

Obsidian (ahb SIHD ee-uhn) is formed when molten rock cools quickly.

Basalt (buh SAWLT) makes up much of Earth's crust beneath the oceans.

Granite (GRAN iht) is molten rock that hardens in the crust.

Sedimentary Rock

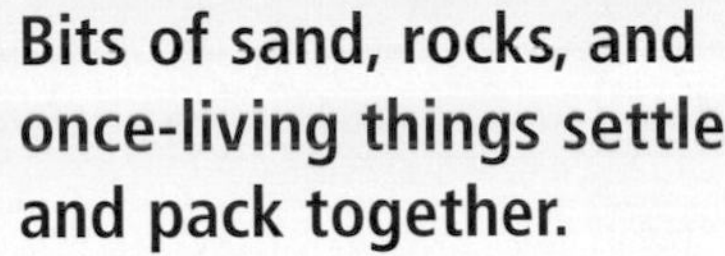
Bits of sand, rocks, and once-living things settle and pack together.

Conglomerate (kuhn GLAHM-ur iht) forms from sediments of different sizes.

Limestone sometimes forms when the remains of ocean animals become cemented together.

Shale forms from thin layers of clay. Shale is smooth and breaks easily into layers.

Sedimentary Rock

Sedimentary (sehd uh MEHN tuh ree) **rock** forms when sand, pieces of rock, bits of soil, and remains of once-living things are pressed together and harden. These materials are called sediment. Rock is broken into sediment by natural forces in a process called **weathering**. Over time, layers of sediment are deposited on top of one another. Over millions of years, the bottom layers become rock.

Sandstone and limestone are two types of sedimentary rock. Both form when sediments are squeezed and then cemented together. Sandstone is made up of grains of weathered rock, or sand. Some limestone is made up of shells and skeletons of ocean animals.

Shale, the most common type of sedimentary rock, is formed from fine particles of clay. The particles are pushed together by pressure.

FOCUS CHECK **Compare conditions that form large and small crystals in igneous rock.**

Metamorphic Rock

Metamorphic (meht uh MAWR fihk) **rock** is rock that forms when existing rocks are changed by extreme heat and pressure. Most metamorphic rock forms deep below Earth's surface. Under the conditions found there, crystals and minerals in existing rocks are changed and grains become flattened.

Gneiss (nys) is a metamorphic rock formed from granite, an igneous rock. Compare the grains of granite and gneiss in the photo. In granite, the mineral grains are rounded. In gneiss, the grains are flattened and form long bands.

Slate is a metamorphic rock formed from shale, a sedimentary rock. Shale is a soft rock that forms in layers. Slate is much harder than shale. With more heat and pressure, slate will change to another metamorphic rock called schist.

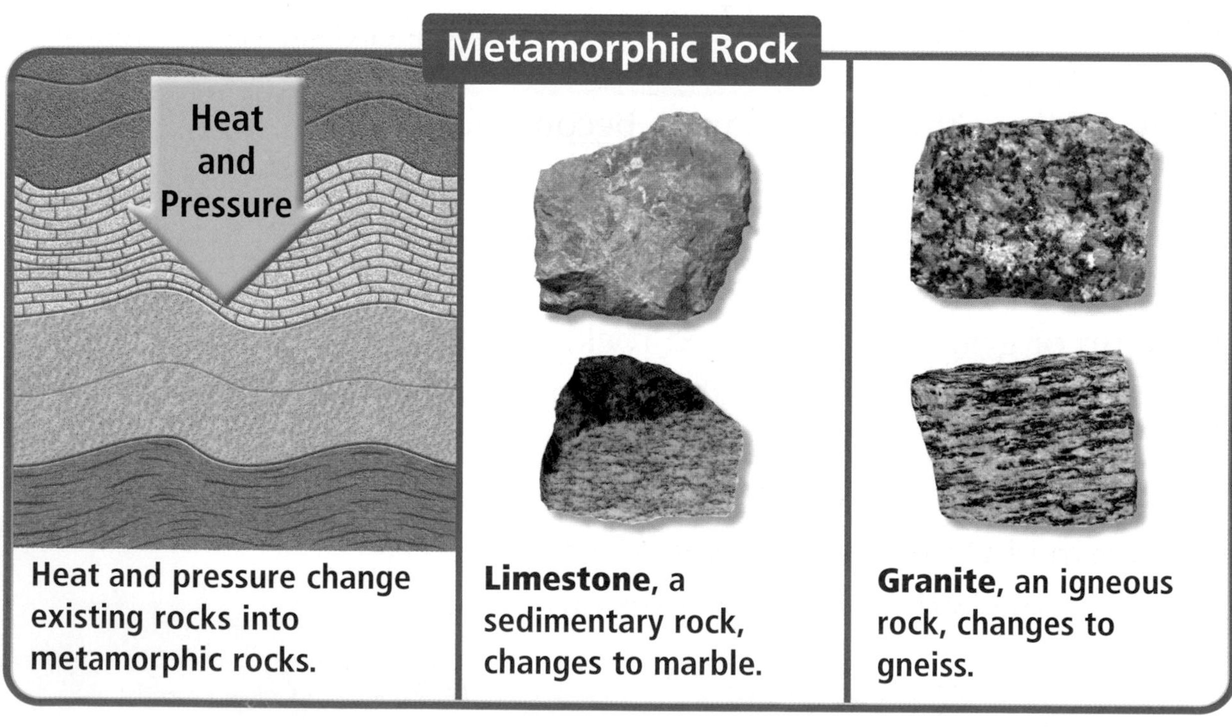

Heat and pressure change existing rocks into metamorphic rocks.

Limestone, a sedimentary rock, changes to marble.

Granite, an igneous rock, changes to gneiss.

Lesson Wrap-Up

Visual Summary

Three basic kinds of rock make up Earth's crust.

Igneous rock forms when melted rock cools and hardens.

granite

basalt

obsidian

Sedimentary rock forms when particles of rock, bits of soil, and remains of once-living things harden.

shale

limestone

conglomerate

Metamorphic rock forms when existing rocks are changed by heat and pressure beneath Earth's surface.

marble

gneiss

Check for Understanding

MAKE A ROCK DISPLAY

Work in groups of three. Each student should find a different kind of rock. Make a display of your rocks. Label each rock with an index card that names the type of rock and tells some of its general characteristics.

0307.7.2

Review

1. **MAIN IDEA** What are the three basic types of rock that make up Earth's crust?
2. **VOCABULARY** Use the terms *weathering* and *sedimentary rock* in a sentence.
3. **READING SKILL: Compare** Compare the ways in which sedimentary rock and metamorphic rock form.
4. **CRITICAL THINKING: Hypothesize** What would happen if heat and pressure were added to sediments?
5. **INQUIRY SKILL: Infer** Suppose you find a rock that contains shells. Which of the three types of rock is it likely to be? Explain your answer.

TCAP Prep

Which of the following is not a mineral?

Ⓐ granite
Ⓑ graphite
Ⓒ gold
Ⓓ feldspar

SPI 0307.7.2

Go Digital Technology

Visit **www.eduplace.com/tnscp** to learn more about identifying rocks.

HEAT From EARTH

Geothermal energy is heat from within Earth. It can be used to warm buildings and produce electricity. The term geothermal is from two Greek roots. Geo means "earth" and therm means "heat." So, geothermal means "earth-heat."

You know that igneous rock forms when melted rock below Earth's surface cools and hardens. If you could travel about 3,048 m (10,000 ft) below ground, you would find that the temperature of the rock is hot enough to boil water. Scientists have found a way to use superheated water and steam from deep within Earth to produce electricity.

Geothermal energy is a clean power source. It can be renewed as long as water can be pumped back into the ground. One drawback is that it is available only where large amounts of underground water are in contact with heated rock.

The Geysers in northern California is the first geothermal power plant in the United States.

Dry Steam Power Plant

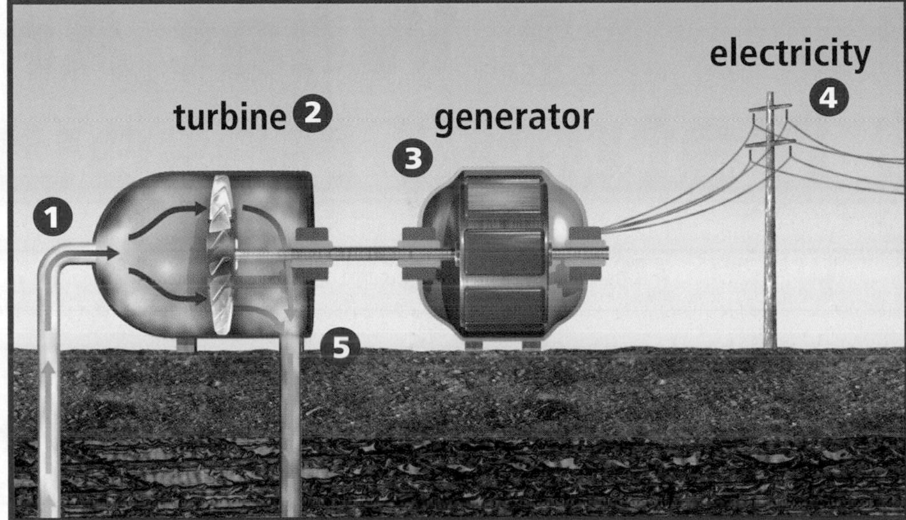

1. Steam is pumped from deep within Earth.
2. The steam turns a device called a turbine.
3. The turbine powers a generator.
4. The generator produces electricity.
5. The cooled steam becomes water and is pumped back into the ground to be reheated.

Sharing Ideas

1. **READING CHECK** What is geothermal energy?
2. **WRITE ABOUT IT** What must be done to keep geothermal energy from being used up?
3. **TALK ABOUT IT** Discuss with your classmates how increased use of geothermal energy could help the environment.

Lesson 3

TENNESSEE STANDARDS

GLE 0307.Inq.3 Organize data into appropriate tables, graphs, drawings, or diagrams.
GLE 0307.7.3 Distinguish between natural and manmade objects.

Guiding Question

What Are Natural Resources?

Why It Matters...

What do an automobile, a pair of eyeglasses, and a doghouse have in common? They are all made of materials such as metal, glass, and wood that come from nature. These natural materials are used to make things that people use every day.

PREPARE TO INVESTIGATE

Inquiry Skill

Classify When you classify, you sort objects into groups according to their properties.

Materials

- set of objects

Science and Math Toolbox

For step 2, review **Making a Chart to Organize Data** on page H10.

Directed Inquiry

What It's Made Of

Procedure

1. **Collaborate** Work with a partner. Get a set of objects from your teacher. Place them on a desk.
2. **Record Data** In your Science Notebook, make a chart like the one shown.
3. **Classify** Examine each object. Group together objects that are made of metal. Then group together objects that are made of wood. Finally, group together objects that are made of materials other than metal or wood.
4. **Record Data** Record your groupings in your chart.

Think and Write

1. **Communicate** Explain why you grouped the objects as you did.
2. **Use Numbers** How many objects are made of metal? How many are made of wood? How many are made of another material?
3. **Infer** Based on your data, what is the most common material that the objects in your set are made of? Make an inference about the effects that a shortage of this material would have on Earth.

✓ **0307.7.5**

STEP 2

Metal	Wood	Other Material

STEP 3

STEP 4

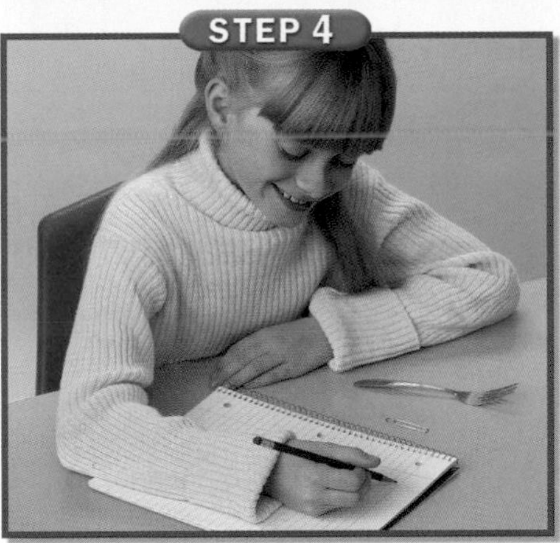

Guided Inquiry

Research List all the different materials that spoons are made of. Use the library or Internet to find out where each material comes from. Share your findings with your classmates.

VOCABULARY

★ natural resource
nonrenewable resource
ore
renewable resource

GRAPHIC ORGANIZER

Main Idea and Details
Write on a chart the main idea and two details from the lesson.

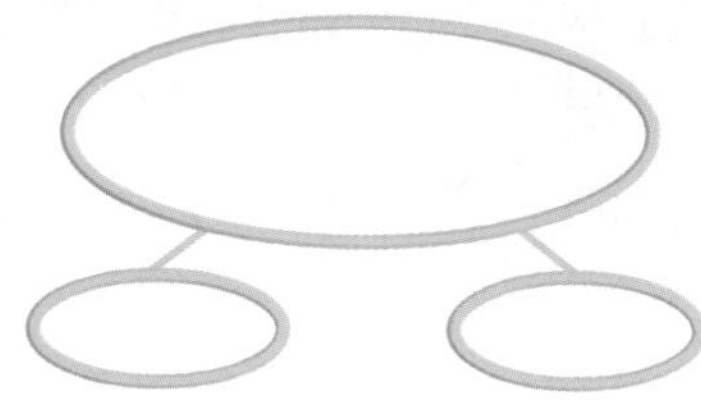

GLE 0307.7.3 Distinguish between natural and manmade objects.

Natural Resources

Earth's Natural Resources

A home-improvement store sells everything you might need to build or fix a home. It has wood for floors and walls, metal pipes and wiring, and glass doors and windows. Where did all these materials come from?

Almost everything around you comes from natural resources. A **natural resource** is a material from Earth that is useful to people. The wood sold as lumber in a home-improvement store comes from trees. The metal used to make pipes and wires comes from ores (awrz). An **ore** is a rock that contains metal or other useful minerals. The glass for the windows is made mostly from melted sand.

Natural resources provide you with the air, water, food, clothing, and shelter you need to live. Materials for books, toys, and sports equipment come from natural resources. Natural resources help provide electricity for television and gas for cars.

FOCUS CHECK Where do natural resources come from?

Using Natural Resources

Natural Resource	Uses	Example
Plants	food, lumber, furniture, paper, cardboard, rubber, cork, beauty products, cotton, medicines	
Animals	food, clothing, wool, leather, fertilizer	
Rocks, Soil, and Minerals	concrete, bricks, growing crops, gardening, salt, talcum powder, gems, glass (melted sand), ceramics (heated clay)	
Oil	plastics, human-made fabrics, food containers, safety equipment, fuel, machine and engine grease, beauty products	
Water	drinking, bathing, washing, cooking, growing crops, gardening	
Metals	tools, building materials, plumbing, transportation, wiring, cans, coins, jewelry	

Renewable and Nonrenewable Resources

Imagine that you pick flowers from a daisy plant. As time passes, the plant grows new flowers. Now imagine that you collect some pebbles from the ground. Unlike the flowers, the stones cannot grow back.

Some resources, like the flowers, are renewable resources. A **renewable resource** is a natural resource that can be replaced by nature. Others are nonrenewable resources. A **nonrenewable resource** is in limited supply. It cannot be replaced, or it takes thousands or even millions of years to be replaced.

This sailboat is powered by the wind, a renewable resource. ▶

Trees are renewable resources. Lumber is made from trees. It is used to construct buildings and make furniture. ▶

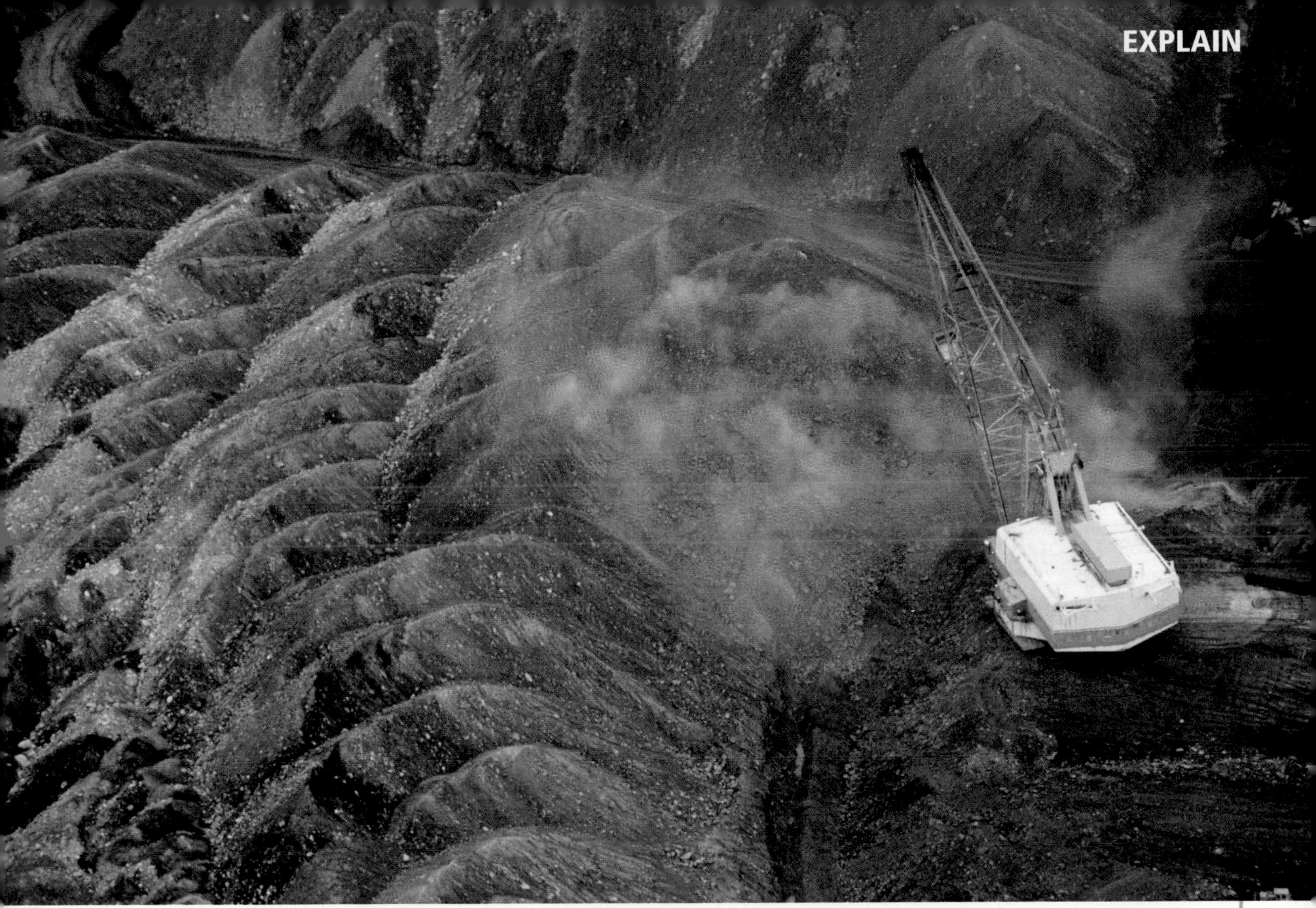

▲ **Coal is removed from Earth in mines, like the one shown.**

Plants are examples of renewable resources. They can grow back. Water and air are also renewable. Fresh water is renewed each time it rains. Air can be used over and over again.

Metal ores and coal are examples of nonrenewable resources. Coal is used to produce electricity and to make iron and steel. Once metal ores and coal are removed from Earth and used, they cannot be replaced.

FOCUS CHECK What are renewable resources?

Express Lab

Activity Card

Categorize Water Uses

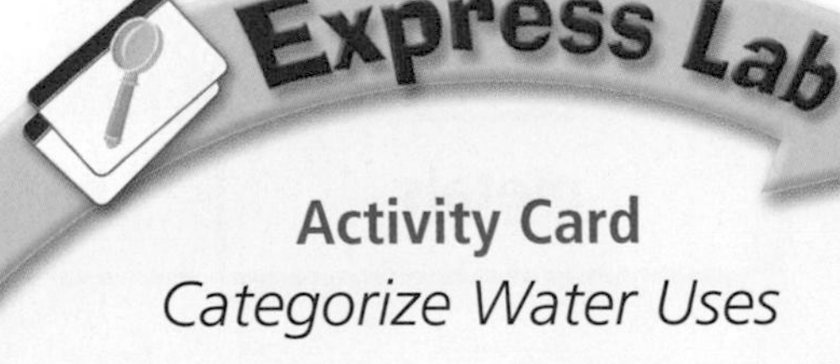

Comparing Resources and Products

The items that people make and use come from renewable or nonrenewable natural resources. Renewable resources include water, plants, animals, and air. Nonrenewable resources include materials from Earth, such as oil, metals, and minerals.

Some things around you are natural, but many are made by people. Plants, rocks, and soil are natural. Light bulbs, desks, and bricks are made by people. Bricks, like other people-made objects, come from a natural resource. A brick is rock changed by people to a more useful form.

FOCUS CHECK Name one renewable and one nonrenewable resource.

Lesson Wrap-Up

Visual Summary

Everything that people use comes from natural resources.

Some natural resources are renewable. They can be replaced.

Some resources are nonrenewable. They cannot be replaced.

Check for Understanding

COMPARE OBJECTS

With your teacher's permission, gather a selection of objects made from different materials. Examine the objects to find out whether they are natural or made by people. Exchange objects with a partner. Use a hand lens to examine the materials. Record your observations. How are the natural objects alike? How are the people-made objects alike? How do the two kinds of objects differ?

✔ 0307.7.3

Review

1. **MAIN IDEA** Why are natural resources important?
2. **VOCABULARY** What is the difference between a renewable resource and a nonrenewable resource?
3. **READING SKILL: Main Idea and Details** Write two details that support the main idea that a natural resource is renewable or nonrenewable.
4. **CRITICAL THINKING: Apply** A boat could be made of metal or wood. Which would you use to save nonrenewable resources? Explain.
5. **INQUIRY SKILL: Classify** Choose ten items in your classroom. Decide whether each item comes from a renewable or nonrenewable resource.

TCAP Prep

Natural resources

Ⓐ are always renewable
Ⓑ are materials found on Earth
Ⓒ can never be used up
Ⓓ are made by people

SPI 0307.7.3

Go Digital Technology

Visit **www.eduplace.com/tnscp** to learn more about natural resources.

Lesson 4

TENNESSEE STANDARDS

GLE 0307.Inq.1 Explore different scientific phenomena by asking questions, making logical predictions, planning investigations, and recording data.

GLE 0307.7.4 Design a simple investigation to demonstrate how earth materials can be conserved or recycled.

How Can Resources Be Conserved?

Why It Matters...

For most people, old milk containers are garbage. And they could be, if they are not reused. These boys used old milk containers to build a boat. Making new things from old materials saves resources.

PREPARE TO INVESTIGATE

Inquiry Skill

Compare When you compare two things, you observe how they are alike and different.

Materials

- 4 plastic bowls
- water
- marking pen
- clock
- plastic-foam packing peanuts
- pieces of crumpled newspaper
- plastic bubble wrap
- cellulose packing peanuts

Science and Math Toolbox

For steps 3 and 4, review **Measuring Elapsed Time** on pages H12–H13.

Directed Inquiry

Long-Lived Litter

Procedure

1. **Collaborate** In your Science Notebook, make a chart like the one shown. Work with a partner. Use a marking pen to label each of four bowls with a different packing material listed in the chart.
2. **Experiment** Fill each bowl halfway with water. Put a few small pieces of each packing material into its labeled bowl.
3. **Record Data** After an hour, look at the packing material in each bowl. Feel whether the material has softened or has begun to break down. Record your observations in your chart.
4. **Observe** Repeat step 3 every few hours for the rest of the day.

STEP 1

Packing Materials	Observation 1	2	3	4
cellulose peanuts				
newspaper				
foam peanuts				
bubble wrap				

STEP 2

STEP 3

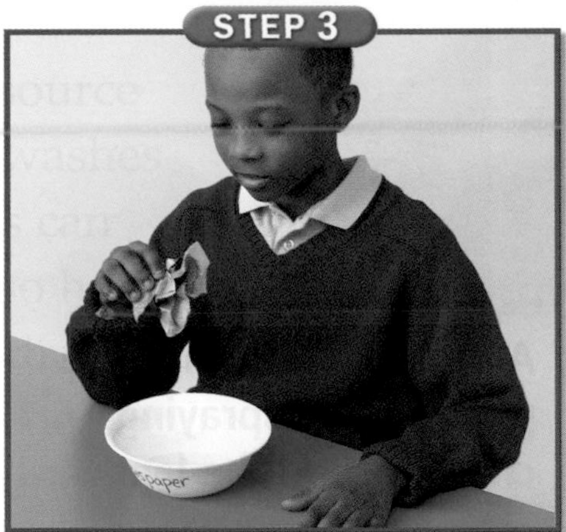

Think and Write

1. **Compare** By the end of the day, which packing materials have begun to break down? Which materials have not?
2. **Infer** Suppose each packing material were thrown away as trash and buried under soil in a landfill. Which packing materials would not break down?

Guided Inquiry

Design an Experiment
How could you break down the newspaper and cellulose peanuts faster? Design an experiment to test your ideas. Get permission from your teacher to carry out your plan.

✓ 0307.T/E.2

Trash Bird

Would you believe this 20-foot tall, 40-foot long sculpture is made entirely out of trash? An artist found an unusual and humorous way to recycle trash, but trash is a serious problem. Most trash is simply thrown out, dumped, or buried. But we are running out of places to put it. Without recycling, we will be buried in our own trash! You can help by following the three R's: Reduce the amount of trash you create. Reuse whatever you can. Recycle the rest.

DID YOU KNOW?

In 1960, the average American family of four discarded about 10 pounds of trash a day. By 2000, that amount had almost doubled to about 18 pounds of trash a day.

GLE 0307.7.2 Recognize that rocks can be composed of one or more minerals. **Math GLE 0306.5.1** Organize, display, and analyze data using various representations to solve problems. **ELA GLE 0301.3.3** Write in a variety of modes and genres, including narration, literary response, personal experience, and subject matter content.

Math Rock Formation

Different types of metamorphic rock form under different conditions of temperature and pressure within Earth. The diagram shows the temperatures at which some metamorphic rocks form. Use it to answer the questions. Provide all answers in both degrees Celsius and Fahrenheit.

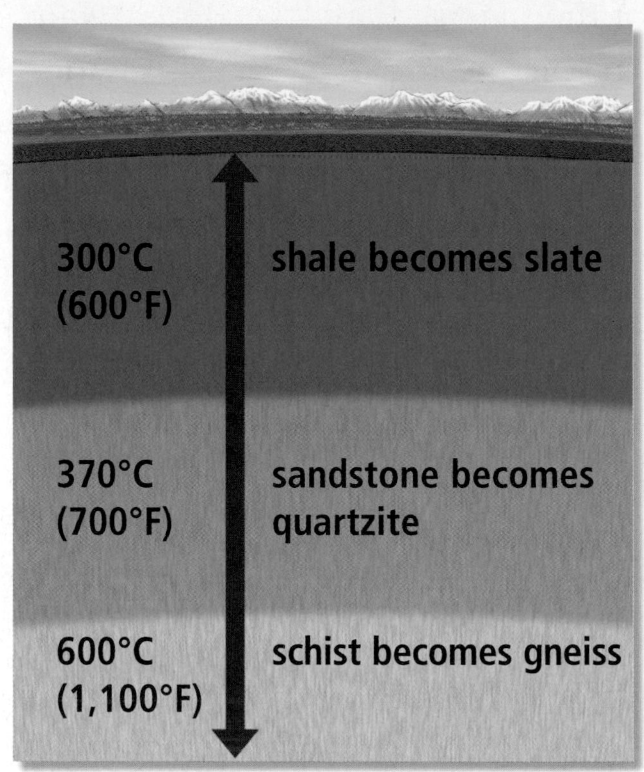

1. What is the difference in temperature at which quartzite and slate form?
2. How does the temperature at which gneiss forms compare with the temperature at which slate forms?
3. Which metamorphic rock forms at 600°C?

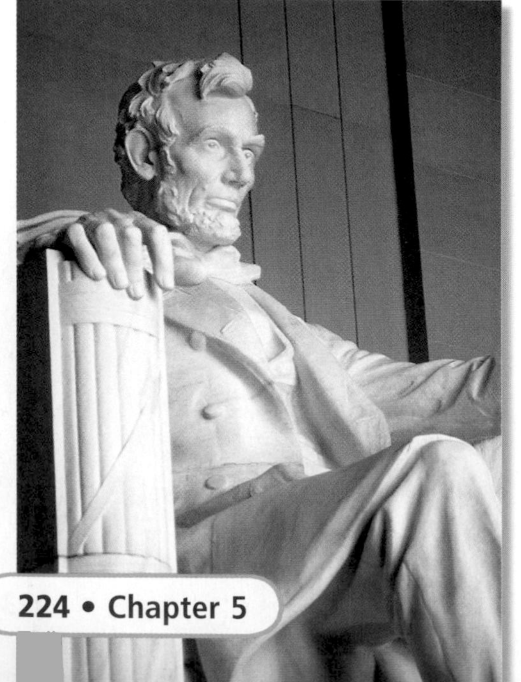

Writing Informational

Many sculptures and statues, such as the famous statue of Abraham Lincoln at the Lincoln Memorial, were carved from marble.

Select a statue or building in your area that is made of or decorated with marble, granite, or other type of rock. Provide a detailed description of the statue or building. Use terms that will give the reader a vivid image of the stone's appearance. Explain which properties make it a good choice for the particular use.

Geologist

Geologists study Earth, how rocks form, and how they change. There are many jobs for geologists. Some geologists advise builders on the construction of skyscrapers, bridges, dams, and tunnels. Certain geologists look for new sources of gas and oil. There are also geologists who study fossils, volcanoes, and earthquakes.

What It Takes!

- A degree in geology, earth science, or geophysics
- Concern for the environment

Land Surveyor

When you see a building, park, or road under construction, you can be sure a land surveyor was there first. Land surveyors measure land to set the boundaries for a piece of property. They prepare maps for legal documents such as deeds and leases.

What It Takes!

- A high-school diploma
- On-the-job training
- Math skills and courses in drafting, drawing, and surveying

Chapter 6

Patterns in Earth's Atmosphere

Lesson Preview

LESSON **1**

How are a puddle, water in a bathtub, and snow on a mountain all connected?

LESSON **2**

It will snow tomorrow and be sunny the day after. How do scientists predict the weather?

LESSON **3**

In January, people in Hawaii are surfing while folks in Maine are ice skating. How do weather patterns vary around the world?

Fun Facts

The highest temperature ever recorded in Tennessee was 113°F.

Vocabulary Preview

★ atmosphere
climate
condensation
equator
evaporation
latitude
polar climate
★ precipitation
temperate climate
temperature
tropical climate
★ water cycle
water vapor
weather

★ = Tennessee Academic Vocabulary

Vocabulary Strategies

Have you ever seen any of these terms before? Do you know what they mean?

↓

Describe, explain, or give an example of the vocabulary terms in your own words.

↓

Draw a picture, symbol, example, or other image that describes the term.

Glossary p. H16

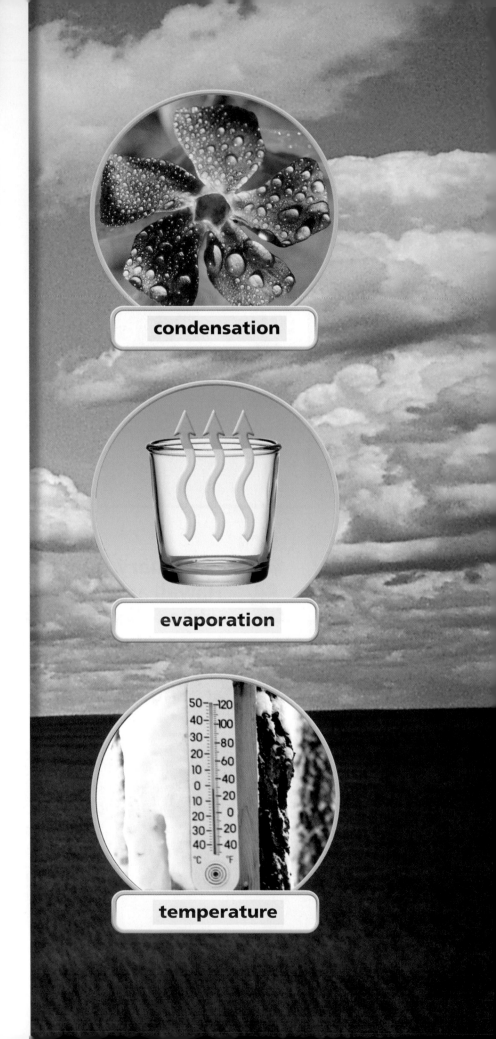

condensation

evaporation

temperature

weather

Start with Your Standards

Inquiry

GLE 0307.Inq.1 Explore different scientific phenomena by asking questions, making logical predictions, planning investigations, and recording data.

GLE 0307.Inq.3 Organize data into appropriate tables, graphs, drawings, or diagrams.

Earth and Space Science

Standard 8 The Atmosphere

GLE 0307.8.1 Recognize that that there are a variety of atmospheric conditions that can be measured.

GLE 0307.8.2 Use tools such as the barometer, thermometer, anemometer, and rain gauge to measure atmospheric conditions.

GLE 0307.8.3 Identify cloud types associated with particular atmospheric conditions.

GLE 0307.8.4 Predict the weather based on cloud observations.

Physical Science

Standard 10 Energy

GLE 0307.10.1 Investigate phenomena that produce heat.

Interact with this chapter.

www.eduplace.com/tnscp

Lesson 1

TENNESSEE STANDARDS

GLE 0307.Inq.1 Explore different scientific phenomena by asking questions, making logical predictions, planning investigations, and recording data.
GLE 0307.8.1 Recognize that there are a variety of atmospheric conditions that can be measured.
GLE 0307.8.2 Use tools such as the barometer, thermometer, anemometer, and rain gauge to measure atmospheric conditions.

What Is the Water Cycle?

Why It Matters...

Fog covers the shoreline of a rocky coast. A lighthouse sends out a powerful beam to warn ships of danger. Some kinds of weather, such as thick fog or violent storms, are not just a bother. They can be deadly. Understanding how weather occurs can help save lives.

PREPARE TO INVESTIGATE

Inquiry Skill

Predict When you predict, you state what you think will happen based on observations and experiences.

Materials

- 2 plastic bowls
- ice cubes
- warm water and cool water
- clock

Science and Math Toolbox

For step 3, review **Measuring Elapsed Time** on pages H12–H13.

Directed Inquiry

Water and Ice

Procedure

1. **Collaborate** Work with a partner. In your Science Notebook, make a chart like the one shown.
2. **Experiment** Fill a plastic bowl halfway with warm water. Fill a second plastic bowl halfway with cool water. Make a label for each bowl.
3. **Use Variables** Place four or five ice cubes in the bowl with the cool water. Set both bowls of water in a warm place for 20 minutes.
4. **Predict** Predict what you think will happen to the bowls of water after 20 minutes. Record your predictions in your chart.
5. **Observe** After 20 minutes, carefully observe both bowls of water. In your chart, record any changes that occurred inside the bowls and on the outside of the bowls.

STEP 1

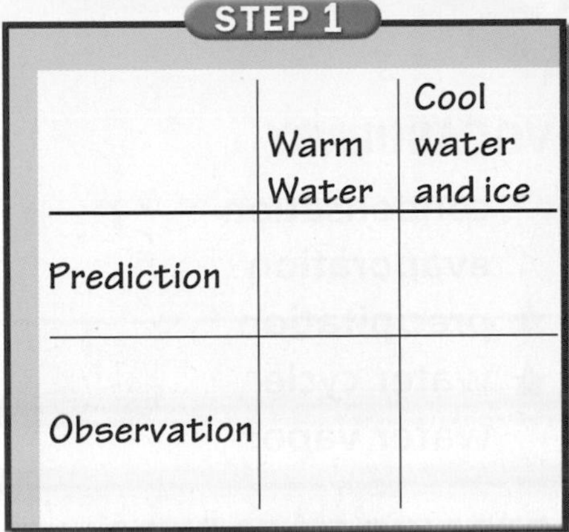

	Warm Water	Cool water and ice
Prediction		
Observation		

STEP 2

STEP 3

Think and Write

1. **Hypothesize** Write a hypothesis to explain what happened to the ice cubes in the cool bowl of water.
2. **Compare** Look at your chart. What was different about the outside of the bowls after 20 minutes?

✓ 0307.10.1

Guided Inquiry

Solve a Problem

During some summers, there is not enough rain to grow crops. Based on what you learned in this experiment, invent a way to get water to crops during a dry summer.

Reading Science

Water Moves

VOCABULARY

condensation
evaporation
★ precipitation
★ water cycle
water vapor

GRAPHIC ORGANIZER

Sequence Use a chart to show events in the water cycle.

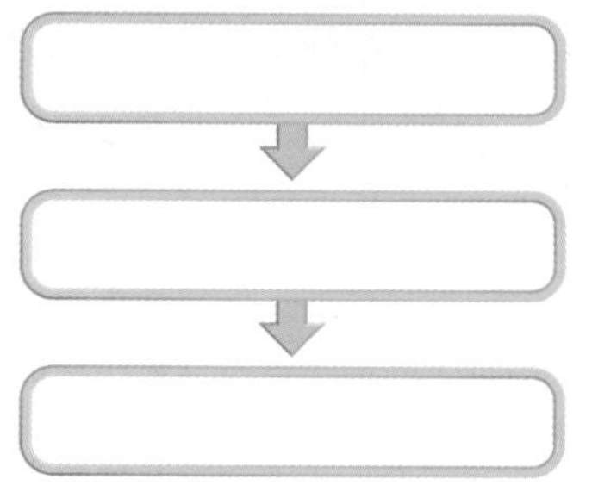

GLE 0307.8.1 Recognize that there are a variety of atmospheric conditions that can be measured.

GLE 0307.8.2 Use tools such as the barometer, thermometer, anemometer, and rain gauge to measure atmospheric conditions.

Changing Water

What do ice, liquid water, and water as a gas have in common? They all are different forms of water. You probably know that ice is the solid form and water is the liquid form. **Water vapor** is water in the form of an invisible gas.

Water is one of the few materials on Earth that can be found in all three forms, or states, under normal conditions. You have probably seen or felt water as a solid, a liquid, and a gas in your daily life.

Water Changes State

Ice

Ice is the solid form of water. When enough heat is removed from liquid water, ice forms.

+ heat
– heat

Water

Liquid water forms when heat is added to ice and when heat is taken away from water vapor.

+ heat
– heat

Water Vapor

Water vapor is invisible. One way it forms is when heat is added to liquid water.

Heat from the sun causes water in a puddle to evaporate.

Have you ever noticed puddles of water in the street after a rainstorm? Sometimes, in a few hours, the puddles disappear. The liquid water in the puddles changes to the gas water vapor. The change of state from a liquid to a gas is called **evaporation** (ih vap uh RAY shuhn).

On a cool morning, you may have noticed drops of water on leaves or on car windshields. This water is dew. Dew does not fall like rain. It forms on cool surfaces from the condensation (kahn dehn SAY shuhn) of water vapor in air. **Condensation** is the change of state from a gas to a liquid.

Heating or cooling water can change it from one state to another. When heat is added to ice, the ice melts and changes to liquid water. When heat is added to liquid water, the water evaporates. That is why wet clothes on a line dry quickly in sunlight on a warm day.

When heat is taken away from water vapor, it condenses to form liquid water. If enough heat is taken away, the liquid water freezes and becomes ice.

FOCUS CHECK What happens when heat is added to ice?

In some dry areas, animals and plants use dew as a water source.

The Water Cycle

As water changes state, it moves between the air and Earth in a process called the **water cycle**. Water is always moving through the water cycle. This process renews Earth's water supply.

As liquid water on Earth evaporates, it forms water vapor in the air. When the water vapor in air cools, it condenses into tiny droplets. These tiny droplets form clouds. Larger water droplets fall back to Earth as precipitation (prih sihp ih TAY shuhn). **Precipitation** is any form of water that falls from clouds to Earth's surface. Precipitation includes rain, snow, sleet, and hail.

Some of the precipitation soaks into the ground, becoming groundwater. Water that does not soak into the ground flows downhill as runoff. Runoff collects in streams and rivers. Streams and rivers empty into ponds, lakes, and oceans.

FOCUS CHECK What happens after water falls to the ground as precipitation?

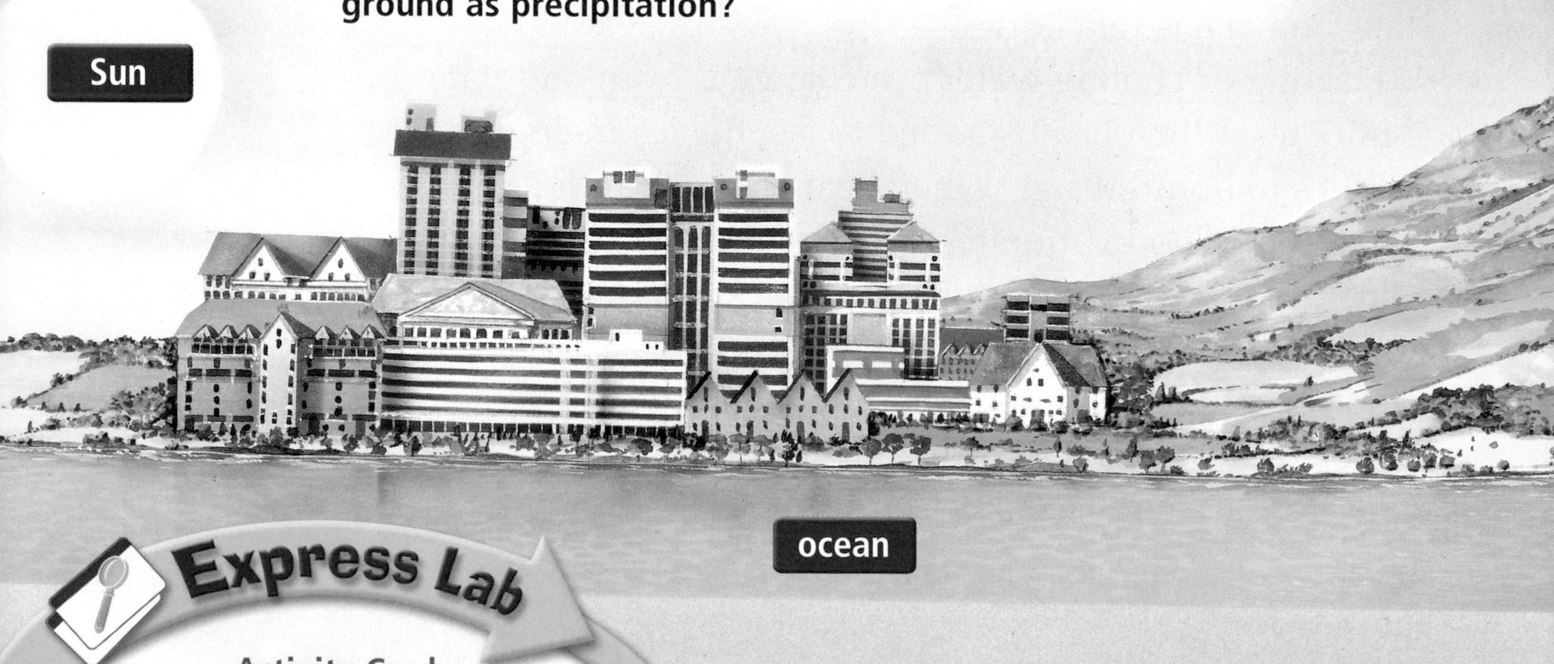

Express Lab

Activity Card
Record Evaporation

Condensation This occurs when water vapor in air cools. The water vapor changes to tiny droplets of liquid water. Clouds are made of these tiny droplets.

Precipitation As more water vapor condenses, the droplets in clouds become larger and heavier. These drops of water fall to the ground as precipitation.

water vapor in the air

lake

runoff

groundwater

Evaporation This occurs when heat from the Sun causes liquid water to change to water vapor, a gas. Water evaporates from oceans, lakes, and rivers.

Living Things and the Water Cycle

Living things are part of the water cycle. All living things need water in order to survive. Plants take in water through their roots. Animals drink water.

Living things also return water to the water cycle. Plants give off large amounts of water through their leaves. Animals, including people, give off water as waste. The water cycle renews this water so that it becomes fresh water again. The graph shows some of the many ways that people use water.

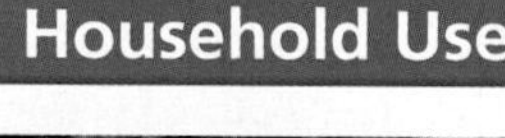

FOCUS CHECK How do living things return water to the water cycle?

Water Usage in the United States

Household Use

People use water in their homes to drink, clean, bathe, and cook.

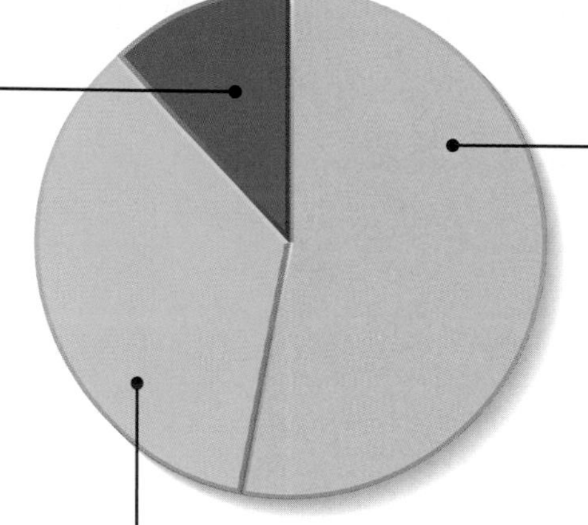

Agriculture

People use large amounts of water to grow food. Most of this water is used for plant crops.

Industry

Factories, power plants, and other industries use water to cool machines, make products, and produce electricity.

Lesson Wrap-Up

Visual Summary

	Water changes state between solid, liquid, and gas when heat is added or taken away.
	The water cycle is a process in which water changes state and moves between the air and Earth.
	Living things take water from the water cycle and return water to the water cycle.

Check for Understanding

INVESTIGATE THE WATER CYCLE

Suppose you put a small bowl of ice cubes on a sunny windowsill. What will happen to the ice cubes after a few hours? What will happen in a few days? Look at the picture of the water cycle on pages 236–237. Which part of the picture does this investigation represent?

✔ **0307.10.1**

Review

1. **MAIN IDEA** Describe what happens to water as it moves through the water cycle.
2. **VOCABULARY** Define the term *water vapor.*
3. **READING SKILL: Sequence** In the water cycle, which event takes place between evaporation and precipitation?
4. **CRITICAL THINKING: Synthesize** Explain how water you drink today may once have been inside the body of a dinosaur.
5. **INQUIRY SKILL: Predict** What would happen to the water cycle if the Sun did not provide heat?

TCAP Prep

Precipitation includes all of the following <u>except</u>

Ⓐ snow
Ⓑ runoff
Ⓒ hail
Ⓓ rain

SPI 0307.8.1

Go Digital Technology

Visit **www.eduplace.com/tnscp** to research more about the water cycle.

Lesson 2

TENNESSEE STANDARDS

GLE 0307.Inq.3 Organize data into appropriate tables, graphs, drawing, or diagrams.
GLE 0307.8.2 Use tools such as the barometer, thermometer, anemometer, and rain gauge to measure atmospheric conditions.
GLE 0307.8.3 Identify cloud types associated with particular atmospheric conditions.

Guiding Question

How Does Weather Change Each Day?

Why It Matters...

What do you think the weather was like when this girl left home? A wet umbrella and puddles are signs that it was raining earlier. Weather affects how you dress and what you do. Having a picnic, playing an outdoor sport, or traveling by airplane are all events that weather can affect.

PREPARE TO INVESTIGATE

Inquiry Skill

Communicate When you communicate, you share information by using words, actions, sketches, graphs, tables, and diagrams.

Materials

- thermometer
- rain and snow gauge
- map of local area

Science and Math Toolbox

For step 4, review **Making a Bar Graph** on page H3.

Directed Inquiry

Weather Report

Procedure

1. **Collaborate** Work in groups of four. Set a thermometer outside in a shady area. Place a rain and snow gauge in an open area outside.

2. **Communicate** In your Science Notebook, make a chart like the one shown. Have each group member keep track of one of the weather conditions listed in the chart.

3. **Observe** Record the weather conditions each day for five days. Observe the kinds of clouds that are in the sky. Note whether they cover more than half or less than half of the sky. Classify the wind as calm, breezy, or strong. Measure and record the temperature and any precipitation.

4. **Communicate** In your Science Notebook, make a bar graph like the one shown to show your data for daily temperature.

STEP 1

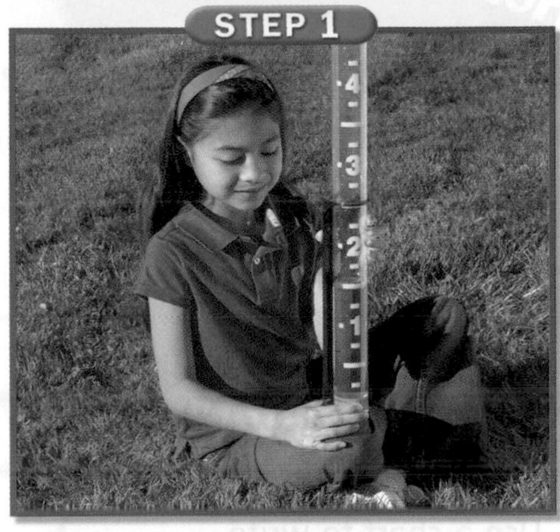

STEP 2

Weather Condition	Day 1	Day 2	Day 3	Day 4	Day 5
Sky					
Wind					
Precipitation					
Temperature					

STEP 4

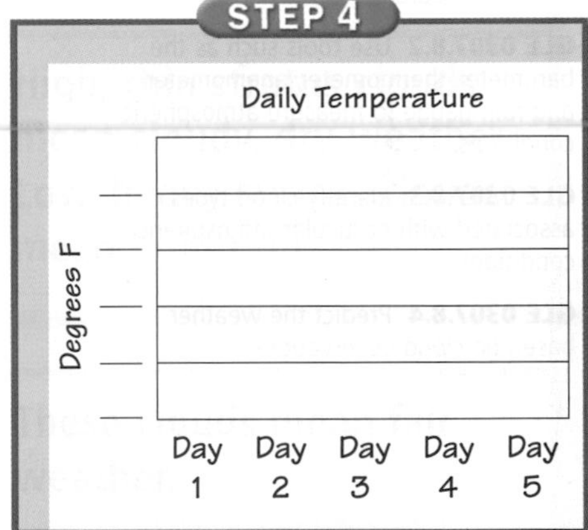

Think and Write

1. **Analyze Data** What was the biggest change in the weather over the week?
2. **Communicate** Use a map of your area to make a weather map for one day. Use symbols such as a sun, a raindrop, or a cloud to stand for the weather conditions.

0307.8.2

Guided Inquiry

Design an Experiment

Continue to record the weather data for the rest of the month. At the end of the month, provide a summary of your data for each weather condition.

Literature

Where do thunder and lightning come from? The Ibibio (ee BEE bee oh) people of southern Nigeria (Ny JIHR ee uh) tell a folktale about thunder and lightning. Read part of it below. In the nonfiction selection, *Hurricanes Have Eyes But Can't See*, you'll learn some science facts about thunder and lightning.

How & Why Stories

by Martha Hamilton and Mitch Weiss

Thunder and Lightning

A mother sheep, Thunder, and her son, Lightning, lived in a village. Lightning often misbehaved by burning farmers' crops. Each time he did this, his mother grew angry and her booming voice shook the village.

The villagers once again complained to the king. He was so angry that he banished Thunder and Lightning from the earth. He sent them to live in the sky....

And so it is to this very day. Whenever there's a thunderstorm, it's because Lightning has grown angry and thrown his bolts down to the earth. Not long after that, you'll hear his mother, Thunder, angrily scolding him with her booming voice.

Hurricanes Have Eyes But Can't See

by Melvin and Gilda Berger

Lightning is a bright, giant spark of electricity that jumps between a cloud and the ground, between two clouds, or within a cloud.

Inside a thunderhead, powerful winds cause drops of water and ice crystals to rub against one another. This creates an electrical charge that grows bigger and bigger. Soon, it is strong enough to make the electricity jump from one place to another. This makes a giant zigzag spark—a streak of lightning.

Thunder always follows lightning. As lightning flashes through the air, it instantly heats the air to 54,000°F (30,000°C). The heated air explodes. It makes a loud crack of thunder, called a thunderclap.

Sharing Ideas

1. **READING CHECK** In the Ibibio folktale, what causes thunder and lightning?
2. **WRITE ABOUT IT** What new facts did you learn about thunder and lightning after reading the nonfiction selection?
3. **TALK ABOUT IT** Discuss a weather factor you have learned about with your classmates.

Lesson 3

TENNESSEE STANDARDS

GLE 0307.Inq.3 Organize data into appropriate tables, graphs, drawings, or diagrams.
GLE 0307.8.1 Recognize that there are a variety of atmospheric conditions that can be measured.

What Is Climate?

Why It Matters...

In many places, children enjoy sledding in the winter. In other places, snow never falls. Knowing the average weather conditions over many years helps people plan activities. It also helps them build the right kinds of houses and plant crops that will grow well.

PREPARE TO INVESTIGATE

Inquiry Skill

Research When you do research, you learn more about a subject by looking in books, searching the Internet, or asking science experts.

Materials

- photo cards
- globe
- world map
- research materials

Directed Inquiry

World Weather

Procedure

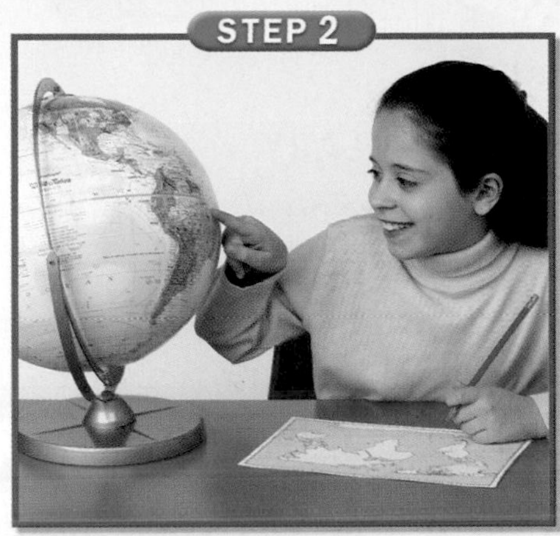
STEP 2

1. **Collaborate** Work in groups of three. Your teacher will give each student in the group one photo card. Your group will share one world map.
2. **Observe** On a globe, find the location of the place shown on your photo card. Use the world map supplied by your teacher to help you.

STEP 3

3. **Research** Use reference books or the Internet to find the latitude (LAT ih-tood), of your location. Latitude tells how far north or south you are from the midpoint of Earth. When you have found the latitude, write it next to the location on the world map. Also find the average summer temperature and the average winter temperature of your location.
4. **Record Data** Work with your group to make a chart like the one shown. Group members should record their data.

STEP 4

Location	Latitude	Average Summer Temperature	Average Winter Temperature
Belem, Brazil			
Tucson, Arizona, USA			
Inuvik, Canada			

Think and Write

1. **Use Numbers** Which location has the greatest difference between its average summer temperature and its average winter temperature?
2. **Infer** How does latitude affect the average summer temperature? How does it affect the average winter temperature?

Guided Inquiry

Research Use books or the Internet to find the places that have had the highest temperature, the lowest temperature, and the lowest yearly precipitation. Label these places on your map.

Reading Science

VOCABULARY

- climate
- equator
- latitude
- polar climate
- temperate climate
- tropical climate

GRAPHIC ORGANIZER

Compare and Contrast
As you read, use a chart to compare and contrast the temperature of different climates.

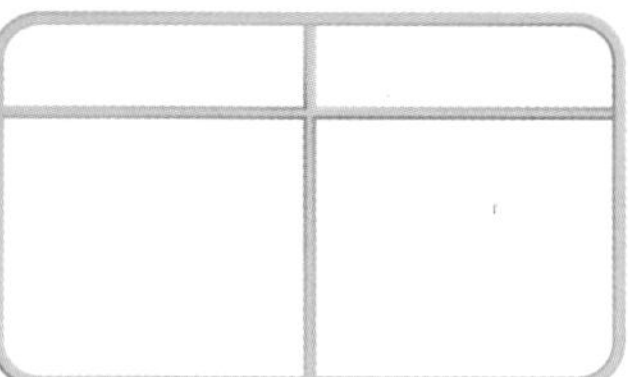

GLE 0307.8.1 Recognize that there are a variety of atmospheric conditions that can be measured.

Climate

Temperature and Precipitation

Suppose you were going on a trip to Alaska in November. Would you pack shorts and T-shirts? Would you pack a winter coat and mittens if you were headed to Hawaii in June? You probably would not. That's because Alaska has a cold climate (KLY miht), and Hawaii has a warm climate. Knowing the climate of a place can help you pack the right clothing for a trip.

A rainforest has a warm, wet climate. ▼

Express Lab

Activity Card
Find Other Climate Factors

Climate is the average weather conditions in an area over a long period of time. Climate is not the same as weather. It is cold in Alaska for many months, year after year. So the climate there can be described as cold. But on a day in summer, the weather in Alaska might be warm enough to wear shorts. Climate depends on average temperature and precipitation. In Hawaii, the average temperature is warm. There is usually a lot of precipitation. You could describe Hawaii's climate as warm and wet. Alaska is often cold, and it gets a lot of rain and snowfall. You could say that Alaska's climate is cold and wet.

FOCUS CHECK How are weather and climate alike?

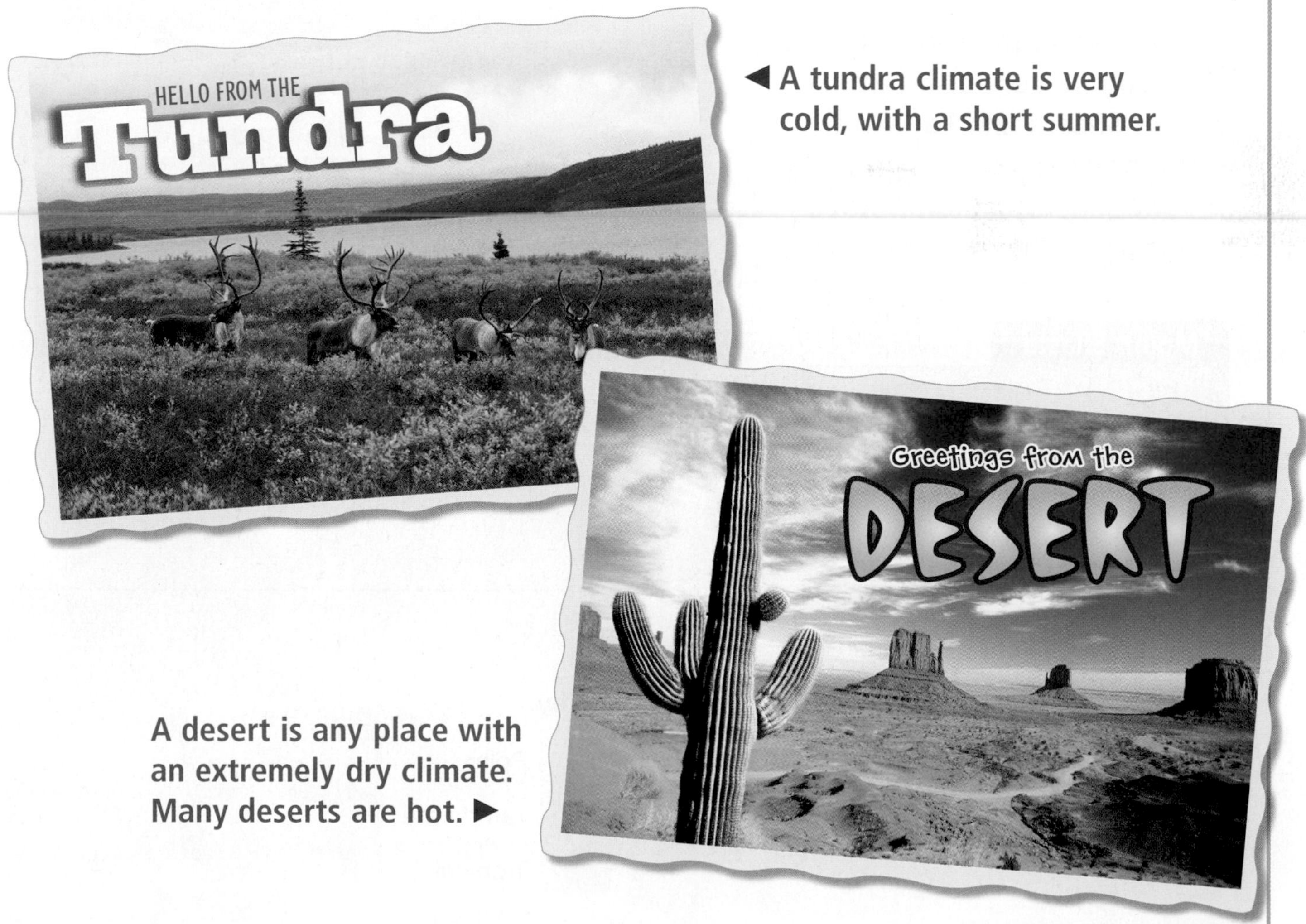

HELLO FROM THE
Tundra
Greetings from the
DESERT

◀ A tundra climate is very cold, with a short summer.

A desert is any place with an extremely dry climate. Many deserts are hot. ▶

Latitude

Climate depends on **latitude** (LAT ih tood), which is the distance north or south of the equator (ih KWAY-tur). The **equator** is an imaginary line around Earth, halfway between the North Pole and the South Pole. Places close to the equator are warmer than places that are farther from the equator.

The areas just north and south of the equator have a tropical (TRAHP ih kuhl) climate. A **tropical climate** is very warm and wet for most of or all of the year.

Places that are halfway between the equator and the poles have a **temperate climate**. In these places, summers are warm or hot, and winters are cool or cold.

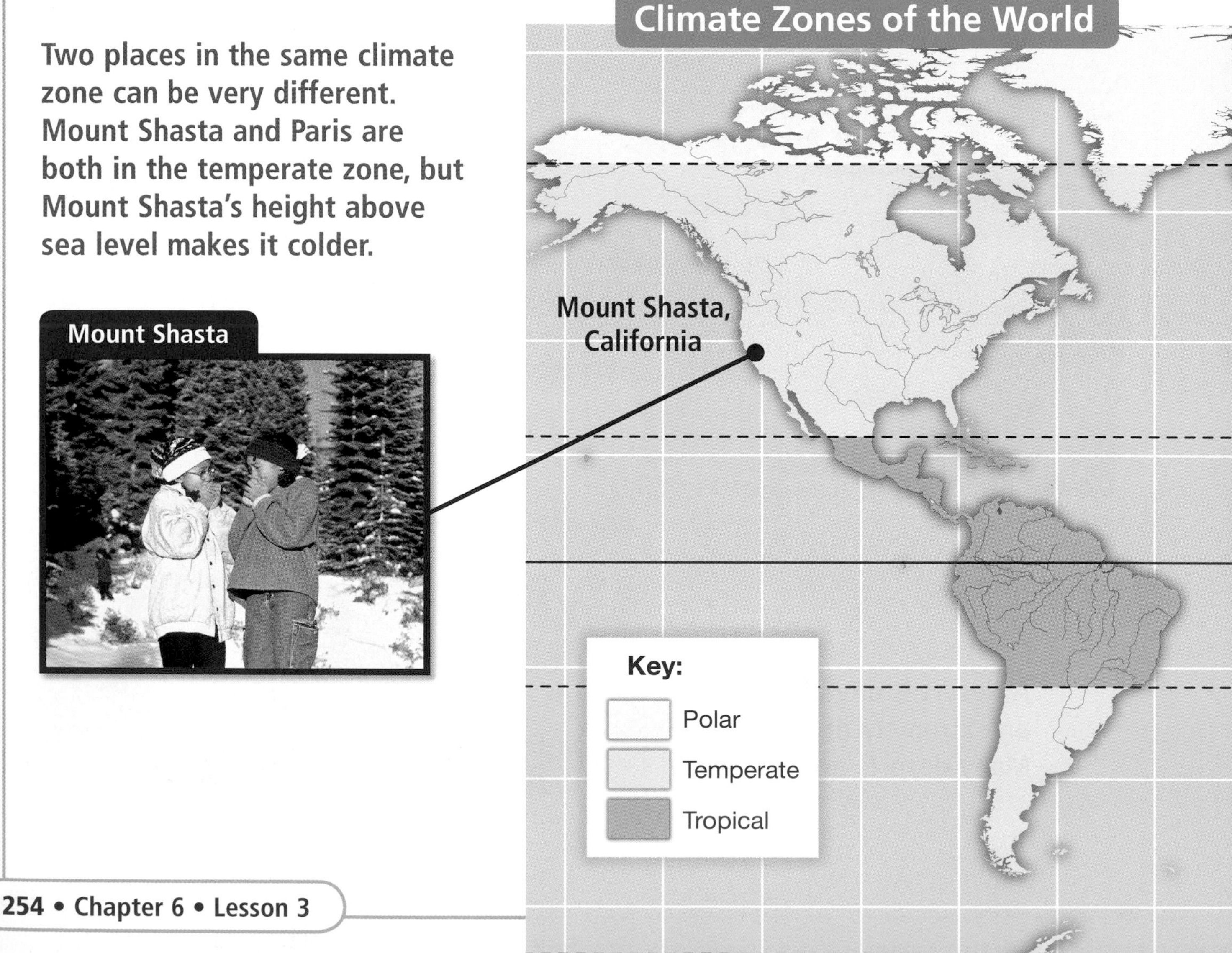

Two places in the same climate zone can be very different. Mount Shasta and Paris are both in the temperate zone, but Mount Shasta's height above sea level makes it colder.

Closest to the poles, the climate is very cold. It is often quite dry. Places with a **polar climate** have long, cold winters and short, cool summers.

Areas within the climate zones may have different climates. For example, the temperate zone includes both dry climates, such as deserts, and moist climates, such as wetlands. Climates may also differ depending on how high the land is. Mountains have colder climates than do low areas.

FOCUS CHECK How do summers differ in a temperate climate and a polar climate?

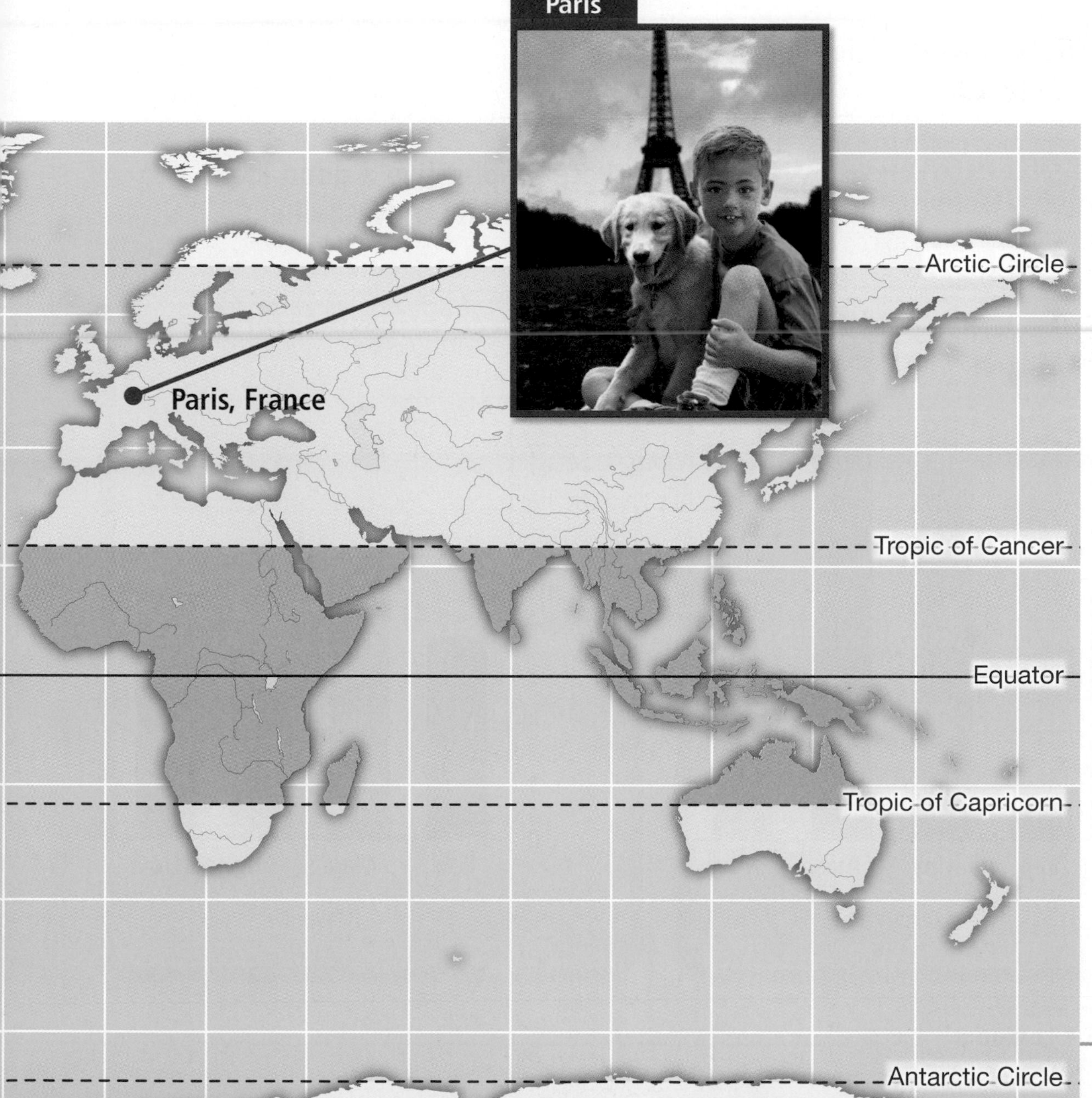

Weather Patterns and Climate

You cannot tell the climate of a place by observing the weather for one day. Even if you look at the weather for a whole year, you may not know the climate. That year may have been warmer, cooler, drier, or wetter than usual.

To learn the climate of a place, scientists look at weather data from many years. The graphs show the average high temperature and average rainfall for Nashville during four months. The data was collected over many years.

FOCUS CHECK How do scientists learn about the climate of a place?

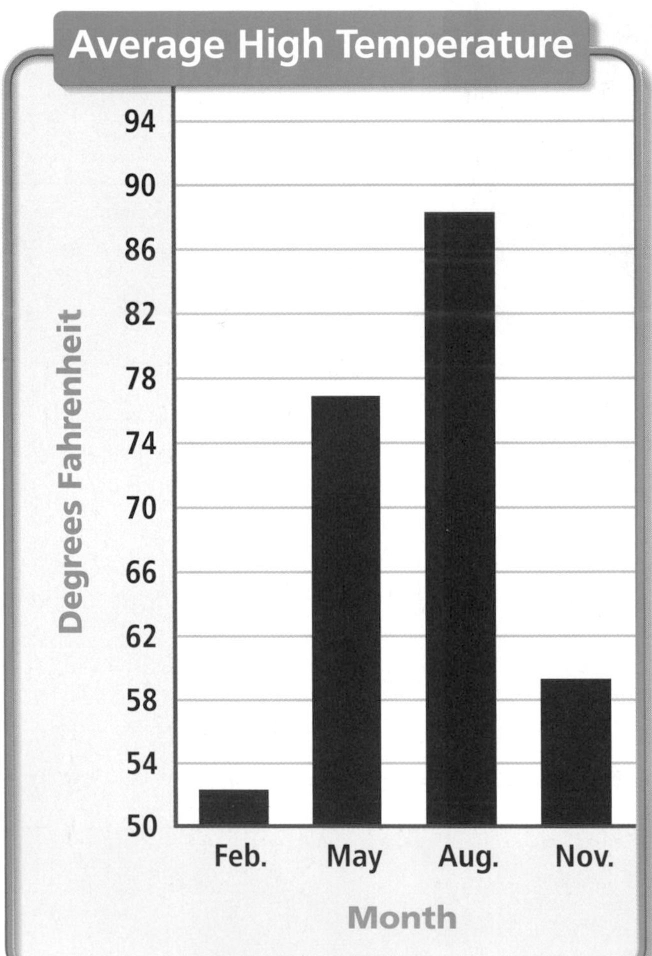

These graphs give a good idea of the climate of Nashville.

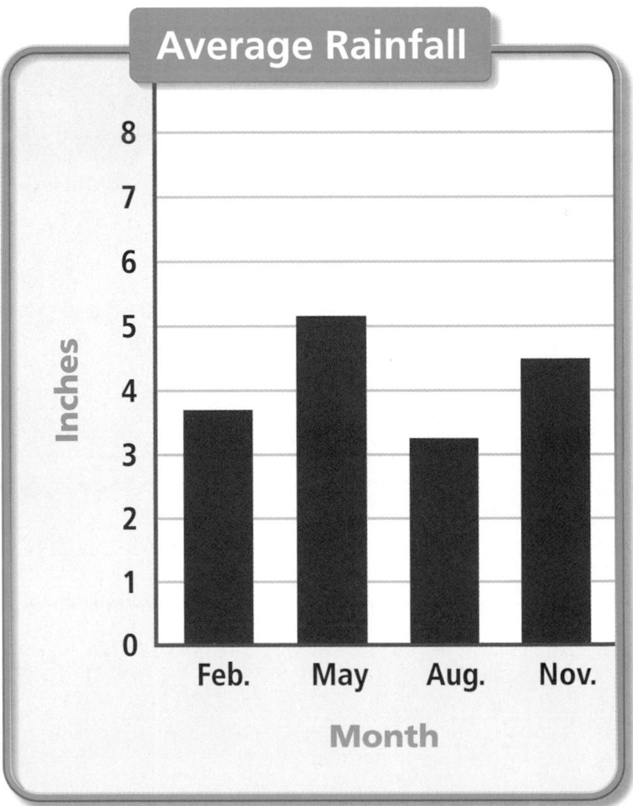

Visual Summary

Climate is the average weather conditions of a place over many years.

Climate zones change with latitude, from tropical to temperate to polar.

Temperatures within a climate zone can vary.

Check for Understanding

TELL ABOUT CLIMATE AND WEATHER
Write a few sentences telling what the climate is like where you live. Then tell what today's weather is like. What tools would you use to find out? What would each tool tell you about the local weather?

✓ **0307.8.1**

Review

1. **MAIN IDEA** How are climate and weather different?
2. **VOCABULARY** What is the equator?
3. **READING SKILL: Compare and Contrast** Describe how the climate of a hot desert and a tropical rainforest are alike and different.
4. **CRITICAL THINKING: Analyze** A person has never seen snow. What can you conclude about the climate where this person lives?
5. **INQUIRY SKILL: Research** Find weather data for your area. What are the yearly weather patterns? How would you describe the climate of your area?

TCAP Prep

In which of these climates would you expect to find a rain gauge with the highest yearly readings?

Ⓐ temperate
Ⓑ desert
Ⓒ polar
Ⓓ tropical

SPI 0307.8.1

Technology

Visit **www.eduplace.com/tnscp** to find out more about climate.

EXTREME Science

SUPER STORMS

Hurricanes are big, powerful windstorms. How big? Look at this photograph of hurricane Ivan taken from space. How large was Ivan? It covered all of Alabama and parts of Tennessee, Georgia, and Florida!

When hurricanes roar ashore, they can do terrible damage with wind, rain, surging tides, and huge waves. Fortunately, most hurricanes don't reach land but stay at sea. But 2004 was an exception. Florida got hit with four powerful hurricanes in less than two months. Hurricane Charley was a category 4. Hurricane Frances was a category 2. Hurricane Ivan was a category 3. Hurricane Jeanne was a category 3. What does this chart tell you about each of these storms?

Strength	Damage	Winds	Storm Surge
Category 1	Minimal	74–95 mph	4–5 feet
Category 2	Moderate	96–110 mph	6–8 feet
Category 3	Extensive	111–130 mph	9–12 feet
Category 4	Extreme	131–155 mph	13–18 feet
Category 5	Catastrophic	>155 mph	>18 feet

Weather scientists divide hurricanes into categories based on wind speed.

The winds in the strongest hurricanes move three times as fast as cars on a freeway!

GLE 0307.8.1 Recognize that there are a variety of atmospheric conditions that can be measured.
Math GLE 0306.3.4 Create and represent patterns using words, tables, graphs, and symbols.
ELA GLE 0301.3.3 Write in a variety of modes and genres, including narration, literary response, personal experience, and subject matter content.

Math Analyze Snowfall Data

The table shows the amount of the average yearly snowfall in four different United States cities. The cities are listed in alphabetical order.

1. Reorder the cities according to the amount of snowfall they receive. Start with the city with the lowest average snowfall. Put the information in a table.
2. About how many inches is the difference between the highest and lowest average yearly snowfalls?
3. What is the exact difference between the highest and lowest average snowfalls?
4. Add a third column to your table, showing the snowfall amounts in feet and inches.

Snowfall Amounts

Location	Average Yearly Snowfall
Anchorage, Alaska	71 inches
Boston, Massachusetts	42 inches
Olympia, Washington	17 inches
Syracuse, New York	116 inches

Narrative

The book *Cloudy with a Chance of Meatballs,* by Judi Barrett, is a tall tale about a town with unusual weather. "It rained things like soup and juice. It snowed mashed potatoes and peas. And sometimes the wind blew in storms of hamburgers." Write your own tall tale about a town with unusual weather. Draw a picture to go with your story.

Kelly Cox

Kelly Cox grew up in an area outside of Maryville, Tennessee. As a child, she liked pretending she was a TV weather forecaster. She gave made-up forecasts using a big spoon as a microphone.

Today Ms. Cox is a meteorologist and a weather forecaster for a Nashville TV station. Ms. Cox is also a storm spotter for the National Weather Service (NWS). That means she observes storms and reports her findings to the NWS and to local safety officials. Ms. Cox earned a degree in Broadcast Meteorology.

Chapter 6 Review and TCAP Prep

Vocabulary

Complete each sentence with a term from the list.

1. The blanket of air that surrounds Earth is the _____.
2. The change of state from a liquid to a gas is _____ .
3. The condition of the atmosphere at a certain place and time is _____.
4. The measure of how hot or cold something is called _____.
5. A place that has long, cold winters and short, cool summers has a/an _____.
6. The change of state from a gas to a liquid is called _____.
7. Water changes state and moves between the atmosphere and Earth in a process called the _____.
8. The imaginary line around Earth halfway between the North Pole and the South Pole is called the _____.
9. Water in the form of an invisible gas is _____.
10. Water that falls from clouds to Earth's surface is _____.

- ★ **atmosphere**
- **climate**
- **condensation**
- **equator**
- **evaporation**
- **latitude**
- **polar climate**
- ★ **precipitation**
- **temperate climate**
- **temperature**
- **tropical climate**
- ★ **water cycle**
- **water vapor**
- **weather**

TCAP Inquiry Skills

11. **Communicate** Make a bar graph using this information. It gives the average temperatures for three cities for the same week in February.

    Memphis 44°F

    Nashville 38°F

    Clarksville 34°

    GLE 0307.Inq.3

12. **Predict** You look out the window and see high, thin wispy clouds. What kind of clouds are they? What kind of weather will you most likely have?

    GLE 0307.8.4

Map the Concept

Tell the kind of weather each cloud usually brings.

Cloud Type	Weather
Cumulus	
Stratus	
Cirrus	
Cumulonimbus	

GLE 0307.8.3

Critical Thinking

13. **Synthesize** Write a paragraph to describe what the weather was like one day this week. Include at least three weather conditions. **GLE 0307.8.1**

14. **Analyze** Humidity and precipitation are alike in a way, but do not mean the same thing. Explain how they are alike and how they are different. **GLE 0307.8.1**

15. **Evaluate** Imagine that a group of people are starting a settlement in a new place. They can only bring three weather instruments. Which three do you think they should bring? Explain. **GLE 0307.8.2**

16. **Apply** It has started raining. If you had checked a barometer over the past few hours, would it have shown that the air pressure was rising, or falling? **GLE 0307.8.2**

Make a Cloud Book

Collect pictures of various cloud types from magazines and the Internet. You may also take your own photos of clouds. Use your textbook to help you identify the clouds. Put the pictures in a scrapbook. Label each type of cloud. Describe the type of weather that is likely to occur when these clouds are seen.

✔ **0307.8.2**

TCAP Prep

Answer the following questions.

17 Which of the following is a kind of precipitation?

Ⓐ rain
Ⓑ weather
Ⓒ temperature
Ⓓ atmosphere **SPI 0307.8.1**

18 The condition of the atmosphere at a certain place and time is

Ⓕ climate
Ⓖ weather
Ⓗ the water cycle
Ⓙ humidity **SPI 0307.8.1**

19 A tool that measures wind speed is a/an

Ⓐ weathervane
Ⓑ anemometer
Ⓒ thermometer
Ⓓ temperature **SPI 0307.8.1**

20 Stratus and cirrus are types of

Ⓕ clouds
Ⓖ precipitation
Ⓗ humidity
Ⓙ evaporation **SPI 0307.8.2**

6 The Universe

Performance Indicator: **SPI 0307.6.1 Identify the major components of the solar system, i.e., sun, planets and moons.**

1 Earth gets light from

Ⓐ the Moon
Ⓑ the Sun
Ⓒ Venus
Ⓓ itself

2 The illustration below most likely shows which planet?

Ⓕ Mars
Ⓖ Mercury
Ⓗ Saturn
Ⓙ Venus

7 The Earth

Performance Indicator: **SPI 0307.7.1 Classify landforms and bodies of water according to their geological features and identify them on a map.**

3 A canyon is a type of

Ⓐ glacier
Ⓑ mountain
Ⓒ plain
Ⓓ valley

7 The Earth

Performance Indicator: **SPI 0307.7.4 Determine methods for conserving natural resources.**

4 The three R's of conservation are reuse, reduce, and

Ⓕ recycle
Ⓖ refill
Ⓗ remove
Ⓙ resource

8 The Atmosphere

Performance Indicator: **SPI 0307.8.1 Choose the correct tool for measuring a particular atmospheric condition.**

5 Which tool is used to measure wind speed?

Ⓐ barometer 

Ⓒ rain gauge 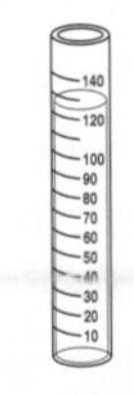

Ⓑ thermometer 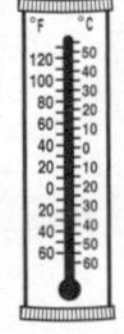

Ⓓ anemometer 

8 The Atmosphere

Performance Indicator: **SPI 0307.8.2 Match major cloud types with specific atmospheric conditions.**

6 Which kind of cloud is likely to mean thunderstorms?

Ⓕ cumulus
Ⓖ cumulonimbus
Ⓗ cirrus
Ⓙ stratus

www.eduplace.com/tnscp

Discover More

Simulate how a dam can change an environment! Building a dam helps some plants and animals but may harm others. When a dam is built, it causes flooding and creates a lake where there used to be dry land. The lake becomes a habitat for fish, birds, and other animals. It may also be a source of water farmers can use for their crops.

The flooding caused by a dam has harmful effects, too. Water may cover land areas that are the homes of plants and animals. Some plants will die, and many animals will have to find new homes.

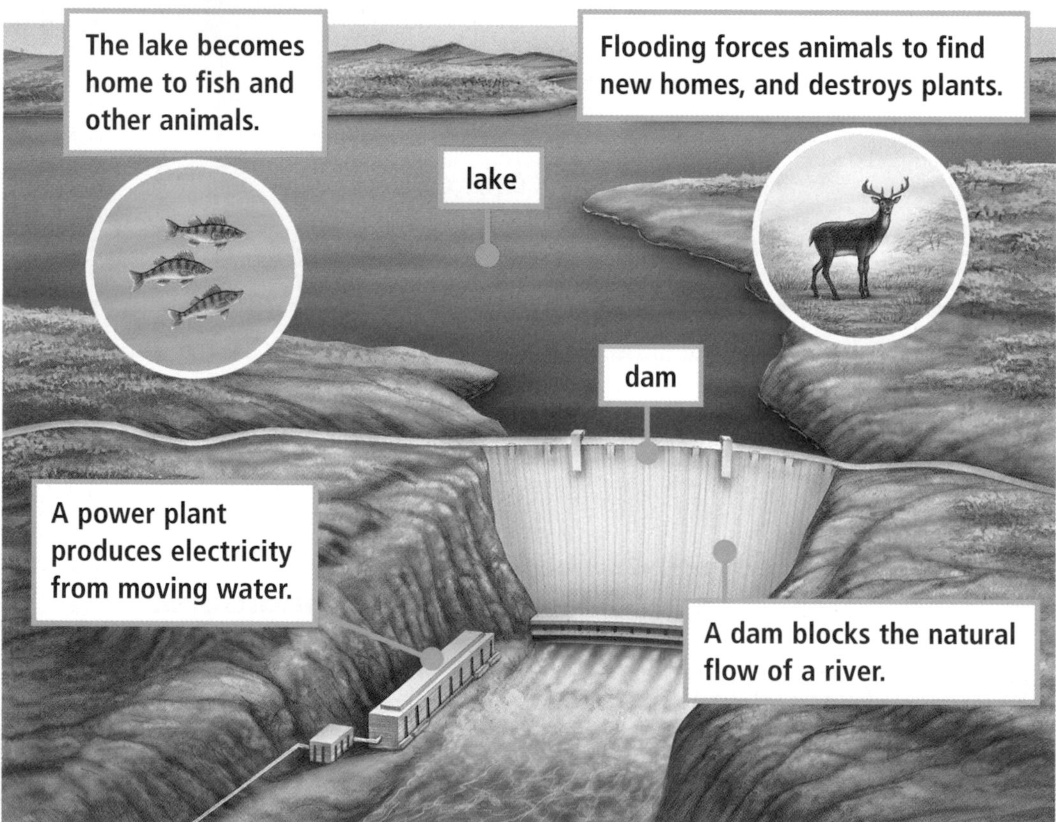
The lake becomes home to fish and other animals.
Flooding forces animals to find new homes, and destroys plants.
lake
dam
A power plant produces electricity from moving water.
A dam blocks the natural flow of a river.

 to learn how a dam impacts the plants and animals in an area.

PHYSICAL SCIENCE

TENNESSEE

Tennessee Excursions and Engineering Project

Mary's Greenhouse

McMinnville, in the heart of Tennessee, is known as the Nursery Capital of the World. There are dozens of plant nurseries in the area that grow everything from daisies to green beans. Mary's Greenhouse is a local favorite.

Mary Hamby started Mary's Greenhouse in the 1970s with two small greenhouses. Growing plants was a hobby she enjoyed. Today, her company has 45 greenhouses that grow plants all year round. Nearly 300 different kinds of plants grow in the greenhouses.

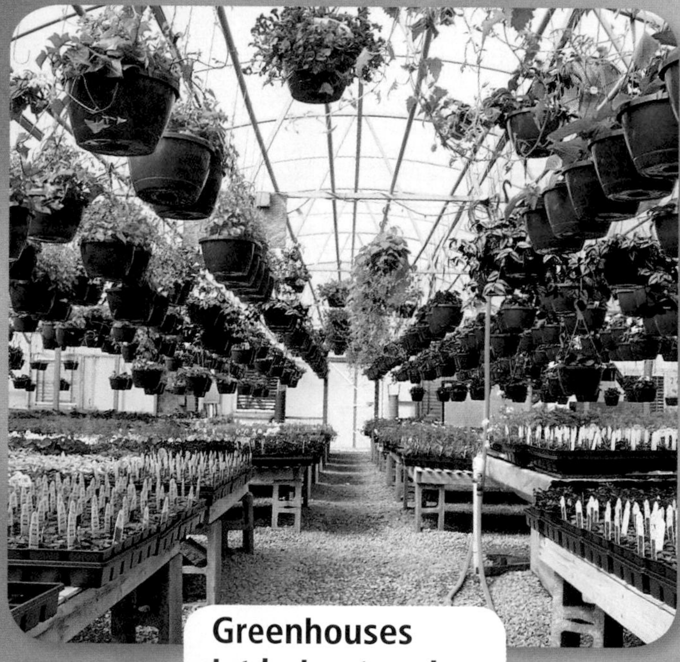

Greenhouses let in heat and light, but keep out diseases and pests.

How Does a Garden Grow?

Many nurseries rely on greenhouses to grow plants. There are many benefits to growing plants in greenhouses. Growers can keep the temperature and humidity constant inside them. This enables them to grow healthy plants, even if it is snowing outside. Greenhouses also keep pests and diseases from harming the plants.

Greenhouses are usually made of glass or plastic that allows sunlight to come through. Plants need sunlight to grow.

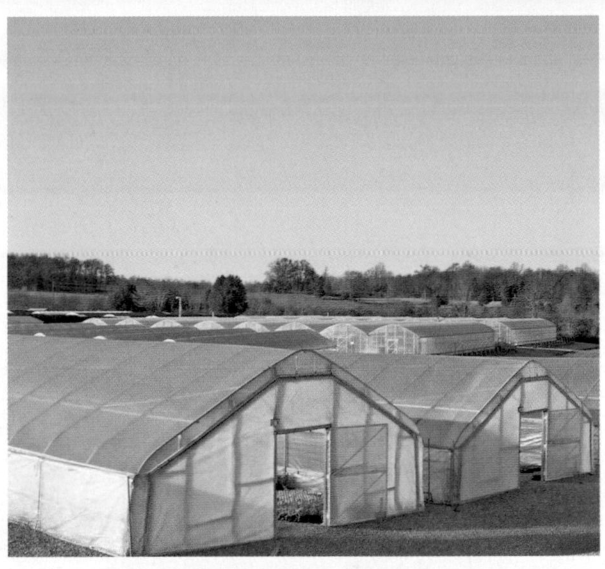

Heat from the Sun warms the air, plants, and tables inside the greenhouse. Because the plants are indoors, they lose heat very slowly. Even on cold days, the Sun keeps the plants warm inside a greenhouse.

Think and Write

1. **Scientific Thinking** What is the source of light and heat in a greenhouse?
2. **Scientific Inquiry** Why is glass a good material for making a greenhouse?

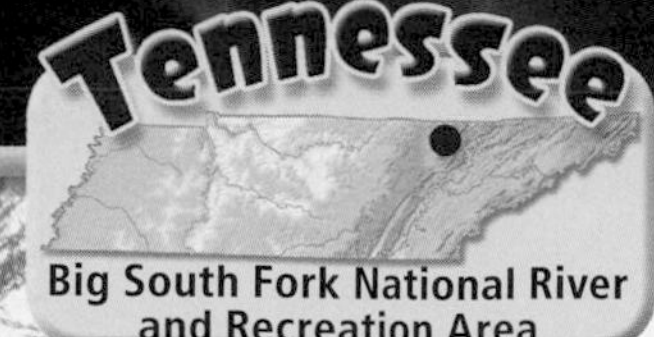

CHARIT CREEK LODGE

The Great Smoky Mountains National Park is known all over the world for its beauty. Nearly nine million people visit the park each year. The views from Charit Creek Lodge are especially grand. But only a handful of people are lucky enough to visit the lodge or spend the night there.

Why do so many people miss this spot? It's because you can't get to Charit Creek Lodge in a car. It can only be reached by bike, on horseback, or on foot.

One of the cabins at the lodge is very old. It was built as a home by settler Jonathan Blevins in 1817. The rest of the cabins were opened in 1987. Since 1989, the lodge has been a hotel.

Because Charit Creek Lodge is far from roads and cities, the environment around it is unspoiled. Visitors can hike on nearby nature trails and go white-water rafting. Guests can even see wildlife such as deer, bears, wild turkeys, and salamanders.

It's Dark in Here!

Charit Creek Lodge cabins do not have electricity. Instead of using electric lights, the cabins have lamps fueled by kerosene, a liquid fuel that burns. Water for bathing is heated in a separate building. Heated water means visitors don't have to worry about taking cold showers.

The winters in Tennessee can be very cold. Each cabin has a wood-burning stove that provides heat to the entire cabin. When wood burns, it gives off thermal energy which is felt as heat. The heat moves from warmer areas, where the fire is, to cooler parts of the cabin.

Think and Write

1. **Scientific Thinking** How are the cabins at Charit Creek Lodge heated?
2. **Science and Technology** Imagine that you and your family are going to vacation at Charit Creek Lodge. Plan several activities for your time there that do not require electricity.

Wood-burning stoves heat the cabins.

Chattanooga Symphony & Opera

Beautiful music has been heard in Chattanooga for nearly 100 years. Early on, small groups of musicians met and played. By 1933, the Chattanooga Symphony began performing a regular season for sold-out crowds. Soon after, an opera company was added. Today, the Chattanooga Symphony and Opera perform for thousands of listeners each year in a specially designed building.

Designers of music halls build spaces that allow people to hear the different sounds made by all the instruments. A music hall shaped like a shoebox is a good design. It is long and high but not very wide. The walls are close to the audience. Music is a form of sound energy. Sound travels through air. When the music strikes the walls of the music hall, it bounces off. Listeners feel surrounded by the music.

Energy travels in sound waves produced by the musicians.

Turn Up the Volume

Different instruments in an orchestra have different volumes and pitches. Volume is a measure of how much energy a sound has. A tuba has a greater volume and can produce sounds that have more energy than those produced by a flute. That is why an orchestra might have only one or two tubas but many flutes.

Pitch is a measure of how high or low a sound is. Tuba sounds have a low pitch. Flute sounds have a high pitch.

Each instrument has a unique sound.

Think and Write

1. **Scientific Thinking** Compare a trombone to a violin. Which one has the higher pitch?
2. **Scientific Inquiry** Describe an activity you might do to learn more about sound.

Build a Musical Instrument

Identify the Problem Suppose you and four friends want to start a band. Sadly, you don't have enough money to buy five musical instruments.

Think of a Solution Your idea is that each band member makes an instrument. List characteristics that each instrument must have so it can play three different pitches. For example, stringed instruments must have strings of different lengths.

Plan and Build Using the ideas from your list, sketch and label your design. Think of materials you could use to make your instrument. Then build it.

Test and Improve Now test your instrument. If necessary, improve it so that it produces at least three pitches.

Communicate

1. Tell whether your instrument design was a success, and explain your response.
2. How did your list help you build your instrument?
3. Describe one improvement you could make to your instrument.

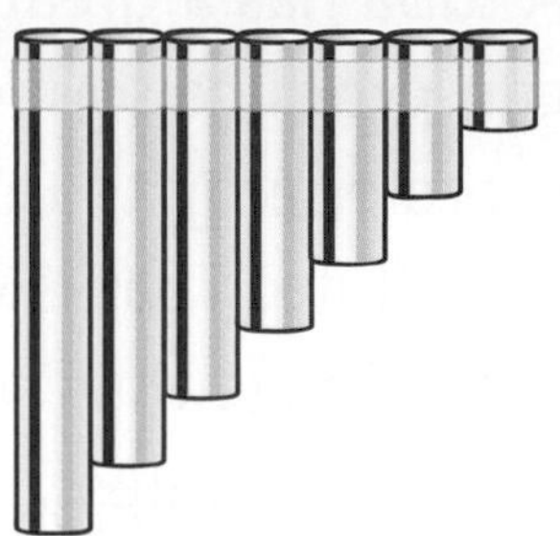

Possible Materials

- masking tape
- sandpaper
- scissors
- tissue paper
- paper-towel rolls
- craft sticks
- glue
- straws
- string
- small boxes
- rubber bands
- scrap cardboard
- drinking glasses
- spoon
- water bottles
- water

GLE 0307.T/E.5 Apply a creative design strategy to solve a particular problem generated by societal needs and wants.

Physical Science

Tennessee

Guiding Question

What is matter, and what happens when objects and forces interact?

Chapter 7

Matter

Lesson Preview

LESSON **1**

A firefighter's coat protects from extreme heat. Basketballs are made to bounce. What are some useful properties of matter?

LESSON **2**

What do a melting ice cube and a paper airplane have in common?

LESSON **3**

In what way are a bowl of soup, a puffy cloud, and a block of concrete alike?

LESSON **4**

How can dirt, water, and a shallow pan help you find gold?

Fun Facts

Diamonds are the hardest natural kind of matter known.

Vocabulary Preview

- condense
- evaporate
- filter
- freeze
- gas
- liquid
- mass
- ★ matter
- melt
- mixture
- ★ physical change
- ★ physical property
- solid
- substance
- volume

★ = Tennessee Academic Vocabulary

Vocabulary Strategies

Have you ever seen any of these terms before? Do you know what they mean?

Describe, explain, or give an example of the vocabulary terms in your own words.

Draw a picture, symbol, example, or other image that describes the term.

Glossary p. H16

physical change

matter

mixture

Start with Your Standards

Inquiry

GLE 0307.Inq.2 Select and use appropriate tools and simple equipment to conduct an investigation.

GLE 0307.Inq.3 Organize data into appropriate tables, graphs, drawings, or diagrams.

GLE 0307.Inq.4 Identify and interpret simple patterns of evidence to communicate the findings of multiple investigations.

GLE 0307.Inq.6 Compare the results of an investigation with what scientists already accept about this question.

Physical Science

Standard 9 Matter

GLE 0307.9.1 Design a simple experiment to determine how the physical properties of matter can change over time and under different conditions.

GLE 0307.9.2 Investigate different types of mixtures.

GLE 0307.9.3 Describe different methods to separate mixtures.

Interact with this chapter.

www.eduplace.com/tnscp

Lesson 1

TENNESSEE STANDARDS

GLE 0307.Inq.2 Select and use appropriate tools and simple equipment to conduct an investigation.
GLE 0307.9.1. Design a simple experiment to determine how the physical properties of matter can change over time and under different conditions.

Guiding Question

What Are Physical Properties?

Why It Matters...

Suppose you lost your sweater. How would you describe it? You might say that it's orange. You might also say that it is made of cotton. You might describe the knitted pattern and explain that the size is medium. You can identify sweaters and other objects by describing them.

Lost and Found

PREPARE TO INVESTIGATE

Inquiry Skill

Compare When you compare things, you observe how they are different and how they are alike.

Materials

- bag of assorted shells
- metric ruler
- hand lens
- poster board
- markers
- glue or tape

Science and Math Toolbox

For step 2, review **Using a Hand Lens** on page H2.

Directed Inquiry

Sorting Shells

Procedure

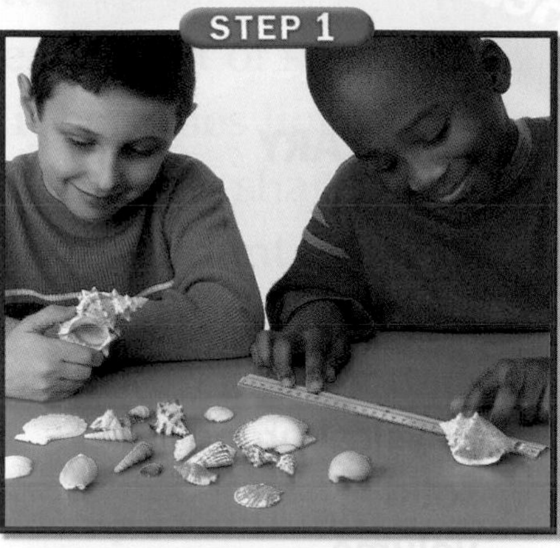
STEP 1

1. **Measure** Work with a partner. Open the bag of shells. Spread out the shells on the desk. Use a metric ruler to measure the length of each shell. Record your measurements in your Science Notebook.

2. **Compare** Use a hand lens to observe the shells. Notice how the shells are alike and different.

STEP 3

3. **Classify** Choose a physical property (FIHZ ih kuhl PRAHP ur tee) and classify the shells based on that property. A **physical property** is a characteristic that can be observed with the senses. Color, shape, and size are physical properties.

STEP 4

4. **Communicate** Make a poster. Glue or tape the groups of shells on the poster. Write a label for each group. The label should describe the physical properties of the shells in that group.

Think and Write

1. **Communicate** What physical properties did you use to classify your shells?

2. **Communicate** Which senses did you use to observe the physical properties of the shells?

Guided Inquiry

Design an Experiment
Think of other ways to describe shells. Does a magnet pull on them? Do they melt in the Sun? Can you see through them? Do they float? List your descriptions.

✓ 0307.9.1

The shape of the sponge is a rectangle.
PEAS & CARROTS
The melon is larger than each lemon.
The tomato is large, red, and smooth.

You can use the physical properties of matter to identify objects.

Observing Matter

Look for the watermelon in the grocery basket. What physical properties of the melon did you use to find it? You might have looked for its color and shape.

Other physical properties you can observe are texture, temperature, hardness, sound, flavor, and size. You observe the physical properties of matter using your five senses—sight, touch, taste, smell, and hearing. If you could pick up the melon and eat it, you might observe that it is smooth, crisp, sweet, and juicy.

Measuring Matter

How would you describe how heavy a marble or a bowling ball is? You can use a measuring device such as a balance or a scale to find an exact measurement.

▲ **The mass of an object equals the sum of the masses of its parts.**

How heavy the marble or the bowling ball is depends on its mass. **Mass** is the amount of matter in an object. A balance measures mass. Mass is given in units called grams (g).

Mass is different from weight (wayt). Weight measures the pull of Earth's gravity (GRAV ih tee) on an object. Mass and weight are both physical properties of matter.

The bowling ball and marble have different masses. They also have different volumes (VAHL-yoomz). **Volume** is the amount of space that matter takes up. Look at the containers below. The same volume of sand has been put into each container. No matter what the container's shape, the sand takes up the same amount of space in each one.

Volume is also a physical property. The volume of a solid is often measured in cubic centimeters (cm^3). Liquid volume is often measured in liters (L).

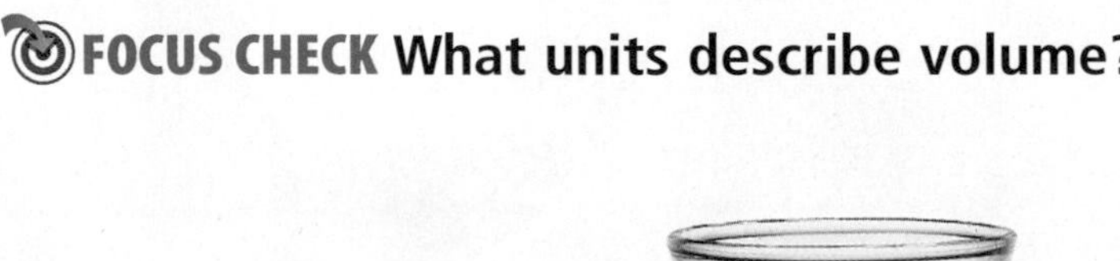

FOCUS CHECK What units describe volume?

Although each container is a different shape and size, the volume of sand in each container is the same.

Useful Properties of Matter

Which would you choose to wear in the rain: a raincoat or a wool sweater? You would probably choose a raincoat because you know raincoats are waterproof. You choose one material over another because of its properties.

The properties of different kinds of matter make them useful for different purposes. You wouldn't cook food on a stove in a plastic pan. A metal pan heats food without melting.

Being magnetic is a useful property of some metals. Some kinds of matter allow electricity to pass through them easily. Glass is a kind of matter that allows light to pass through it.

▲ A basketball is made from matter that is unbreakable and springy.

FOCUS CHECK What are two useful properties of matter?

The boaters' raincoats, as well as many parts of the boat, are made from waterproof materials. ▶

The swimmer's goggles are made from matter that is clear, unbreakable, and waterproof.

Lesson Wrap-Up

Visual Summary

	Three states of matter are solid, liquid, and gas.
	You can describe physical properties of matter by using your five senses and by measuring.
	The properties of matter make matter useful for different purposes.

Check for Understanding

COMPARE COMMON SUBSTANCES
Work with a partner. Each of you should prepare two small samples, about 50 mL, of a common and safe substance. For example, you might choose liquid detergent and mouthwash or salt and peppercorns. Be sure your teacher approves your samples.

Exchange samples with your partner. Record a list of as many of the properties of each sample as you can observe. **Safety:** Do not taste the samples. Use all your senses, except taste, to make your observations. Compare the lists of properties. Then make an educated guess about the identity of each sample.

✓ **0307.9.1**

Review

1. **MAIN IDEA** List four physical properties of an apple.
2. **VOCABULARY** Using your own words, describe what matter is.
3. **READING SKILL: Classify** Is vinegar a solid, a liquid, or a gas? Explain your choice.
4. **CRITICAL THINKING: Synthesize** Water becomes a solid below 0°C and a gas above 100°C. What is its state at 50°C?
5. **INQUIRY SKILL: Compare** How are mass and volume different?

TCAP Prep

How would you test a metal to learn if it would make a good wire for a lamp?

Ⓐ Pour water on it.
Ⓑ Shine a light on it.
Ⓒ Try to pass electricity through it.
Ⓓ Hold a magnet near it.

SPI 0307.Inq.1

Go Digital Technology

Visit **www.eduplace.com/tnscp** to find out more about the physical properties of matter.

High-Tech Hang Gliding

Get a bird's-eye view. A hang glider is like a kite that a person can hang from and ride through the air without an engine. Today's hang gliders are faster, lighter, and easier to use than ever before. The V-shaped gliders are made from new materials and have high-tech designs.

Hang glider designers use computers to design better wings. Some of the fastest hang gliders have wings covered with a type of polyester film. Two physical properties of this material are that it is light and strong.

Many hang gliders have parts made from carbon fiber—a material that is strong, lightweight, and flexible. Flexible material can bend without breaking. Hang gliders made with carbon fiber are faster and easier to control than older models.

GLE 0307.9.1 Design a simple experiment to determine how the physical properties of matter can change over time and under different conditions.

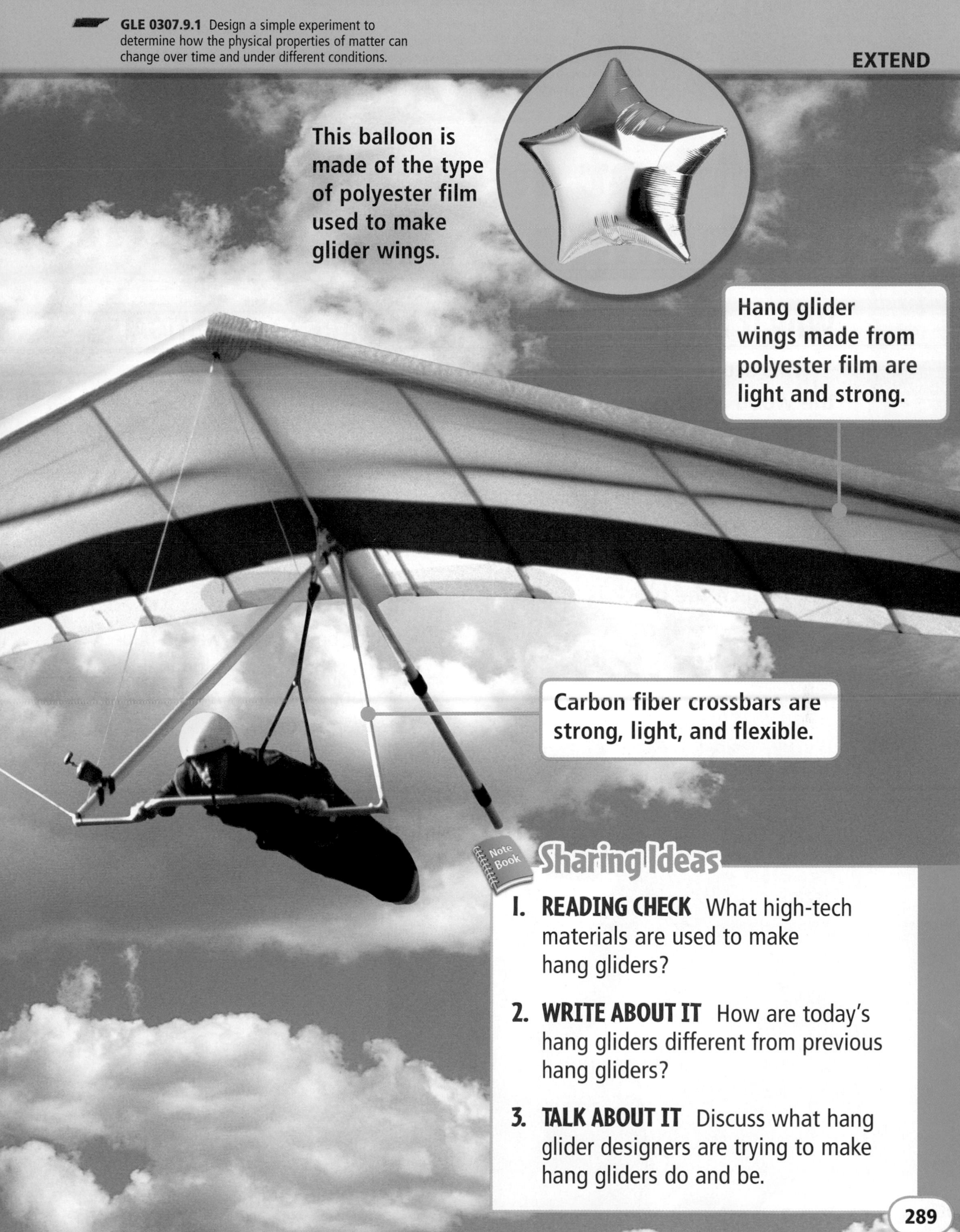

This balloon is made of the type of polyester film used to make glider wings.
Hang glider wings made from polyester film are light and strong.
Carbon fiber crossbars are strong, light, and flexible.
Note Book

Sharing Ideas

1. **READING CHECK** What high-tech materials are used to make hang gliders?
2. **WRITE ABOUT IT** How are today's hang gliders different from previous hang gliders?
3. **TALK ABOUT IT** Discuss what hang glider designers are trying to make hang gliders do and be.

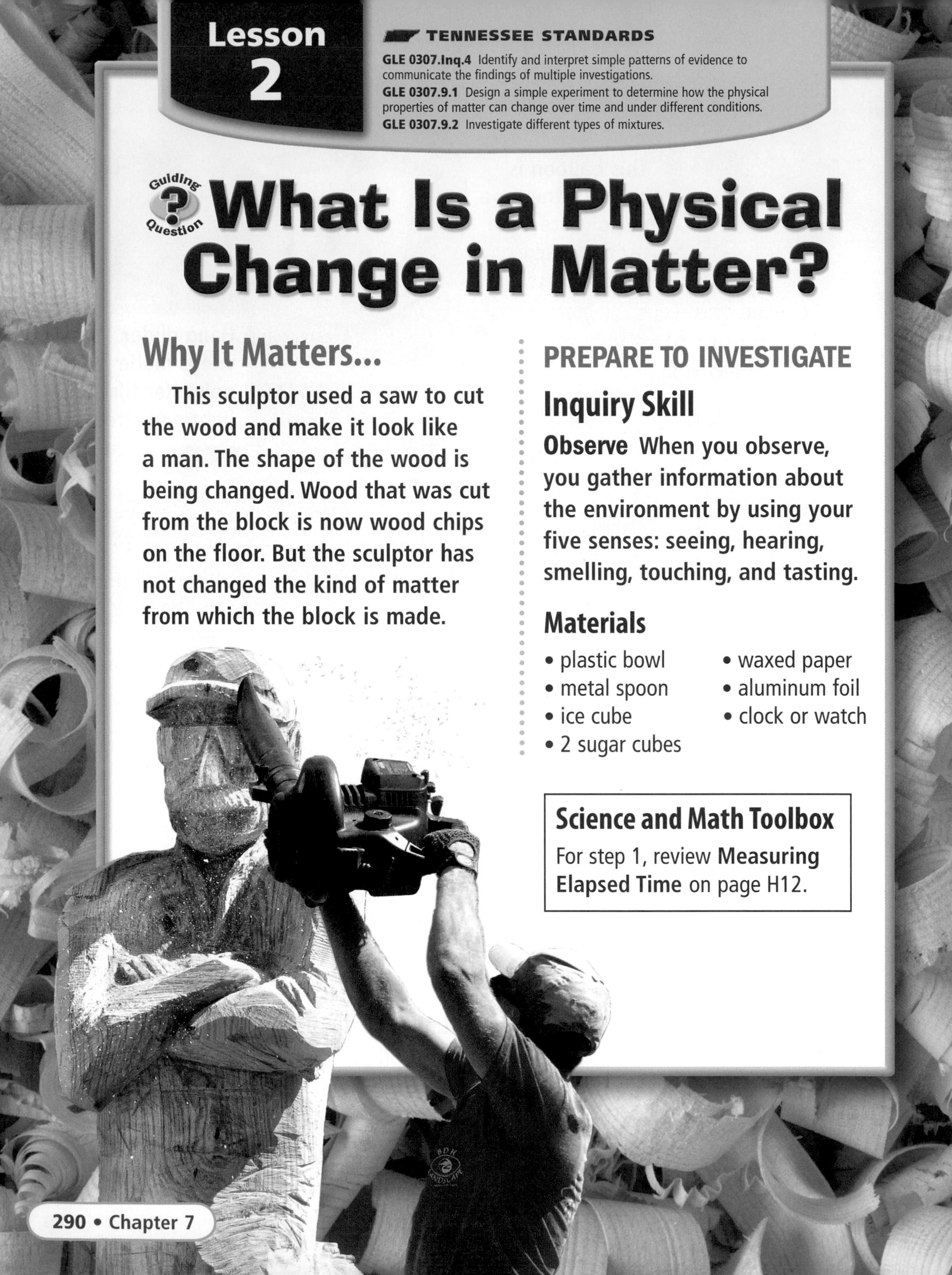

Lesson 2

TENNESSEE STANDARDS

GLE 0307.Inq.4 Identify and interpret simple patterns of evidence to communicate the findings of multiple investigations.

GLE 0307.9.1 Design a simple experiment to determine how the physical properties of matter can change over time and under different conditions.

GLE 0307.9.2 Investigate different types of mixtures.

Guiding Question

What Is a Physical Change in Matter?

Why It Matters...

This sculptor used a saw to cut the wood and make it look like a man. The shape of the wood is being changed. Wood that was cut from the block is now wood chips on the floor. But the sculptor has not changed the kind of matter from which the block is made.

PREPARE TO INVESTIGATE

Inquiry Skill

Observe When you observe, you gather information about the environment by using your five senses: seeing, hearing, smelling, touching, and tasting.

Materials

- plastic bowl
- metal spoon
- ice cube
- 2 sugar cubes
- waxed paper
- aluminum foil
- clock or watch

Science and Math Toolbox

For step 1, review **Measuring Elapsed Time** on page H12.

Directed Inquiry

Change It

Procedure

1. **Collaborate** Work with a partner. Place an ice cube in a plastic bowl. Observe the ice cube after 10 minutes. Record your observations in your Science Notebook.
2. **Compare** Use a metal spoon to crush a sugar cube wrapped in waxed paper. Unwrap the crushed cube and compare it to an uncrushed one. Record how they are alike and different.
3. **Observe** Record how a sheet of aluminum foil looks. Then gently crumple the foil into a loose ball. Again record how the foil looks.
4. **Compare** Now carefully pull apart the crumpled foil ball. Flatten and smooth it. Record how the foil was changed in steps 3 and 4.

STEP 1

STEP 2

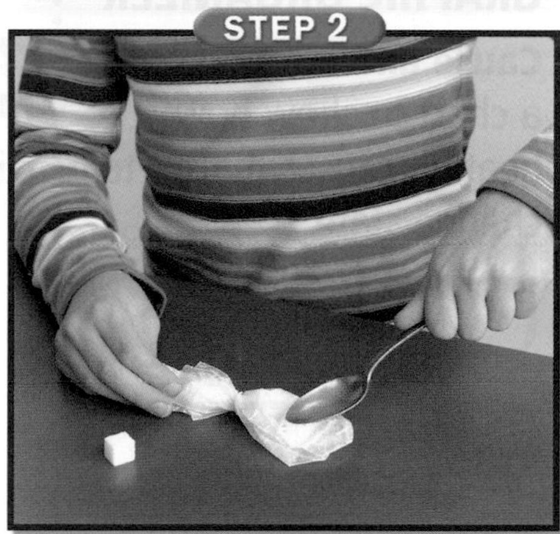

STEP 4

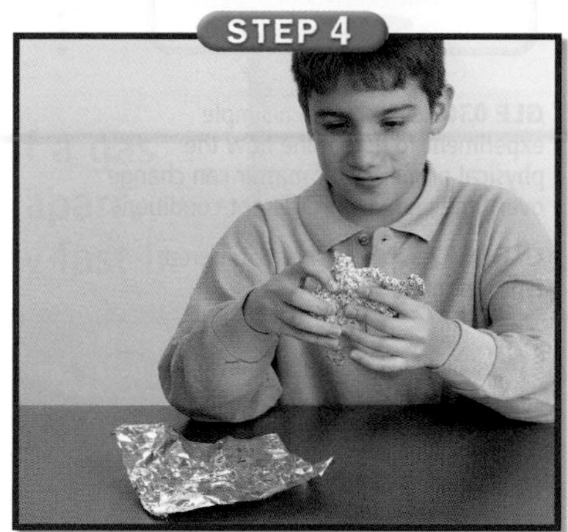

Think and Write

1. **Infer** What caused the ice cube to change in step 1?
2. **Compare** How are the changes in the ice cube and the sugar cube alike? How are they different?
3. **Compare** How are the changes in the aluminum foil and the sugar cube alike? How are they different?

✓ 0307.9.2, ✓ 0307.9.3

Guided Inquiry

Design an Experiment

How would the melted ice cube change if you put it in a freezer? Design and carry out an experiment to find out. Then compare your results to the original ice cube.

Icy Blooms

Many flowers bloom in the spring. But frost flowers, or ice flowers, appear in cold weather in late fall or early winter.

Actually, frost flowers aren't really flowers. They are delicate ribbons of ice. They appear when the air is cold but the ground is not yet frozen.

Frost flowers form when the sap in some kinds of plants freezes and then expands. This action causes cracks to open along the stem. Water in the stem pushes out through the cracks. When it freezes, thin ice "petals" with amazing shapes form.

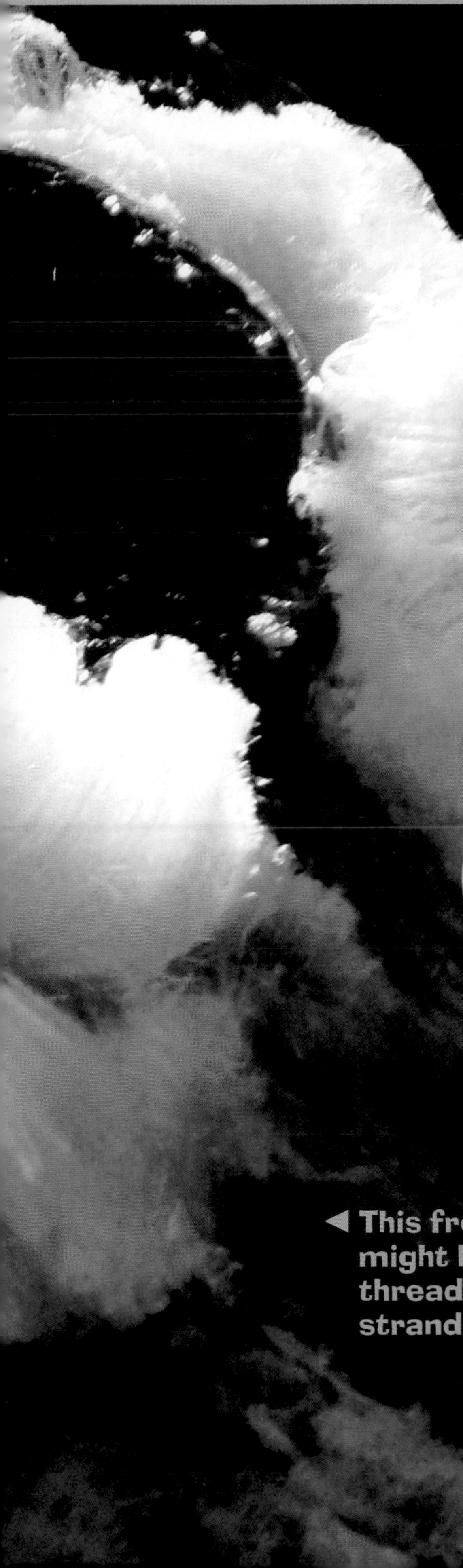

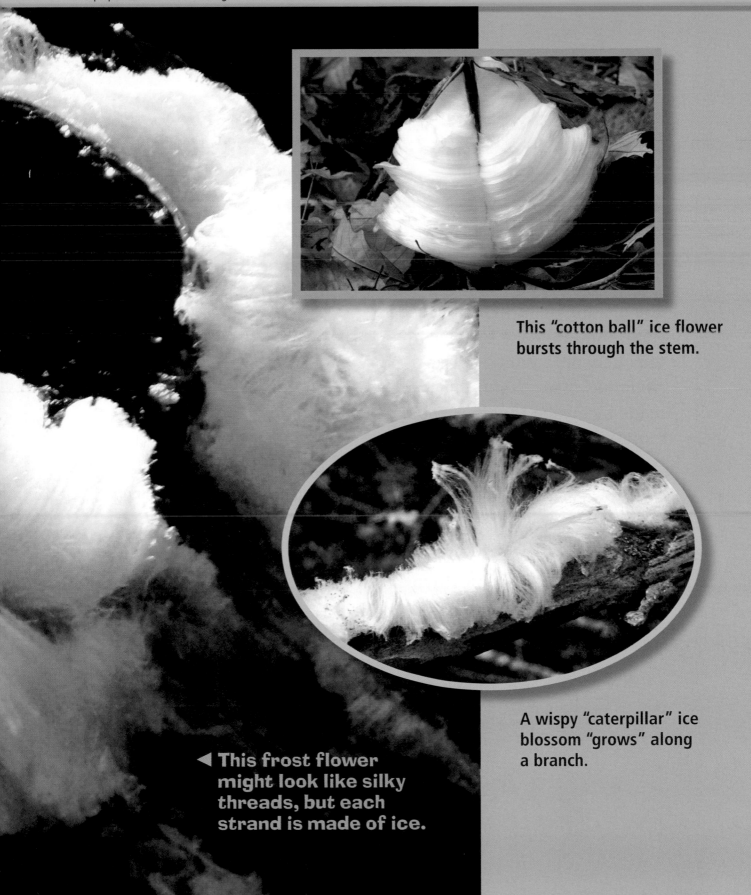

This "cotton ball" ice flower bursts through the stem.

A wispy "caterpillar" ice blossom "grows" along a branch.

◀ **This frost flower might look like silky threads, but each strand is made of ice.**

Lesson 3

TENNESSEE STANDARDS

GLE 0307.Inq.3 Organize data into appropriate tables, graphs, drawings, or diagrams.
GLE 0307.9.1 Design a simple experiment to determine how the physical properties of matter can change over time and under different conditions.
GLE 0307.9.2 Investigate different types of mixtures.

Guiding Question

How Are Mixtures Made?

Why It Matters . . .

You gather milk, strawberries, and ice to make a fruit smoothie. You mix the items in a blender. The items used to make the smoothie look very different now. Like a smoothie, many useful things are made by mixing together two or more kinds of matter.

PREPARE TO INVESTIGATE

Inquiry Skill

Observe When you observe, you gather information using your five senses: sight, smell, touch, taste, and hearing.

Materials

- paper clips
- toothpicks
- dry beans
- rice
- water
- salt
- plastic spoon
- 6 small plastic bowls

Science and Math Toolbox

For step 1, review **Making a Chart to Organize Data** on page H10.

Directed Inquiry

The Great Mix-Up

Procedure

1. **Collaborate** Work in a small group. In your Science Notebook, make a chart like the one shown.
2. Fill each of five small plastic bowls halfway with one of the following materials: paper clips, toothpicks, dry beans, rice, and water. Put a spoonful of salt into a sixth bowl.
3. **Observe** Look at the material in each bowl. Smell and touch it. Record your observations in your chart. **Safety:** Do not taste any materials.
4. **Record Data** Pour the paper clips into the bowl of toothpicks and stir them together. Observe and record the properties of the mixed materials.
5. **Record Data** Repeat step 4, pouring the beans into the rice.
6. **Record Data** Repeat step 4, pouring the salt into the water.

STEP 1

Material	Properties before mixing	Properties after mixing
paper clips		
toothpicks		
beans		
rice		
salt		
water		

STEP 4

STEP 5

Think and Write

1. **Analyze Data** Which materials changed when you mixed them together? How did they change?
2. **Predict** What will happen if you mix beans and paper clips?

✓ 0307.9.4

Guided Inquiry

Design an Experiment

Mix together three or more of the materials. Have the properties of the materials changed after being mixed together? Give reasons for your answer.

Lesson 4

TENNESSEE STANDARDS

GLE 0307.Inq.2 Select and use appropriate tools and simple equipment to conduct an investigation.
GLE 0307.9.2 Investigate different types of mixtures.
GLE 0307.9.3 Describe different methods to separate mixtures.

How Can Mixtures Be Separated?

Why It Matters...

Some people still pan for gold in the American West. They scoop up sand and water into a shallow pan. Then they swirl the mixture around. Gold dust is heavier than the rest of the sand. As the pan is swirled, the gold dust sinks to the bottom. Panning is one way to separate a mixture.

PREPARE TO INVESTIGATE

Inquiry Skill

Record Data **When you record data, you write measurements, predictions, and observations about an experiment.**

Materials

- mixtures from Lesson 3
- magnet
- strainer
- clock or watch with second hand

Science and Math Toolbox

For steps 2 and 3, review **Measuring Elapsed Time** on pages H12–H13.

Directed Inquiry

Un-mixing Mixtures

Procedure

1. **Collaborate** Work with a partner. In your Science Notebook, make a chart like the one shown.

2. **Record Data** Separate a mixture of paper clips and toothpicks by hand. Have your partner time you. Record the time in your chart.

3. **Measure** Mix the toothpicks and paper clips together again. Keep time as your partner uses a magnet to separate the mixture. Record the time in your chart.

4. **Measure** Repeat steps 2 and 3 with a mixture of beans and rice. For step 3, use a strainer instead of the magnet.

5. **Observe** Put two spoonfuls of water in a dish. Mix in one spoonful of salt. Leave the mixture in a sunny spot until the water evaporates. Record how long it takes for the water to dry up.

STEP 1

Mixture	By Hand	Using a Tool
Paper clips and toothpicks		
Beans and rice		

STEP 2

STEP 4

Think and Write

1. **Analyze Data** In steps 2–5, which method of separating mixtures was fastest?

2. What property was used to separate the paper clips from the toothpicks in step 3?

3. **Infer** How do you know the properties of the salt and water did not change when they were mixed?

0307.9.5

Guided Inquiry

Design an Experiment

How could you speed up the separation of the salt and water? Plan an experiment and ask your teacher to help you conduct it.

Reading Science

▶ VOCABULARY

filter

▶ GRAPHIC ORGANIZER

Problem-Solution Use a chart to list one type of mixture and to describe how it could be separated.

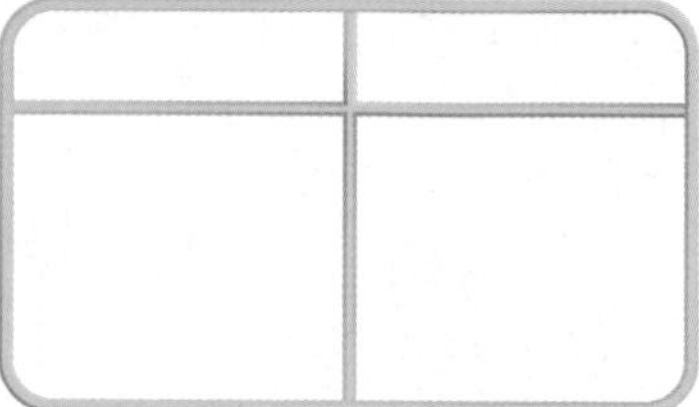

GLE 0307.9.2 Investigate different types of mixtures.

GLE 0307.9.3 Describe different methods to separate mixtures.

Separating Mixtures

Picking by Hand

If you're making a necklace, how do you choose which beads to use? You might look for beads with a certain color, shape, or size. Or maybe you want to use only beads made of wood or glass.

You have learned that color, shape, and size are physical properties. Wood has physical properties that make it different from metal, glass, or plastic. You can use the physical properties of substances in a mixture to choose the ones you want to take out, or separate, from the mixture.

You can separate the beads by color.

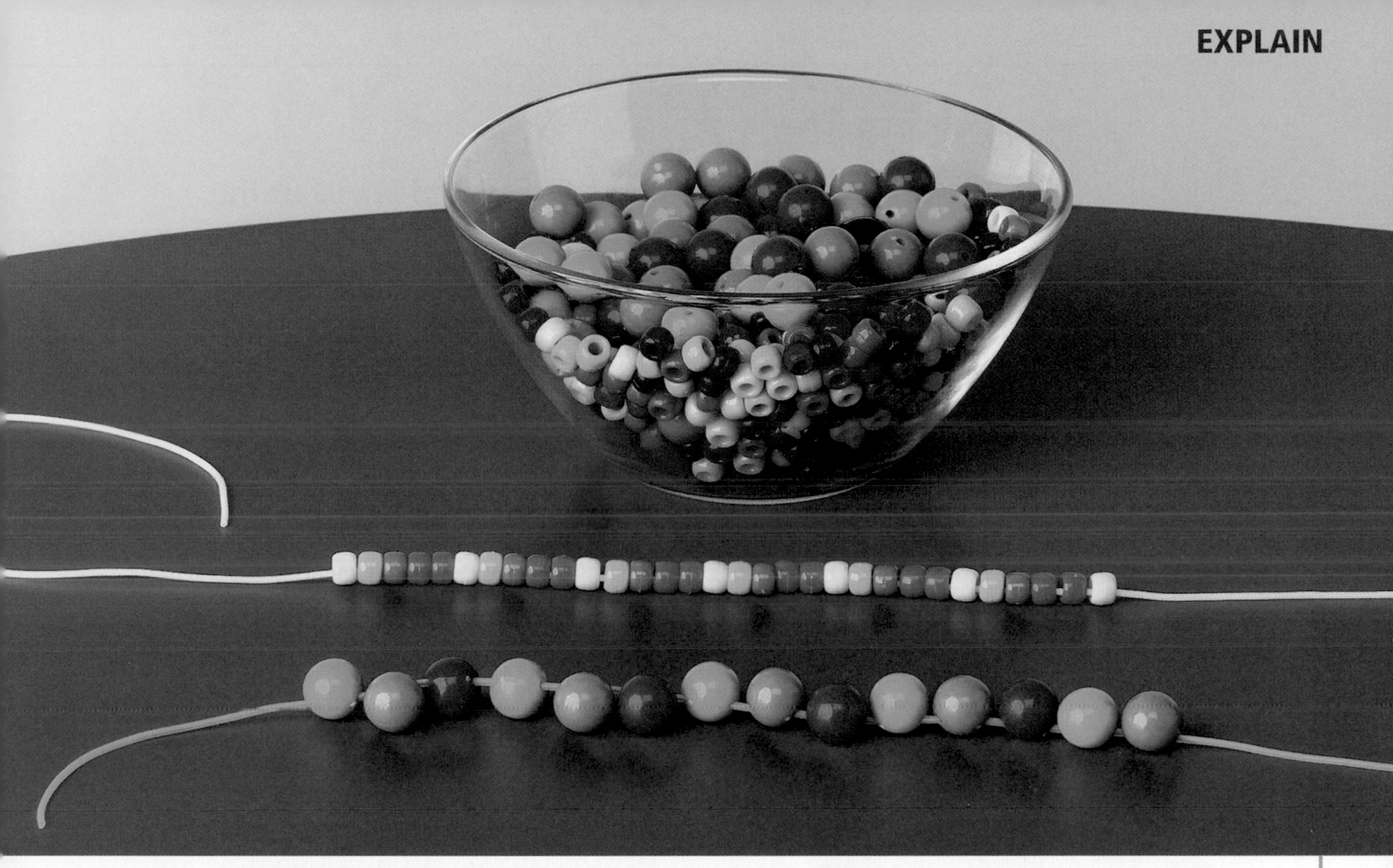

▲ **You can separate the beads by size, shape, or color.**

Sometimes the properties of substances in a mixture are easy to see and easy to handle. You can separate those substances by hand. You can easily pick out all the red beads or all the wooden beads. But suppose the beads were tiny, like grains of sand, or as large as boulders. Then it would be quite difficult to separate them by hand.

Mixtures made of solids are often easy to separate by hand. You can also separate some liquid mixtures and liquid-solid mixtures by hand. For a mixture of oil and water, you can skim most of the oil from the top of the water. You can pick out the rocks in a mixture of water and gravel. You can also carefully pour the water off.

FOCUS CHECK What physical properties make beads easy to separate by hand?

Using Tools

If you've ever sifted sand to find shells at the beach, then you've used a tool to separate a mixture. If the parts of a mixture are hard to see or to hold, you use tools to separate them. Using tools also saves time. At the beach, you can use a strainer to find shells. A strainer is a container that has many holes of the same size. When you put a mixture in a strainer, anything smaller than the holes falls through them. Anything larger stays in the strainer.

A strainer is a kind of filter (FIHL tur). A **filter** is a device or material that traps some substances and allows others to pass through. Water can pass through a coffee filter, but the coffee grounds cannot.

It would take a long time to dig through all of the sand-and-shell mixture in the pail to find every shell. The strainer quickly separates the sand from the shells.

A magnet can be used to quickly separate the paper clips from this mixture. ▶

Strainers and filters separate a mixture by the size of its parts. Other tools separate mixtures by other properties of the materials in the mixture. A magnet is a tool that attracts, or pulls on, objects that contain iron. A magnet can be used to pick up only the objects in a mixture that contain iron. Other objects that do not contain iron are left behind.

The temperature at which a substance melts is another property that can be used to separate substances in a mixture. Most metals are found mixed with rock in the earth. To separate the metal from the rock, the rock is heated until the metal melts and flows away. The rock melts at a higher temperature than the metal, so the rock stays solid.

FOCUS CHECK Identify two tools that are used to separate mixtures.

Express Lab

Activity Card
Separate a Mixture

Using Water

Water is another tool that can be used to separate mixtures. Some objects float in water. Other objects sink. You can use water to easily separate a mixture of corks and marbles in a container. If you pour water into the container, the corks float to the top and the marbles sink.

Some materials will mix completely and evenly with water. Other materials will not. You can separate a mixture of sand and salt by mixing it with water. The salt will mix completely with the water, seeming to disappear. The sand can be removed by filtering it from the salty water. But the salt cannot be separated by filtering. The pieces of salt have become so small, they will pass through any filter. How can you remove the salt from the water? If you allow the water to evaporate, the salt will be left behind.

FOCUS CHECK How can water be used to separate a mixture?

Corks and marbles have different properties. You can use water to separate a mixture of corks and marbles.

Lesson Wrap-Up

Visual Summary

A mixture can be separated by using the properties of the substances in the mixture.

Some mixtures can be easily separated by hand. Other mixtures can be separated by using tools.

Water is another tool that is used to separate mixtures.

Check for Understanding

SEPARATE MIXTURES

Work with a partner. Investigate different ways to separate a sand-and-water mixture. You will need clear plastic containers, water, sand, and a coffee filter. Make a new but identical mixture each time you experiment.

Try separating the mixture by allowing the sand to settle and then pouring off the water. Also try evaporating the water. Try a third method, using the coffee filter. Record all your observations. Which method gave the best results?

✓ 0307.9.5

Review

1. **MAIN IDEA** How can substances in a mixture be separated?
2. **VOCABULARY** What is a filter?
3. **READING SKILL: Problem-Solution** How can a mixture of rocks and sand be separated?
4. **CRITICAL THINKING: Apply** How could you quickly separate a mixture of steel thumbtacks and erasers without pricking your fingers on the sharp thumbtacks?
5. **INQUIRY SKILL: Record Data** Count the different mixtures mentioned in this lesson. Decide how many can be separated by hand, by evaporation, by using tools, and by using water. Record the data in a table.

TCAP Prep

To separate parts of a mixture by size, you would use a

Ⓐ magnet
Ⓑ cup of water
Ⓒ pan
Ⓓ strainer

SPI 0307.9.2

Go Digital Technology

Visit **www.eduplace.com/tnscp** to find out more about how mixtures can be separated.

LINKS for Home and School

GLE 0307.9.1 Design a simple experiment to determine how the physical properties of matter can change over time and under different conditions. **Math GLE 0306.4.4** Use appropriate units, strategies and tools to solve problems involving perimeter of linear units and capacity units. **ELA GLE 0301.3.3** Write in a variety of modes and genres, including narration, literary response, personal experience, and subject matter content.

Math Measure Physical Properties

The physical properties of matter include size, volume, and mass. Scientists use different tools to measure the physical properties of solids. A ruler can be used to measure length, width, and height. A balance can be used to measure mass.

Physical Properties of a Solid				
Length	Width	Height	Volume	Mass

1. Make a chart like the one shown. Record all your data in your chart. Use a ruler to measure a small box, a wood block, or a textbook. Measure and record the length, width, and height of the object.

2. Find the volume of the box by multiplying the length times the width times the height. Record your data.

3. Use a balance to find the mass of the box. Record your data.

Narrative

Window screens are a kind of filter. The small holes allow fresh air to pass through. At the same time, they keep out insects and other tiny pests. Imagine that you are the inventor of the window screen. Write an advertisement for your invention. Be sure you explain how it works.

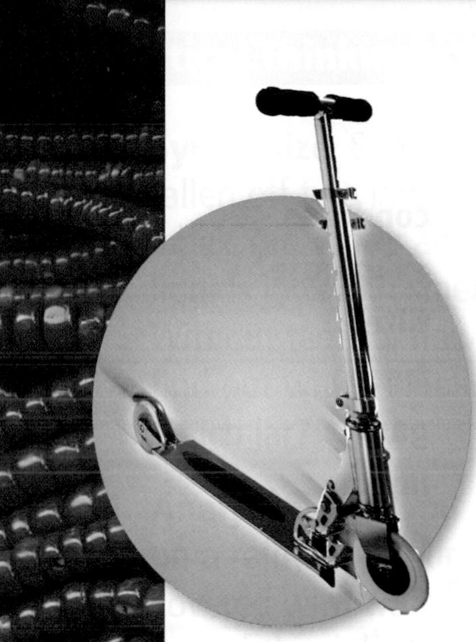

Metallurgist

What do bicycles, toasters, and cars have in common? They are all made with metal. Metallurgists are scientists who work with metals, usually at companies that make metal products. They know how to get metals out of rocks and how to create and use alloys.

What It Takes!

- A degree in metallurgical engineering, materials science, or materials engineering
- Strong problem-solving skills

Jewelry Designer

Creating jewelry is part art and part science. Jewelry designers use artistic abilities to craft pieces that will attract customers' attention. They use science knowledge to work with all sorts of precious metals and gems. For example, to shape rings into different sizes, jewelry designers must have an understanding of the properties of metals like gold and silver.

What It Takes!

- A high-school diploma
- Courses in gemology, jewelry manufacturing, and jewelry design

Chapter 8

Heat and Sound Energy

Lesson Preview

LESSON

1

On a cold day you drink a cup of hot cocoa to feel warm. What is heat, how is it produced, and how does it move?

LESSON

2

Music travels through the air and echoes bounce off walls. What is sound and how does it move?

Fun Facts

A lightning bolt heats the air so that it is three times hotter than the surface of the Sun.

Vocabulary Preview

conductor
crest
friction
heat
pitch
thermal energy
trough
vibrate
volume
wave

Vocabulary Strategies

Have you ever seen any of these terms before? Do you know what they mean?

↓

Describe, explain, or give an example of the vocabulary terms in your own words.

↓

Draw a picture, symbol, example, or other image that describes the term.

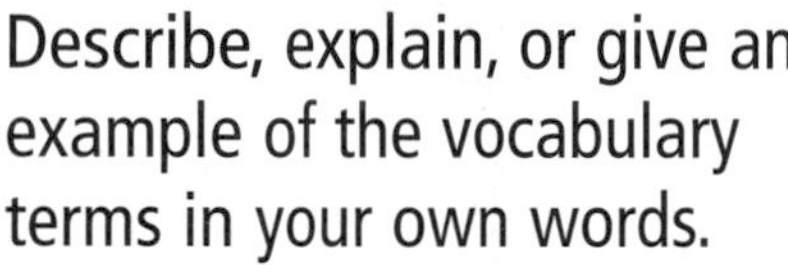

Glossary p. H16

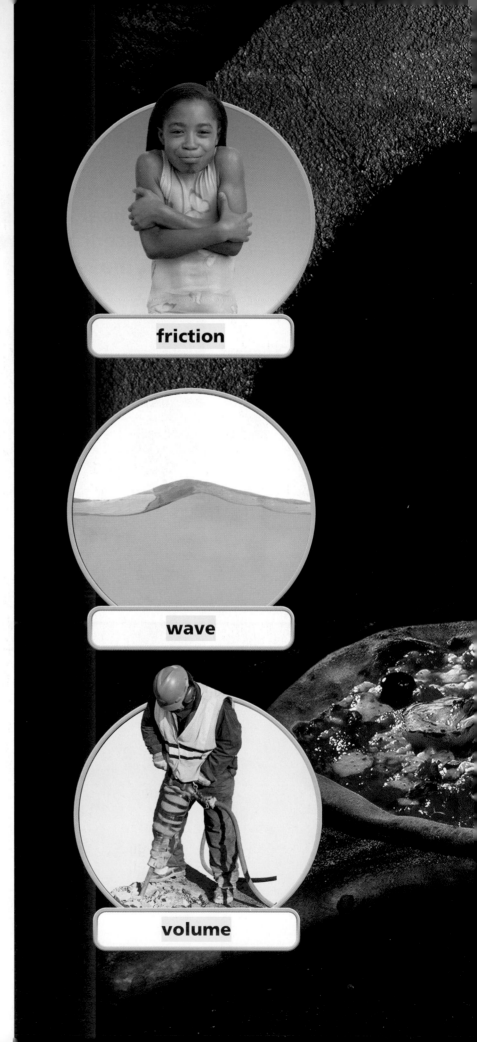

friction

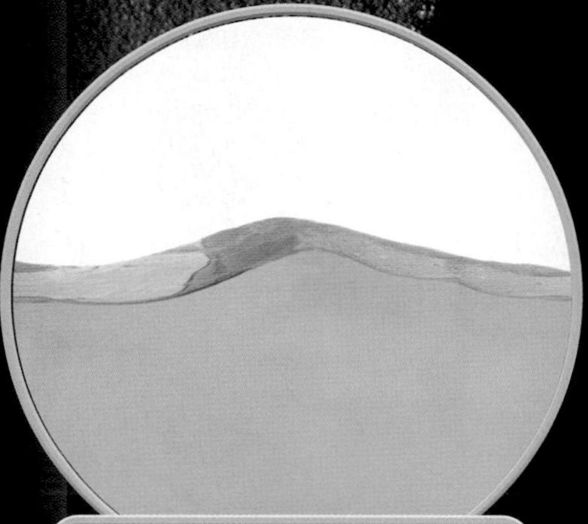

wave

volume

thermal energy

Start with Your Standards

Inquiry

GLE 0307.Inq.4 Identify and interpret simple patterns of evidence to communicate the findings of multiple investigations.

GLE 0307.Inq.6 Compare the results of an investigation with what scientists already accept about this question.

Physical Science

Standard 10 Energy

GLE 0307.10.1 Investigate phenomena that produce heat.

GLE 0307.10.2 Design and conduct an experiment to investigate the ability of different materials to conduct heat.

Standard 11 Motion

GLE 0307.11.3 Investigate how the pitch and volume of a sound can be changed.

Interact with this chapter.

www.eduplace.com/tnscp

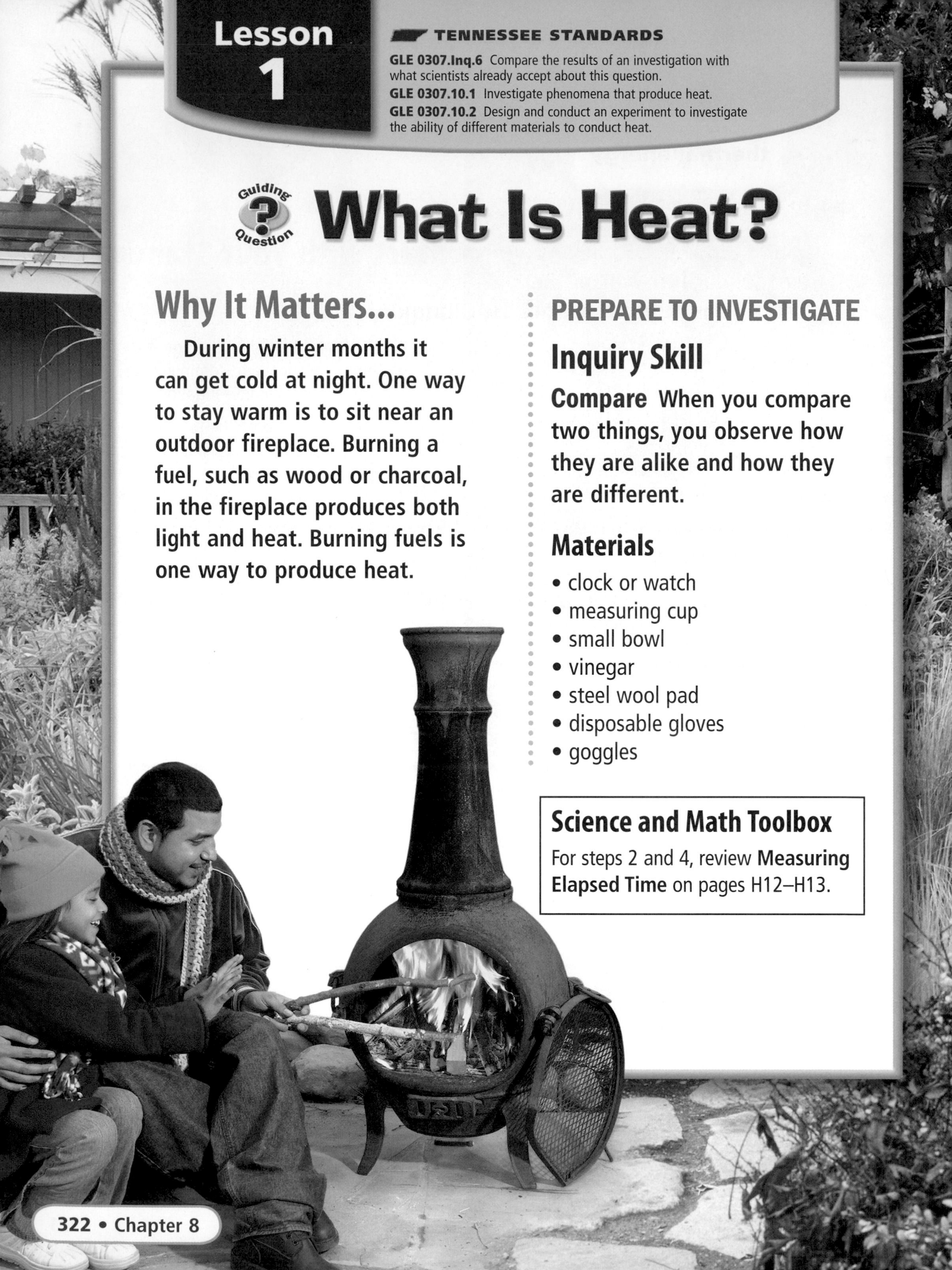

Lesson 1

TENNESSEE STANDARDS

GLE 0307.Inq.6 Compare the results of an investigation with what scientists already accept about this question.

GLE 0307.10.1 Investigate phenomena that produce heat.

GLE 0307.10.2 Design and conduct an experiment to investigate the ability of different materials to conduct heat.

Guiding Question

What Is Heat?

Why It Matters...

During winter months it can get cold at night. One way to stay warm is to sit near an outdoor fireplace. Burning a fuel, such as wood or charcoal, in the fireplace produces both light and heat. Burning fuels is one way to produce heat.

PREPARE TO INVESTIGATE

Inquiry Skill

Compare When you compare two things, you observe how they are alike and how they are different.

Materials

- clock or watch
- measuring cup
- small bowl
- vinegar
- steel wool pad
- disposable gloves
- goggles

Science and Math Toolbox

For steps 2 and 4, review **Measuring Elapsed Time** on pages H12–H13.

Directed Inquiry

Feel the Heat

Procedure

1. **Observe** Hold your hands together. Do they feel cool or warm? Record your observations in your Science Notebook.
2. **Compare** Rub your hands together very quickly for 10 seconds. Notice whether they feel cooler or warmer than they did before. Record your observations.
3. **Observe** Pick up a steel wool pad and hold it in your hands. Record whether it feels cool or warm.
4. **Measure** Pour $\frac{1}{4}$ cup of vinegar into a bowl. Place the steel wool pad in the bowl for 2 minutes. Then remove the pad and squeeze it out over the bowl. Place the pad on a paper towel to dry for 5 minutes. **Safety:** Wear goggles and disposable gloves.
5. **Compare** Remove the gloves and feel the steel wool pad. Record whether it feels different than it did in step 3.

STEP 2

STEP 3

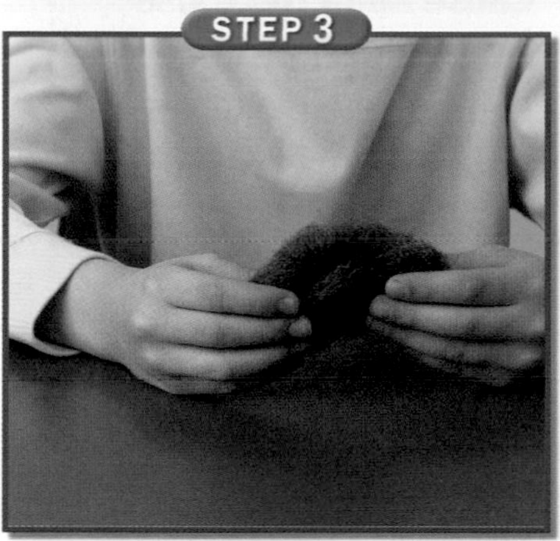

STEP 4

Think and Write

1. **Infer** What was the effect of rubbing your hands together in step 2?
2. **Infer** Mixing two kinds of materials can cause them to change and produce heat. Infer whether materials changed in steps 4 and 5. Explain your inference.

✓ 0307.Inq.4

Guided Inquiry

Experiment Find out how a coin feels before and after rubbing it against sandpaper, cement, and cloth. Then research what scientists know about the kind of energy produced when surfaces rub. Compare this with your results.

Reading Science

Heat

▶ VOCABULARY

- conductor
- friction
- heat
- thermal energy

▶ GRAPHIC ORGANIZER

Cause and Effect Use a chart to show how thermal energy moves from a warmer object to a cooler object.

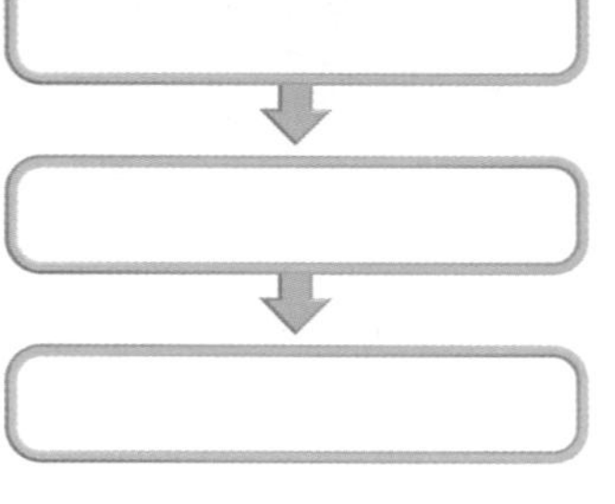

GLE 0307.10.1 Investigate phenomena that produce heat.

GLE 0307.10.2 Design and conduct an experiment to investigate the ability of different materials to conduct heat.

Thermal Energy

All the things around you are made of matter. All matter is made of tiny invisible particles that are always moving. The energy of moving particles in matter is called **thermal energy**. The more thermal energy an object has, the faster its particles move.

You feel thermal energy as heat. **Heat** is the flow of thermal energy from warmer objects to cooler objects. Thermal energy is sometimes called heat energy.

You know that heat energy moves because you know that cold objects get warmer. Think about what happens when you eat a frozen juice pop on a hot day.

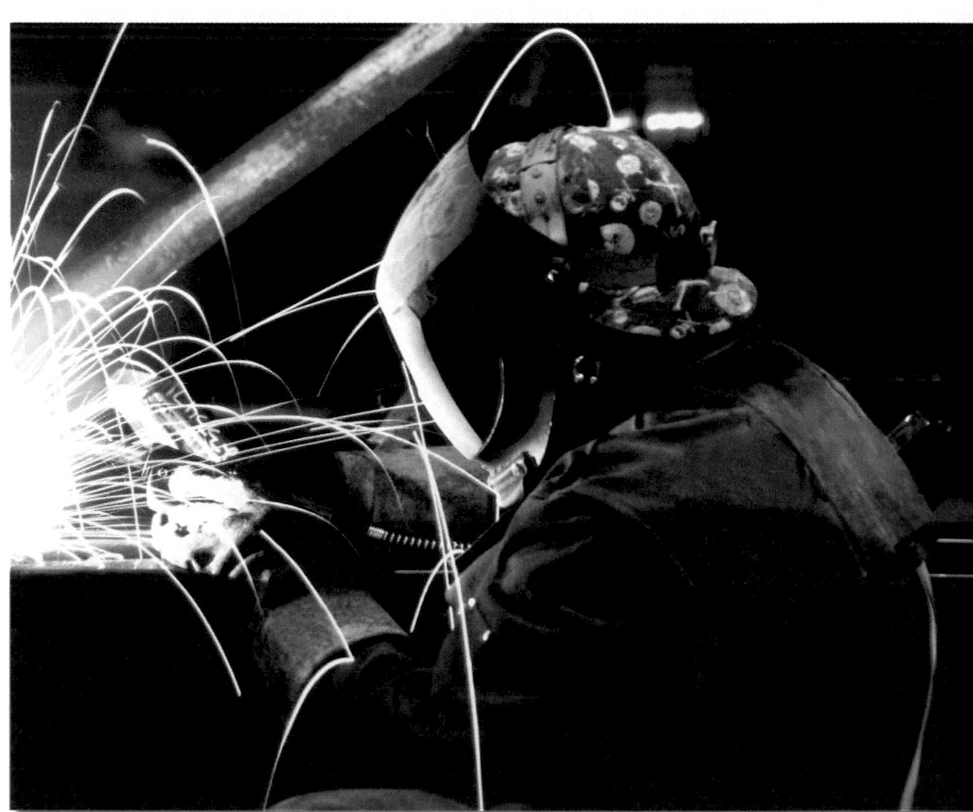

A welder uses heat to melt metal. ▶

Why does your hand feel cold when you hold an ice cube? Heat moves from your hand to the ice cube. The ice melts because its particles gain thermal energy. A mug of hot chocolate heats your hands because heat moves from the warm mug to your cooler hands.

Look below to see how heat moves from hot cereal. After a few minutes, the cereal is cooler. The spoon, which was placed in the cereal, is now warmer. If you held your hand over the cereal, you would feel the heat.

The spoon and the air have gained heat, so they have become warmer. The cereal has lost heat, so it has become cooler. This flow of heat will continue until the cereal, the air, and the spoon are all equally warm.

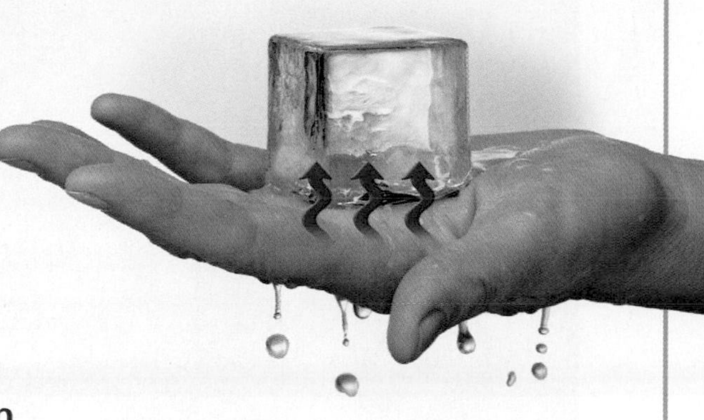

▲ **When you hold an ice cube, heat from your warm hand moves to the cold ice. Your hand feels cold because it has lost heat.**

FOCUS CHECK What causes an object to feel warm when you touch it?

◀ **Heat moves from the hot cereal to the cooler spoon and to the surrounding air.**

Express Lab

Activity Card
Observe Effects of Friction

▲ A heat lamp gives off enough energy to keep these chicks warm.

Producing Heat

There are many ways to produce heat. You can produce heat by rubbing your hands together quickly. You know that heat has been produced because your hands feel warm. The reason rubbing your hands together produces heat is because of friction (FRIHK shuhn). **Friction** is a force that occurs when one object rubs against another object. Friction slows down and stops motion between two surfaces that touch.

Look at the photo of the baby chicks. It shows heat being produced in another way. Electricity moving through the lamp bulb changes to heat, which warms the chicks. Toasters, electric stoves, and hair dryers all use electricity to produce heat.

Another way to produce heat is to mix different kinds of matter. Mixing matter can produce a change in the matter, called a chemical change. Often when a chemical change occurs, heat is given off.

There are many examples of changes in matter that produce heat. When a piece of steel wool is placed in vinegar, a change occurs. Heat can be felt when the steel wool is touched. A heat pack, such as the one in the photo, is another example. When the pack is squeezed, different kinds of matter mix together and change. The heat that is produced can be used to warm hands on a cold day.

Burning fuels is another way to produce heat. Think about why you feel heat from a campfire. When wood is burned, the wood changes to another kind of matter and heat is given off. Many homes are heated by burning fuel oil or natural gas.

▲ **How does this hand warmer heat pack get warm?**

FOCUS CHECK What causes your hands to get warm when you rub them together?

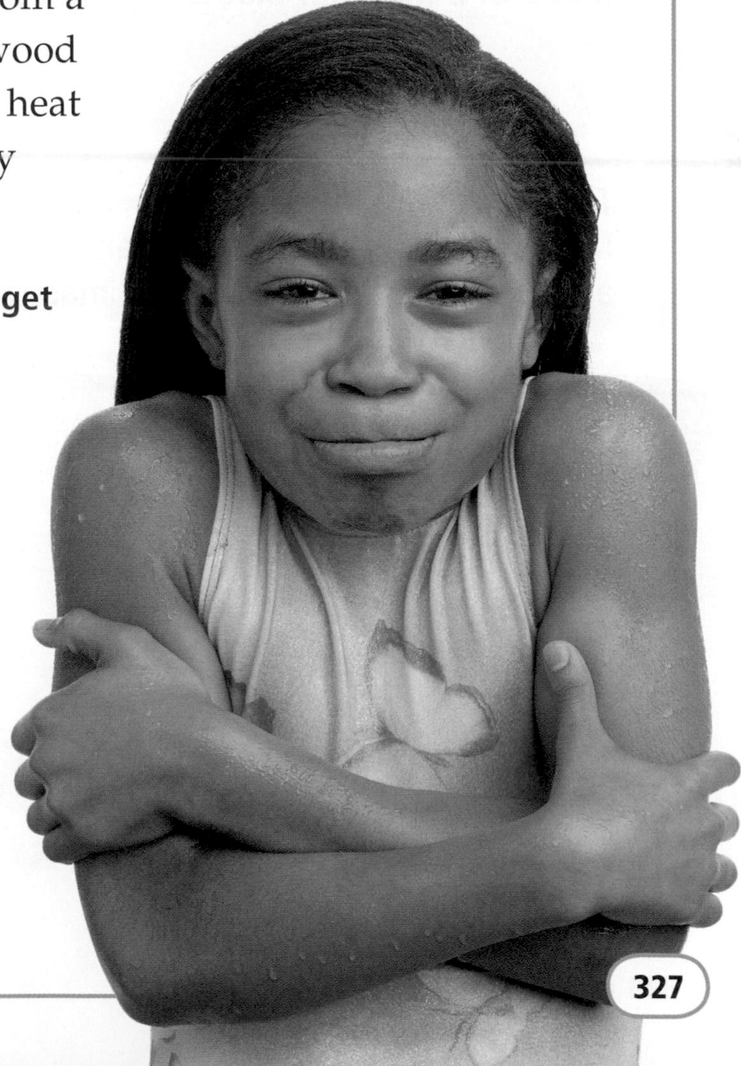

Quickly rubbing your arms can make you feel warmer when you are cold. Friction between your moving hands and your arms produces heat. ▶

Conductors

Heat moves more easily through some materials than through others. Any material that allows heat to move through it easily is called a **conductor**. Most metals are good heat conductors. That is why pots and pans are usually made of such metals as steel and aluminum. Heat can move quickly from the heat source, through the pot, and into the uncooked food.

Glass and ceramic materials also conduct heat, but not as easily as most metals do. Pans made of these materials heat up more slowly than those made of metal. They also take longer to cool. So once a glass or ceramic pan is removed from a heat source, it will keep food inside it warmer for a longer time.

FOCUS CHECK Why are most pots and pans made of a material that is a good conductor?

These pans are made of different conductors. Metal conducts heat better than glass or ceramic, and will heat faster than these materials.

Lesson Wrap-Up

Visual Summary

	Heat is the flow of thermal energy from warmer objects to cooler objects.
	Heat can be produced by rubbing, by electricity, by burning fuels, and by mixing matter.
	Some materials are good heat conductors. Metal conducts heat better than glass does.

Check for Understanding

OBSERVE SOURCES OF HEAT
Work with a partner to carry out these investigations.

- Have an ice-cube-melting race. Put one ice cube on a paper plate in a sunny window. At the same time, put another ice cube on a plate in a cool, shady location. Time the melting of each ice cube. Record your results. Explain any difference in melting time.
- Sharpen a pencil. Quickly feel the sharpened end and describe what you feel. Explain the result.
- Take turns shaking a small, closed can of metal washers for 3 minutes. Open the can. Feel the washers. Explain the result. ✓ **0307.10.1**

Review

1. **MAIN IDEA** What is one way to produce heat?
2. **VOCABULARY** What is friction?
3. **READING SKILL: Cause and Effect** What effect does putting a metal spoon in hot water have on the spoon?
4. **CRITICAL THINKING: Evaluate** You hold a cup of ice, and your hand becomes cold. A friend says that cold from the cup moved to your hand. Is your friend's statement correct? Explain.
5. **INQUIRY SKILL: Compare** How is the way a toaster produces heat different from the way a campfire produces heat?

TCAP Prep

Grilling vegetables on a fire fueled by charcoal is an example of heat produced by

Ⓐ friction
Ⓑ burning
Ⓒ mixing different kinds of matter
Ⓓ electricity

SPI 0307.10.1

Go Digital Technology

Visit **www.eduplace.com/tnscp** to learn more about heat.

Almost Not There!

Hey! Why aren't those crayons melting?

The answer can be found in that strange stuff they're sitting on. It looks like blue smoke, but it's actually a solid called aerogel. Aerogel is the lightest solid in the world. It is mostly air, and is the best insulator ever invented. Insulators don't allow heat to move through them easily.

Why does aerogel provide such great insulation? It has a spongelike structure that traps pockets of air. Trapped air is a good insulator. Aerogel insulates in the way that a puffy jacket does. One day aerogel may be used in the walls of your home to keep you warm.

Ghostly cube
How light is aerogel? A cube of aerogel 20 ft by 20 ft would weigh less than a ten-year-old child!

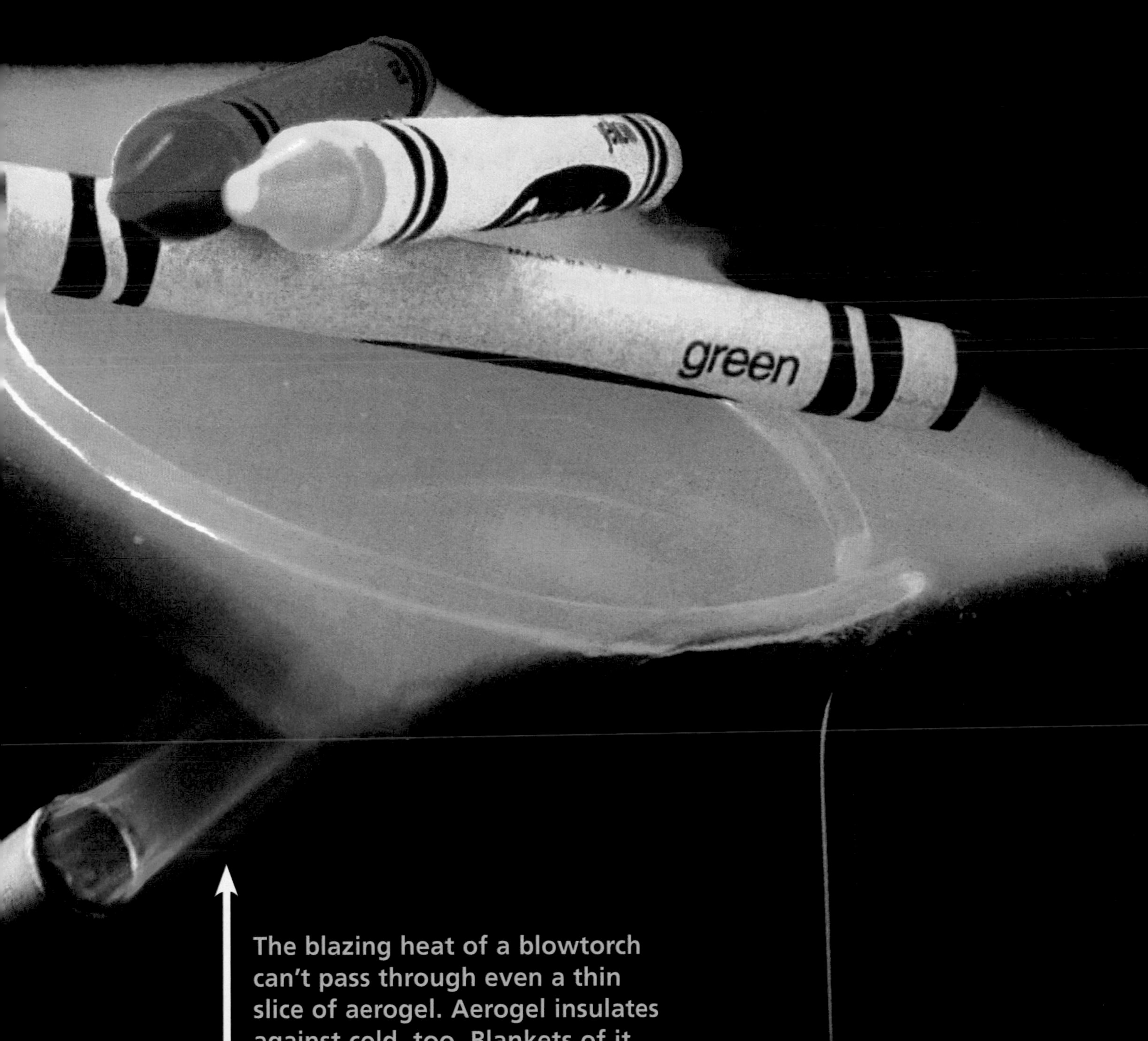

The blazing heat of a blowtorch can't pass through even a thin slice of aerogel. Aerogel insulates against cold, too. Blankets of it keep electronic instruments from freezing in outer space.

Lesson 2

TENNESSEE STANDARDS

GLE 0307.Inq.4 Identify and interpret simple patterns of evidence to communicate the findings of multiple investigations.
GLE 0307.11.3 Investigate how the pitch and volume of a sound can be changed.

What Is Sound?

Why It Matters...

You may have made waves in a parachute in gym class. You have probably made waves on water. Waves are a way energy moves from one place to another. Many familiar forms of energy, including sound, move in waves.

PREPARE TO INVESTIGATE

Inquiry Skill

Observe When you observe, you gather information about the environment, using your five senses: seeing, hearing, smelling, touching, and tasting.

Materials

- empty coffee can
- metal spoon
- large washer
- string
- hand lens
- sand
- goggles

Science and Math Toolbox

For step 2, review **Using a Hand Lens** on page H2.

Directed Inquiry

Seeing Sounds

Procedure

1. **Collaborate** Work with a partner. Turn an empty coffee can upside down. Have your partner tap the bottom of the can with a spoon. In your Science Notebook, record what happens. **Safety**: Wear goggles.

2. **Observe** Place a few grains of sand on the bottom of the can. As your partner taps the can with the spoon, use a hand lens to observe the grains of sand. Record your observations.

3. **Record Data** Hold a metal washer by the edge. Use the spoon to tap the washer. Record your observations.

4. **Observe** Now tie one end of a string to the washer. Have your partner hold the other end of the string so that the washer hangs. Tap the washer with the spoon. Record your observations.

STEP 1

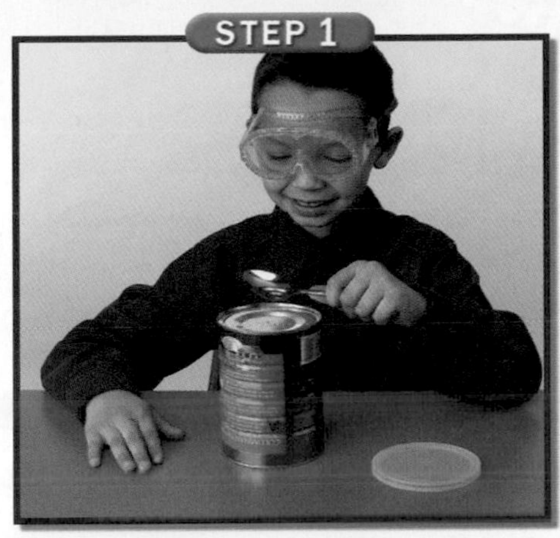

STEP 2

STEP 4

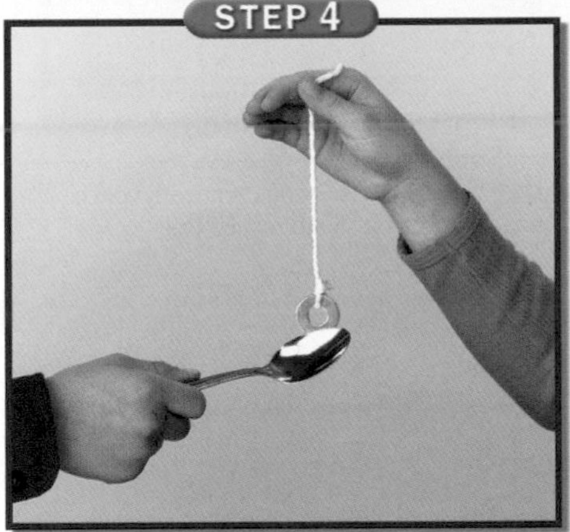

Think and Write

1. **Observe** What happened to the sand grains in step 2? What do you think caused this?
2. **Compare** How did the noise the washer made differ in steps 3 and 4?
3. **Hypothesize** What might explain the difference in the sounds?

Guided Inquiry

Research Use the Internet or library to find information about musical instruments made from common objects, unusual materials, or junk. Describe how musicians use the objects to make music.

Reading Science

Waves

VOCABULARY

crest
pitch
trough
vibrate
volume
wave

GRAPHIC ORGANIZER

Draw Conclusions Use a chart to record what you can tell about a sound wave from the pitch and volume of the sound.

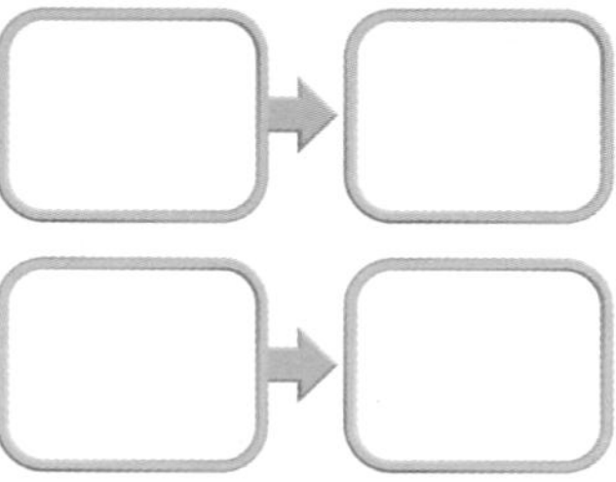

GLE 0307.11.3 Investigate how the pitch and volume of a sound can be changed.

How Energy Travels

Suddenly the side of a mountain slides into the ocean. It's a landslide! The energy of the moving rocks and soil creates waves in the ocean. These waves reach a distant island, where they push water onto the shore. How did the energy of the landslide move through the water? It traveled in waves. A **wave** is a movement that carries energy from one place to another.

Many forms of energy can travel in waves. Mechanical energy, heat energy, light energy, and sound energy can all travel in waves.

This wave moves particles of water up and down. The toy boat moves up and down as the wave's energy passes through the water.

water particles

wave energy

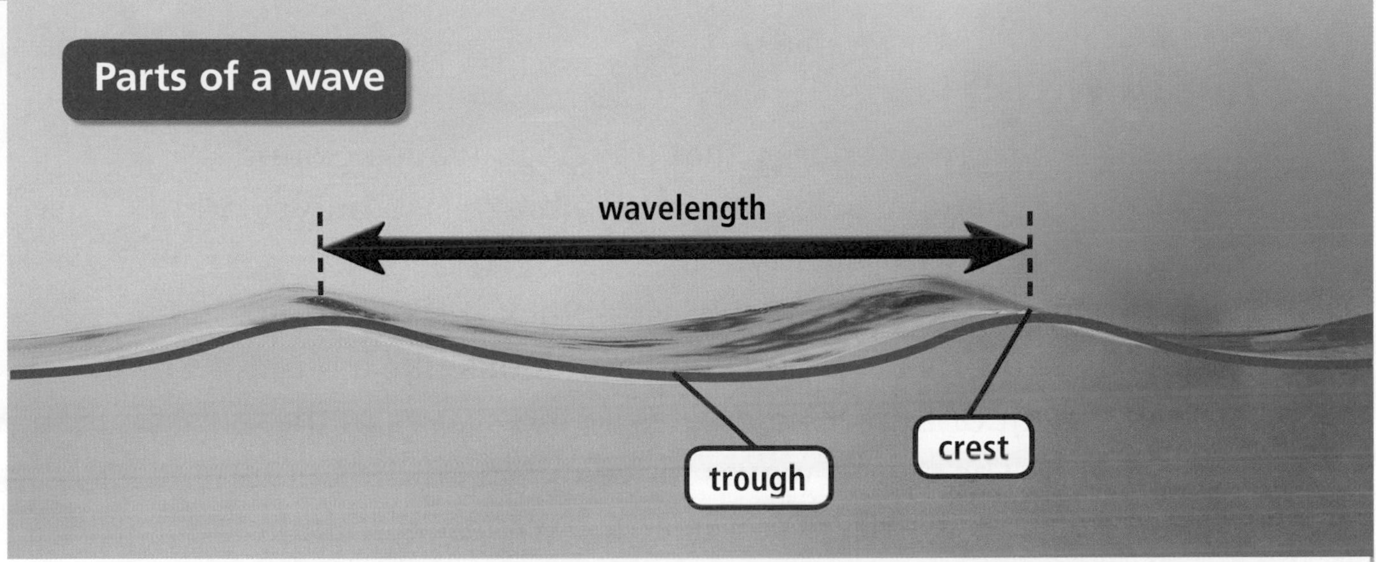

Measuring Waves

All waves have traits that can be measured. The **crest** of a wave is its highest point. The **trough** (trawf) of a wave is its lowest point. Waves with more energy have higher crests and deeper troughs.

The wavelength of a wave is the distance between one crest and the next crest or one trough and the next trough. Waves with shorter wavelengths have crests and troughs that are closer together. When crests (or troughs) are close together, each crest is followed quickly by the next. You can count how many crests pass by in a given time. This is the frequency (FREE kwuhn see) of the wave.

FOCUS CHECK If a wave has high crests and deep troughs, what can you conclude about how much energy the wave has?

Express Lab

Activity Card
Model a Sound Wave

Sound Waves

Sound is a form of energy that travels in waves. Sound is produced when particles of matter **vibrate** (VY brayt), or move back and forth quickly.

A guitar string vibrates when you pluck it. The string moves back and forth so quickly that it looks like a blur. The movement of the string creates sound waves in the air around it. The sound waves move out in all directions from the vibrating string. You hear the waves as sounds.

When a guitar string is plucked, it vibrates. The energy of the vibrations travels through the air as sound waves.

A sound wave moves particles of matter back and forth. It is like a spring that is squeezed and then released. As the sound wave travels through matter, particles of matter squeeze together and then spread apart. This happens over and over again as the wave moves away from its source. A crest is where particles of matter are bunched close together. A trough is where particles are spread far apart.

When a sound wave travels from its source, the particles that carry the wave do not travel with the wave. The particles move back and forth, but stay in the same general location. For this reason, a sound wave can travel only through matter. It cannot travel through empty space.

FOCUS CHECK Can noise from Earth travel to other planets in the solar system? Why or why not?

A sound wave moves particles of matter back and forth. Particles of air squeeze together and then spread apart as a sound wave passes through.

High and Low Sounds

There is a big difference between the tweet of a songbird and the growl of a lion. Vibrating matter produces both sounds. But one sound is much higher than the other. How high or low a sound seems is called **pitch** (pihch).

Pitch depends on the frequency of sound waves. High-pitched sounds have high-frequency sound waves. Low-pitched sounds have low-frequency sound waves. Small objects vibrate more quickly and make high-pitched sounds. Large objects vibrate more slowly and make low-pitched sounds.

▲ The shorter bars of the xylophone make higher-pitched sounds than the longer bars do.

◀ Blowing across the bottle openings produces sounds of different pitch. The pitch depends on the amount of air vibrating in the bottles. A small amount of air produces a high-pitched sound.

Loud and Soft Sounds

How loud or soft a sound seems is called **volume** (VAHL yoom). Volume depends on the size of the crests and troughs of sound waves. A sound with high volume, such as a siren, has waves with high crests and deep troughs. A sound with low volume, such as a whisper, has low crests and shallow troughs. Waves with high crests and deep troughs have more energy than waves with low crests and shallow troughs. You hear this difference in energy as a difference in volume.

FOCUS CHECK What can you conclude about sound waves that produce a high-pitched sound?

A jackhammer produces very loud sounds. High-volume sounds can hurt your ears. Ear protectors reduce the amount of sound that reaches the ears. ▼

▲ A mouse makes soft, high-pitched sounds.

Dolphins use sound to communicate. Dolphins can communicate over long distances because sound waves travel a long way through water.

Sound Moves Through Matter

Most of the time, you hear sound waves that travel through the air, which is gas. Sound waves can also travel through liquids. Dolphins use sound waves to communicate with each other under water. Sounds can also travel through solids, such as a wooden door. Sound waves travel faster through solids than liquids. They travel faster through liquids than gases.

Sound waves can reflect (rih FLEHKT), or bounce, off objects. Reflected sound waves are called echoes (EHK ohz). You can hear echoes when sound waves bounce off the face of a large building or the walls of a gym.

FOCUS CHECK Will a sound wave travel fastest through air, water, or wood?

Lesson Wrap-Up

Visual Summary

Waves are up-and-down or back-and-forth movements that carry energy.

Sound is the energy of vibrating matter. Sound travels as waves through matter.

Pitch depends on the frequency of sound waves. Volume depends on the size of the crests and troughs.

Check for Understanding

PLAY A SOUND GAME

Play a pitch and volume game with a partner. Get three plastic containers with lids. Place paper clips in one, plastic buttons in another, and pencil erasers in the third. Put the lid on each container.

With your partner's eyes closed, either shake one container very gently and then hard, or shake it hard and then gently. Your partner must tell which sound was louder—the first or second. Next, your partner must use the pitch of the sounds made to help identify the objects in the container. Then reverse roles with your partner. ✔ **0307.11.2**

Review

1. **MAIN IDEA** How does sound travel?
2. **VOCABULARY** What is the pitch of a sound?
3. **READING SKILL: Draw Conclusions** A jet engine produces a loud sound. What can you conclude about how much energy the engine produces?
4. **CRITICAL THINKING: Evaluate** A spaceship in a movie flies in outer space, where there is no matter. Its engines make a loud sound. Why is this not correct?
5. **INQUIRY SKILL: Observe** An organ has small and large pipes. Describe the pitch of the sounds produced by the different pipes.

TCAP Prep

Which property of a sound depends on the frequency of a sound wave?

Ⓐ pitch
Ⓑ volume
Ⓒ height
Ⓓ energy

SPI 0307.11.3

Go Digital Technology

Visit **www.eduplace.com/tnscp** to learn more about waves.

Sound Safari

What happens in a sound studio?

The setting is a classroom. A group of students is about to make its own sound studio. The students need to produce all kinds of sounds—growls, chirps, thunder, rattles, and echoes. How will they do it? Let's listen in!

Characters

Mr. Lee: teacher

Elaine, **Rena**, **Rico**, **David**: students

Sound Studio

Elaine: I have a question. Who decided we should put on a play called *Lost in the Jungle Cave*? I mean, couldn't we just do something simple? How about *Lost in the Library*? You don't need monkey sounds for that.

Rena: True, but you don't need a sound-effects team for that either. Libraries are pretty silent, remember?

Mr. Lee: All right, everybody, let's focus on the jungle, not the library. Rena, tell about the play, *Lost in the Jungle Cave*.

Rena: Okay. In the play, MuMu the Monkey runs into a cave after a thunderstorm. Her friend LuLu the Lion looks for her in the jungle. That means we need a monkey, a thunderstorm, a lion, and other jungle noises.

Rico: This is going to be great! I can make just about any animal sound. Squeak! Chirrrrrrp! GROWWWWL!

Rena: Is that supposed to be a lion? Lions don't GROWWWWL. They ROARRRR.

David: Does anybody know what a monkey sounds like? I read someplace that monkeys are really loud. Let me give it a try. I-I-I-I-EEEK-EEEK!

Rena: The script says that MuMu the monkey calls to LuLu from inside that cave. But all she can hear is her own echo! How can we make an echo?

Mr. Lee: We can make an echo in the gym later. Now, let's take a look in this bag of tricks *[pulls out a bag]*. I've got coconut shells, copper sheets, bits of tinfoil... .

Rena: These are for sound effects?

Mr. Lee: Think about sounds you might hear in the jungle.

David: What about bees? BUZZZZZZZZ. How's that?

Mr. Lee: Nice try, but not all animals make sounds the way we do. Bees wings move so fast that the air vibrates—and you hear a buzzing sound. Thunder works in a similar way.

Rena: *[confused]* But thunder doesn't buzz!

Mr. Lee: When lightning heats air, it makes the air vibrate. That creates sound waves and makes a loud boom.

Rico: So how can we make a thunder sound for the play?

Mr. Lee: In the 1700s, a fellow named John Dennis hung a large sheet of thin copper from the ceiling by wires. When he rattled it, it sounded like thunder. When someone copied Dennis's idea, he accused the man of "stealing my thunder!" It's a famous saying now.

Rena: I have an idea for the coconut shells. Listen. The lion is running to find MuMu. *[knocks coconut shell halves on table]*

David: Umm, that sounds like a horse running. There are no horses in the play.

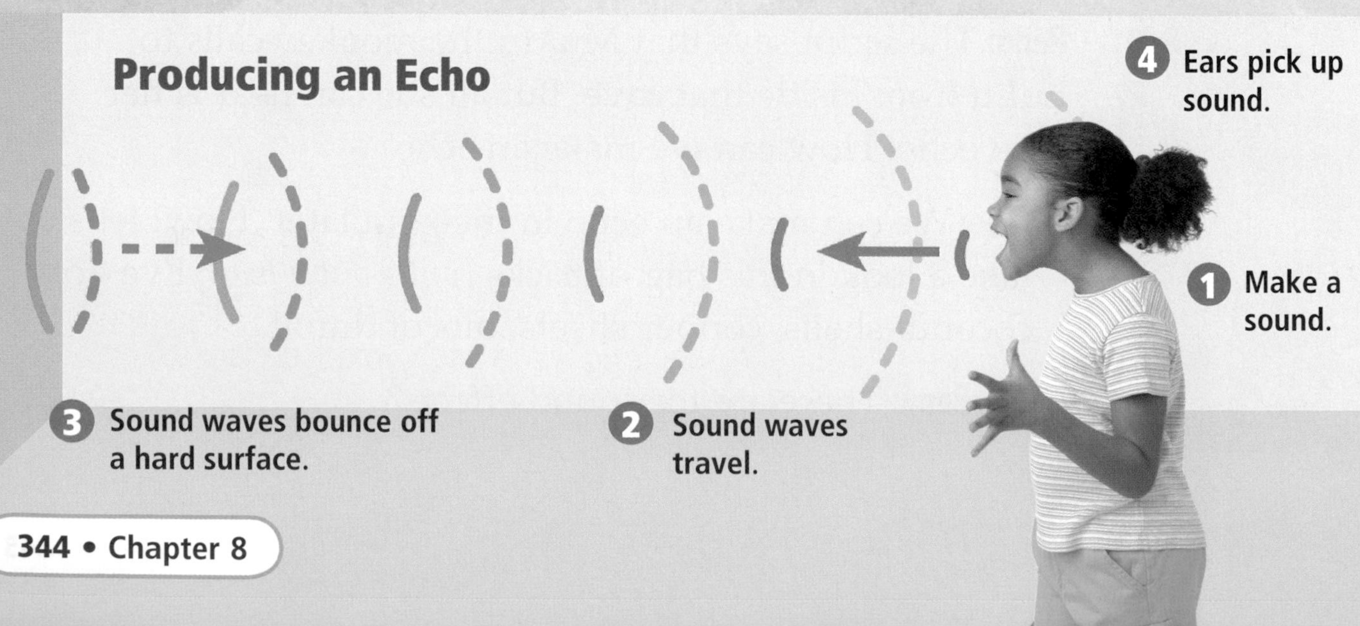
Producing an Echo
4 Ears pick up sound.
1 Make a sound.
3 Sound waves bounce off a hard surface.
2 Sound waves travel.

Elaine: Hey, if I rustle these bits of tinfoil, it sounds like animals running through leaves.

Rena: OK. MuMu is in the cave. From a distance, she hears Lulu. ROAR!

Elaine: When she is far away, the sound is soft. But she follows the sound. *[stirs the tinfoil]* As she gets closer...

David: The roar gets louder. ROOOOOOARRR! Finally, LuLu finds MuMu!!!!! ROOOOOOOAAAARRRRR! I-I-I-I-EEEK-EEEK!

Mr. Lee: Good job, team. Now all we need is the echo!

David: We need a big area with a flat wall that sound waves can bounce off, like the gymnasium.

[MR. LEE and STUDENTS walk to the gymnasium.]

David: Okay. This is when MuMu runs into the dark, scary cave. *[dramatically]* She cries out, but all she hears is her own echo!

David: *[shouts toward the wall]* I-I-I-I-EEEK-EEEK, I-I-I-I-EEEK-EEEK!

[They hear the echo: I-I-I-I-EEEK-EEEK, I-I-I-I-EEEK-EEEK.]

Mr. Lee: Congratulations kids, I think we're ready for the play!

1. **READING CHECK** What makes an echo?
2. **WRITE ABOUT IT** Compare the ways that a lion and a bee each produces sound.
3. **TALK ABOUT IT** Discuss new ways to create sound effects with everyday objects.

GLE 0307.10.1 Investigate phenomena that produce heat. **Math GLE 0306.3.4** Create and represent patterns using words, tables, graphs and symbols. **ELA GLE 0301.3.3** Write in a variety of modes and genres, including narration, literary response, personal experience, and subject matter content.

MATH Make a Bar Graph

Rhea used an outdoor thermometer to measure the temperature outside her window several times over the course of one day. She recorded each temperature and the time it was taken. Make a bar graph of her data. Use a scale of 2 degrees. Below your graph, write a sentence that describes any trends you observe.

Time	Temperature
8 A.M.	68°F
10 A.M.	71°F
Noon	74°F
2 P.M.	75°F
4 P.M.	74°F
6 P.M.	70°F

Narrative

Some composers use sounds to represent people, animals, ideas, and feelings. For example, in the symphony *Peter and the Wolf*, a flute represents a little bird, French horns are a wolf, a hunter is drums, and an oboe is a duck. Create your own short story with several characters. Write the story and tell what musical instrument you would use to represent each character.

Dr. Lonnie Johnson

When Lonnie Johnson was in high school, he built a robot from scrap metal. His robot won first prize in a national contest. Since then, Dr. Johnson has made a career as an inventor.

As a NASA scientist, Dr. Johnson invented a cooling system. It uses a water-based heat pump and is ideal for long missions in space.

Today, Dr. Johnson runs his own company in Atlanta. He and his team research and develop many products. One is a new type of cooling system that does not use harmful chemicals used in most refrigerators. Some of Dr. Johnson's inventions are just for fun, such as a popular water toy called the SuperSoaker®.

Chapter 8 Review and TCAP Prep

Vocabulary

Complete each sentence with a term from the list.

conductor
crest
friction
heat
pitch
thermal energy
trough
vibrate
volume
wave

1. The force produced when one object rubs against another object is _____.
2. The highest point of a wave is the _____.
3. The energy of moving particles in matter is called _____.
4. To move back and forth quickly is to _____.
5. How high or low a sound seems is its _____.
6. The flow of thermal energy from warmer objects to cooler objects is called _____.
7. A movement that carries energy from place to place is a _____.
8. A material that heat moves through easily is called a _____.
9. The lowest point of a wave is the _____.
10. How loud or soft a sound seems is its _____.

TCAP Inquiry Skills

11. **Infer** Three ice cubes are melting in a metal pan. When they are placed in a plastic-foam cup, the ice cubes don't melt as quickly. What can you infer about the plastic foam? **GLE 0307.10.2**
12. **Predict** Sandpaper is rubbed on a wooden board for several minutes. How will this affect the temperature of the sandpaper? Explain. **GLE 0307.10.1**
13. **Infer** The noise of an engine suddenly increases in both volume and pitch. What has happened to the crests, troughs, and frequency of the sound waves made by the engine? **GLE 0307.11.3**

Map the Concept

Label the diagrams, using the terms below.

trough	1. __________
wavelength	2. __________
vibrate	3. __________
crest	4. __________

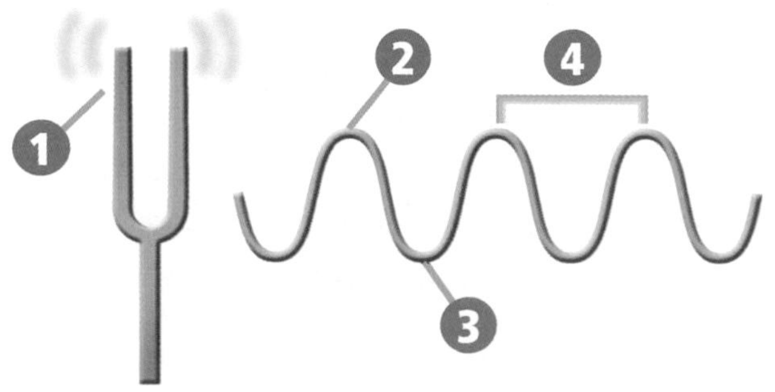

GLE 0307.11.3

Critical Thinking

14. **Synthesize** A cold juice box is placed in direct sunlight. What change will take place in the thermal energy of the particles that make up the juice? Explain. **GLE 0307.10.2**

15. **Analyze** Bicycle brakes use friction to slow or stop the wheels. If a rider uses the brakes often, how will the temperature of the brakes change? Explain. **GLE 0307.10.1**

16. **Hypothesize** When guitar strings are tight, the sound they make has a high pitch. Suppose guitar strings are plucked in exactly the same way before and after they are tightened. When will the sound waves have a greater frequency? **GLE 0307.11.3**

Check for Understanding

Test for Heat Conduction

Work in a group. Collect containers made of different materials to see which are good heat conductors. Look for containers that are about the same size and made from glass, plastic, plastic foam, ceramic, wood, and various metals.

Place an ice cube in each container. Record the time it takes for each ice cube to melt. Make a chart to show the rank of each material as a heat conductor. Assign number 1 to the best conductor.

✓ **0307.10.2**

TCAP Prep

Answer the following questions.

17 Which material would be the poorest heat conductor?

Ⓐ plastic foam
Ⓑ steel
Ⓒ copper
Ⓓ glass

SPI 0307.10.2

18 Look back at the photo on page 326. Which of these is the source of heat being used?

Ⓕ friction
Ⓖ chemical change
Ⓗ electricity
Ⓙ burning fuel

SPI 0307.10.1

19 When struck, which object would produce a sound with the lowest pitch?

Ⓐ thin steel wire
Ⓑ large solid steel door
Ⓒ steel nail
Ⓓ solid steel bat

SPI 0307.11.4

20 The walls in a building contain a material that is a poor heat conductor. The material

Ⓕ keeps cold air from moving into the building
Ⓖ keeps thermal energy from moving out of the building
Ⓗ easily conducts thermal energy
Ⓙ causes thermal energy to move into the building

SPI 0307.10.2

Chapter 9

Force and Motion

Lesson Preview

LESSON 1

The wind pushes on a sail and moves a sailboat. A dog pulls on a toy as it plays with its owner. What forces cause a change in motion?

LESSON 2

A running cheetah and a racing car are in motion. How are distance, direction, and speed used to describe motion?

LESSON 3

Magnets can hold a picture on a metal door or lift a heavy object. What are magnets and how do they work?

Fun Facts

It takes a cheetah just 3 seconds to go from standing still to running 70 miles an hour.

Vocabulary Preview

attract
direction
distance
★ force
gravity
magnet
★ magnetism
magnetic poles
motion
permanent magnet
speed
temporary magnet

★ = Tennessee Academic Vocabulary

Vocabulary Strategies

Have you ever seen any of these terms before? Do you know what they mean?

Describe, explain, or give an example of the vocabulary terms in your own words.

Draw a picture, symbol, example, or other image that describes the term.

Glossary p. H16

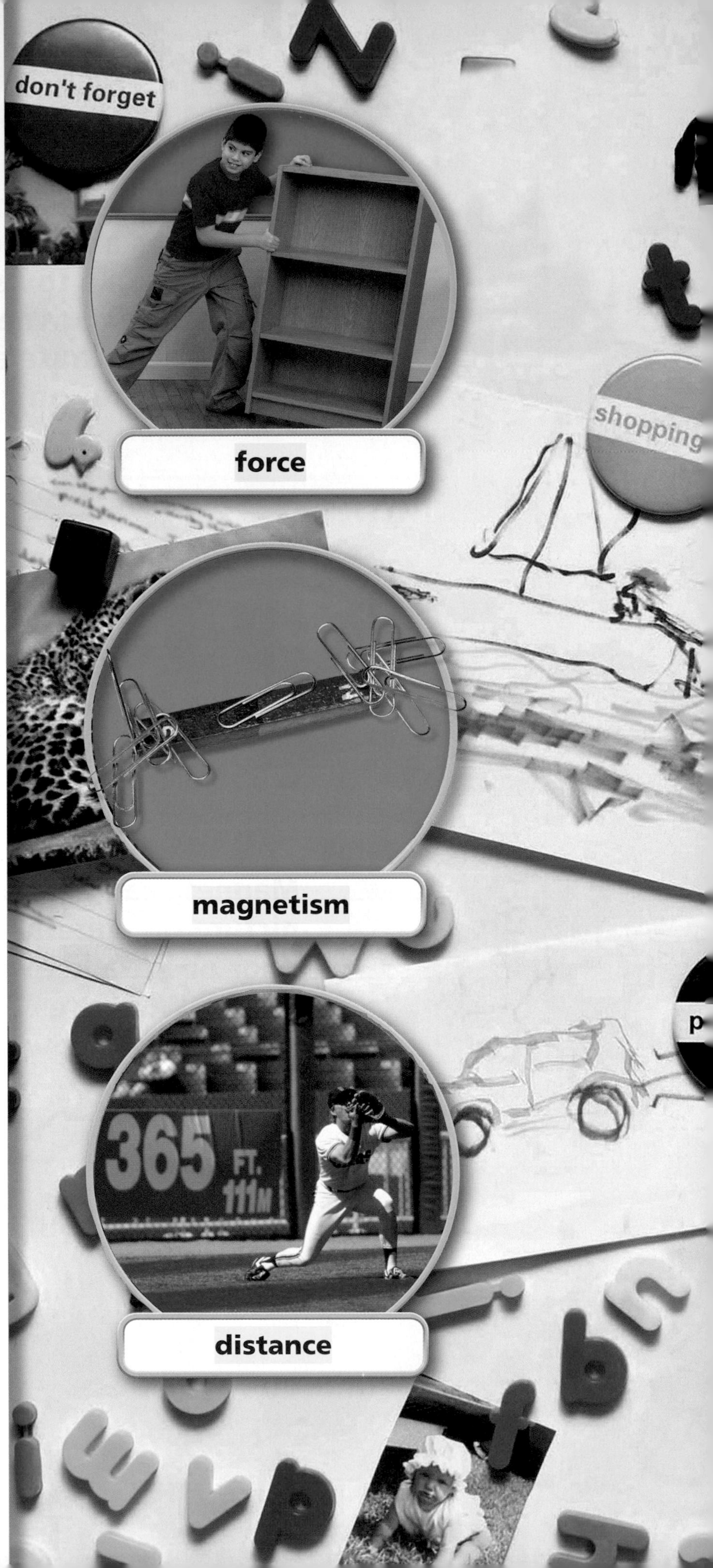

force

magnetism

distance

permanent magnet

Start with Your Standards

Inquiry

GLE 0307.Inq.1 Explore different scientific phenomena by asking questions, making logical predictions, planning investigations, and recording data.

GLE 0307.Inq.3 Organize data into appropriate tables, graphs, drawings, or diagrams.

GLE 0307.Inq.4 Identify and interpret simple patterns of evidence to communicate the findings of multiple investigations.

Physical Science

Standard 11 Motion

GLE 0307.11.1 Explore how the direction of a moving object is affected by unbalanced forces.

GLE 0307.11.2 Recognize the relationship between the mass of an object and the force needed to move it.

Standard 12 Forces in Nature

GLE 0307.12.1 Explore how magnets attract objects made of certain metals.

Interact with this chapter.

www.eduplace.com/tnscp

Lesson 1

TENNESSEE STANDARDS

GLE 0307.Inq.4 Identify and interpret simple patterns of evidence to communicate the findings of multiple investigations.

GLE 0307.11.1 Explore how the direction of a moving object is affected by unbalanced forces.

GLE 0307.11.2 Recognize the relationship between the mass of an object and the force needed to move it.

Guiding Question

How Do Forces Affect Objects?

Why It Matters...

Have you ever played the game of tug of war, in which two teams test their strength? Forces decide who wins the game. Each team pulls on a rope as hard as they can. The winning team pulls the other team over a line on the ground. Forces affect all parts of your life.

PREPARE TO INVESTIGATE

Inquiry Skill

Predict When you predict, you state what you think will happen based on your observations and experiences.

Materials

- toy cart
- rubber band
- classroom objects
- tape
- ruler
- goggles

Directed Inquiry

Make Things Move

Procedure

1. **Measure** Place two strips of tape 15 cm apart on the floor. Put a chair leg next to one strip of tape. Put a rubber band around the chair leg. Stretch the rubber band as shown in step 1. **Safety:** Wear goggles.

2. **Observe** Place a toy cart against the stretched rubber band. Pull the cart back so it goes behind the second line on the floor. Let it go. Use tape to mark the spot where the cart stops.

3. **Compare** Put an object on the cart. Repeat step 2. Compare the distances.

STEP 1

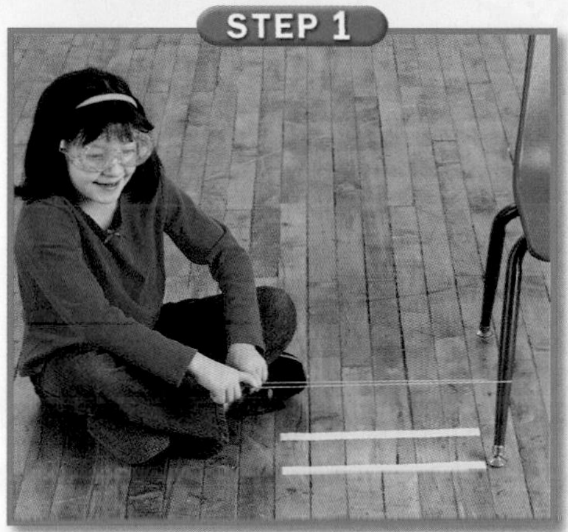

STEP 2

STEP 3

Think and Write

1. **Infer** Why do you think the cart went different distances?

2. **Predict** How could you make the heavier cart go the same distance as the lighter cart?

Guided Inquiry

Experiment Put other objects on the cart, one at a time. Repeat step 2 for each object. Record the distance that the cart moves for each object. Make a chart of your results and compare them.

✓ 0307.11.1

Reading Science

Forces

VOCABULARY

★ force
gravity
motion

GRAPHIC ORGANIZER

Cause and Effect Use a chart to describe the effect of each force that you read about.

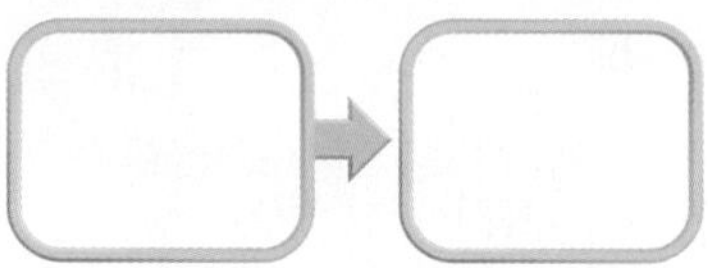

GLE 0307.11.1 Explore how the direction of a moving object is affected by unbalanced forces.

GLE 0307.11.2 Recognize the relationship between the mass of an object and the force needed to move it.

Motion, Pushes, and Pulls

Suppose your chair is next to the wall, but you want the chair to be near your desk. How would you get it there? You would move it, of course. Moving it would change its position, or place. The change in position of an object is called **motion** (MOH shuhn). Motion occurs any time an object moves from one position to another. The chair and bookcase in the room are in motion. The children who are moving the furniture are also in motion.

These children are using forces to move the furniture in the room.

PUSH

PULL

The children are using forces to arrange the books.

Think again about moving your chair. To change the chair's position, you would have to use a force on it. A **force** is a push or a pull. A push moves an object away from you. A pull moves an object toward you.

Any change in motion needs a force. You use a force to start a motion. You also use a force to speed up, slow down, or stop a motion. And you use a force to change the direction of a motion. Using a stronger force causes a bigger change in the motion.

FOCUS CHECK What is needed to change a motion?

Balanced and Unbalanced Forces

To describe a force, you must know two things. You must know the size of the force. You must also know which way the force is directed. Look at the picture on the right. It shows a soccer player about to kick a ball. The girl will apply an unbalanced force to the ball. The force will send the ball moving quickly in the direction of the kick.

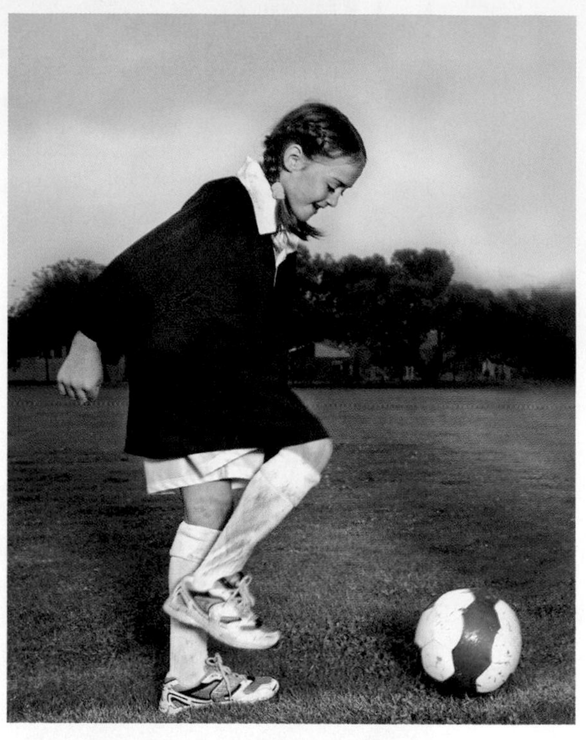

▲ An unbalanced force will be applied when the girl kicks the ball. That's why the ball will move.

Now look at the picture at the bottom of the page. You can see two players about to kick the ball in opposite directions. Suppose their feet hit the ball at the same time, and with the same force. Then the ball will not move. That's because the forces being applied to the ball are balanced.

FOCUS CHECK What happens to an object that has an unbalanced force applied to it?

If the players kick the ball at the same time with equal force, the ball will not move. That's because the forces on the ball will be balanced. ►

Gravity

What force affects all matter on Earth, even air? The force is gravity (GRAV ih tee). **Gravity** is a force that pulls objects toward each other. For example, Earth's gravity pulls objects toward the center of Earth. It causes objects to fall to the ground and water to flow downhill. Gravity exists between all objects, not just between Earth and other objects.

Gravity acts on objects without touching them. For example, Earth's gravity pulls on objects in space, such as the space shuttle or the Moon. The strength of gravity depends on the mass of each object. There is more gravity between objects that have greater masses. Earth has a large mass, so there is a strong pull between Earth and other objects on or near it.

An object's weight is a measure of how strongly Earth's gravity pulls on that object. Objects with greater mass are heavier than objects with less mass. The greater the mass of an object, the more force is needed to move it.

◀ **When the table is moved, the glass tips over. Gravity pulls the glass toward the center of Earth.**

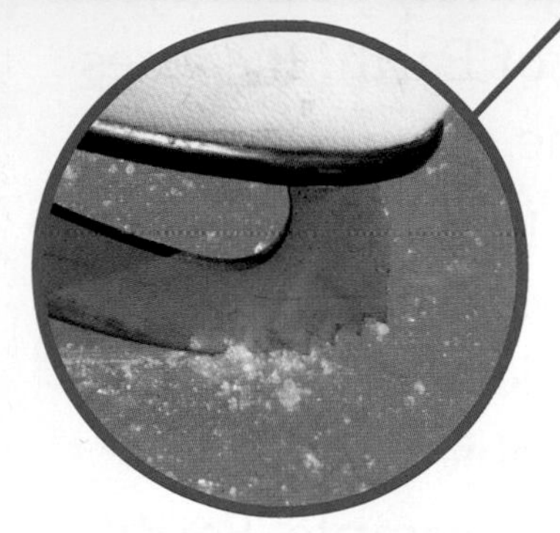

▲ The smooth blade reduces friction with the ice. The rough tip increases friction. It helps the skater to start and stop.

Friction

Friction is a force that slows down and stops motion between two surfaces that touch. There is more friction between rough or sticky surfaces than between smooth surfaces.

Friction can be useful. Without friction, your feet would slip and slide on the floor when you tried to walk. Sometimes friction is not useful. Friction can slow down machines and wear out their parts. Many machines use oil to make surfaces slippery and reduce friction.

FOCUS CHECK What types of surfaces have little friction between them?

The soft cloth and smooth slide reduce friction, allowing a fast ride. ▼

Express Lab

Activity Card
Find How Friction Varies

Lesson Wrap-Up

Visual Summary

A force is needed to change a motion. Gravity pulls objects toward each other.

An unbalanced force will cause an object to move. Balanced forces will not cause movement.

Friction is a force that slows down and stops the motion of two surfaces that touch.

Check for Understanding

INVESTIGATE FORCES

Bend a paper clip into the shape of a hook. Hang it on a rubber band. Then attach a large washer to the hook. When the washer stops moving, it has balanced forces acting on it. One force, gravity, is pulling down on the washer. The other force, the rubber band, is pulling up. Now add two more washers to the paper clip. What effect does adding mass have? What causes this result?

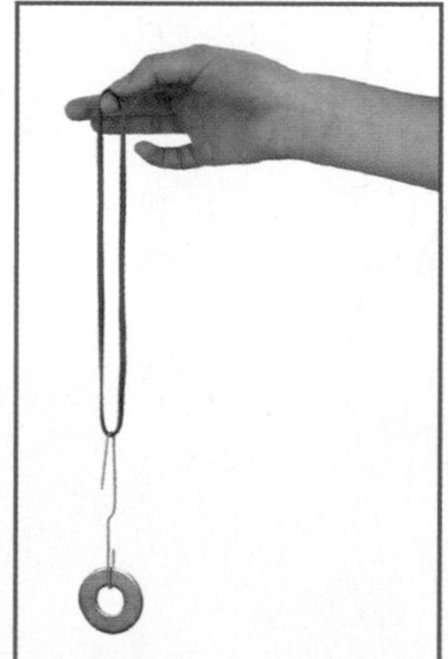

 0307.11.1

Review

1. **MAIN IDEA** What is a force?
2. **VOCABULARY** Define the term *motion*.
3. **READING SKILL: Cause and Effect** What effect does Earth's gravity have on objects on or near it?
4. **CRITICAL THINKING: Apply** The brakes of a train grind against its wheels to stop the train. What force is in use?
5. **INQUIRY SKILL: Predict** You push a box across a rough concrete floor. Your friend pushes the same box across a smooth tile floor. Predict which box will slide more easily.

TCAP Prep

The mass of an object is increased. How does that affect the forces acting on that object?

(A) The forces become unbalanced.

(B) There is no effect on the forces.

(C) The forces become balanced.

(D) The force of gravity decreases.

SPI 0307.11.2

Go Digital Technology

Visit **www.eduplace.com/tnscp** to find out more about forces.

Lesson 2

TENNESSEE STANDARDS

GLE 0307.Inq.3 Organize data into appropriate tables, graphs, drawings, or diagrams.

GLE 0307.11.1 Explore how the direction of a moving object is affected by unbalanced forces.

How Can Motion Be Described?

Why It Matters...

How would you describe the motion of the athlete in this picture? Fast? In a straight line? You can describe motion by saying how far something moves, in what direction it is moving, and how fast it travels.

PREPARE TO INVESTIGATE

Inquiry Skill

Communicate When you communicate, you share information by using words, actions, sketches, graphs, tables, and diagrams.

Materials

- 2 marbles
- shallow bowl
- metric ruler

Science and Math Toolbox

For step 4, review **Using a Tape Measure or Ruler** on page H6.

Directed Inquiry

Moving Marbles

Procedure

1. **Observe** Place one marble against the inside of a bowl. Push the marble so that it spins around the inside of the bowl. Observe the marble's motion as it moves inside the bowl.
2. **Communicate** In your Science Notebook, describe the motion of the marble. Describe its speed and its direction.
3. **Observe** Set two marbles next to each other on the floor. Gently push one of the marbles straight ahead. Then push the second marble straight ahead, but with more force. Describe how far each marble moved.
4. **Experiment** Set both marbles on the floor, about 10 cm apart. Gently roll the second marble so that it strikes the first marble. Describe the motions of the two marbles.

STEP 1

STEP 3

STEP 4

Think and Write

1. **Analyze Data** In step 1, how did the marble move inside the bowl?
2. **Analyze Data** In step 4, how did the first marble behave when the second marble struck it?
3. **Communicate** Draw diagrams to show the motions of the marbles in steps 1, 3, and 4.

✓ **0307.Inq.3**

Guided Inquiry

Be an Inventor Invent a device that uses marbles in a fun way. Your device should use different types of motion. Draw a sketch that uses arrows to show how the marbles move.

Ups and Downs

Wheeeeee! In 1884, shouts of excitement rang through the air at Coney Island, New York. The first gravity-powered roller coaster raced up and down over tracks.

The *Gravity Switchback Railway*, as it was called, traveled at almost 10 km (about 6 mi) in an hour. The train had two flat steel tracks that were nailed to wooden planks. It used the force of gravity to move. The ride started up high, and the car picked up speed as the tracks dipped.

The riders had to do some work, too. To board the roller coaster, they had to climb stairs to a platform at the top of the first hill. At only five cents a ride, getting a thrill and some exercise was a bargain!

This painting shows what it was like to ride a roller coaster in the 1800s.

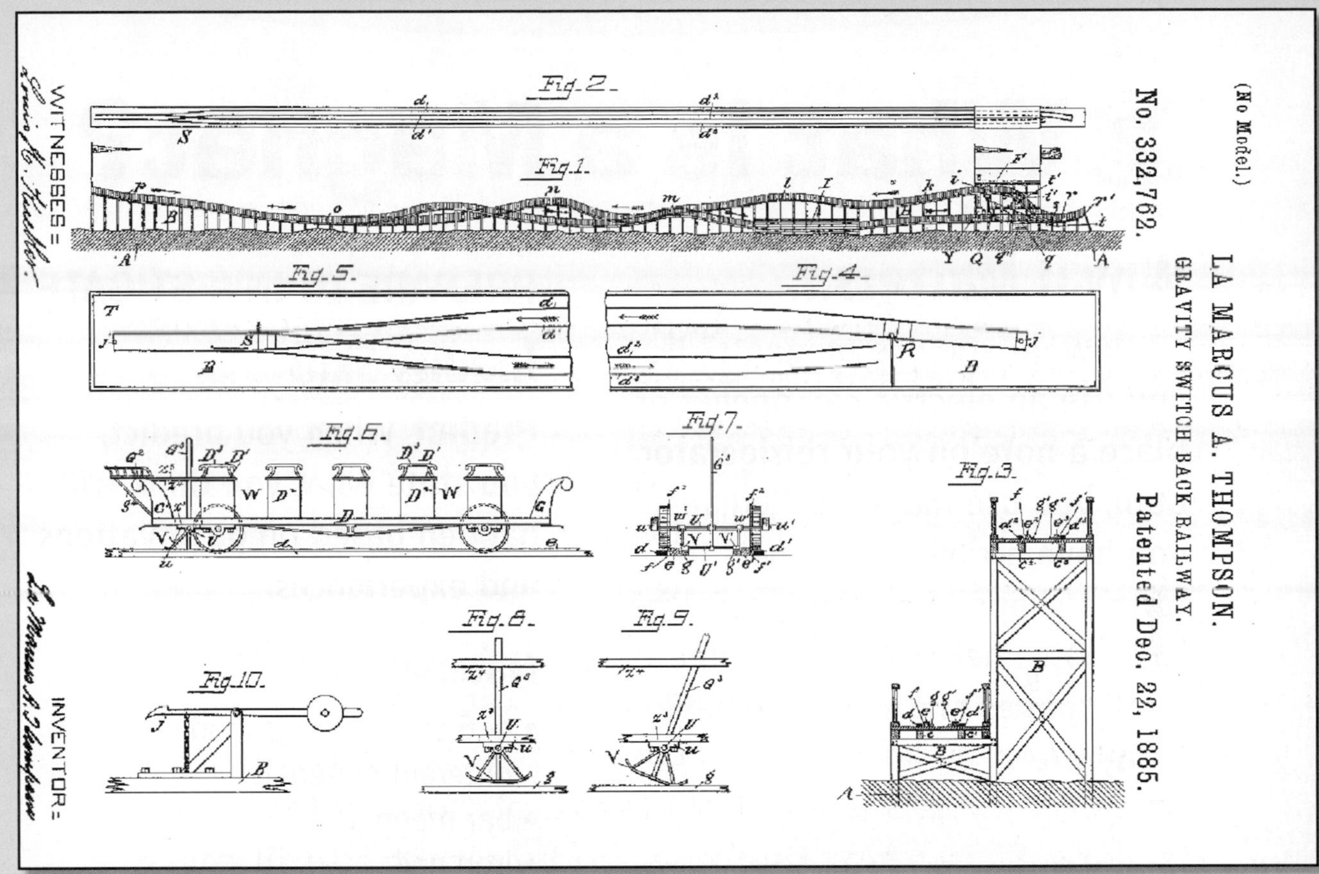

▲ **LaMarcus Thompson's 1885 patent describes the materials and design of the *Gravity Switchback Railway.***

▲ **Thompson designed many other coasters. This is a drawing from his patent for the *Pleasure Cable Railway.***

Sharing Ideas

1. **READING CHECK** Where was the Gravity Switchback Railway located?
2. **WRITE ABOUT IT** What force did Thompson's roller coaster use to move?
3. **TALK ABOUT IT** Discuss how it may have felt to ride on the first gravity-powered roller coaster.

Lesson 3

TENNESSEE STANDARDS

GLE 0307.Inq.1 Explore different scientific phenomena by asking questions, making logical predictions, planning investigations, and recording data.

GLE 0307.12.1 Explore how magnets attract objects made of certain metals.

What Is a Magnet?

Why It Matters...

How do you use magnets? If you use an electric can opener or place a note on your refrigerator door, you use magnets. Perhaps you have arranged magnets to form a shape or pattern, as in the toy shown here. Magnets come in all shapes and sizes and have many uses.

PREPARE TO INVESTIGATE

Inquiry Skill

Predict When you predict, you state what you think will happen based on observations and experiences.

Materials

- 4–6 small objects made of different materials
- bar magnet
- iron nail

Science and Math Toolbox

For steps 1, 3 and 4, review **Making a Chart to Organize Data** on page H10.

Directed Inquiry

Make a Magnet

Procedure

1 **Collaborate** Work with a partner. Place several small objects on your desk. In your Science Notebook, make a chart titled *Magnet* like the one shown. Record each object in your chart.

2 **Predict** With your partner, predict what objects the magnet will pull toward it, or **attract**. These objects will stick to the magnet. Record your predictions as "yes" or "no" in your chart. Then move a magnet close to each object. Record your observations.

3 **Predict** Make a chart titled *Nail* like the one in step 1. Repeat step 2, using an iron nail in place of the magnet. **Safety:** Be careful when handling the nail.

4 Stroke the nail with one end of the magnet 30 times. Stroke in one direction only. Make a chart titled *Stroked Nail*. Then repeat step 2, using the stroked nail. Record your predictions and observations.

STEP 1

MAGNET

What Objects Are Attracted?		
Object	Prediction	Observation

STEP 2

STEP 4

Think and Write

1. **Analyze Data** How did stroking the nail with the magnet affect the nail?

2. **Infer** What can you infer about the objects that the magnet and the stroked nail attracted?

✓ 0307.12.2

Guided Inquiry

Experiment Find out how many paper clips the stroked nail can pick up. Then predict what will happen if the nail is stroked 20 times and then 30 more times. Test your predictions.

Reading Science

Magnets

VOCABULARY

attract
magnet
★ magnetism
magnetic poles
permanent magnet
temporary magnet

GRAPHIC ORGANIZER

Cause and Effect As you read, complete the chart with examples of ways that magnets affect different objects.

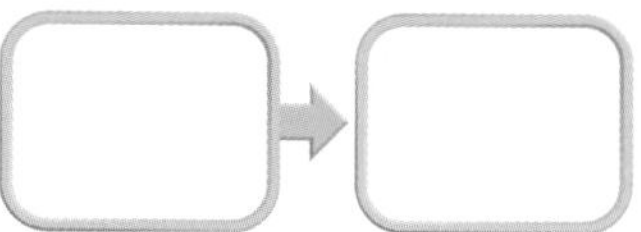

GLE 0307.12.1 Explore how magnets attract objects made of certain metals.

Uses of Magnets

Have you ever used an electric can opener? If so, you probably noticed that one part of the can opener holds the can lid once it is removed. That part is a magnet. In the toy shown below, a magnet is used to move around tiny metal particles to form a picture.

A **magnet** is any object that pulls certain metals toward it. Two metals that magnets pull toward them, or **attract,** are iron and nickel. A magnet's ability to attract these metals is called **magnetism,** or magnetic attraction. Materials that are nonmetals, such as rubber, paper, wood, glass, and plastic, are not attracted to a magnet.

▲ The removed can lid is held by a magnet on the can opener.

Metal particles in this toy are moved with a magnetic wand to form a picture. ▼

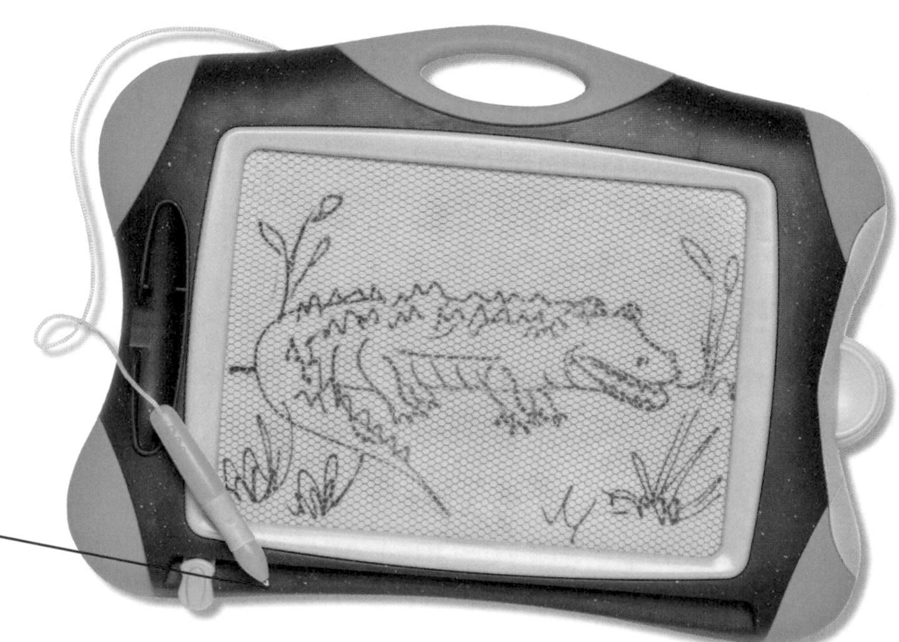

▲ Permanent magnets decorate this refrigerator door.

Two Kinds of Magnets

The kind of magnet you find holding papers to a refrigerator door is called a permanent magnet. A **permanent magnet** is an object that keeps its magnetism for a long time. A permanent magnet can be made from a mixture of iron and other metals. Most permanent magnets are made in factories. But some permanent magnets occur in nature as rocks.

Metal objects made of iron or nickel can be magnetized, or made into magnets. Look at the paper clip holding the metal objects. The paper clip has been stroked with a magnet. It has become a temporary magnet. A **temporary magnet** is an object that loses its magnetism after a short time.

▲ A paper clip has become a temporary magnet.

FOCUS CHECK What effect does a magnet have on objects made of iron and nickel?

Express Lab

Activity Card

Compare the Strengths of Magnets

Poles of a Magnet

What happens if you scatter a handful of metal paper clips over a magnet? Most of the clips will be attracted to the ends of the magnet. The ends of a magnet are the **magnetic poles,** the areas of a magnet where its force of attraction is strongest.

All magnets have two poles—a north pole and a south pole. Suppose you tie a string around the middle of a bar magnet. Then you hold the end of the string and allow the magnet to swing freely. The magnet will turn until one end points toward the north. That end is the north-seeking pole, or north pole of the magnet. The other end of the magnet points south. This is the magnet's south-seeking pole, or south pole.

FOCUS CHECK Why do magnetic objects tend to be attracted to the ends of a magnet?

More paper clips are clustered around the poles of the magnets because the magnetic force is strongest at the poles. ►

Lesson Wrap-Up

Visual Summary

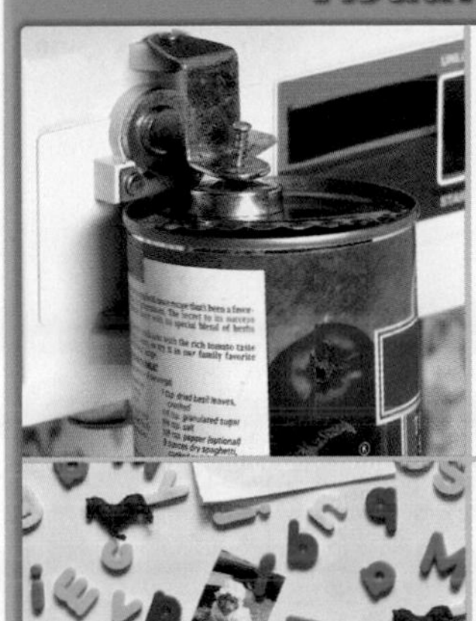

A magnet is an object that attracts certain metals, mainly iron and nickel.

A permanent magnet keeps its magnetism for a long time. A temporary magnet soon loses its magnetism.

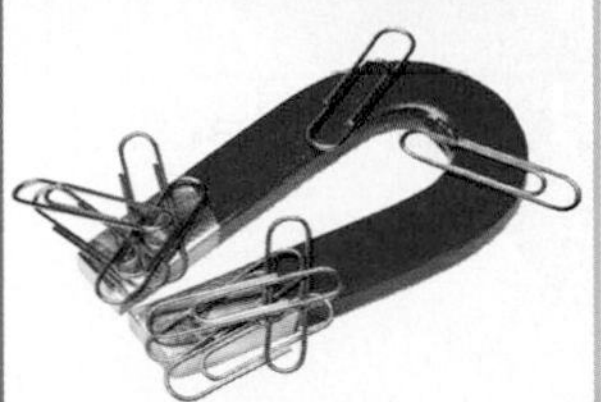

A magnet's force of attraction is strongest at its poles.

Check for Understanding

TEST MAGNETS AND DISTANCE

Find out how distance affects magnetic attraction. You will need a strong magnet. Tie one end of a thread to a paper clip. Tape the other end of the thread to a desktop. Use the strong magnet to hold the clip up without touching it. The thread should be taut. Slowly move the magnet away from the clip. Notice how far you can move the magnet before the clip falls. **✔ 0307.12.1**

Review

1. **MAIN IDEA** What kinds of objects do magnets attract?
2. **VOCABULARY** What is a temporary magnet?
3. **READING SKILL: Cause and Effect** What effect does a magnet have on objects made of rubber and plastic?
4. **CRITICAL THINKING: Apply** Suppose you lower a magnet into a pile of staples mixed with plastic toothpicks. When you pull out the magnet, what would you expect to see on it?
5. **INQUIRY SKILL: Predict** A bar magnet is used to pick up paper clips. To which part of the magnet will the paper clips tend to stick?

TCAP Prep

Which of the following materials will not be attracted to a magnet?

Ⓐ plastic eyeglass lens
Ⓑ iron lock
Ⓒ steel ball bearing
Ⓓ nickel bracelet

SPI 0307.12.2

Technology

Visit **www.eduplace.com/tnscp** to learn more about magnets and their uses.

Train or Plane?

Can you fly without leaving the ground? Yes, if you're riding China's Maglev train. This train can reach great speeds—up to 310 miles per hour!

More amazing still, the Maglev has no engine and no wheels! What's the secret? Magnets! "Maglev" stands for magnetic levitation. Powerful opposing magnets lift, or "levitate," the train off the track. The Maglev floats about 0.5 in. above a guideway. Powerful magnets in the guideway push and pull the Maglev along. That's why the Maglev has no need for an engine or to carry fuel, as other kinds of trains do.

Speed Comparison America's Amtrak Acela train can travel 150 miles per hour. The high-speed French TGV train and the Japanese "bullet" train hit almost 186 miles per hour in commercial use. China's commercial Maglev easily cruises at 267 miles per hour!

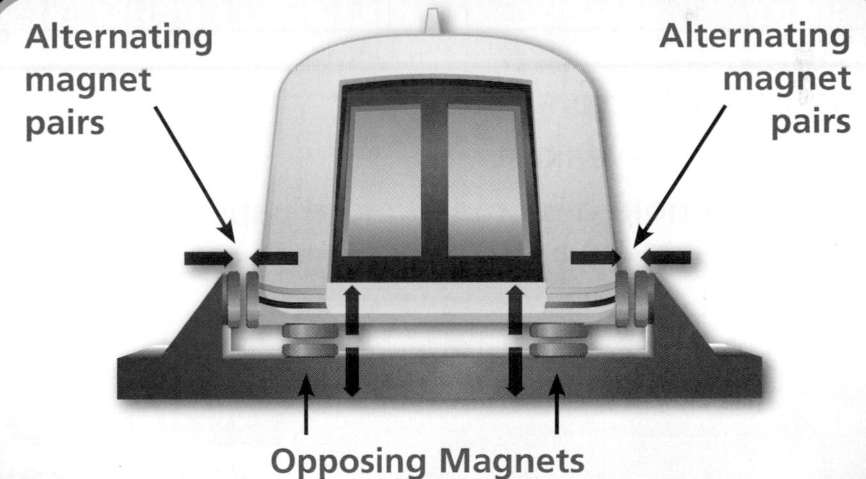

The Maglev's magnetic drive is based on the principle that opposite poles of magnets attract and like poles repel.

GLE 0307.12.1 Explore how magnets attract objects made of certain metals.
Math GLE 0306.5.1 Organize, display, and analyze data using various representations to solve problems.
ELA GLE 0301.3.1 Write for a variety of purposes and to a variety of audiences.

Math Graph Magnet Strength

The table lists how many paper clips seven horseshoe magnets can attract. The number of clips attracted shows how strong each magnet is compared to the others. Use the data to make a pictograph. Each symbol on your graph should stand for 3 paper clips.

Strengths of Some Magnets							
Magnet	A	B	C	D	E	F	G
Number of Paper Clips Attracted	21	6	30	3	33	15	18

1. Which magnet is strongest?
2. Which magnet is weakest?
3. Magnet *C* can hold how many more paper clips than Magnet *G*?

Narrative

Write a paragraph that describes a trip you have taken in a car, bus, train, boat, or airplane. Use direction words such as *right, left, up, down, north, south, east,* and *west*. Use speed words such as *fast* and *slow*. Use distance words such as *kilometers, near, far, long,* and *short*.

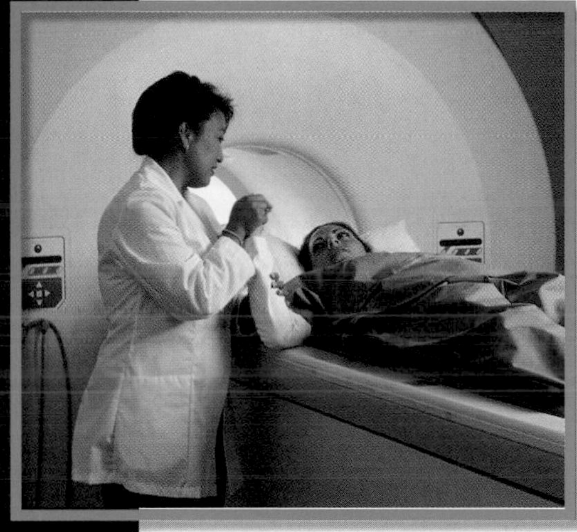

MRI Technician

MRI stands for *magnetic resonance imaging*. In hospitals, an MRI machine uses powerful magnets to view, or scan, large areas inside the human body. MRI technicians are the people who operate the machine that does the scan.

What It Takes!

- Training at a technical school
- Skills for dealing with machines and people

Mechanical Engineer

Mechanical engineers design, test, and improve all types of machines. They work on machines such as engines and generators. They also work on the kinds of machines that you have in your home, such as food mixers and toys that move.

What It Takes!

- A degree in mechanical engineering
- Drafting, drawing, design, and problem-solving skills
- Knowledge of computer systems

Chapter 9 Review and TCAP Prep

Vocabulary

Complete each sentence with a term from the list.

1. How fast or slow an object is moving is its ______.
2. A magnet that keeps its magnetism is a/an ______.
3. A change in an object's position is called ______.
4. An object that pulls certain metals toward it is a/an ______.
5. A magnet that loses its magnetism quickly is a/an ______.
6. The measure of how far an object has traveled is ______.
7. A magnet's ability to attract certain metals is called ______.
8. A force that pulls objects toward the center of Earth is ______.
9. The ends of a magnet, where the force of attraction is greatest, are called the ______.
10. The path a moving object follows is its ______.

attract
direction
distance
★ **force**
gravity
magnet
★ **magnetism**
magnetic poles
motion
permanent magnet
speed
temporary magnet

TCAP Inquiry Skills

11. **Predict** You sprinkle iron filings over a horseshoe magnet. Where would you expect most of the filings to collect? Explain. **GLE 0307.12.1**

12. **Infer** Two dogs are pulling on opposite ends of a toy. Dog A gets the toy away from Dog B. Explain how Dog A got the toy in terms of balanced or unbalanced forces. **GLE 0307.11.1**

13. **Hypothesize** You place one end of a magnet into a pile of paper clips. No clips stick to the magnet. Hypothesize a reason for this result. **GLE 0307.12.1**

Map the Concept

Use the words below to label the diagram.

distance **speed**
motion **force**
direction

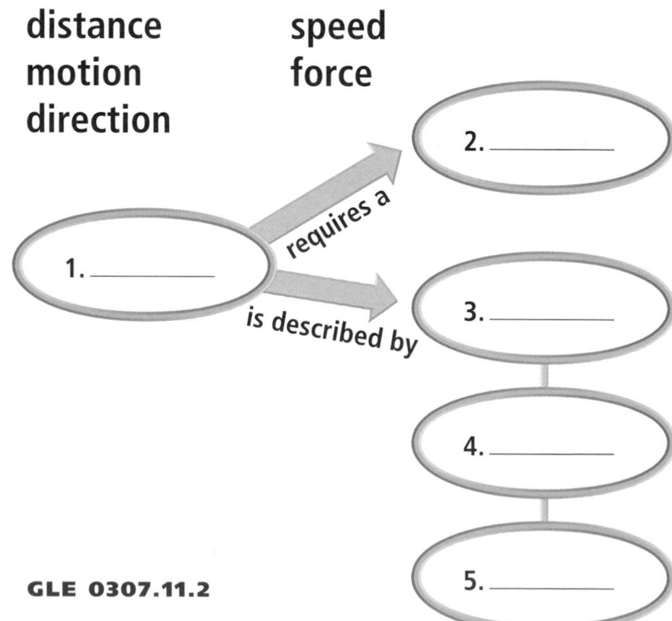

GLE 0307.11.2

Critical Thinking

14. Synthesize You magnetize a nail by stroking it with a magnet. Another student has magnetized the same kind of nail, but its magnetism is stronger. What might have caused this difference? **GLE 0307.12.1**

15. Evaluate Your friend says that a soccer ball stops rolling along the grass because the force of your kick stops acting on the ball. Is this statement correct? If not, what force stops the ball? **GLE 0307.11.1**

16. Apply A classmate tells you how to get to her house from school. Her instructions tell you how far to go and which way to turn. Which description of motion is not included in her instructions? **GLE 0307.11.1**

Check for Understanding

Test for Magnetism

Gather a variety of different objects to test with a magnet. Be sure to include several metal objects, such as coins, buttons, screws, and washers. Make a chart. Record the kind of material from which each object is made. You may need to check with an adult to find out this information. In your chart, record whether or not each material is attracted by a magnet. **✔ 0307.12.2**

TCAP Prep

17. An object made of which material will be attracted to a magnet?

Ⓐ wood
Ⓑ iron
Ⓒ paper
Ⓓ glass

SPI 0307.12.2

18. A marble moving in a straight line hits a wall. It keeps moving, but there is a change in its

Ⓕ friction
Ⓖ magnetism
Ⓗ gravity
Ⓙ direction

SPI 0307.11.1

19. Which are forces that can act on objects without touching them?

Ⓐ gravity and friction
Ⓑ magnetism and friction
Ⓒ magnetism and gravity
Ⓓ gravity and motion

SPI 0307.12.1

20. Three friends weigh the same. Two get on sled A. One gets on sled B. What will happen if each sled is given an equal push?

Ⓕ Sled A will go faster.
Ⓖ Sled B will go faster.
Ⓗ Both sleds will go at the same speed.
Ⓙ Sled A will go faster at first and then it will go slower than sled B.

SPI 0307.11.2

UNIT C TCAP Prep

9 Matter

Performance Indicator: **SPI 0307.9.2 Identify methods for separating different types of mixtures.**

1 Which is a way to separate the parts of a salt-water mixture?

Ⓐ Use a magnet to pull out the salt.
Ⓑ Evaporate the water.
Ⓒ Pick out the salt by hand.
Ⓓ Freeze the water.

10 Energy

Performance Indicator: **SPI 0307.10.2 Classify materials according to their ability to conduct heat.**

2 Which material should the handle of a pan be made out of so the handle will be safe to hold when the pan is heated?

Ⓕ copper
Ⓖ nickel
Ⓗ wood
Ⓙ iron

11 Motion

Performance Indicator: **SPI 0307.11.1 Identify how the direction of a moving object is changed by an applied force.**

3 When a pitched baseball is hit by a bat, the ball first

Ⓐ slows down
Ⓑ changes direction
Ⓒ stops moving
Ⓓ speeds up

11 Motion

Performance Indicator: **SPI 0307.11.4 Identify how sounds with different pitch and volume are produced.**

4 A student blows across each bottle with equal force. Which bottle will produce the sound with the lowest pitch?

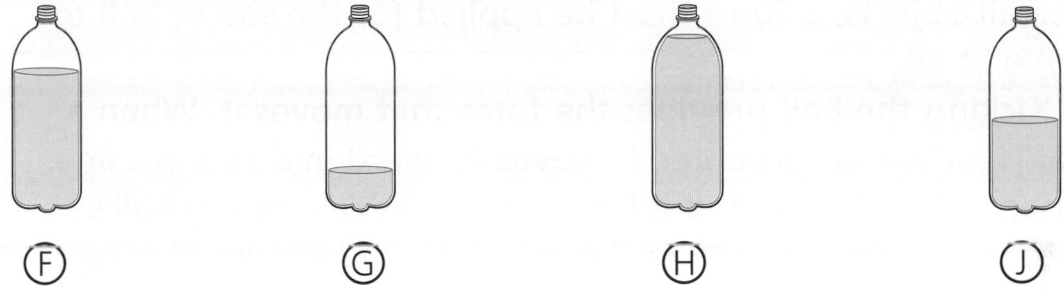

5 A sound wave with high crests and deep troughs produces a sound that has a

Ⓐ loud volume
Ⓑ high pitch
Ⓒ soft volume
Ⓓ low pitch

12 Forces in Nature

Performance Indicator: **SPI 0307.12.2 Identify objects that are attracted to magnets.**

6 Which of the following objects would a magnet attract?

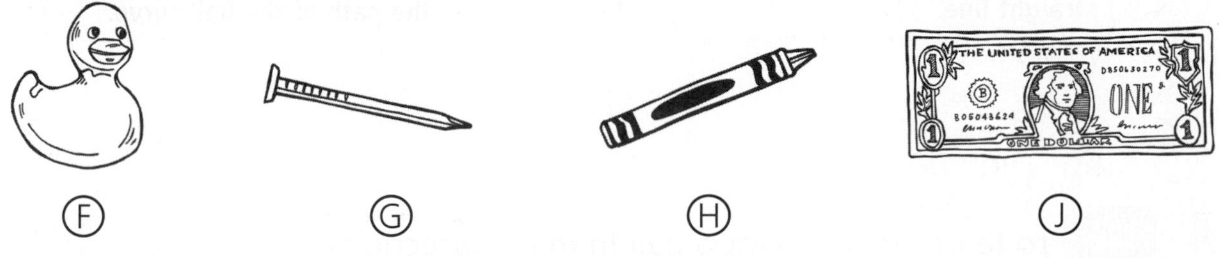

www.eduplace.com/tnscp

Discover More

Simulate kicking a soccer ball. How a soccer ball moves is a result of the way the soccer player kicks that ball. Like all objects, a force must be applied for the soccer ball to move at all.

Kicking the ball provides the force that moves it. When a ball is kicked at its center, it moves forward in a straight line. When it is kicked to the left or right of its center, the ball's path curves to one side or the other. That's because kicking the ball left or right of its center causes the ball to spin. This spin causes the ball to move in a curved path.

Straight Path

Kicking the center of the soccer ball moves the ball forward in a straight line.

Curved Path

Kicking to the left or right of the soccer ball's center makes the path of the ball curve.

to learn how to kick a ball in many directions.

Science and Math Toolbox

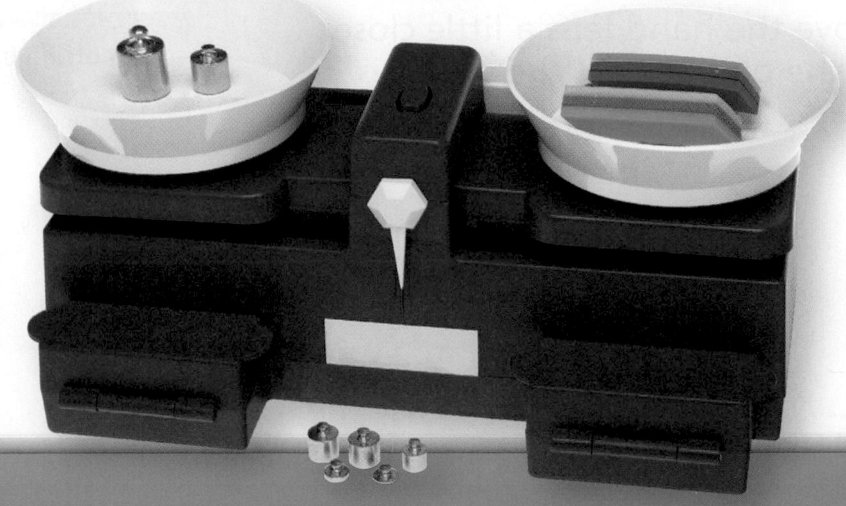

Using a Hand Lens

A hand lens is a tool that magnifies objects, or makes objects appear larger. This makes it possible for you to see details of an object that would be hard to see without the hand lens.

Look at a Coin or a Stamp

1. Place an object such as a coin or a stamp on a table or other flat surface.

2. Hold the hand lens just above the object. As you look through the lens, slowly move the lens away from the object. Notice that the object appears to get larger and a little blurry.

3. Move the hand lens a little closer to the object until the object is once again in sharp focus.

Making a Bar Graph

A bar graph helps you organize and compare data.

Make a Bar Graph of Animal Heights

Animals come in all different shapes and sizes. You can use the information in this table to make a bar graph of animal heights.

Heights of Animals

Animal	Height (cm)
Bear	240
Elephant	315
Cow	150
Giraffe	570
Camel	210
Horse	165

1. Draw the side and the bottom of the graph. Label the side of the graph as shown. The numbers will show the height of the animals in centimeters.

2. Label the bottom of the graph. Write the names of the animals at the bottom so that there is room to draw the bars.

3. Choose a title for your graph. Your title should describe the subject of the graph.

4. Draw bars to show the height of each animal. Some heights are between two numbers.

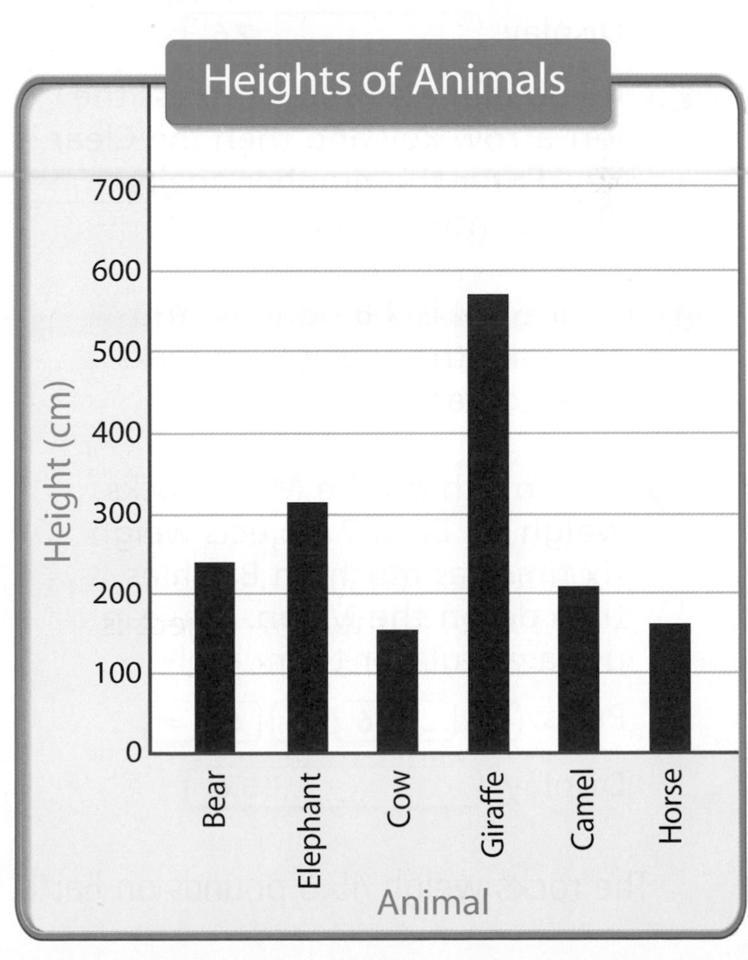

Using a Calculator

After you've made measurements, a calculator can help you analyze your data.

Add and Multiply Decimals

Suppose you're an astronaut. You may take 8 pounds of Moon rocks back to Earth. Can you take all the rocks in the table? Use a calculator to find out.

Weight of Moon Rocks

Moon Rock	Weight of Rock on Moon (lb)
Rock 1	1.7
Rock 2	1.8
Rock 3	2.6
Rock 4	1.5

1. To add, press:
   1 . 7 + 1 . 8 +
   2 . 6 + 1 . 5 =
   Display: 7.6
2. If you make a mistake, press the left arrow key and then the Clear key. Enter the number again. Then continue adding.
3. Your total is 7.6 pounds. You can take the four Moon rocks back to Earth.
4. How much do the Moon rocks weigh on Earth? Objects weigh six times as much on Earth as they do on the Moon. You can use a calculator to multiply.
   Press: 7 . 6 × 6 =
   Display: 45.6

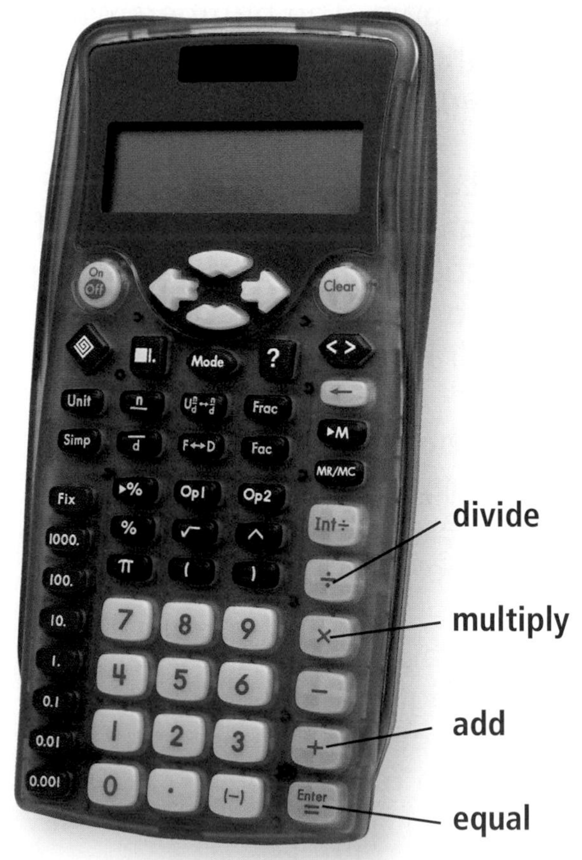

The rocks weigh 45.6 pounds on Earth.

Making a Tally Chart

A tally chart can help you keep track of items you are counting. Sometimes you need to count many different items. It may be hard to count all of the items of the same type as a group. That's when a tally chart can be helpful.

Make a Tally Chart of Birds Seen

A group of bird watchers made a tally chart to record how many birds of each type they saw. Here are the tallies they have made so far.

- Every time you count one item, make one tally.
- When you reach five, draw the fifth tally as a line through the other four.
- To find the total number of robins, count by fives and then ones.
- You can use the tally chart to make a chart with numbers.

Birds Seen

Type of Bird	Tally
Cardinal	||
Blue jay	𝍸 𝍸 𝍸
Mockingbird	||||
Hummingbird	𝍸 ||
House sparrow	𝍸 𝍸 𝍸 𝍸 |
Robin	𝍸 𝍸 ||

What kind of bird was seen most often?

- Now use a tally chart to record how many cars of different colors pass your school.

Birds Seen

Type of Bird	Number
Cardinal	2
Blue jay	15
Mockingbird	4
Hummingbird	7
House sparrow	21
Robin	12

Using a Tape Measure or Ruler

Tape measures and rulers are tools for measuring the length of objects and distances. Scientists most often use units such as meters, centimeters, and millimeters when making length measurements.

Use a Tape Measure

1. Measure the distance around a jar. Wrap the tape around the jar.
2. Find the line where the tape begins to wrap over itself.
3. Record the distance around the jar to the nearest centimeter.

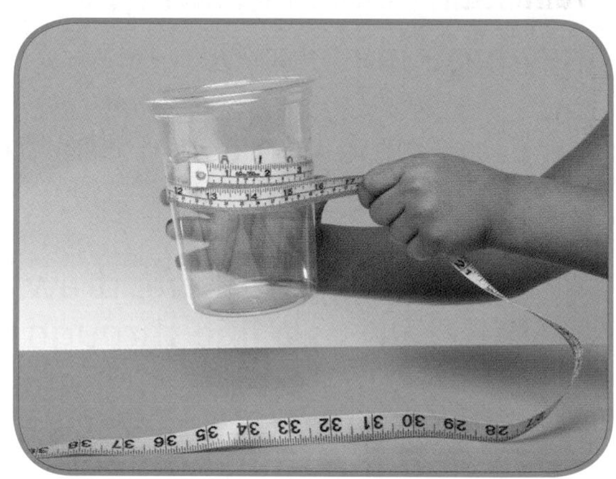

Use a Metric Ruler

1. Measure the length of your shoe. Place the ruler or the meterstick on the floor. Line up the end of the ruler with the heel of your shoe.
2. Notice where the other end of your shoe lines up with the ruler.
3. Look at the scale on the ruler. Record the length of your shoe to the nearest centimeter and to the nearest millimeter.

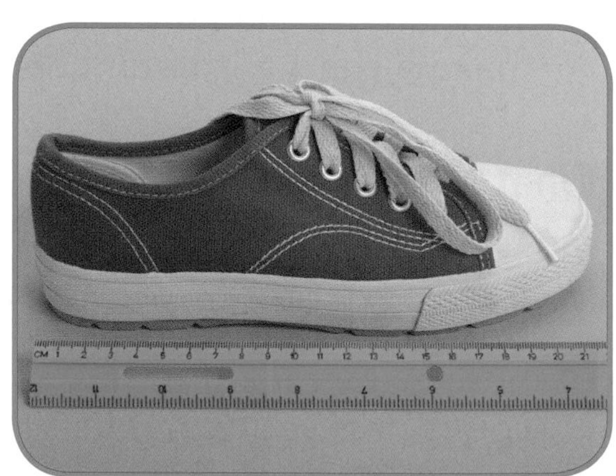

Measuring Volume

A beaker, a measuring cup, and a graduated cylinder are used to measure volume. Volume is the amount of space something takes up. Most of the containers that scientists use to measure volume have a scale marked in milliliters (mL).

Beaker 50 mL

Measuring cup 50 mL

Graduated cylinder 50 mL

Measure the Volume of a Liquid

1. Measure the volume of juice. Pour some juice into a measuring container.

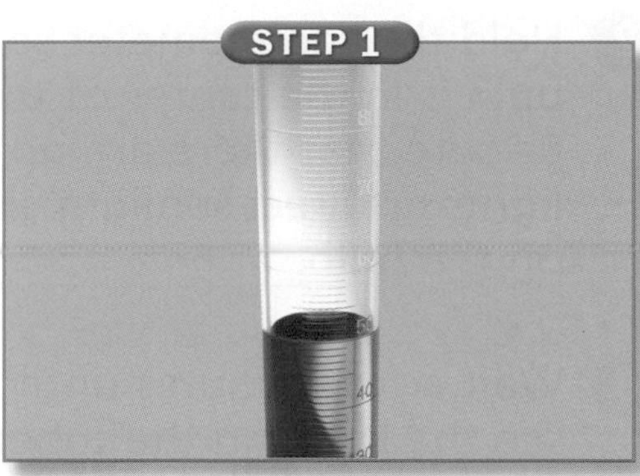

STEP 1

2. Move your head so that your eyes are level with the top of the juice. Read the scale line that is closest to the surface of the juice. If the surface of the juice is curved up on the sides, look at the lowest point of the curve.

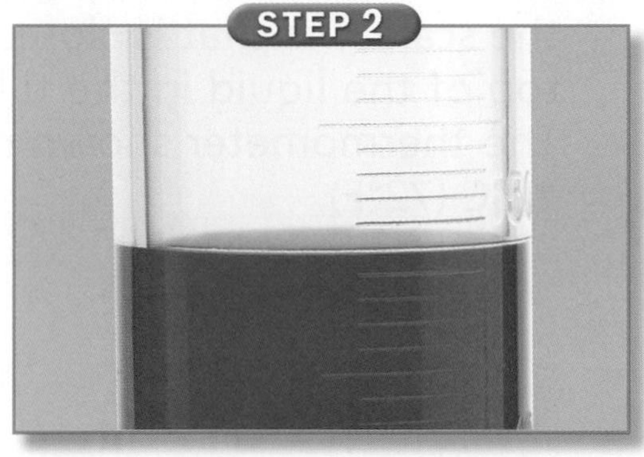

STEP 2

3. Read the measurement on the scale. You can estimate the value between two lines on the scale.

Using a Thermometer

A thermometer is used to measure temperature. When the liquid in the tube of a thermometer gets warmer, it expands and moves farther up the tube. Different scales can be used to measure temperature, but scientists usually use the Celsius scale.

Measure the Temperature of a Liquid

1. Half fill a cup with warm tap water.

2. Hold the thermometer so that the bulb is in the center of the liquid. Be sure that there are no bright lights or direct sunlight shining on the bulb.

3. Wait a few minutes until you see the liquid in the tube of the thermometer stop moving. Read the scale line that is closest to the top of the liquid in the tube. The thermometer shown reads 22°C (72°F).

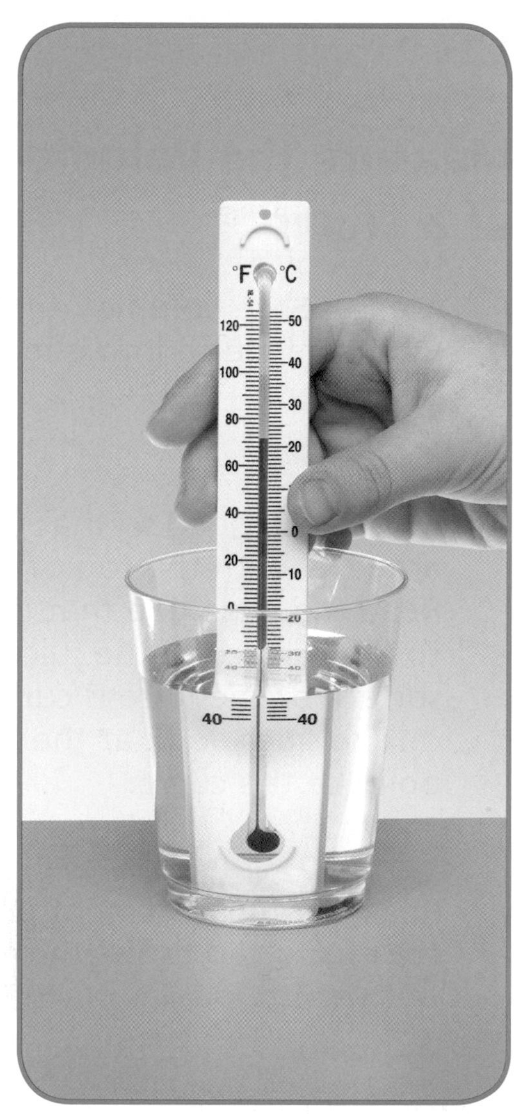

Using a Balance

A balance is used to measure mass. Mass is the amount of matter in an object. To find the mass of an object, place it in the left pan of the balance. Place standard masses in the right pan.

Measure the Mass of a Ball

1. Check that the empty pans are balanced, or level with each other. When balanced, the pointer on the base should be at the middle mark. If it needs to be adjusted, move the slider on the back of the balance a little to the left or right.
2. Place a ball on the left pan. Then add standard masses, one at a time, to the right pan. When the pointer is at the middle mark again, each pan holds the same amount of matter and has the same mass.
3. Add the numbers marked on the masses in the pan. The total is the mass of the ball in grams.

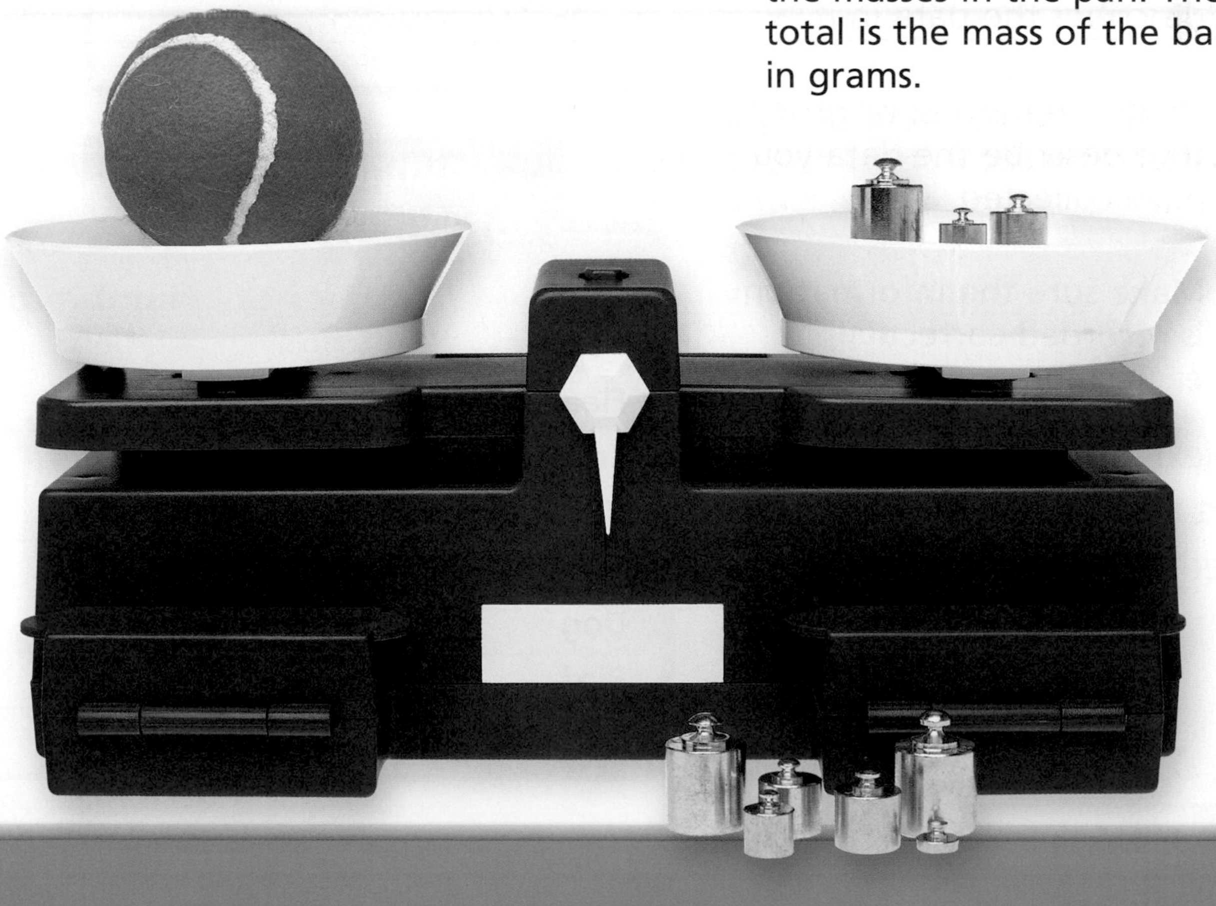

Making a Chart to Organize Data

A chart can help you keep track of information. When you organize information, or data, it is easier to read, compare, or classify it.

Classifying Animals

Suppose you want to organize this data about animal characteristics. You could base the chart on the two characteristics listed—the number of wings and the number of legs.

1. Give the chart a title that describes the data in it.
2. Name categories, or groups, that describe the data you have collected.
3. Make sure the information is recorded correctly in each column.

Next, you could make another chart to show animal classification based on number of legs only.

My Data

Fleas have no wings. Fleas have six legs.

Snakes have no wings or legs.

A bee has four wings. It has six legs.

Spiders never have wings. They have eight legs.

A dog has no wings. It has four legs.

Birds have two wings and two legs.

A cow has no wings. It has four legs.

A butterfly has four wings. It has six legs.

Animals–Number of Wings and Legs

Animal	Number of Wings	Number of Legs
Flea	0	6
Snake	0	0
Bee	4	6
Spider	0	8
Dog	0	4
Bird	2	2
Butterfly	4	6

Reading a Circle Graph

A circle graph shows a whole divided into parts. You can use a circle graph to compare the parts to each other. You can also use it to compare the parts to the whole.

A Circle Graph of Fuel Use

This circle graph shows fuel use in the United States. The graph has 10 equal parts, or sections. Each section equals $\frac{1}{10}$ of the whole. One whole equals $\frac{10}{10}$.

Estimated Fuel Use in the United States

Oil Of all the fuel used in the United States, 4 out of 10 parts, or $\frac{4}{10}$, is oil.

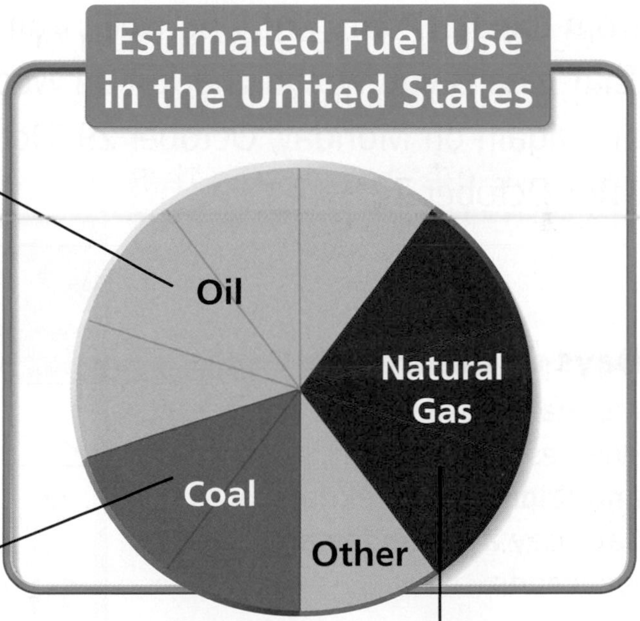

Coal Of all the fuel used in the United States, 2 out of 10 parts, or $\frac{2}{10}$, is coal.

Natural Gas Of all the fuel used in the United States, 3 out of 10 parts, or $\frac{3}{10}$, is natural gas.

Measuring Elapsed Time

A calendar can help you find out how much time has passed, or elapsed, in days or weeks. A clock can help you see how much time has elapsed in hours and minutes. A clock with a second hand or a stopwatch can help you find out how many seconds have elapsed.

Using a Calendar to Find Elapsed Days

This is a calendar for the month of October. October has 31 days. Suppose it is October 22 and you begin an experiment. You need to check the experiment two days from the start date and one week from the start date. That means you would check it on Wednesday, October 24, and again on Monday, October 29. October 29 is 7 days after October 22.

October

Sunday	Monday	Tuesday	Wednesday	Thursday	Friday	Saturday
	1	2	3	4	5	6
7	8	9	10	11	12	13
14	15	16	17	18	19	20
21	22	23	24	25	26	27
28	29	30	31			

Days of the Week
Monday, Tuesday, Wednesday, Thursday, and Friday are weekdays. Saturday and Sunday are weekends.

Last Month
Last month ended on Sunday, September 30.

Next Month
Next month begins on Thursday, November 1.

Using a Clock or a Stopwatch to Find Elapsed Time

You need to time an experiment for 20 minutes.

It is 1:30 P.M.

Stop at 1:50 P.M.

You need to time an experiment for 15 seconds. You can use the second hand of a clock or watch.

Start the experiment when the second hand is on number 6.

Stop when 15 seconds have passed and the second hand is on the 9.

You can use a stopwatch to time 15 seconds.

Press the reset button on a stopwatch so that you see 0:00oo.

Press the start button. When you see 0:15oo, press the stop button.

Measurements

Volume

1 L of sports drink is a little more than 1 qt.

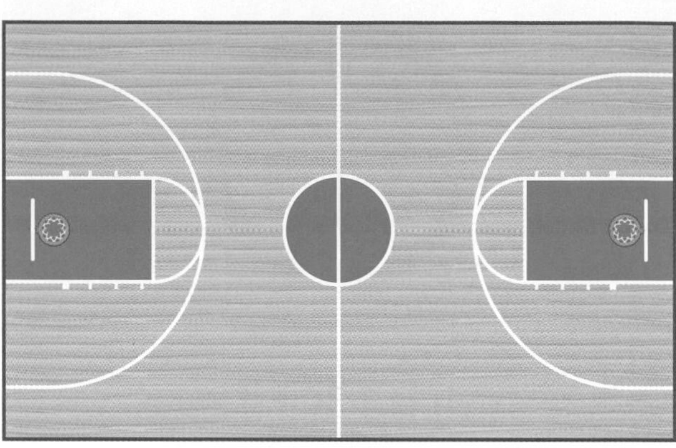

Area

A basketball court covers about 4,700 ft^2. It covers about 435 m^2.

Metric Measures

Temperature

- Ice melts at 0 degrees Celsius (°C)
- Water freezes at 0°C
- Water boils at 100°C

Length and Distance

- 1,000 meters (m) = 1 kilometer (km)
- 100 centimeters (cm) = 1 m
- 10 millimeters (mm) = 1 cm

Force

- 1 newton (N) = 1 kilogram × 1(meter/second) per second

Volume

- 1 cubic meter (m^3) = 1 m × 1 m × 1 m
- 1 cubic centimeter (cm^3) = 1 cm × 1 cm × 1 cm
- 1 liter (L) = 1,000 milliliters (mL)
- 1 cm^3 = 1 mL

Area

- 1 square kilometer (km^2) = 1 km × 1 km
- 1 hectare = 10,000 m^2

Mass

- 1,000 grams (g) = 1 kilogram (kg)
- 1,000 milligrams (mg) = 1 g

Temperature
The temperature at an indoor basketball game might be 27°C, which is 80°F.

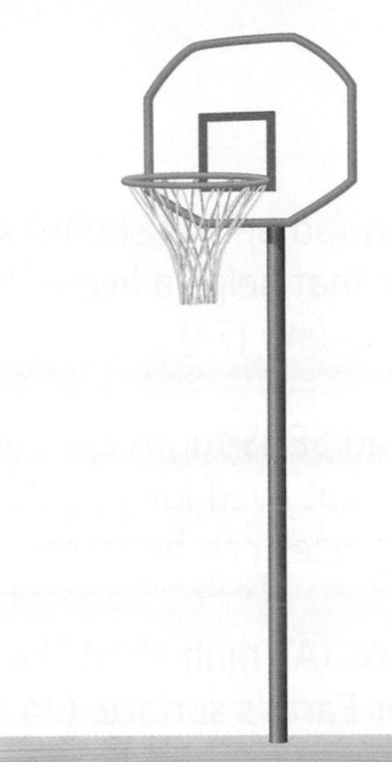

Length and Distance
A basketball rim is about 10 ft high, or a little more than 3 m from the floor.

Customary Measures

Temperature
- Ice melts at 32 degrees Fahrenheit (°F)
- Water freezes at 32°F
- Water boils at 212°F

Length and Distance
- 12 inches (in.) = 1 foot (ft)
- 3 ft = 1 yard (yd)
- 5,280 ft = 1 mile (mi)

Weight
- 16 ounces (oz) = 1 pound (lb)
- 2,000 pounds = 1 ton (T)

Volume of Fluids
- 8 fluid ounces (fl oz) = 1 cup (c)
- 2 c = 1 pint (pt)
- 2 pt = 1 quart (qt)
- 4 qt = 1 gallon (gal)

Metric and Customary Rates
km/h = kilometers per hour
m/s = meters per second
mph = miles per hour

Glossary

adaptation (ad ap TAY shuhn) A behavior or body part that helps a living thing survive in its environment. (74)

ancestor (an SEHS tur) A species or a form of a species that lived long ago and to which modern species can be traced. (118)

★ **atmosphere** (AT muh sfihr) The layers of air that cover Earth's surface. (242)

attract (uh TRAKT) To pull toward. (374)

behavior (bih HAYV yur) The way that an organism typically acts in a certain situation. (74)

cell (sehl) The smallest and most basic unit of a living thing. (18)

climate (KLY miht) The average weather conditions in a certain area over a long period. (253)

community (kuh MYOO nih ee) A group of plants and animals that live in the same area and interact with each other. (67)

condensation (kahn dehn SAY shuhn) The change of state from gas to liquid. (235)

condense (kuhn DEHNS) To change state from gas to liquid. (293)

conductor (kuhn DUHK tuhr) Any material that allows heat to move through it easily. (328)

conifer (KAHN uh fur) A plant that makes seeds inside of cones. (30)

★ **conservation** (kahn sur VAY shuhn) The safekeeping and wise use of natural resources. (220)

crest (krehst) The highest point of a wave. (335)

direction (dih REHK shuhn) The path an object follows. (367)

distance (DIHS tuhns) A measure of length. (366)

ecosystem (EE koh SIHS tuhm) All of the living and nonliving things that exist and interact in one place. (62)

endangered species (ehn DAYN jurd SPEE-sheez) A species that has so few members that the entire species is at risk of dying out. (104)

★ **energy** (EHN ur jee) The ability to cause change. (59)

environment (ehn VY ruhn muhnt) All the living and nonliving things that surround and affect an organism. (62)

equator (ih KWAY tuhr) An imaginary line around Earth, halfway between the North Pole and the South Pole. (254)

era (IHR uh) A major division of time. (110)

evaporate (ih VAP uh rayt) To change state slowly from liquid to gas. (293)

evaporation (ih vap uh RAY shuhn) The change of state from liquid to gas. (235)

★ **extinct species** (ihk STIHNGKT SPEE sheez) A species that has died off. (100)

filter (FIHL tur) A device or material that traps some substances and allows others to pass through it. (310)

★ **force** (fawwrs) A push or a pull. (357)

fossil (FAHS uhl) The very old remains of a plant or an animal. (108)

freeze (freez) To change state from liquid to solid. (293)

friction (FRIHK shuhn) A force that occurs when one object rubs against another. (326)

fruit (froot) The part of a plant that contains the seeds. (28)

gas (gas) Matter that has no definite shape and that does not take up a definite amount of space. (283)

gas giant (gas JY ent) A very large planet made up mostly of gases. (172)

★ **geological feature** (jee uh LAHJ ihk uhl FEE-chur) A part of Earth's surface, either land or water, that has a certain shape and that is formed naturally. (192)

gravity (GRAV ih tee) A force that pulls an object toward another object. (359)

habitat (HAB ih tat) The place in which an organism lives. (84)

heat (heet) The flow of thermal energy from warmer objects to cooler objects. (324)

igneous rock (IHG nee uhs rahk) A kind of rock that forms when melted rock from inside Earth cools and hardens. (202)

individual (ihn duh VIHJ yoo uhl) A single member of a species. (44)

inner planet (IHN ur PLAN iht) Any of the four planets (Mercury, Venus, Earth, Mars) closest to the Sun. (158)

larva (LAHR vuh) The second, wormlike, stage in an insect's life cycle. (34)

latitude (LAT ih tood) The distance north or south of the equator. (254)

leaf (leef) The part of a plant that collects sunlight and gases from the air and uses them to make food for the plant. (18)

★ = Tennessee Academic Vocabulary

★ **life cycle** (lyf SY kuhl) The series of changes that a living thing goes through during its lifetime. (28)

liquid (LIHK wihd) Matter that takes the shape of its container and takes up a definite amount of space. (283)

magnet (MAG niht) Any object that pulls certain metals to it. (374)

magnetic poles (mag NEHT ihk pohlz) The areas of a magnet where the force of attraction is strongest. (376)

★ **magnetism** (MAG nuh tihz uhm) Also called magnetic attraction. A magnet's ability to attract certain metals. (374)

magnify (MAG nuh fy) To make an object appear larger. (148)

mass (mas) The amount of matter in an object. (285)

★ **matter** (MAT ur) Anything that has mass and takes up space. Matter is found in three states: solid, liquid, and gas. (282)

melt (mehlt) To change state from solid to liquid. (293)

metamorphic rock (meht uh MAWR fihk-rahk) Rock that forms when other rock is changed by heat and pressure. (204)

mineral (MIHN ur uhl) A material that is found in nature and that has never been alive. (198)

mixture (MIHKS chur) Matter that is made up of two or more substances or materials that are physically combined. (301)

moon (moon) A small, rounded body that orbits a planet. (157)

motion (MOH shuhn) A change in the position of an object. (356)

★ **natural resource** (NACH ur uhl REE sawrs) A material from Earth that is useful to people. (210)

nonrenewable resource (nahn rih NOO uh buhl REE sawrs) A natural resource that is in limited supply and that cannot be replaced or that takes thousands of years to be replaced. (212)

nutrient (NOO tree uhnt) A substance that living things need in order to survive and grow. (17)

★ **observe** (UHB zuhrv) To use tools and the senses to gather information and to determine the properties of objects or events. (S6)

★ **offspring** (AWF sprihng) The living thing made when an animal reproduces. (36)

★ **orbit** (AWR biht) To move in a path, usually around a planet or star. Also, the path itself. (157)

ore (awr) Rock that contains metal or other useful minerals. (210)

★ **organism** (AWR guh nihz uhm) Any living thing. (60)

outer planet (OW tur PLAN iht) Any of the four planets (Jupiter, Saturn, Uranus, Neptune) farthest from the Sun. (159)

paleontologist (pay lee ahn TAHL uh jihst) A scientist who studies fossils and organisms that lived long ago. (109)

permanent magnet (pur muh nuhnt MAG-niht) An object that keeps it magnetism for a long time. (375)

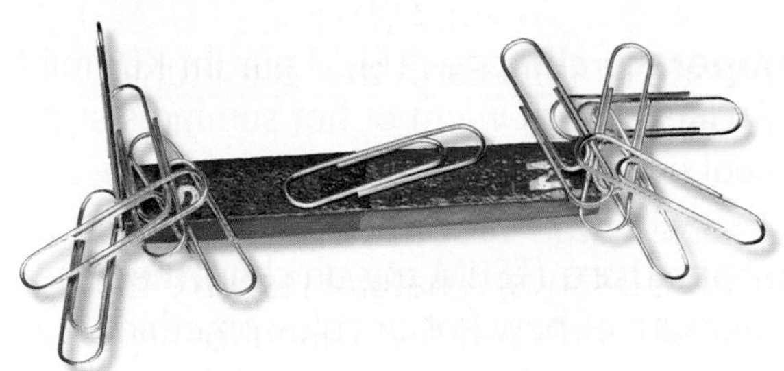

★ **photosynthesis** (foh toh SIHN thih sihs) The process by which a plant makes food. (21)

★ **physical change** (FIHZ ih kuhl chaynj) A change in the size, shape, or state of matter. (292)

★ **physical property** (FIHZ ih kuhl PRAHP ur-tee) A characteristic of matter that can be measured or observed with the senses. (283)

pitch (pihch) How high or low a sound seems. (338)

planet (PLAN iht) A large body in space that orbits a star. (156)

polar climate (POH lur KLY miht) A climate with long, cold winters and short, cool summers. (255)

★ **pollution** (puh LOO shuhn) The addition of harmful materials to the environment. (86, 218)

population (pahp yuh LAY shuhn) All the organisms of the same kind that live in an ecosystem. (66)

★ **precipitation** (prih sihp ih TAY shuhn) Any form of water that falls from clouds to Earth's surface. (236)

★ **predator** (PREHD uh tur) An animal that hunts other animals for food. (70)

★ **prey** (pray) Any animal that is hunted for food by a predator. (70)

pupa (PYOO puh) The third stage of an insect's life cycle, during which it changes into an adult. (34)

recycle (ree SY kuhl) To collect old materials, process them, and use them to make new items. (220)

relative (REHL uh tihv) A species that shares a common ancestor with another species. (119)

renewable resource (rih NOO uh buhl REE-sawrs) A natural resource that can be replaced by nature. (212)

rock (rahk) A solid material made up of one or more minerals. (200)

root (root) The part of a plant that takes in water and nutrients and that provides support for the plant. (18)

★ **rotation** (roh TAY shuhn) A complete spin, or turn, of a planet or other body. (160)

★ = **Tennessee Academic Vocabulary**

sedimentary rock (sehd uh MEHN tuh ree-rahk) Rock that forms when sediment is pressed together and hardens. (203)

seed (seed) The first stage in the life cycle of most plants. (28)

★ **solar system** (SOH lur SIHS tuhm) The Sun and the planets, moons, and other objects that orbit the Sun. (157)

solid (SAHL ihd) Matter that has a definite shape and that takes up a definite amount of space. (283)

space probe (SPAYS prohb) A craft that explores outer space carrying instruments, but not people. (168)

species (SPEE sheez) A group of the same type of living thing that can mate and produce other living things of the same kind. (100)

speed (speed) A measure of how fast or slowly something is moving. (368)

stem (stehm) The part of a plant that holds up the leaves and carries water and nutrients through the plant. (18)

substance (SUHB stuhns) A single kind of matter that has certain properties. (300)

Sun (suhn) The nearest star to Earth. (156)

telescope (TEHL ih skohp) A tool that makes distant objects appear to be larger and sharper. (148)

temperate climate (TEHM pur iht KLY miht) A climate with warm or hot summers and cool or cold winters. (254)

temperature (TEHM pur uh chur) The measure of how hot or cold something is. (244)

temporary magnet (TEHM puh rair ee-MAG neht) An object that loses its magnetism after a short time. (375)

thermal energy (THUR muhl ehn ur jee) The energy of moving particles in matter. (324)

trait (trayt) A feature such as a body part or a behavior. (119)

tropical climate (TRAHP ih kuhl KLY miht) A climate that is very warm and wet for all or most of the year. (254)

trough (trawf) The lowest point of a wave. (335)

vibrate (VY brayt) To move back and forth quickly. (336)

volume (VAHL yoom) 1. The amount of space that matter takes up. (285); 2. How loud or soft a sound seems. (339)

★ **water cycle** (WAW tur SY kuhl) The movement of water between the air and Earth as it changes state. (236)

water vapor (WAW tur VAY pur) Water in the form of an invisible gas. (234)

wave (wayv) A movement that carries energy from one place to another. (334)

weather (WEHTH ur) The condition of the atmosphere at a certain place and time. (244)

★ **weathering** (WEHTH ur ihng) The breaking up or wearing away of rock. (203)

★ = Tennessee Academic Vocabulary

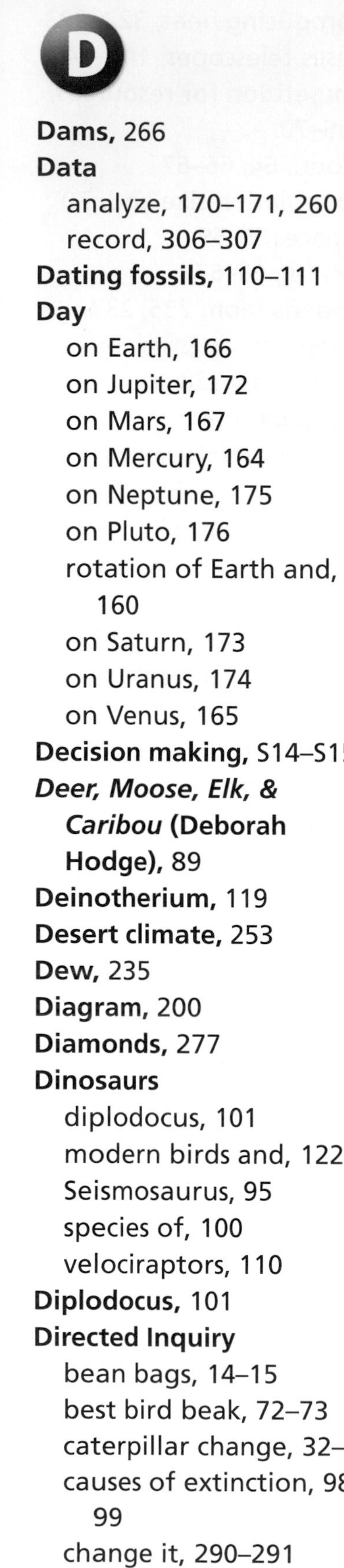

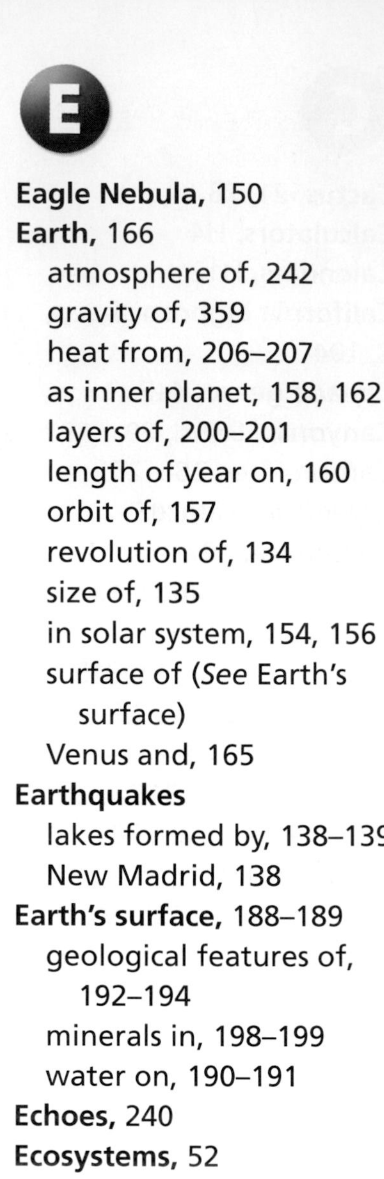

F

N

O

T

Y

Z

Permission Acknowledgments

KEY: (t) top, (tl) top left, (tr) top right, (c) center, (cl) center left, (cr) center right, (b) bottom, (bl) bottom left, (br) bottom right, (bg) background.

Cover: (front) © 2004 Alexander Haas/ imagequestmarine.com; (bg) Raymond Gehman/National Geographic/Getty Images: (spine) © 2004 Alexander Haas/ imagequestmarine.com.

Nature of Science: S1 (bg) Jim Cummins/ Corbis; S2-S3 (bg) Andy Rouse/Photo Researchers, Inc.; S3 (br) Courtesy of Dr. Caitlin O'Connell-Rodwell; S4-S5 (bg) Doug McCutcheon/LGPL/Alamy Images; S6-S7 (bg) Andreas Hart/OKAPIA/Photo Researchers, Inc.; S10-S11 (bg) Courtesy of Jonathan Santos; S10 (tr) Courtesy of Jonathan Santos; S11 (br) NASA/Roger Ressmeyer/Corbis; S12-S13 (bg) Holos/The Image Bank/Getty Images; S14-S15 (bg) Peter Pinnock/ImageState/Picturequest.

Life Excursions: 2 (bg) Pat O'Hara/Corbis; 3 (inset) Shedd Aquarium/ www.fishphotos.org; 4 (bg) Willard Clay Photography, Inc.; 4 (inset) Jeffrey Rich Nature; 5 (tr) Byron Jorjorian/Alamy; 5 (cr) Courtesy of Clayton Ferrell/USFWS; 6 (bg) D'Arcy Evans; 6 (inset) Andre Jenny/Alamy; 7 (inset) Karen Pulfer Focht/Getty Images; 8 (inset) John Van Decker/Alamy.

Unit A: 9 Robert Pickett/Corbis; 11 (tr) Burke/Trilio/Brand X/Jupiter Images; 11 (cl) William Manning/Corbis; 11 (cr) Dwight Kuhn; 11 (bl) Renee Stockdale/Animals Animals; 12-13 S and D and K Maslowski/ Minden Pictures; 16-17 (bg) Charles O'Rear/Corbis; 16-17 (bg) Terry W. Eggers/ Corbis; 18 (c) Dwight Kuhn; 19 (cr) Microfield Scientific Ltd Science Photo Library/Photo Researchers, Inc.; 19 (r) Dwight Kuhn; 20 (tl) John Elk/Bruce Coleman, Inc.; 20-21 (b) Nature's Images/ Photo Researchers, Inc.; 21 (tr) Peter Chadwick/DK Images; 21 (br) Dave King/ DK Images; 23 (t) Charles O'Rear/Corbis; 23 (t) Terry W. Eggers/Corbis; 24 (frame) Image Farm; 24 (tl) The Granger Collection, New York; 24 (br) The Granger Collection, New York; 24-25 (b) 1998 From the Warnock Library. Imaged by Octavo (www.Octavo.Com). Used with Permission/Octavo; 25 (tl) Eye of Science/Photo Researchers; 25 (tr) Susumu Nishinaga/ Photo Researchers; 25 (cr) Omikron/Photo Researchers, Inc.; 29 (bg) Martin Ruegner, Imagestate/Alamy Images; 29 (t) Maryann Frazier/Photo Researchers, Inc.; 29 (cl) Nigel Cattlin/Holt Studios International Ltd/Alamy Images; 29 (cr) Stephen P. Parker/Photo Researchers, Inc.; 29 (bl) Dwight Kuhn; 29 (br) Foodfolio/Alamy Images; 31 (t) Maryann Frazier/Photo Researchers, Inc.; 32-33 (bg) Robert Gill/ Papilio/Corbis; 32 (bl) Mitch Reardon/ Stone/Getty Images; 34 (cl) Robert Pickett/ Alamy Images; 35 (t) Stephen Dalton/ Photo Researchers, Inc.; 35 (cl) Stephen Dalton/Photo Researchers, Inc.; 35 (cr) George Bernard/Photo Researchers, Inc.; 35 (b) George Bernard/Photo Researchers, Inc.; 36 (tl) Jane Burton/DK Images; 36 (tr) Jane Burton/DK Images; 36 (cr) Jane Burton/DK Images; 36 (bl) Cyril Laubscher/ DK Images; 36 (br) Jane Burton/DK Images; 38-39 (bg) Roger De La Harpe/Animals Animals; 39 (inset) Anup Shah/naturepl.com; 40-41 (bg) Ricky John Molloy/Stone/Getty Images; 42 (l) Bios/Peter Arnold; 42 (r) Ernest A. Janes/Bruce Coleman, Inc.; 43 (t) Frank Lukasseck/Corbis; 43 (b) Jeff Foott/ Bruce Coleman, Inc.; 44 (tl) Richard Shiell; 44 (bl) Ulrike Schanz/Photo Researchers, Inc.; 44 (bc) Jacana/Photo Researchers, Inc.; 44 (br) Rolf Kopfle/Bruce Coleman, Inc.; 45 (tr) Piet Opperman/Piet Opperman; 45 (cr) Colin Seddon/Nature Picture Library; 45 (br) Steven David Miller/Nature Picture Library; 45 (bl) Carolyn A. McKeone/Photo Researchers, Inc.; 45 (br) John Daniels/ Bruce Coleman, Inc.; 46 (t) Michael Newman/PhotoEdit; 46 (tc) Fancy Photography/Veer; 46 (bc) Juice Images Photography/Veer; 46 (b) Erik Isakson / Jupiter Images; 47 (t) Bios/Peter Arnold; 47 (c) Richard Shiell; 47 (bl) Michael Newman/ PhotoEdit; 49 (tl) Kaz Mori/The Image Bank/Getty Images; 49 (b) Holger Winkler/ zefa/Corbis; 52-53 (bg) Jeff Lepore/Photo Researchers; 53 (tl) Ron Stroud/Masterfile; 53 (tr) Gary Vestal/Stone/Getty Images; 53 (bl) Eric Soder/Photo Researchers, Inc.; 53 (br) John Foster/Masterfile; 54 (tl) blickwinkel/Alamy; 56-57 (bg) Nancy G Photography/Alamy; 56 (bl) Tim Fitzharris/ Minden Pictures; 60 (bl) Clive Streeter/DK Images; 61 (tr) Michael Wickes/Bruce Coleman, Inc.; 61 (cl) Jeff L. Lepore/Photo Researchers, Inc.; 61 (br) Burke/Triolo Productions/Foodpix/Jupiter Images; 63 (c) Inga Spence/Visuals Unlimited; 64-65 (bg) Eric Von Weber/Stone/Getty Images; 64 (bl) Photri-Microstock; 66-67 (bg) John Shaw/ Bruce Coleman, Inc.; 66 (t) John Hawkins; Frank Lane Picture Agency/Corbis; 66 (cl) blickwinkel/Alamy; 66 (cr) W. Perry Conway/Corbis; 66 (b) Joe McDonald/ Corbis; 67 (tr) Jim Brandenburg/Minden Pictures; 67 (cr) M. Loup/Peter Arnold; 68 (tr) Dale Wilson/Masterfile; 68 (b) Konrad Wothe/Minden Pictures; 69 (tr) Richard Laird/Taxi/Getty Images; 69 (b) Clark James Mishler; 70 Nancy G Photography/Alamy; 71 (t) Jim Brandenburg/Minden Pictures; 71 (c) Konrad Wothe/Minden Pictures; 71 (b) Nancy G Photography/Alamy; 72-73 (bg) Jack Dermid/Photo Researchers, Inc.; 72 (bl) Michael & Patricia Fogden/Corbis; 74 (l) Susanne Danegger/Photo Researchers, Inc.; 74 (r) Scott Camazine/Photo Researchers, Inc.; 75 (t) Howard Miller/ Photo Researchers, Inc; 75 (b) moodboard/ Corbis; 78 (t) Mark J. Barrett/Alamy; 78 (b) Jeffrey Rotman/Photo Researchers, Inc.; 80-81 (bg) Brandon Cole; 80 (inset) Peter Parks/Image Quest 3-D; 82-83 (bg) Steve Holt/Stockpix.Com; 84 Sumio Harada/ Minden Pictures; 86 B. Blume/Unep/Peter Arnold; 87 (t) Sumio Harada/Minden Pictures; 87 (b) B. Blume/Unep/Peter Arnold; 91 (bg) Gerald Cubitt; 91 (tr) Gary Conner/Photo Edit, Inc.; 94-95 (bg) Kokoro Dinosaurs; 95 (tr) B. Moose Peterson/ Ardea, London, Ltd.; 95 (cl) Jeff Vanuga/ naturepl.com; 97 (t) Demetrio Carrasco/DK Images; 97 (c) G. Bernard/Photo Researchers, Inc.; 97 (b) Tom Bean/Corbis; 98-99 (bg) Japack Company/Corbis; 98 (bl) Keren Su/China Span/Alamy Images; 101 (b) Peter Arnold, Inc./Alamy Images; 102 (b) Joyce & Frank Burek/Animals Animals-Earth Scenes; 103 (tl) Paris Museum of Natural History; 103 (tr) G. Bernard/Photo Researchers, Inc.; 104 (cr) Jonathan Gale/ Getty Images; 104 (br) Colin Keates/DK Images; 105 (t) G. Bernard/Photo Researchers, Inc.; 106 (bl) Tom Bean/Corbis; 108 (bl) Demetrio Carrasco/DK Images; 108 (br) Peter Chadwick/DK Images; 109 (bl) DEA Picture Library/Getty Images; 111 (t) Demetrio Carrasco/DK Images; 111 (c) DEA Picture Library /Getty Images; 114 (br) Phil Degginger/Bruce Coleman, Inc.; 115 (cr) Natural History Museum, London; 115 (bl) Ken Lucas/Getty Images; 116-117 (bg) Jonathan Blair/Corbis; 119 (br) SuperStock, Inc./SuperStock; 120 (cr) Fritz Prenzel/ Animals Animals; 120 (bl) ZSSD/Minden Pictures; 121 (t) Colin Keates/DK Images; 121 (b) Art Wolfe/Photo Researchers, Inc.; 122 (l) Sally A. Morgan; Ecoscene/Corbis; 122 (r) Malcolm Schuyl/Alamy; 124-125 (bg) Don Foley; 126 SuperStock, Inc./ SuperStock; 127 (bg) Courtesy of the Museum of Paleontology; 127 (tr) Courtesy of the Museum of Paleontology; 132 (bl) Elvele Images/Alamy Images.

Earth Excursions: 134 (bg) Shigemi Numazawa/Atlas Photo Bank/Photo Researchers, Inc.; 134 (inset) Corbis; 135 (inset) Will and/or Lissa Funk/Alpine Aperture; 136 (bg) Eastcott Momatiuk/ Getty Images; 136 (inset) Courtesy of WATE TV 6; 137 (inset) Courtesy of WATE TV 6; 138 (bg) Byron Jorjorian/www.bciusa.com; 139 (inset) Adam Jones/Visuals Unlimited; 140 (inset) M Stock/Alamy.

Unit B: 141 (bg) Stockli, Nelson, Hasler/ NASA; 142-143 (bg) GoodShoot/SuperStock; 143 (tr) Tony Freeman/Photo Edit, Inc.; 143 (cl) SPL/Photo Researchers, Inc.; 143 (cr) JPL/NASA; 143 (bl) AP Photo/NASA; 143 (br) Handout/Reuters/Corbis; 144-145 (bg) NASA/Getty Images; 144 (c) U.S. Geological Survey/Photo Researchers, Inc.; 144 (b) Jupiter Images/Brand X/Alamy Images; 146-147 (bg) Taxi/Getty Images; 148 Steve Vidler/Superstock; 149 (t) Dr. Seth Shostack/Photo Researchers, Inc.; 149 (b) Denis Scott/Corbis; 151 (t) Jupiter Images /Brand X/Alamy; 151 (c) Steve Vidler/SuperStock; 151 (b) Denis Scott/ Corbis; 152-153 (bg) Dennis Di Cicco/Peter Arnold; 152 (inset) NASA; 153 (inset) Detlev Van Ravenswaay/Photo Researchers, Inc.; 154 (bl) ESA./NASA/SOHO; 158-159 (bg) Michael Siebert/zefa/Corbis; 158 (tr) Digital Vision Ltd./SuperStock; 158 (cl) USGS/Photo Researchers, Inc.; 158 (cr) Digital Vision Ltd./SuperStock; 159 (tr) GoodShoot/SuperStock; 159 (cl) Pixtal/ SuperStock; 159 (bl) NASA/Photo Researchers, Inc.; 159 (br) NASA-JPL; 161 (tl) USGS/Photo Researchers, Inc.; 161 (tr) Pixtal/SuperStock; 161 (tcl) Digital Vision Ltd./SuperStock; 161 (tcr) NASA/Photo Researchers, Inc.; 161 (cr) GoodShoot/ SuperStock; 161 (bcl) Digital Vision Ltd./ SuperStock; 161 (br) NASA-JPL; 162-163 (bg) Bill Frymire/Masterfile; 162 (bl) US Geological Survey/Photo Researchers, Inc.; 164 (c) USGS/Photo Researchers, Inc.; 165 (c) Digital Vision Ltd./SuperStock; 165 (b) Photri-Microstock; 166 (cr) Digital Vision Ltd./SuperStock; 166 (b) Thomas Ligon/ARC Science Simulations/Photo Researchers, Inc.; 167 (b) MPI/Getty Images; 168 (tl) NASA/Photri; 168 (tr) NASA; 168 (b) Handout/Reuters/Corbis; 169 (tl) USGS/ Photo Researchers, Inc.; 169 (tcl) Digital

Vision Ltd./SuperStock; 169 (bcl) Digital Vision Ltd./SuperStock; 170-171 (bg) Pixtal/SuperStock; 172 (bl) Pixtal/SuperStock; 172 (cr) Pixtal/SuperStock; 173 (t) Digital Vision Ltd./SuperStock; 173 (cr) JPL/NASA; 174 (cr) Denis Scott/Corbis; 174 (br) Denis Scott/Corbis; 175 (t) NASA-JPL; 176 (cr) NASA-JPL; 177 (tl) Pixtal/SuperStock; 177 (tr) NASA-JPL; 177 (tcl) JPL/NASA; 177 (bcl) Denis Scott/Corbis; 178-179 (bg) Courtesy the W.M. Keck Observatory; 178 (b) Forest J. Egan; 181 Gary Hochman, NET Television, Lincoln, Nebraska, for the Wonderwise Project; 184-185 (bg) Craig Tuttle/Corbis; 185 (tr) David Paterson/Alamy Images; 185 (cl) Bio Associates/Photo Researchers, Inc.; 185 (cr) Robert Harding World Imagery/Alamy Images; 185 (bl) Thinkstock/Getty Images; 186-187 (bg) William Manning/Corbis; 188-189 (bg) Layne Kennedy/Corbis; 188 (bl) Richard A. Cooke/Corbis; 190-191 (b) Panoramic Images/Getty Images; 191 Bill Arron/Photo Edit, Inc.; 194 (cr) Arco Images/Alamy; 194 (br) Jay Dickman/Corbis; 194 (bl) DY Riess MD/Alamy; 196-197 (bg) Alan Schein Photography/Corbis; 196 (bl) Tony Freeman/Photo Edit, Inc.; 198 (t) Dirk Wiersma/Photo Researchers; 198 (bl) Jacana/Photo Researchers; 198 (bc) Jean-Claude Revy/ISM/Phototake; 198 (br) Mark A. Schneider; 199 (tr) The Natural History Museum/Alamy; 199 (tcr) Ben Johnson/Photo Researchers; 199 (cr) Daniel Sambraus/Photo Researchers; 199 (bcr) Gc Minerals/Alamy Images; 199 (br) Wayne Scherr/Photo Researchers, Inc.; 202 (t) Breck P. Kent / Animals Animals– Earth Scenes; 202 (c) Andrew J. Martinez/Photo Researchers, Inc.; 202 (b) Breck P. Kent/Animals Animals– Earth Scenes; 203 (t) Joyce photographics/Photo Researchers, Inc.; 203 (c) Breck P. Kent / Animals Animals– Earth Scenes; 203 (b) Getty Images/Dorling Kindersley; 204 (tl) Breck P. Kent / Animals Animals– Earth Scenes; 204 (tr) Granite Vermont; 204 (bl) Michael Szoenyi; 204 (br) Andrew J. Martinez/Photo Researchers; 205 (tl) Granite Vermont; 205 (tc) Andrew J. Martinez/Photo Researchers, Inc.; 205 (tr) Breck P. Kent / Animals Animals– Earth Scenes; 205 (cl) Getty Images/Dorling Kindersley; 205 (c) Breck P. Kent / Animals Animals– Earth Scenes; 205 (cr) Joyce photographics/Photo Researchers, Inc.; 205 (bl) Michael Szoenyi; 205 (br) Andrew J. Martinez/Photo Researchers; 206-207 (bg) Inga Spence/Index Stock; 208-209 (bg) K YamashitaPan Stock/Panoramic Images; 208 (bl) David Young-Wolff/Photo Edit Inc; 211 (tr) Chromosohm/Photo Researchers, Inc.; 211 (tcr) Victoria Pearson/Taxi/Getty Images; 211 (c) A. Schein/Masterfile; 211 (cr) Ingram Publishing/Alamy Images; 211 (bcr) Steve Prezant/Masterfile; 211 (br) Ron Chapple/Thinkstock/Alamy Images; 212 (c) Rob Reichenfeld/DK Images; 212 (br) IFA Bilderteam/Estock Photo; 213 (t) Jim Richardson/Corbis; 214 (tl) Brian Miller/Bruce Coleman, Inc.; 214 (tc) Michael Townsand/Photographer's Choice/Getty Images; 214 (tr) Steve & Dave Maslowski/Photo Researchers, Inc.; 214 (bl) Brand X RF; 214 (bc) Michael Newman/PhotoEdit; 214 (br) Foodfolio/Alamy; 215 (t) Ron Chapple/Thinkstock/Alamy Images; 215 (c) Michael Townsand/Photographer'S Choice/Getty Images; 215 (b) Brand X RF; 216-217 (bg) Karl Weatherly/Corbis; 218 (b) John CrallTranstock Inc./Alamy Images; 219 (l) Dorris De Witt Stone/Getty Images; 219 (r) David Ball/Corbis; 220 (b) Bill Bachmann/Photri, Inc.; 221 (t) Dorris De Witt Stone/Getty Images; 221 (c) Bill Bachmann/Photri, Inc.; 222-223 (bg) AP Photo/The Albuquerque Journal, Olin Calk; 223 (t) Jose Azel/Aurora Photos; 224 (bl) Vic Bider /Photo Edit, Inc.; 225 (bg) Photo Link/Picturequest/Jupiter Images; 225 (tr) Fred Glick, Stringer/Ap Photo; 228 Stuart & Cynthia Pernick /SuperStock ; 229 (tr) Larry Fisher/Masterfile; 229 (cl) Mehau Kulyk/Photo Researchers, Inc.; 229 (br) Warren Bolster/Stone/Getty Images; 230-231 (bg) Digital Stock; 232-233 (bg) Mike Dobel/Masterfile; 235 (t) John Kaprielian/Photo Researchers; 235 (b) John Grant/Photri, Inc.; 238 (l) Kevin Dodge/Masterfile; 238 (b) Scott Berner/Photri-Microstock; 238 (r) Corbis; 239 (b) Kevin Dodge/Masterfile; 240-241 (bg) Cleve Bryant/Photo Edit; 240 (bl) Lawrence Migdale/Photo Researchers, Inc.; 242-243 (bg) Digital Vision Ltd./SuperStock; 243 (tcl) David R. Frazier/Photo Researchers, Inc.; 243 (bcl) Joyce Photographics/Photo Researchers; 243 (bl) Tony Freeman/Photo Edit, Inc.; 244 (b) Steve Terrill/Corbis; 245 (tl) Cindy Charles/Photo Edit, Inc.; 245 (tr) Tony Freeman/Photo Edit, Inc.; 245 (bl) Felicia Martinez/Photo Edit, Inc.; 245 (br) David Young-Wolf/Photo Edit, Inc.; 246 (tl) NASA/Corbis; 247 (t) Digital Vision Ltd./Superstock; 247 (c) Cindy Charles/Photo Edit, Inc.; 250-251 (bg) SuperStock; 250 (bl) Rommel/Masterfile; 252 (b) Tom Brakefield/Corbis; 253 (br) Bob Anderson/Masterfile; 254 (bl) Mark Gibson/Gibson Stock Photography; 255 (c) Nicola Tree/Alamy Images; 255 (c) Comstock Images/Alamy Images; 257 (t) Bob Anderson/Masterfile; 257 (c) Rolf Hicker/age fotostock; 257 (b) Nicola Tree/Alamy Images; 257 (b) Comstock Images/Alamy Images; 258-259 (bg) NOAA; 261 (tc) News Channel 5 Nashville; 261 (bg) Chuck Eckert/Alamy.

Physical Excursions: 268 (bg) David McGlynn/Getty Images; 268 (inset) Courtesy of Mary's Greenhouse; 269 (cr) Courtesy of Mary's Greenhouse; 269 (bl) Courtesy of Mary's Greenhouse; 270 (bg) Will and/or Lissa Funk/Alpine Aperture; 271 (inset) Arco Images/Alamy; 272 (bg) Steve Porter/Alamy; 272 (inset) Courtesy of the Chattanooga Symphony & Opera; 273 (inset) Courtesy of Chattanooga Symphony & Opera.

Unit C: 276-277 (bg) Michael Venture/Photo Edit, Inc.; 277 (tr) Anton Vengo/SuperStock; 277 (cl) C Squared Studios/Getty Images; 280-281 (bg) Craig Aurness/Corbis; 286 (tl) Mark Dadswell/Getty Images; 286 (cr) Sharon Green/Pacific Stock; 286 (b) Peter Griffith/Masterfile; 287 (b) Sharon Green/Pacific Stock; 288-289 (bg) Wills Wing, Inc.; 290-291 (bg) Siedie Pries/Getty Images; 290 (bl) Jason Plotkin/The York Dispatch/Ap Wide World Photos; 292 (b) Dave King/DK Images; 293 (l) Dave King/DK Images; 293 (r) Dave King/DK Images; 295 (t) Dave King/DK Images; 296-297 (bg) Property of bobbi fabellano; 298-299 (bg) Tom Pantages; 302 (tl) Thomas Michael Corcoran/PhotoEdit; 302 (b) Lynn Stone/Bruce Coleman, Inc.; 303 (t) Douglas E. Walker/Masterfile; 304 (tr) Plainpicture/Lobster/Alamy Images; 304 (b) J. Spillane/Photri, Inc.; 305 (b) Plainpicture/Lobster/Alamy Images; 306-307 (bg) Bruce Heinemann/Photodisc/Getty Images; 306 (bl) DK Images; 315 (bg) Macduff Everton/Corbis; 315 (tl) William Whitehurst/Corbis; 315 (cr) Ainaco/Corbis; 315 (br) Ainaco/Corbis; 318-319 (bg) Gary I. Rothstein/epa/Corbis; 319 (t) Element Photo/Stockfood America; 319 (b) Lawrence Migdale; 320-321 (bg) Eisenhut & Mayer/Food Pix/Getty Images; 320 (c) DK Images; 322-323 (bg) Mark Turner/Botanica/Getty Images; 324 (b) Ingram Publishing/SuperStock; 326 (t) Pat Morris/Ardea; 329 (c) Pat Morris/Ardea; 330-331 (bg) Nasa; 330 (inset) Nasa; 332-333 (bg) Tom Pantages; 334 (b) DK Images; 335 (t) DK Images; 336 (l) Tony Freeman/Photo Edit, Inc.; 336 (r) Image Source/Corbis; 338 (t) Spencer Grant/Photo Edit, Inc.; 338 (b) Mike Dunning/DK Images; 339 (l) Lothar Lenz/Masterfile; 339 (r) Alan Schein/Alamy; 341 (t) DK Images; 341 (c) Image Source/Corbis; 341 (b) Mike Dunning/DK Images; 346 (cr) © Susan Van Etten/Photo Edit, Inc.; 347 (bg) Courtesy of Dr. Lonnie Johnson; 350 (bg) Ron Fehling/Masterfile; 351 (t) Paul Wayne Wilson/Photo Stock File/Alamy Images; 351 (c) David Noton/Masterfile; 351 (b) Unicorn Stock Photos; 354-355 (bg) Rolf Bruderer/Corbis; 358 (cr) MM Productions/Corbis; 358 (br) MM Productions/Corbis; 360 (tl) Radlund & Amp; Associates/Brand X Pictures/Jupiter Images; 360 (cl) Ken Wardius/Index Stock Imagery; 360 (br) Gary Conner/Photo Edit, Inc.; 361 (b) Ken Wardius/Index Stock Imagery; 362-363 (bg) Robert W. Ginn/Photo Edit, Inc.; 364-365 (b) Mark Scott/Taxi/Getty Images; 366 (b) David Madison Sports Images, Inc.; 367 (tr) Kimm Anderson, St. Cloud Times/Associated Press/ApWideworld; 367 (bl) K. Leidorf/Masterfile; 368 (tl) Michael & Patricia Fogden/Minden Pictures; 368 (bl) T. Allofs/Zefa/Masterfile; 368 (br) Tim Fitzharris/Masterfile; 369 (t) Mark Scott/Taxi/Getty Images; 369 (c) Kimm Anderson, St. Cloud Times/Associated Press/ApWideworld; 369 (b) T. Allofs/Zefa/Masterfile; 370 (b) The Granger Collection, Ny; 371 (t) United States Patent And Trademark Office; 371 (b) United States Patent And Trademark Office; 374 (bl) Phil Degginger/Bruce Coleman, Inc.; 375 (t) Jonathan Kitchen/Digital Vision/Getty Images; 377 (t) Phil Degginger/Bruce Coleman, Inc.; 377 (c) Jonathan Kitchen/Digital Vision/Getty Images; 378-379 (bg) AP Photo/Str; 380 (bl) Nicola Tree/Getty Images; 381 (t) Gaber Palmer/Corbis.